NEGOTIATION AND SETTLEMENT ADVOCACY

A Book of Readings

By

Charles B. Wiggins
Professor of Law
University of San Diego, School of Law

and

L. Randolph Lowry
Professor of Law
Pepperdine University

WEST GROUP

Bancroft Whitney • Clark Boardman Callaghan
Lawyers Cooperative Publishing • WESTLAW • West Publishing

*TEXT IS PRINTED ON 10% POST
CONSUMER RECYCLED PAPER*
1st Reprint–1998

Dedication

To Marion B. Wiggins
Who Taught Her Son Nearly Everything He
Has Done Well In This Life

C.B.W.

To My Parents—Ila Stroud and Lloyd Lowry
Who Began My Negotiation Training Early and Have
Lovingly Encouraged Me Throughout Life

L.R.L.

The authors wish to thank the staff of the Straus Institute for Dispute Resolution at Pepperdine University School of Law. Professor Wiggins especially thanks Donna Silverberg for her loving encouragement. Monica Pierce of the University of San Diego is as responsible as anyone for the publication of this book. Without her energy, administrative talent and persistence, these materials would remain as several piles of papers in boxes. Thank you.

*

Foreword

This book of readings celebrates over a quarter century's exploration of the interpersonal communication process we call negotiation. The first major effort to systematize this field for lawyers, by Judge Harry Edwards and Professor James J. White of Michigan, appeared in 1978. Since then, others have continued this steady inquiry. Until recently, however, the impact of negotiation analysis on the profession has been modest by comparison to the juggernaut of adjudication analysis that dominates the legal horizon.

This litigation ideology is ubiquitous. From the first day of law school we come to value a command of trial procedure. Skills courses customarily stress how to take a useful deposition, influence the trier of fact with a powerful opening statement, or conduct a withering cross-examination. After law school, a large and lucrative cottage industry of trial advocacy training ministers to the practicing Bar. And yet, the reality of legal practice is that we spend most of our lives as lawyers negotiating with others.

Almost all law schools now offer a course in negotiation, though this is a relatively recent phenomenon. A friend tells the story of his attempt only a few years ago to persuade his law faculty to approve a negotiation course. He had done his homework and arrived at the critical faculty meeting armed with a comprehensive syllabus and reading list. After making an impassioned presentation, one faculty member from another generation raised his hand. "If our students need a course like negotiation, they can go to the local business college and take it. We should not give academic credit for this stuff." Just as our friend thought all was lost, another of his colleagues said: "Yes, but if we don't offer the course, our students will lose all their negotiations to the people who went to that business college." Logic, faculty vision and a pinch of Darwinism carried the day in this negotiation.

At present, negotiation teaching and training is having its day. Thanks largely to social scientists as well as professional school researchers, we are learning a great deal about why certain bargaining techniques are successful. We can identify predictable structures of negotiation behavior that people use to plan transactions or resolve conflict. In contrast to what Gertrude Stein said in another context, there is now much "there, there" when it comes to academic negotiation analysis.

Lawyers and their clients are also increasingly attracted to dispute resolution techniques like negotiation and settlement advocacy that offer a positive alternative to adjudication. For generations, attorneys looked only to the courtroom when their clients needed conflict management assistance. As a consequence, because the only tool in the attorney's tool kit was the hammer of litigation, all client problems began to look suspiciously like nails. Clients now know that increasing delay, soaring costs, unpredictability and soured relationships are unacceptable consequences of adjudication. Likewise, clients are concerned about the appropriateness of scorched earth approaches when putting transactions together. Thus, negotiation, and its facilitated cousin mediation, are recognized both as efficient alternatives to the courtroom and as flexible tools to obtain mutually satisfactory business deals.

This book collects negotiation materials from what we consider the most instructive and provocative writings in the field. While our bias has been toward including authors with a legal orientation, we have searched more broadly as well. The excerpts include descriptions of bargaining structure, assessments of effective behavior, interesting case studies and intriguing treatments of peripheral topics. We let the readings speak for themselves, and minimize the use of footnotes. Each chapter is introduced by a short conceptual orientation. We have organized these materials to reflect over a decade of our experience teaching in several law schools, and providing negotiation training for law firms, businesses, bar associations, and government officials. The organizational format has proved resilient across cultures, in work conducted for political, academic, social and business leaders throughout Central Europe, the former Soviet Union, Asia and India.

We believe that negotiation is not just an essential skill for lawyers; it is an indispensable life skill for every person. Being a more competent negotiator means being a more competent co-worker, parent, child, spouse, neighbor, citizen and friend. As we become more self-conscious of our own bargaining behavior, and of how to use the principles developed in this collection, we can dramatically enhance our negotiating proficiency. These principles of effective negiation operate like a smooth perfume. While the fragrance of sound bargaining knowledge may be universal, the scent takes on the individual characteristics of each bargainer's personality and orientation when put into everyday practice.

We hope that this collection of readings provides a basis for understanding effective negotiation techniques, whether in the classroom or by individual study. Teachers will want to use these materials as a foundation from which to build their own supplemental collection. All curious people should read William Ury's *Getting Past No,* Howard Raiffa's *The Art and Science of Negotiation* and James Lax and David Sebenius' *The Manager as Negotiator.* A more complete biography appears at the end of the materials.

The field of negotiation analysis is rich and growing. This volume provides a useful starting point for a lifetime of learning.

Acknowledgments and Copyrights

CHAPTER ONE

1. Gulliver, Phillip H., Disputes and Negotiations: A Cross-Cultural Perspective, 81–89 (1979); reprinted with the permission of Academic Press, Inc.

2. Sander, Frank E.A. & Rubin, Jeffrey, The Janus Quality of Negotiation: Dealmaking and Dispute Settlement, 4 Negot. J. 109–12 (1988); reprinted with the permission of Plenum Publishing Corporation and authors.

3. Gifford, Donald, A Context-Based Theory of Strategy Selection in Legal Negotiation, 46 Ohio St. L.J. 41, 45–48 (1985); reoriented with the permission of Ohio State Law Journal and author.

4. Gifford, Donald, Legal Negotiation: Theory and Applications, 32–35 (1989); reprinted with the permission of West Publishing Corporation.

5. Murray, John, Understanding Competing Theories of Negotiation, 2 Negot. J. 179, 182–85 (1986); reprinted with the permission of Plenum Publishing Corporation and author.

6. Nyerges, Janos, Ten Commandments for a Negotiator, 3 Negot. J. 21, 21–26 (1987); reprinted with the permission of Plenum Publishing Corporation and author.

CHAPTER TWO

1. Excerpts from Metamagical Themas: Computer Tournaments of the Prisoner's Dilemma Suggest How Cooperation Evolves by Douglas Hofstadter, Scientific American 16–19 (May 1983); copyright © 1985 by Basic Books, Inc.; reprinted with the permission of Basic Books, a division of Harper Collins Publishers, Inc.

2. Excerpts from The Evolution of Cooperation by Robert Axelrod, 109–23 (1984); copyright © 1984 by Robert Axelrod; reprinted with the permission of Basic Books, a division of Harper Collins Publisher, Inc.

3 Lax, David & Sebenius, James, The Manager as Negotiator: Bargaining for Cooperation and Competitive Gain, 29–35 (1986); abridged and reprinted with the permission of The Free Press, a Division of Simon & Schuster, copyright © 1986 by David A. Lax and James K. Sebenius.

4. Bass, Thomas, Forgiveness Math, Discover Magazine, 62–67 (May 1993); Thomas Bass/© 1993 The Walt Disney Co., reprinted with the permission of Discover Magazine.

5. Frank, Robert H., Gilovich, Thomas & Regan, Dennis, Does Studying Economics Inhibit Cooperation?, 7 J. of Economic Perspectives 159–71 (1993); reprinted with the permission of American Economic Association and authors.

6. Passell, Peter, The Law as the Free Market's Rogue: Hostage to the Prisoner's Dilemma, The New York Times, March 25, 1994, B–18; reoriented with the permission of The New York Times.

7. Gilson, Ronald J. & Mnookin, Robert H., Disputing Through Agents: Cooperation and Conflict Between Lawyers in Litigation. This article originally appeared at 94 Colum. L. Rev. 509 (1994); reprinted by permission.

CHAPTER THREE

1. Raiffa, Howard, The Art and Science of Negotiation, 35–43, 47–50 (1982); reprinted by permission Harvard University Press, copyright © 1982 by the President and Fellows of Harvard College; all rights reserved.

2. Gifford, Donald, A Context-Based Theory of Strategy Selection in Legal Negotiation, 46 Ohio St. L.J. 41, 48–52 (1985); reprinted with the permission of Ohio State Law Journal and author.

3. Meltsner, Michael & Schrag, Philip, Negotiating Tactics for Legal Services Lawyers, 7 Clearinghouse Review 259–62 (1973); reprinted with the permission of National Clearinghouse for Legal Services, Inc. and authors.

4. Craver, Charles, Negotiation Techniques: How to Keep Br'er Rabbit Out of the Brier Patch, Trial 65, 67–74 (June 1988); reprinted with the permission of Trial Magazine.

5. Lax, David & Sebenius, James, The Manager as Negotiator: Bargaining for Cooperation and Competitive Gain 123–30 (1986); abridged and reprinted with the permission of The Free Press, a Division of Simon & Schuster from The Manager as Negotiator: Bargaining for Cooperation and Competitive Gain by David A. Lax and James K. Sebenius, copyright © 1986 by David A. Lax and James K. Sebenius.

6. Lowenthal, Gary, A General Theory of Negotiation Process, Strategy and Behavior, 31 U. Kan. L. Rev. 69, 76–77 (1982); reprinted with the permission of University of Kansas Law Review.

CHAPTER FOUR

1. Gifford, Donald, A Context-Based Theory of Strategy Selection in Legal Negotiation, 46 Ohio St. L.J. 41, 52–57 (1985); reprinted with the permission of Ohio State Law Journal and author.

2. Menkel-Meadow, Carrie, Toward Another View of Legal Negotiation: The Structure of Problem Solving, 31 UCLA L. Rev. 754, 794–817 (1984); originally published in 31 UCLA L. Rev. 754; copyright © 1984, The Regents of the University of California; all rights reserved.

3. Greenhalgh, Leonard, The Case Against Winning in Negotiations, 3 Negot. J. 167 (1987); reprinted with the permission of Plenum Publishing Corporation and author.

4. Pruitt, Dean, Achieving Integrative Agreements, in Negotiation in Organizations, Max Bazerman & Roy Lewicki, eds., 36–44 (1983); copyright © 1983 by Sage Publications, Inc.; all rights reserved; reprinted by permission of Sage Publications, Inc.

5. Lax, David & Sebenius, James, Interests: The Measure of Negotiation, 2 Negot. J. 76, 78–91 (1986); reprinted with the permission of Plenum Publishing Corporation and authors.

6. De Waal, Frans, Peacemaking Among Primates, 231–39, 269–71 (1989); reprinted by permission from Harvard University Press, copyright © 1989 by Frans B., M. De Waal; all rights reserved.

7. Condlin, Robert J., Bargaining in the Dark: The Normative Incoherence of Lawyer Dispute Bargaining Role, 51 Md. L. Rev. 1, 26–49 (1992); reprinted with the permission of Maryland Law Review and author.

CHAPTER FIVE

1. Gifford, Donald, A Context Based Theory of Strategy Selection in Legal Negotiation, 46 Ohio St. L.J. 41, 58–71 (1985); reprinted with the permission of Ohio State Law Journal and author.

2. Condlin, Robert J., Bargaining in the Dark: The Normative Incoherence of Lawyer Dispute Bargaining Role, 51 Md. L. Rev. 1, 7–11 (1992); reprinted with the permission of Maryland Law Review and author.

3. Excerpts from Getting Past No: Dealing With Difficult People by William Ury; copyright © 1991 by William Ury; used by permission of Bantam Books, a division of Bantam Doubleday Dell Publishing Group, Inc.

4. Lax, David & Sebenius, James, The Power of Alternatives or the Limits to Negotiation, 1 Negot. J. 163 (1985); reprinted with the permission of Plenum Publishing Corporation and authors.

5. Gifford, Donald, Legal Negotiation: Theory and Applications, 50–54 (1989); reprinted with the permission of West Publishing Corporation.

CHAPTER SIX

1. Greenhalgh, Leonard, Relationships in Negotiations, 3 Negot. J. 235, 235–43 (1987); reprinted with the permission of Plenum Publishing Corporation and author.

2. Fisher, Roger & Davis, Wayne H., Six Basic Interpersonal Skills for a Negotiator's Repertoire, 3 Negot. J. 117, 117–22 (1987); reprinted with the permission of Plenum Publishing Corporation and authors.

3. Mnookin, Robert H., Why Negotiations Fail: An Exploration of the Barriers to the Resolution of Conflict, 8 Ohio St. J. on Dispute Resolution, 235–235–47 (1993); reprinted with the permission of Ohio State Journal on Dispute Resolution and author.

4. Bazeman, Max H., Negotiator Judgment, 27 Am Beh. Scientist 211, 211–24 (1985); copyright © 1985 by Sage Publications, Inc.; reprinted by permission of Sage Publication, Inc.

CHAPTER TEN

1. Freund, James, Bridging Troubled Waters: Negotiating Disputes, Litigation, Vol. 12, No. 2, pp. 43–46 (1986); copyright © 1986 by The American Bar Association; reprinted by permission; all rights reserved.

2. Gifford, Donald, A Context-Based Theory of Strategy Selection in Legal Negotiation, 46 Ohio St. L.J. 41, 82–88 (1985); reprinted with the permission of Ohio State Law Journal and author.

3. Gross, Samuel R. & Syverud, Kent D., Getting to No: A Study of Settlement Negotiations and the Selection of Cases for Trial, 90 Mich. L. Rev. 319, 320–25, 327–29, 333, 341, 378–85 (1991); reprinted with permission of Michigan Law Review and authors.

4. Fisher, Roger, What About Negotiation as a Specialty, 69 ABA J. 121, 122–24 (1983); copyright © 1983 by The American Bar Association.

5. Cochran, Robert, Legal Representation and the Next Steps Toward Client Control: Attorney Malpractice for the Failure to Allow the Client to Control Negotiation and Pursue Alternatives to Litigation, 47 Wash. & Lee L. Rev. 818, 823–4, 854–4, 859–63, 867–8, 876–7 (1990); reprinted with the permission of Washington & Lee Law Review.

6. Riskin, Leonard, The Represented Client in a Settlement Conference: The Lessons of G. Heileman Brewing Co. v. Joseph Oat Corp., 69 Wash. U.L. Rev. 1059, 1062–5, 1097–105 (1991); reprinted with the permission of Washington University Law Review and author.

7. Kritzer, Herbert, Fee Arrangements and Negotiation, 21 L. & Soc. Rev. 341, 341–7 (1987); reprinted by permission of the Law and Society Association.

CHAPTER ELEVEN

1. Fiss, Owen M., Against Settlement, 93 Yale L.J. 1073, 1073–1090; reprinted by permission of The Yale Law Journal Company and Fred B. Rothman & Company.

2. Luban, David, Settlements and the Erosion of the Public Realm, 83 Geo. L.J. 2619, 2621–42 (1995); reprinted with the permission of Georgetown University Law Journal and author.

3. McMunigal, Kevin C., The Costs of Settlement: The Impact of Scarcity of Adjudication on Litigating Lawyers, 37 UCLA L. Rev. 833, 834–61 (1990). Copyright © 1990, The Regents of the University of California, all rights reserved.

4. Menkel-Meadow, Carrie, Whose Dispute Is It Anyway?: A Philosophical and Democratic Defense of Settlement (In Some Cases), 83 Geo. L.J. 2663, 2663–85 (1995); reprinted with the permission of Georgetown University Law Journal and author.

CHAPTER TWELVE

1. Norton, Eleanor Holmes, Bargaining and the Ethics of Process, 64 N.Y.U.L. Rev. 493, 506–8, 524–5, 535–6, 538 (1989); reprinted with the permission of New York University Law Review.

2. White, James J., Machiavelli and the Bar: Ethical Limitations on Lying in Negotiation, 1980 American Bar Foundation Research Journal 926, 926-38; copyright © 1980 American Bar Foundation; reprinted with permission.

3. Model Rules of Professional Conduct, Rule 4.1 and Comment and ABA Commission on Evaluation of Professional Standards (Kutak Commission), Model Rules of Professional Conduct (Proposed Final Draft, Jan. 30, 1980), Proposed Rule 4.2(a)&(b) and Comment; copyright © 1980 by The American Bar Association; reprinted by permission of The American Bar Association; all rights reserved.

4. Hazard, Geoffrey C. Jr., The Lawyer's Obligation to Be Trustworthy When Dealing With Opposing Paries, 33 So. Car. L. Rev. 181, 192–96 (1981); reprinted with the permission of South Carolina Law Review.

5. Lowenthal, Gary, Truthful Bargaining by Lawyers, 2 Geo. J. of Legal Ethics 411, 423–7 (1988); reoriented with the permission of Georgetown Journal of Legal Ethics and author.

6. Gordon, Robert, Private Settlement as Alternative Adjudication: A Rationale for Negotiation Ethics, 18 U. Mich. J. of Law Reform 503, 530–6 (1985); reprinted with the permission of University of Michigan Journal of Law Reform.

7. Lax, David A. & Sebenius, James K., Three Thecal Issues in Negotiation, 2 Negot. J. 363–70 (1986); reprinted with the permission of Plenum Publishing Corporation and authors.

8. Hartwell, Steven, Understanding and Dealing With Deception in Legal Negotiation, 6 Ohio St. J. On Disp. Res. 171, 182–7 (1991); reprinted with the permission of the Ohio State Journal on Dispute Resolution and author.

9. Peters, Geoffrey, The Use of Lies in Negotiation, 48 Ohio St. L.J. 1, 8–13 (1987); reprinted with the permission of Ohio State Law Journal and author.

10. Perschbacher, Rex, Regulating Lawyers' Negotiations, 27 Ariz. L. Rev. 75, 77–9, 137–8 (1985); copyright © 1985 by the Arizona Board of Regents; reprinted by permission.

Table of Contents

NEGOTIATION AND SETTLEMENT ADVOCACY

A Book of Readings

*

Section I

NEGOTIATION AS A STRUCTURED PROCESS OF INTERPERSONAL COMMUNICATION

Some negotiators are more successful than others. Many people think that negotiating success is a skill related to an excellent physician's bedside manner or to a major league baseball player's ability to hit the curve ball. Some have natural ability, and some do not. Perhaps it has to do with how each person was raised, or to genetics, or just to chance.

In fact, however, when people negotiate, their behavior frequently follows predictable patterns. Some successful negotiators follow the patterns unconsciously, while others work to bring them to consciousness and use this information to their advantage. For most of us, unless we are conscious about what is occurring, it is difficult to see these recurring themes.

This section elucidates the predictable patterns of negotiation. The materials in Chapter One orient us to the topic of negotiation. They place bargaining in its social and behavioral context, and introduce us to both descriptive and prescriptive approaches to negotiation analysis. We are then ready to move to understand the recurring patterns of negotiation structure.

In Chapter Two we will learn about a technique, derived from social and behavioral experimentation, that is the foundation of all sound bargaining techniques. If we are self-conscious of this technique, we can assure that—at worst—we will never be exploited in our bargaining. It is comforting to know that no matter what else happens in a negotiation, we will not do far worse than we should.

This baseline of avoiding exploitation is just the starting point for becoming self conscious about effective negotiation behavior. In the next two chapters we will learn techniques that will allow us to do much better than merely survive. In Chapter Three we will discover that people frequently bargain to distribute a single unit of value, like money, where gain for one party comes primarily at another's expense. In these competitive contexts, people follow a predictable process of making opening offers, responding with counteroffers, bargaining for concessions, making commitments, and using tactics. By understanding the predictability of bargaining in this context, and by being self conscious about how to use this predictability strategically, we can materially enhance our negotiation outcomes.

In Chapter Four we will see that these predictable patterns of competitive negotiation provide a useful but an incomplete picture of bargaining dynamics. There are times in most negotiations when opportunities arise to create additional value or to expand the range of available options for settlement. By recognizing when these opportunities arise, and by taking advantage of them to craft a creative and elegant solution, we can again enhance our negotiation outcomes.

Finally, in Chapter Five, the last Chapter in this Section, we will discuss how parties can work with their bargaining opposites to move between the available strategies and achieve the best possible outcome. We will also learn how to develop external reference points to the present negotiation that will enable us to gauge our possibilities for success in this interaction. By using all these tools of negotiation structure, by being self conscious, we can dramatically increase the likelihood of reaching optimal negotiated outcomes.

Chapter 1

THE NEGOTIATION PROCESS—
GENERAL OBSERVATIONS

Negotiation can be defined as a communication process that people use to plan transactions and resolve conflict. If this definition is satisfactory, then much of human behavior involves negotiating. Indeed, almost all of our interactions with others involve some kind of negotiation. The readings in this first chapter introduce several preliminary themes that will be amplified in great detail throughout the volume.

In the first selection, Phillip Gulliver, the noted anthropologist, describes two patterns of communication in negotiation that appear to be universal across cultures. Gulliver describes how bargainers employ cyclical and sequential communication patterns as they interact with others.

Frank Sander and the late Jeffrey Rubin next characterize more concretely the two primary contexts in which people negotiate. Bargainers sometimes enter into deal-making transactions, looking forward to build future relationships; and sometimes enter into dispute settlement transactions, looking backward to resolve past conflicts. Strategies effective in one context may be counterproductive in another. They introduce several important concepts, such as the difference between issues and interests, and the power of a good alternative, that we will amplify in later chapters. Effective negotiators recognize the characteristic attributes and opportunities of each bargaining context, and "eventually come to know both faces of the negotiation process."

Lawyers spend much of their professional life working in the transaction planning and the dispute resolution contexts described by Sander and Rubin. Two excerpts from Donald Gifford's writing introduce us to the strategic choices available to lawyers when they negotiate in these contexts. In the first selection, Gifford labels the three typical strategic approaches, and distinguishes between negotiation strategies and negotiator styles. Then, Gifford observes that lawyers' bargaining behavior frequently has a predictable rhythm. This rhythm is influenced by their perception of the relevant bargaining context. He highlights the customary phases of this behavior, and shows how mistakes as to context can make bargaining more difficult.

In our next reading, John Murray builds upon this analysis by offering a typology of the strengths and the weaknesses of competitive and problem-solving bargaining behavior. Experts disagree as to the number of types of bargaining contexts facing the negotiator. For example, Murray sees two, whereas Gifford sees three. All experts agree, however, that effective negotiators must understand the distinctive characteristics of the various bargaining contexts. They can then assess how best to proceed in any negotiation, with appreciation for the upsides and the downsides of their strategy selection. Murray's writing introduces this concept, again to be amplified in later chapters.

Finally, we end this introductory chapter with a personal reflection. Drawing upon his extensive international experience, the late Hungarian diplomat Nyerges Janos provides a list of practical tips for effective negotiating. They provide helpful organizing principles to guide the skilled bargainer.

Readings

1. Phillip H. Gulliver, Disputes and Negotiations: A Cross–Cultural Perspective 81–89 (1979).

2. Frank E.A. Sander & Jeffrey Rubin, *The Janus Quality of Negotiation: Dealmaking and Dispute Settlement,* 4 Negot.J. 109–13 (1988).

3. Donald Gifford, *A Context–Based Theory of Strategy Selection in Legal Negotiation,* 46 Ohio St.L.J. 41, 45–48 (1985).

4. Donald Gifford, Legal Negotiation: Theory and Applications 32–35 (1989).

5. John Murray, *Understanding Competing Theories of Negotiation,* 2 Negot.J. 179, 182–85 (1986).

6. Janos Nyerges, *Ten Commandments for a Negotiator,* 3 Negot.J. 21, 21–6 (1987).

7. For Further Reading

    a. Robert J. Condlin, *"Cases on Both Sides:" Patterns of Argument in Legal Dispute–Negotiation,* 44 Md.L.Rev. 65 (1985).

    b. Robert Ellickson, Order Without Law: How Neighbors Settle Disputes (1991).

    c. Phillip H. Gulliver, *Anthropological Contributions to the Study of Negotiations,* 4 Negot.J. 247 (1988).

    d. Jeffrey Hartje, *Lawyer's Skills in Negotiations: Justice in Unseen Hands,* 1984 J. of Disp.Res. 119.

    e. Geoffrey Martin, *The "Practical" and the "Theoretical" Split in Modern Negotiation Literature,* 4 Negot.J. 45 (1988).

    f. Dean Pruitt, *Strategic Choice in Negotiation,* 27 Am.Beh.Sci. 167 (1983).

    g. Jeffrey Rubin, *Negotiation,* 27 Am.Beh.Sci. 135 (1983).

    h. James K. Sebenius, *Negotiation Analysis: A Characterization and Review,* 38 Manag.Sci. 18 (1992).

    i. I. William Zartman, *Common Elements in the Analysis of the Negotiation Process,* 4 Negot.J. 31 (1988).

PHILLIP H. GULLIVER, DISPUTES AND NEGOTIATIONS: A CROSS-CULTURAL PERSPECTIVE

81–88 (1979).

... [W]hen a dispute emerges and negotiations begin, the two parties start at a distance from one another, in disagreement, opposition, and conflict, with disparate ideas and expectations about an acceptable outcome. Through the processes of negotiation the parties gradually may be able to come together into coordination and collusion and, in the end, to some agreement on the issues between them.

. . .

In negotiation there are two distinct though interconnected processes going on simultaneously: a repetitive, cyclical one and a developmental one. A simple analogy is a moving automobile. There is the cyclical turning of the wheels (linked to the cyclical action of valves, pistons, etc., in the motor) that enables the vehicle to move, and there is the actual movement of the vehicle from one place to another. The latter process depends on the former but the raison d'être of the automobile is its spatial movement. In negotiation, somewhat similarly, there is a cyclical process comprising the repetitive exchange of information between the parties, its assessment, and the resulting adjustments of expectations and preferences; there is also a developmental process involved in the movement from the initiation of the dispute to its conclusion—some outcome—and its implementation.

. . .

It is logically appropriate to discuss first the model of the cyclical process since by analogy it is the turning of the wheels that makes movement of the vehicle possible. Because the two processes are intimately interconnected, references to the developmental process are unavoidable in the following exposition, though they are kept to a minimum so as to avoid confusion.

The Cyclical Model

Briefly, the pattern of repetitive exchange is that, in turn, each party receives information of various kinds from the other and in response offers information to him. There is, however, more than merely communication. There is cognition and learning. Received information is interpreted and evaluated by a party and added to what he already knows or thinks he knows. Thus a party may be able to learn more about his own expectations and preferences, about those of his opponent, and about their common situation and possible outcomes. Learning may induce changes in the party's preference set and his strategies or it may reinforce his existing position. Learning may raise the need for more information from the opponent and/or the need to give further information to him so that he may be induced to learn and therefore be persuaded to shift his position to something more favorable to the party. Depending on the kind of learning, the party makes a tactical choice concerning the purpose and content of his next message, which is then proffered to his opponent. In turn, the other party goes through the same procedure and then offers his information to the first party ... and so on. Thus, one might say, the wheels turn and the vehicle moves.

. . .

The Exchange of Information

In negotiation there is a continual need both to give and to receive information. There is a need to give it in order to tell the opponent about one's own demands and strengths and to attempt to induce him to shift his demands toward one's own. There is a need to obtain information in order to get a better understanding of the opponent—his expectations and demands, his attitudes, strategies, strengths, and weaknesses, together with any changes in all these matters. In order to obtain needed information, a party has to give information to his opponent. In order to give information, he needs to receive information from his opponent. Receiving information creates the opportunity, but also the necessity perhaps, to learn and to adjust expectations and demands. That in turn induces the party to offer further information and to seek to obtain more.

Thus there is and has to be exchange of information, or more accurately, of messages. Strictly speaking, information is not exchanged but shared since the giver himself retains that which is given, in contrast with economic exchange of goods. A party must respond and wishes to respond to the receipt of messages by giving his own in return. As in other kinds of social reciprocity, a party offers messages in order to obtain a response and to be able to claim a response, or at least some kind of reaction that carries a message. Refusal to exchange messages may, in the short run, draw further messages from the opponent and may be intended to do so. Continued refusal—or what is effectively the same thing, mere repetition of previous messages—leads to impasse and the possible breakdown of negotiations.

Yet these desires and needs to give and to receive information create a persisting dilemma for each party. How much information should be given and when? What information is required and how can it be obtained? Moreover, as Iklé has pointed out, "It is an essential feature of negotiations that the process of finding out the opponent's terms (and of revealing one's own) is also part of the process of inducing him to soften his terms (and of making one's own more acceptable to him)." While seeking to persuade or coerce his opponent, a party lays himself open to persuasion and coercion. He may, therefore, attempt to defend himself by the offer of further information and his opponent proceeds likewise.

. . .

An inherent problem in these exchanges is that each party tends to edit in his own favor the information he offers. He wishes to show and substantiate his demands and to emphasize his strengths and determination but without disclosing his weaknesses, his truer expectations, or his minimal requirements. Thus he usually stresses and exaggerates the more advantageous features of his case while discounting or ignoring the disadvantageous ones. A party must expect that the messages he receives are similarly edited. The flow of information is therefore distorted in some degree. Moreover, the exchange of messages always carries the possibility that unintended information will be conveyed at the same time. On the one hand, a party may not say what he intended, or he may say more than he intended as information is carried between the lines and, as an affectual penumbra, colors what is said.

On the other hand, his opponent may misreceive and misinterpret messages and obtain wrong information.

. . .

The kinds of information exchanged depend a good deal on the current phase of the negotiation: that is, on the mode and focus of interaction and purpose at the time (as explained in the developmental model). Some kinds of subject matter are more likely to be confined to particular phases. For instance, information concerning procedural rules is more pertinent to earlier phases when procedure is being established, although it is never altogether excluded from later phases if the parties consider it important. Factual information similarly is more emphasized in earlier phases, whereas messages carrying threats, promises, and other persuasion are likely to be more common in later ones. Yet the subject matter and even the overt content of messages are often much the same in different phases even though the information transmitted can be quite different. "This is my best offer," or "We cannot agree to your claim," carry and are more or less intended to carry different information in earlier and later phases. During final bargaining a "final offer" may indeed be just that or something very near it, but earlier it is nothing like so definitive and usually it is not intended to be so. Earlier, the information is something like a show of the importance of the particular issue in dispute and of the strength of resistance intended. It may in fact be little more than putting a toe in the water to test it, an attempt to get reaction and response from the opponent in order to learn more about his expectations and preferences. It relates, in the earlier phases, to attempts by parties to perceive where the main differences lie and what the maximal limits are to the range of reference on the issue in question. That is to say, messages are to be understood, and are so interpreted by the receiver, depending on what is already known and not known by the parties about each other. A message and its information are very largely contextual, as of course is the case in most ordinary conversation.

Assessment of messages is necessary to complete the transference of information and so make it usable. Some or even all of a message may not be received. What is received is subject to appraisal. For instance, what is its content, overtly and covertly? What is the probable degree of validity of fact, opinion, affectual state, and ignorance? What did the opponent intend to convey and with what force? What did he convey unwittingly and why in the fashion he used? What is absent from the message and why? Such assessment can be carried out quite carefully and analytically or, at the other extreme, it may be largely unconsidered gut reaction. Some messages are highly complex, containing information that cannot be immediately assessed or its implications understood. Such information may have to be set aside for the moment until more information is accumulated or until a later phase of the negotiations. Other messages are so simple that, in one sense, their content is clear; yet the alert negotiator is prepared to acknowledge that the simplicity may be deceptive, deliberately or not on the part of the sender. "No" can indicate or be understood to indicate a variety of information: "yes" or "yes but" or "I do not know" among others, or it can indicate a less certain denial than hitherto and so reveal some degree of change in the sender's expectations or determination.

For instance, an observation on the weather or a humorous anecdote may—though it may not—carry an expression of friendliness and willingness to be cooperative or an expression of antagonism and derision. It can show a desire to break tension, to pause awhile, or to change topic and tactics. It can be a sign of a lack of further ideas or of frustration, and many other things, according to the current phase of the negotiations and the relationship between the parties. Though seemingly trivial, it affords a party a possibility of indicating something about his position, attitude, and expectations. It may, at a particular point in the negotiations, be quite crucial to an improvement of understanding that in context is no less significant than the party's forthright declaration on some matter. Yet the message may be unimportant, offering little that is new or helpful to the other.

. . .

In terms of the cyclical model, the supply of more or less assessed information can be seen as flowing in two directions. First, received information may affect a party's behavior as a result of causing changes in knowledge, preferences, attitudes, and strategy—in brief, as a result of changes in his preference set. Second, the information may affect a party's behavior as a result of his assessment of his opponent's future behavior—his expectations of his opponent. Both are liable to be affected and changed by each new piece of information received.

FRANK E. A. SANDER AND JEFFREY Z. RUBIN, THE JANUS QUALITY OF NEGOTIATION: DEALMAKING AND DISPUTE SETTLEMENT

4 Negot. J. 109–13 (1988).

In this brief column, we will explore the simple difference between negotiation over entry into a relationship (what we will refer to as Deal–Making Negotiation, or DMN) and negotiation over remaining in or leaving a relationship (what we will refer to as Dispute Settlement Negotiation, or DSN). We will first look at the critical distinguishing characteristics between DSN and DMN, and then consider briefly some of the practical consequences of this distinction for more effective negotiation.

By definition, DMN arises when parties embark upon a deal. Typically this means the parties *have had no prior dealings,* and the *focus is on their future relationship* (e.g., A negotiates for the purchase of B's house; C Corp. agrees to sell its business to D Corp.). Although the second factor is critical in this definition, the first is not. The deal-making parties *may* have had a prior relationship. Indeed sometimes the deal grows out of, or is based on, a prior relationship (e.g., Union X makes a new contract with Company Y; Father F enters an arrangement with Son S for shoveling the sidewalk or putting out the trash), but the thrust of the dealmaking—and hence of the negotiations that lead to the deal—is forward-looking. The parties typically have come together in order to reach agreement, and anticipate a future relationship under the umbrella of the deal that has been struck.

. . .

By contrast, dispute settlement negotiation (DSN) is a *backward*-looking transaction because dispute settlement, in the sense the term is used here, means a dispute arising under an existing agreement. If a dispute arises in the course of any of the previously described deals (e.g., the house to be sold is damaged in a fire, and the question is who bears the risk of that event), then the resulting negotiation is a DSN. A DSN addresses the rights (both substantive and procedural) established under a previous agreement....

Note, finally, that although the distinction between DMN and DSN is fairly clear, there is often a symbiotic interplay between the two. A DMN creates rights that may later form the norms of DSN. Conversely, some disputes arising under an agreement can best be resolved by creating a new relationship (or formulating a new agreement) between the parties, thereby turning a DSN into a new deal.

What are some of the practical implications of these distinctions?

1. As suggested above, DSN looks more to rights (established under the previously made deal); parties in a DSN pay attention to what they feel *entitled* to. In contrast, DMN looks more to interests (because there often aren't any "rights" governing a deal that has not yet been struck). This distinction is attenuated by the symbiotic relationship point made above. That is, in a typical DSN one can look backward to the rights established under the agreement or look forward by creating a new deal. This is a particular problem for lawyers, who are all too prone in cases of dispute settlement to look backward to the legal rights of the disputants (i.e., the court outcome) rather than seeing the case as an opportunity for a new agreement that meets the future needs of the parties and downplays their rights vis-á-vis the present agreement.

Theoretically, negotiations over interests (as in DMN) should be easier to move to agreement than negotiations over rights (as in DSN). Interests can be satisfied in multiple ways, by devising creative options for joint gain, and thus tend to be non-zero sum in nature; rights, although they need not be construed as zero sum, are typically so interpreted by protagonists: Either I win or you win—but not both.

2. In most dispute settlement negotiations, the Best Alternative to a Negotiated Agreement (or BATNA) is fairly clear—what would happen, absent a negotiated settlement, under the terms of the previously made deal.... In deal-making negotiations, however, the vistas are much wider. If A doesn't enter into the deal with B, A may not sell his house at all. Or A may sell it to P or Q.

On the one hand, the deal-making negotiator has a much harder task than the dispute settlement negotiator (because the alternatives are so wide open); on the other hand, there is a far greater opportunity for inventive solutions that meet the needs and interests of the other party....

Note also that in DSN, both parties' BATNAs are usually the same, though their assessments of it may well diverge. But in DMN, each party's BATNA is likely to be different; hence it becomes much more difficult to ascertain the other's BATNA.

. . .

3. Another consequence is that in DSN there is more likely to be an adversarial flavor to the proceedings. In the words of Lax and Sebenius' *The*

Manager as Negotiator (1986), DSN is often about the "claiming" of resources that are in dispute under the terms of an agreement. DMN, in contrast, is often concerned with "creating" opportunities that make negotiated settlement an attractive outcome.

. . .

4. The *mode of discourse* and the *external frames of reference* are also likely to be quite different in the two types of negotiation. In DMN, the parties have wide-ranging opportunities to explore each other's interests and options. The mode of discourse will therefore tend to be informal, reasonably friendly, and focused on a frame of reference that lies in the future: What happens to us if we should go ahead and agree to reach agreement? The focus of activity is devising an agreement that you are ready to "live with" later on.

In contrast, DSN is characterized by a more formal, less friendly mode of discourse—as when one appeals to the formal proceedings of arbitration to bring about the settlement of a dispute under an agreement. And the frame of reference, as we earlier observed, is in the past—usually including a canvass of all the sins of commission and omission that have led the disputants into their present quandary.

DONALD GIFFORD, A CONTEXT–BASED THEORY OF STRATEGY SELECTION IN LEGAL NEGOTIATION

46 Ohio St.L.Rev. 41, 45–48 (1985).

A Basic Typology of Negotiation Strategies

The type of negotiation strategy likely to yield the most favorable outcome for a client is an important question, because the attorney is professionally obligated to seek an advantageous result for her client in all negotiations. During the last twenty years, negotiation theorists from various disciplines including law, social psychology, economics, and international relations have debated vigorously the attributes of various approaches to negotiation. This section defines the characteristics of three primary negotiation strategies and suggests that the negotiator's view of his relationship with the other party is the primary determinant that identifies each theory and distinguishes it from the others. The competitive negotiator seeks to force the opposing party to a settlement favorable to the negotiator by convincing the opponent that his case is not as strong as previously thought and that he should settle the case. The cooperative strategy mandates that the negotiator make concessions to build trust in the other party and encourage further concessions on his part. The third strategy, integrative bargaining, seeks to find solutions to the conflict which satisfy the interests of both parties.

The cooperative and integrative strategies are separate and distinct, even though some legal negotiation theorists fail to distinguish them. The two noncompetitive strategies are similar; the goal of both is to create a nonadversarial atmosphere in which the parties can work toward an agreement. Aside from sharing this objective, however, the strategies involve quite different tactics. Under the cooperative strategy, the negotiator makes concessions in anticipation that his opponent will reciprocate and that the parties will move closer to a compromise resolution. The cooperative strategy is the noncompetitive strategy most likely to be used in a "share bargaining" or "distributive bargaining" situation, that is, where the parties must divide a fixed quantity of resources. The integrative strategy, on the other hand, is not a concession based strategy that seeks to divide a fixed pie; rather, it maximizes the parties' potential for problem-solving in order to increase the joint benefit and expand the pie. It is incorrect, however, to view the cooperative and integrative strategies solely as aspects of a single accommodative or collaborative strategy functioning in two different contexts. Even in an apparently distributive or share bargaining situation, the integrative negotiator strives to identify problem-solving solutions which are not readily perceived. In contrast, the cooperative negotiator initiates the concession swapping process.

Negotiation strategies must be distinguished from the personal styles of negotiators. Professor Gerald Williams' recent text on legal negotiations tends to blur this distinction by using the same descriptive labels, cooperative and competitive, to describe both negotiators' styles and negotiation strategies. Professor Williams' work focuses on an empirical study of effective attorneys' characteristics as evaluated by other attorneys. He labels negotiators who are described by other attorneys as being forthright, trustful, logical (not emotional), courteous, personable, friendly, and tactful as *cooperative*. On the other hand, Professor Williams describes the competitive negotiator as dominant, forceful, aggressive, attacking, ambitious, egotistical, arrogant, and clever. Professor Williams' focus on the personal characteristics of the attorney leads him to the cynical and confining conclusion that "[i]ndividual negotiators may not have much choice about the basic approach they use, which may be determined largely by one's own personality and experience."

A negotiation strategy is a separate and distinct concept from the negotiator's personal characteristics; a strategy is the negotiator's planned and systematic attempt to move the negotiation process toward a resolution favorable to his client's interests. Negotiation strategy consists of the decisions made regarding the opening bid and the subsequent modifications of proposals. Admittedly, strategy and personal style are frequently intertwined. A negotiator who has a "forceful, aggressive, and attacking" personal style frequently will succeed in causing an opponent to lose confidence in himself or his case thereby inducing substantial unilateral concessions, a goal of the competitive strategy. In another instance, however, a negotiator who is "courteous, personable, and friendly" may, through competitive strategic moves such as high opening demands and infrequent concessions, be even more successful in destroying the opponent's confidence in his case and inducing unilateral concessions from the opponent. Usually, a negotiator's personal characteristics positively correlate with his preferred negotiating strategy. Separating personal style and negotiation strategies, however, yields new flexibility for the negotiator. It is possible for negotiators with cooperative personal characteristics to adopt a competitive strategy when it would be advantageous, and naturally competitive individuals can adopt a cooperative strategy. Further, a negotiator should often make competitive, cooperative, and integrative moves within a single negotiation. If negotiation strategies are recognized as something distinct from the personal style of negotiators, then the essential elements of each strategy can be disseminated in writing and taught to prospective negotiators. Short of psychoanalysis, however, it might be difficult or impossible to transform a naturally "courteous, personable, and friendly" individual, even temporarily, into someone who is "attacking, forceful, and aggressive."

DONALD GIFFORD, LEGAL NEGOTIATION: THEORY AND APPLICATIONS
32–35 (1989).

STAGES OF A NEGOTIATION

Many social scientists and legal scholars studying negotiation have noted that the negotiation process appears to progress through a series of developmental stages. Although it probably is impossible to impose a rigid structural model of negotiation, the beginning lawyer should be careful that her negotiating behavior is appropriate for the specific phase of the negotiation. In particular, it is important to acknowledge that negotiation often progresses from phases dominated by competitive tactics to stages dominated by cooperative and problem-solving tactics.

According to those who study the negotiation process, bargaining typically begins with an *orientation and positioning* phase during which the negotiators usually set the "tone" for the negotiations. Initial encounters between the negotiators are likely to be indicative of both the negotiators' *styles* and the *tactics* that will follow. For example, if the attorneys share *competitive* styles at this stage, the negotiation is likely to be a nasty one. As a part of this orientation and positioning process, the negotiators also make initial presentations to each other about how they view the merits of the transaction or case being negotiated. This often is followed by initial proposals for resolving the disputes between the parties; these early proposals usually are not to be taken as serious attempts to resolve the issues in dispute.

Negotiation then progresses through a phase which many negotiation theorists refer to as *exploration of the issues*. Both lawyers present arguments and selectively disclose information supporting their proposals. At the same time, each negotiator engages in an important information-gathering process concerning the other side's interests and attitudes towards the issues being negotiated. She also learns about facts previously known only by the other side. This stage of the negotiation also includes the initial narrowing of differences between the parties as the two negotiators begin to make concessions from their initially extreme positions and drop their arguments on behalf of issues or positions in which their clients are not genuinely interested.

These two phases, *orientation and initial proposals* and *exploration of the issues,* often are contentious and time-consuming. It is typical in personal injury negotiations, for example, for these stages to go on for many months—and frequently for several years—and then to have the remaining stages of the negotiation take place in weeks, days or even hours. In these cases, it is important for the beginning negotiator not to mistake anything that happens until this point in the negotiations as a serious effort to resolve the case. These two early phases are also typically more competitive, particularly in negotiations involving fields such as personal injury cases and labor negotiations, than are the later stages.

It is not until a subsequent stage, variously referred to as *"bargaining"* or *"convergence"* that most serious attempts to resolve the differences between the parties occur. Realizing that deadlock is near, one of the parties typically makes a realistic proposal on one or more of the issues—an offer that is intended to be the basis for a final agreement as opposed to a strategic move. Realistic proposals, involving considerable modifications of earlier unrealistic proposals, flow back and forth. Both sides typically make concessions or suggest problem-solving alternatives. This is not to say that all is sweetness and light. Threats and arguments continue; each negotiator still hides her minimal or "bottom line" settlement requirements. The issues which are genuinely disputed separate out from issues on which compromise or other agreement can be more easily achieved. Then the negotiators move on to trading concessions on issues that the clients would rather not concede, or to deciding that they would rather give up something than have the negotiation stalemate.

Eventually, the negotiation reaches a final stage in which the parties either reach agreement or terminate the negotiation. If the parties successfully negotiate an agreement, the final stage often includes resolving a number of details that have been ignored pending closure on the major issues in dispute.

For someone approaching legal negotiation as a practitioner, and not predominantly as a scholarly observer, two points are critical. First, many—but certainly not all—negotiations follow a pattern of proceeding from *competitive* phases to more *cooperative* or *problem-solving* stages. Second, legal negotiations are often lengthy, and *cooperative* and *problem-solving* techniques sometimes can be risky early in the negotiation unless the negotiator can be sure that such techniques will not lead to exploitation by a *competitive* negotiator.

Competitive tactics early in the negotiation, perhaps ironically, sometimes increase the prospects for successful use of cooperative or problem-solving tactics later in the negotiation.

In summary, the negotiator should consider *timing* as an essential factor in deciding whether to use competitive tactics or the more collaborative tactics of the cooperative and problem-solving methods. In the earliest stages of the negotiation, cooperative and problem-solving tactics are less likely to be reciprocated than later in the negotiation. Early in the process, cooperative moves may be regarded by some negotiators as signs of weakness or inexperience. This is not to assert that meaningful collaborative negotiation is necessarily impossible before extended haggling occurs, but rather to suggest that the negotiator must be realistically confident that the other party is also willing to use cooperative or problem-solving tactics.

JOHN S. MURRAY, UNDERSTANDING COMPETING THEORIES OF NEGOTIATION

2 Negot.J. 179, 182–85 (1986).

EXPLANATION OF NEGOTIATING BEHAVIOR

. . .

The competitive negotiator appears to have a narrow perspective on the negotiation as a whole, but broad and flexible standards for selecting strategies and manipulating the process. Competitive theory is reflected in behavior when the negotiator:

1. Maximizes own return in present transaction.

2. Considers needs/interests/attitudes of opponent as not legitimate, and only relevant when usable to achieve # 1 above.

3. Views all disputing processes and strategies as equally valuable and useful if helpful in achieving # 1 above.

4. Behaves cooperatively only if it helps achieve # 1 above.

5. Chooses processes and strategies similar to military maneuvers. The focus is on the process of winning, not on the resolution of disputes.

6. Presents a strong defense against opponent's tactics.

7. Must control the negotiating process for proper manipulation.

The problem-solving negotiator, on the other hand, holds a broad perspective on the negotiation as a whole, combined with more rigid limits on acceptable strategies and conduct. Some of the key behavioral elements for the problem-solver are:

1. Maximizes own return within the larger time and community context.

2. Considers needs/interests/attitudes of other side as both relevant and legitimate to resolving the dispute.

3. Is competitive but not antagonistic.

4. Tries to discover and share any joint gains available.

5. Concentrates on the substance of the dispute or decision.

6. Considers negotiation and other voluntary processes as superior to nonvoluntary methods (adjudication).

These separate behavioral characteristics contain significant strengths within the bargaining situation. The competitive negotiator can be focused and single-minded, with no details being materially relevant other than the present dispute and the party/client. This concentration allows the competitive negotiator to prepare fully for a specific settlement conference. He or she can come armed with a solid offer and fixed negotiation strategies. The opponent's perspective and tactics will not affect the opening position or strategies; they are important only for the manner and rate of concessions, should the negotiator decide to make any at all. Such knowledge gives the negotiator a reassuring sense of control that translates into confidence that is impressive in the negotiation setting.

Another strength follows directly from this disregard for the opponent's position and tactics. The competitive negotiator has analyzed the facts, determined the position, and made the case. The opponent cannot dislodge or defeat this preparation by any means of persuasion based on the merits. Having such an unbreachable defensive position permits the competitive negotiator to stress an aggressive offense aimed at persuading, coercing, deceiving or otherwise manipulating the opponent to an acceptable agreement.

There is also strength in the competitive negotiator's flexibility in selecting strategies. Everything is acceptable, including the alternative of not negotiating, with the only limit being the express violation of ethical obligations. The ultimate selection is based directly on which strategy yields the maximum expected gain for the party/client. A significant element of bargaining power is the attractiveness of a good alternative to negotiating with the opponent. The competitive negotiator does not hesitate to choose that alternative when it is perceived as yielding a bigger gain, even if that choice places the party/client in a psychologically costly court trial. The relevant standards are quantitative: the size of gain expected from the alternative, discounted to reflect any time delay, compared to what appears possible in settlement. The competitive negotiator thereby avoids the confusion and indecision fostered by the impact of intangible or psychological factors and the normative arguments of fairness, wisdom, durability, and efficiency.

Finally, there is psychological strength in the excitement of doing battle. Like a military general, the competitive negotiator concentrates full attention on manipulating the tools and processes available within the negotiation setting. The goal is victory over the opponent on the field of battle. Resolving the underlying disagreements between parties/clients is left to others. With no responsibility for resolving these underlying problems, the negotiator can savor the excitement and challenge of the negotiation chase as if it were only a game, like baseball, chess or poker.

On the other side, the problem-solving negotiator also brings strengths to the bargaining table. Concentration on the merits of the dispute gives the problem-solver a sense of legitimacy, centrality and purpose. The problem-solver is responsible not only for tactical decisions within the negotiation setting but also for helping resolve the underlying problems of the party/client. Such a central role to the life of the party/client makes the negotiator's efforts less like a game and more like a serious human responsibility. In addition, using the merits as the central negotiating focus establishes a more objective and predictable control mechanism than can be achieved by relying on manipulation of the personal strategy and style decisions of the negotiators.

The problem-solving negotiator also generates strength by recognizing the importance of common interests and joint gains. Such objectives can be shared among negotiators and parties/clients in a mutually positive and reinforcing way, quite different than the competitive effect that the goal of victory has.

Finally, successful problem-solving is a satisfying experience on a human level. Since the intended outcome of the negotiation is a win-win result, the accomplishment of creating an innovative solution that maximizes joint as well as individual gains can be shared with the other side. The process of reaching this goal is psychologically unifying, rather than divisive. Negotiating is thus an enjoyable and challenging personal experience, rather than a highly stressful battle of wits and words.

DOWNSIDE RISKS

Each behavioral pattern exhibits weaknesses as well as strengths.... The significance of recognizing these risks lies in understanding negotiator vulnerabilities, identifying possible threats to consistently good outcomes, and developing appropriate responses or changes to improve the result.

· · ·

It is especially enlightening to analyze the downside risks with the objective of devising actions that might decrease or eliminate them. For the competitive negotiator, adopting actions intended to lessen the risks appears to change negotiating behavior from a competitive to a problem-solving mode.

For example, actions aimed at reducing the harmful effects of frustration, anger, mistrust, misinformation and misjudgment must of necessity include building a better working relationship between the negotiators. The objective would be to identify and eliminate possible breakdowns that are based on emotional and communication problems and not due to the inability to find an outcome that maximizes the party/client gain. The result of adopting such actions would be to improve the amount and credibility of information exchanged, increase the grounds for trust, and lessen the use of manipulation based on process rather than substance.

The success of misrepresentation and deceit as a strategy to elicit information leading to joint gains depends largely on an inequality in the relative level of negotiator competence, which is not a solid base for generating consistently good outcomes. Therefore, actions intended by the competitive negotiator to uncover joint gains would need to include improvement in active listening and acceptance of the opponent's legitimacy.

Reducing brinkmanship would help eliminate impasses where settlement at the party/client's maximum is possible but is frustrated by the psychological impact of the frequent use of threats. Pulling back from the brink requires fewer threats of impasse, less psychological tension, and more recognition of substantive fairness.

The competitive negotiator who tries to counter these downside risks becomes more problem-solving than competitive in orientation, thereby exhibiting more of the characteristics and strengths associated with problem-solving theory.

On the other side, analysis of the downside risks of problem-solving theory suggests that corrective actions will lead to a strengthening of problem-solving skills, not to a change in basic negotiating behavior. The theories are in this way asymmetrical.

For example, the tendency toward unwarranted compromise and accommodation is countered not by confrontation and stubbornness but by more thorough preparation on the merits and a stronger commitment to an identifiable substantive standard. Indefinite aspiration levels and bottom lines pose serious problems for the problem-solving negotiator at all stages of negotiation, from the initial planning to post-agreement evaluation. Corrective steps include the development and use of more accurate analysis of the subject matter, not a shift to process manipulation and positional bargaining.

Viewing impasse not as failure but as a better alternative than agreeing to an unfair settlement does not force a negotiator to be confrontational in a competitive sense. Rather, it causes the problem-solver to be even more committed to a recognized standard of fairness and more flexible in strategy selection.

One of the most feared downside risks for the problem-solver is vulnerability to deception and manipulation by a competitive opponent. The result can be not only an inequitable outcome but also a residual sense of personal and professional embarrassment. Reciprocating with equally deceptive and competitive behavior may be the easiest response, but such reciprocity is defensive in nature, not corrective. Actions to detect and counter deception and manipulation must focus on ways to build confidence in the truthfulness of information exchanged and in the identification of various negotiating tactics.

Personal confidence in the negotiator's own ability and judgment is a prerequisite for effective problem-solving. The negotiator builds such confidence by acquiring up-to-date knowledge of both substance and process, preparing rigorously for each case, and seeking practical negotiating experiences.

Negotiation for the problem-solver who tries to correct for downside risks does not shift to a more competitive and confrontational mode but rather retains and enhances problem-solving characteristics.

JANOS NYERGES, TEN COMMANDMENTS
FOR A NEGOTIATOR

3 Negot.J. 21, 21–26 (1987).

Toward the end of my professional career—I was Special Representative of the Hungarian Government to International Economic Organizations—I was asked by my younger colleagues about the "secret" of my negotiation ability. This question, though flattering, took me by surprise because, as a matter of fact, I never gave much thought to how I did what I did.

. . .

The question of what makes a good negotiator continues to intrigue me. Based on my experience, observation, and study I've developed my own "Ten Commandments for a Negotiator." Here they are:

. . .

1. You Shall Love and Cherish Your Trade

. . .

It is obvious that involvement and dedication to a cause are not enough; in fact, without a strong sense of professionalism, this type of adherence can be a liability. Professionalism, to my mind, is not simply the fact that a good negotiator has a high professional standing. I view professionalism as an intellectual and emotional involvement and commitment to the profession itself. True negotiators are enthusiastic about negotiation, just as good lawyers, doctors, engineers, and teachers are in love with their trade.

. . .

2. BE COURAGEOUS

A good negotiator must command respect. Respect cannot be conferred by rank or functions; it is due to character. Nothing confers respect more than courage, which is the readiness to accept responsibilities and to make decisions.

In German terms, there are two different qualifications: *Entschlussfähig* (i.e., capable to make decisions) and *Entshlussfreudig* (i.e., enjoys making decisions). Being capable of making decisions seems obvious. In reality, however, many negotiators are not born to negotiate, nor even trained to do so. . . .

One of my former ministers was once negotiating with his colleague in a foreign country. As he made a proposal that was a bit unusual, his partner picked up the phone on his desk and, after a quick exchange with the person at the other end of the line, turned to my minister and said: "I am sorry, I cannot accept." Throughout the long discussions, this little scene was repeated several times, with different answers. Finally, my minister had had enough. He turned to his colleague and said, "Couldn't you give me, dear colleague, that phone number?" Enjoying decision making is a quality that's rarely found. It is a sign of a sovereign will, of self-confidence.

. . .

3. THE EAGLE'S EYE MUST BE YOURS

Needless to say, courage and acceptance of the challenges are not enough. Good judgment, quick assessment of the situation—"the eagle's eye" of my third commandment—is also necessary. Without it, courage remains blind. For a negotiator, quick assessment of the situation is what a targeting device is to a guided missile.

I would like to emphasize that good judgment, the correct assessment being a precondition for making an appropriate decision, has a specific importance in the context of the negotiation. More often than not in negotiation, the real situation is far from being clear. Among the factors that obscure the truth are inconsistent behavior on the other side, the irresistible impact of one's own patterns of thinking, the smokescreen of purposely created impressions by the other side, and lack of information. There frequently are few "redcoats" on this battlefield that reveal the positions of the other party.

Speed of assessment is vital because time is the eternal enemy of the negotiator. Sometimes one can buy time, but such a purchase often involves a price that may later turn out to be too high. Instead of buying time, speed in recognizing the real situation *gains* time.

. . .

One word of warning: Quick assessment does not always mean a quick answer. The answer of the good negotiator, once the assessment is quickly made, must be subordinated to tactical considerations.

4. THERE ARE NO PROBLEMS, ONLY OPPORTUNITIES

This very wise advice was quoted to me as having originally been said by a former president of Trans World Airlines. Problems often hypnotize the negotiator, just as the cold eyes of the snake immobilize the little rabbit. However, I believe there are no situations, no problems that do not offer opportunities—if you look for them. By viewing a problem as an opportunity, you often discover new, sometimes surprising proposals. Last but not least, this kind of opportunity can help you convert a seemingly zero sum situation into a non-zero sum situation. The only thing that a good negotiator must do is *look* for these opportunities. If this is how you view "problems," you will find opportunities.

5. BE HONEST UNDER ALL CIRCUMSTANCES

The "commandments" described thus far apply not only to negotiators, but also to the military and boxing champion. These are rules for fighting persons.

Negotiation is a fight—I have no doubt about this—but not a fight alone. It is a fight with a specific character. The good negotiator is not simply a fighter for victory, but a fighter who seeks to win the mind, the sympathy, and the cooperation of his or her opposite number.

Therefore, the most needed quality—without which a negotiator is doomed to fail—is honesty, both intellectual and moral. Honesty has many manifestations and it's a quality that a good negotiator displays on each and every occasion. Negotiators should never have to say "Look how honest I am!" Such a protestation, in fact, places in question the honesty of the person speaking. Instead, honesty should be manifested by faithful observance of the rules of the game, loyalty shown in the way arguments are put forward, and giving the benefit of the doubt to the other party. Honesty is unconditional.

. . .

Interaction cannot be regarded only as the development of mutual sympathy based on personal understanding and esteem. It is an intellectual process as well. In addition, the presentation of facts in negotiation should be handled in a way that strengthens the feeling that the negotiators are *partners* rather than *opponents*.

6. LOVE YOUR OPPONENT EVEN IF YOU RECEIVE SOMETHING LESS IN RETURN

Negotiators are in a contradictory situation: Each wants the problem resolved in a self-interested way. This separates them. On the other hand, each of them has to resolve the same problem, and this unites them. Negotiators are like two workers carrying the same burden: Whether they like it or not, they are part of the same "chain-gang." The negotiator who dislikes or is rude to the other side adds to the mutual burden instead of alleviating it. The better negotiator, on the other hand, respects the other side.

7. PUT YOURSELF IN THE SHOES OF YOUR OPPONENT, BUT DO NOT REMAIN THERE TOO LONG

The good negotiator feels the necessity to put himself or herself into the situation of the other side. This feeling is a natural byproduct of the negotiating process itself. Negotiation involves personal contact, communication, and interaction. . . .

Knowing it is one thing. Reacting to it is another. An inexperienced negotiator is sometimes tempted to use the internal difficulty of the negotiating partner as a welcome occasion to exert pressure. A good negotiator knows that this attitude is more often than not counter-productive. Instead, the good negotiator will try to understand and to alleviate this embarrassing situation. This attitude is sometimes mingled with a kind of sympathy and compassion.

Here lies the danger: Having put oneself in the shoes of the other fellow can lead to the road on which those shoes were marching—that is, seeking solutions which risk being beneficial to the other party alone. The right attitude in such a situation is to find answers that alleviate the burden of the other party while also providing satisfaction for yourself. Therefore, the more willing a negotiator is to assimilate, to feel the problems of the other side, the more that negotiator has to bear in mind the self-interested goals.

8.   CONVERT YOUR OPPONENT INTO YOUR PARTNER

Every negotiator needs help, and the person who is in the best position to give this help is the opponent. Hence, the importance of the conversion of the opponent into a negotiating *partner*. This comes almost automatically, if the previous three commandments were successfully observed. Combined, these precepts yield the indispensable element in any negotiation: trust. Even in extreme cases where the partners are known to each other as criminals or outlaws, they must trust each other, to a minimal extent at least, if the negotiations are to succeed.

9.   DO NOT ACT BEFORE YOU FIND OUT WHAT YOUR PARTNER'S AIMS ARE

In my mind, bargaining in negotiation begins when substantial discussion occurs, offers are made, positions are taken. But—and this mistake occurs very often—what happens if your partner's position is not what you believed it was? You made overtures, your promises, and your threats are all in vain. The harm is greater in such cases than to lose time and opportunity. By revealing your ignorance, you cease to be a competent negotiator.

Therefore, the first stage of the negotiations has to be to find out, to the greatest extent possible, what the partner really wants to achieve. Once you know it, start the bargaining.

10.   YOUR PARTNER IS AT LEAST AS INTELLIGENT AS YOU ARE; BUT YOU MUST HAVE MORE WILL

The good negotiator never underestimates the intellectual capacity of any opponent. Rather, a good negotiator closely observes every move of the partner, giving very serious attention to each action. Soon a good negotiator will realize that negotiation is not a contest of intelligence but a contest of will.

. . .

The good negotiator sees such crises coming, and is prepared to meet them. The better negotiator prepares for such crises, taking good care that the stakes and risks on the other side are greater than his or her own.

Chapter 2

THE PRISONER'S DILEMMA— AVOIDING EXPLOITATION IN THE MIXED–MOTIVE EXCHANGE

Chapter One gave us a general overview of the ubiquitous communication process people use to plan transactions or resolve conflict. In this chapter, we begin to identify more specifically the key ingredients of effective bargaining. Our starting point is the thesis that we would all appreciate a simple prescription that would permit us to avoid being exploited when we negotiate. In the chapters following this one, we will detail how to move upward from this baseline of avoiding exploitation and attain more satisfying outcomes.

Negotiators typically begin their dealings with a number of potentially conflicting motives about how best to proceed. On the one hand, they want to do well, to win as much as they can, for themselves or their client, firm or cause. Aggressive bargaining strategies may help them accomplish these goals successfully. On the other hand, bargainers also recognize that they must interact, however minimally, in order to reach agreement. Typically, enlightened self-interest, not altruism, pulls in this more cooperative direction. Even when people are in bitter dispute, they know that better outcomes might be possible if only their bargaining relationship could be fostered. This cooperative interaction could bring a double benefit. It might lead to a better result in the present negotiation. It might also encourage more successful outcomes in any future dealings.

These mixed motives create a predicament for participants as they develop a preferred negotiating strategy. Many competitive bargaining tactics are hard on the alliance of the parties, and may chill collaborative opportunities. Unfortunately, however, collaborative strategies can leave one open to exploitation by negotiators who do not place a similar premium on a good working relationship. In the face of this inevitable uncertainty, how should an effective negotiator proceed?

For over fifty years a broad range of scholars and practitioners have been intrigued by this strategic puzzle. It has a name: "The Prisoner's Dilemma." Game theorists, mathematicians, political scientists, psychologists and practitioners of negotiation have analyzed the puzzle in detail. Recently, these researchers have advanced some intriguing hypotheses about managing the mixed motives inherent in the prisoner's dilemma. The following materials describe the Prisoner's Dilemma, discuss possible strategies for dealing with it successfully, and raise provocative questions about its general applicability. The readings provide effective bargainers with a theoretical foundation upon which to commence any negotiation with the assurance that they can at least avoid being exploited.

Douglas Hofstadter, a longtime contributor to *Scientific American,* describes the ways in which people confront the puzzle of the Prisoner's Dilemma. His writing highlights research from two linked computer tournaments conducted by Michigan's Robert Axelrod to test how best to manage the Prisoner's Dilemma. In the next reading, Axelrod introduces us to the winner of the computer tournaments; the simple program called "Tit-for-Tat." He develops the implications of this winning program and makes prescriptive suggestions for how to manage the Prisoner's Dilemma most effectively. His four suggestions are thus grounded in the analytical results of game theoretic model testing. They can help every bargainer avoid exploitation when making strategic decisions under typical conditions of uncertainty.

In a passage from a book that should be read by everyone curious about the bargaining process, David Lax and James Sebenius build upon Axelrod's theoretical work to analyze the "Negotiator's Dilemma" with characteristic clarity. Tit-for-Tat's moves either to defect or cooperate in rounds of the iterated prisoner's dilemma are analogous to negotiator's decisions to employ competitive or cooperative strategies during any bargaining process. Negotiators are pulled between the impulse to claim value and to create value. Lax and Sebenius advise us to think of the two strategies not as mutually inconsistent but as Siamese twins, equally valid, symbiotic in the process of negotiating effectively.

Three summaries of recent research complete our theoretical look at the Prisoner's Dilemma. In the first, new game theoretic research on the impact of Axelrod's computer tournament amplifies Tit-for-Tat. The weakness of that program is clear when both players are locked in a competitive embrace. There is no way for either party to test the waters of cooperation by inviting a different response. This new research augments Axelrod's data. The results suggest that occasional efforts to induce the negotiating opposite to cooperate, called "Generous" Tit-for-Tat, are analytically preferable to lockstep and unyielding competition.

In the next two selections, researchers designed instruments to assess the negotiating preferences of people with shared academic expertise. The implications of these studies should receive close scrutiny by legal educators and lawyers. They suggest the critical role of professional socialization in determining bargaining behavior, and the complexity added by lawyer participation in negotiations.

In our final reading in this chapter, two of our best negotiation theorists combine to demonstrate how the Prisoner's Dilemma can have practical implications. We know lawyers routinely negotiate as agents for their clients. We know little about how this agency relationship affects bargaining outcomes. Ronald Gilson and Robert Mnookin use the Prisoner's Dilemma to help explain the "increase in contentiousness" observable in contemporary commercial litigation practice.

Readings

1. Douglas Hofstadter, *Metamagical Themas: Computer Tournaments of the Prisoner's Dilemma Suggest How Cooperation Evolves,* Scientific American 16–19 (May 1983).

2. Robert Axelrod, The Evolution of Cooperation 109–23 (1984).

3. David Lax & James Sebenius, The Manager as Negotiator 29–35 (1986).

4. Thomas Bass, *Forgiveness Math,* Discover Magazine 62–67 (May 1993).

5. Robert H. Frank, Thomas Gilovich & Dennis Regan, *Does Studying Economics Inhibit Cooperation?,* 7 J. of Econ.Persp. 159–71 (1993).

6. Peter Passell, *The Law as the Free Market's Rogue: Hostage to the Prisoner's Dilemma,* The New York Times, March 25, 1994, at B–18.

7. Ronald J. Gilson & Robert H. Mnookin, *Disputing Through Agents: Cooperation and Conflict Between Lawyers in Litigation,* 94 Colum.L.Rev. 509, 534–40 (1994).

8. For Further Reading

    a. Robert Axelrod, *Effective Choice in the Prisoner's Dilemma,* 24 J.Conflict Res. 3 (1980).

    b. Robert Axelrod, *More Effective Choice in the Prisoner's Dilemma,* 24 J.Conflict Res. 379 (1980).

    c. Ian Ayres, *Playing Games With the Law,* 42 Stan.L.Rev. 1291 (1990).

    d. Douglas G. Baird, Robert H. Gertner & Randal C. Picker, Game Theory and the Law (1994).

    e. Jonathan Bendor, *Uncertainty and the Evolution of Cooperation,* 37 J.Conflict Res. 709 (1993).

    f. Jonathan Bendor, Roderick M. Kramer & Suzanne Stout, *When In Doubt: Cooperation in a Noisy Prisoner's Dilemma,* 35 J.Conflict Res. 691 (1991).

    g. Robyn M. Davies & John M. Orbell, *The Benefit of Optional Play in Anonymous One Shot Prisoner's Dilemma Games,* in Barriers to Conflict Resolution 63 (Kenneth Arrow, *et al.,* eds. (1995)).

    h. Jack Hirshleifier & Juan Carlos Martinez Coll, *What Strategies Can Support the Evolutionary Emergence of Cooperation,* 32 J. Conflict Res. 367 (1988).

    i. Ronald J. Gilson & Robert H. Mnookin, *Cooperation and Competition In Negotiation: Can Lawyers Dampen Conflict,* in Barriers to Conflict Resolution 184 (Kenneth Arrow, *et al.,* eds. (1995)).

    j. H.C.J. Godfrey, *The Evolution of Forgiveness,* 355 Nature 206 (1992).

    k. Jane J. Mansbridge, Beyond Self Interest (1990).

    l. Manfred Milinski, *Tit for Tat in Sticklebacks and the Evolution of Cooperation,* 325 Nature 433 (1987).

m. J. Keith Murnighan, Bargaining Games (1992).

n. Craig D. Parks & Anh D. Vu, *Social Dilemma Behavior of Individuals from Highly Individualist and Collectivist Cultures,* 38 J.Conflict Res. 708 (1994).

o. Martin Patchen, *Strategies for Eliciting Cooperation from an Adversary,* 31 J.Conflict.Res. 164 (1985).

p. William Poundstone, Prisoner's Dilemma (1992).

q. Howard Raiffa, The Art and Science of Negotiation (1982).

r. Anatol Rapoport & Albert M. Chammah, Prisoner's Dilemma (1965).

s. David Warsh, *How Selfish Are People—Really?,* 67 Harv.Bus. Rev., May/June 1989.

DOUGLAS R. HOFSTADTER, METAMAGICAL THEMAS: COMPUTER TOURNAMENTS OF THE PRISONER'S DILEMMA SUGGEST HOW COOPERATION EVOLVES

Scientific American 16–19 (May 1983).

Life is filled with paradoxes and dilemmas. Sometimes it even feels as if the essence of living is the sensing—indeed the savoring—of paradox. Although all paradoxes seem somehow related, some seem abstract and philosophical whereas others touch on life directly. A very lifelike paradox is the Prisoner's Dilemma, discovered in about 1950 by Merrill M. Flood and Melvin Dresher, and later formalized by Albert W. Tucker. I shall present it first as a metaphor and then as a formal problem.

The original formulation in terms of prisoners is a little less clear to the uninitiated, in my experience, than the following one. Assume you possess large quantities of some item (money, for example) and want to obtain some amount of another item (stamps, groceries, diamonds). You arrange a mutually agreeable trade with the only dealer of that item known to you. You are both satisfied with the amounts you will be giving and getting. For some reason, though, the exchange must take place in secret. Each of you agrees to leave a bag at a designated place in the woods and to pick up the other's bag at the other's designated place. Suppose it is clear to both of you that you will never meet or have further dealings with each other again.

Clearly there is something for each of you to fear, namely that the other one will leave an empty bag. Obviously if you both leave full bags, you will both be satisfied, but equally obviously it is even more satisfying to get something for nothing. You are therefore tempted to leave an empty bag. In fact, you can even reason it through with seeming rigor this way: "If the dealer brings a full bag, I'll be better off having left an empty bag, because I'll have got all I wanted and given away nothing. If the dealer brings an empty bag, I'll be better off having left an empty bag, because I'll not have been cheated. I'll have gained nothing but lost nothing either. Thus it seems that *no matter what the dealer chooses to do* I'm better off leaving an empty bag. And so I'll leave an empty bag."

The dealer, meanwhile, being in more or less the same boat (although at the other end of it), thinks analogous thoughts and comes to the parallel conclusion that it is best to leave an empty bag. And so both of you, with your impeccable (or seemingly impeccable) logic, leave empty bags and go away empty-handed. How sad, because if you had both just cooperated, you could each have gained something you wanted to have. Does logic prevent cooperation? That is the issue presented by the Prisoner's Dilemma.

. . .

Let us now go back to the original metaphor and slightly alter its conditions. Suppose both you and the dealer very much want to have a regular supply of what the other has to offer, and so before conducting your first exchange you agree to carry on a lifelong exchange once a month. You still expect never to meet face to face. In fact, neither of you has any idea how old the other is, so that you cannot be sure how long this lifelong agreement will last, but it seems safe to assume it will last for a few months anyway, and quite likely for years.

Now, what do you do on your first exchange? Bringing an empty bag seems fairly nasty as the opening of a relationship; hardly an effective way to build up trust. Suppose you bring a full bag and the dealer brings one too. All is bliss—for a month. Then you both must go back. Will your next bag be empty or full? Each month you have to decide whether to "defect" (bring an empty bag) or to "cooperate" (bring a full one). Suppose one month, unexpectedly, your dealer defects. Now what do you do? Will you decide that the dealer can never be trusted again and that from now on you will always bring an empty bag, in effect totally giving up on the entire project? Or will you pretend you didn't notice and continue being friendly? Or will you try to punish the dealer by some number of defections of your own? One? Two? A random number? An increasing number, depending on how many defections you have experienced? Just how mad will you get?

This is the Iterated Prisoner's Dilemma. It is a very difficult problem. It can be, and it has been, rendered more quantitative and in that form studied with the methods of game theory and computer simulation.

ROBERT AXELROD, THE EVOLUTION OF COOPERATION
109–23 (1984).

This chapter offers advice to someone who is in a Prisoner's Dilemma. From an individual's point of view, the object is to score as well as possible over a series of interactions with another player who is also trying to score well. Since the game is a Prisoner's Dilemma, the player has a short-run incentive to defect, but can do better in the long run by developing a pattern of mutual cooperation with the other. The analysis of the Computer Tournament and the results of the theoretical investigations provide some useful information about what strategies are likely to work under different conditions, and why. The purpose of this chapter is to translate these findings into advice for a player.

The advice takes the form of four simple suggestions for how to do well in a durable iterated Prisoner's Dilemma:

1. Don't be envious.
2. Don't be the first to defect.

3.   Reciprocate both cooperation and defection.

4.   Don't be too clever.

1.   DON'T BE ENVIOUS

People are used to thinking about zero-sum interactions. In these settings, whatever one person wins, another loses. A good example is a chess tournament. In order to do well, the contestant must do better than the other player in the game most of the time. A win for White is necessarily a loss for Black.

But most of life is *not* zero-sum. Generally, both sides can do well, or both can do poorly. Mutual cooperation is often possible, but not always achieved. That is why the Prisoner's Dilemma is such a useful model for a wide variety of everyday situations.

.   .   .

Asking how well you are doing compared to how well the other player is doing is not a good standard unless your goal is to destroy the other player. In most situations, such a goal is impossible to achieve, or likely to lead to such costly conflict as to be very dangerous to pursue. When you are not trying to destroy the other player, comparing your score to the other's score simply risks the development of self-destructive envy. A better standard of comparison is how well you are doing relative to how well someone else could be doing in your shoes. Given the strategy of the other player, are you doing as well as possible? Could someone else in your situation have done better with this other player? This is the proper test of successful performance.

TIT FOR TAT won the tournament because it did well in its interactions with a wide variety of other strategies. . . . TIT FOR TAT won the tournament, not by beating the other player, but by eliciting behavior from the other player which allowed both to do well. TIT FOR TAT was so consistent at eliciting mutually rewarding outcomes that it attained a higher overall score than any other strategy.

So in a non-zero-sum world you do not have to do better than the other player to do well for yourself. This is especially true when you are interacting with many different players. Letting each of them do the same or a little better than you is fine, as long as you tend to do well yourself. There is no point in being envious of the success of the other player, since in an iterated Prisoner's Dilemma of long duration the other's success is virtually a prerequisite of your doing well for yourself.

Congress provides a good example. Members of Congress can cooperate with each other without providing threats to each other's standing at home. The main threat to a legislator is not the relative success of another legislator from another part of the country, but from someone who might mount a challenge in the home district. Thus there is not much point in begrudging a fellow legislator the success that comes from mutual cooperation.

Likewise in business. A firm that buys from a supplier can expect that a successful relationship will earn profit for the supplier as well as the buyer. There is no point in being envious of the supplier's profit. Any attempt to reduce it through an uncooperative practice, such as by not paying your bills on time, will only encourage the supplier to take retaliatory action. Retaliatory action could take many forms, often without being explicitly labeled as punishment. It could be less prompt deliveries, lower quality control, less forthcoming attitudes on volume discounts, or less timely news of anticipated changes in market conditions. The retaliation could make the envy quite expensive. Instead of worrying about the relative profits of the seller, the buyer should consider whether another buying strategy would be better.

2.   DON'T BE THE FIRST TO DEFECT

Both the tournament and the theoretical results show that it pays to cooperate as long as the other player is cooperating.

The tournament results ... are very striking. The single best predictor of how well a rule performed was whether or not it was nice, which is to say, whether or not it would ever be the first to defect. In the first round, each of the top eight rules were nice, and not one of the bottom seven were nice. In the second round, all but one of the top fifteen rules were nice (and that one ranked eighth). Of the bottom fifteen rules, all but one were not nice.

.   .   .

The theoretical results provide an important qualification to the advantages of using a nice strategy. When the future of the interaction is not important enough relative to immediate gains from defection, then simply waiting for the other to defect is not such a good idea.... Therefore, if the other player is not likely to be seen again, defecting right away is better than being nice.

This fact has unfortunate implications for groups who are known to move from one place to another. An anthropologist finds that a Gypsy approaches a non-Gypsy expecting trouble, and a non-Gypsy approaches a Gypsy suspiciously, expecting double-dealing.

For example, a physician was called in to attend a very sick Gypsy baby; he was not the first doctor called, but he was the first willing to come. We escorted him toward the back bedroom, but he stopped short of the threshold of the patient's room. "This visit will be fifteen dollars, and you owe me five dollars from the last time. Pay me the twenty dollars before I see the patient," he demanded. "Okay, okay, you'll get it—just look at the baby now," the Gypsies pleaded. Several more go-arounds occurred before I intervened. Ten dollars changed hands and the doctor examined the patient. After the visit, I discovered the Gypsies, in revenge, did not intend to pay the other ten dollars.

.   .   .

Short interactions are not the only condition which would make it pay to be the first to defect. The other possibility is that cooperation will simply not be reciprocated. If everyone else is using a strategy of always defecting, then a single individual can do no better than to use this same strategy. But ... if even a small proportion of one's interactions are going to be with others who are using a responsive strategy like TIT FOR TAT, then it can pay to use TIT FOR TAT rather than to simply defect all the time like most of those in the population.

.   .   .

Of course, one could try to "play it safe" by defecting until the other player cooperates, and only then starting to cooperate. The tournament results show, however, that this is actually a very risky strategy. The reason is that your own initial defection is likely to set off a retaliation by the other player. This will put the two of you in the difficult position of trying to extricate yourselves from an initial pattern of exploitation or mutual defection. If you punish the other's retaliation, the problem can echo into the future. And if you forgive the other, you risk appearing to be exploitable. Even if you can avoid these long-term problems, a prompt retaliation against your initial defection can make you wish that you had been nice from the start.

. . .

3.   RECIPROCATE BOTH COOPERATION AND DEFECTION

The extraordinary success of TIT FOR TAT leads to some simple, but powerful advice: practice reciprocity. After cooperating on the first move, TIT FOR TAT simply reciprocates whatever the other player did on the previous move. This simple rule is amazingly robust. It won the first round of the Computer Tournament for the Prisoner's Dilemma by attaining a higher average score than any other entry submitted by professional game theorists. And when this result was publicized for the contestants in the second round, TIT FOR TAT won again. The victory was obviously a surprise, since anyone could have submitted it to the second round after seeing its success in the first round. But obviously people hoped they could do better—and they were wrong.

. . .

In responding to a defection from the other player, TIT FOR TAT represents a balance between punishing and being forgiving. TIT FOR TAT always defects exactly once after each defection by the other, and TIT FOR TAT was very successful in the tournament. This suggests the question of whether always doing exactly one-for-one is the most effective balance. It is hard to say because rules with slightly different balances were not submitted. What is clear is that extracting more than one defection for each defection of the other risks escalation. On the other hand, extracting less than one-for-one risks exploitation.

. . .

The moral of the story is that the precise level of forgiveness that is optimal depends upon the environment. In particular, if the main danger is unending mutual recriminations, then a generous level of forgiveness is appropriate. But, if the main danger is from strategies that are good at exploiting easygoing rules, then an excess of forgiveness is costly. While the exact balance will be hard to determine in a given environment, the evidence of the tournament suggests that something approaching a one-for-one response to defection is likely to be quite effective in a wide range of settings. Therefore it is good advice to a player to reciprocate defection as well as cooperation.

4. Don't Be too Clever

The tournament results show that in a Prisoner's Dilemma situation it is easy to be *too* clever. The very sophisticated rules did not do better than the simple ones. In fact, the so-called maximizing rules often did poorly because they got into a rut of mutual defection. A common problem with these rules is that they used complex methods of making inferences about the other player—and these inferences were wrong. Part of the problem was that a trial defection by the other player was often taken to imply that the other player could not be enticed into cooperation. But the heart of the problem was that these maximizing rules did not take into account that their *own* behavior would lead the other player to change.

In deciding whether to carry an umbrella, we do not have to worry that the clouds will take our behavior into account. We can do a calculation about the chance of rain based on past experience. Likewise in a zero-sum game, such as chess, we can safely use the assumption that the other player will pick the most dangerous move that can be found, and we can act accordingly. Therefore it pays for us to be as sophisticated and as complex in our analysis as we can.

Non-zero-sum games, such as the Prisoner's Dilemma, are not like this. Unlike the clouds, the other player can respond to your own choices. And unlike the chess opponent, the other player in a Prisoner's Dilemma should not be regarded as someone who is out to defeat you. The other player will be watching your behavior for signs of whether you will reciprocate cooperation or not, and therefore your own behavior is likely to be echoed back to you.

. . .

One way to account for TIT FOR TAT's great success in the tournament is that it has great clarity: it is eminently comprehensible to the other player. When you are using TIT FOR TAT, the other player has an excellent chance of understanding what you are doing. Your one-for-one response to any defection is an easy pattern to appreciate. Your future behavior can then be predicted. Once this happens, the other player can easily see that the best way to deal with TIT FOR TAT is to cooperate with it. Assuming that the game is sufficiently likely to continue for at least one more interaction, there is no better plan when meeting a TIT FOR TAT strategy than to cooperate now so that you will be the recipient of a cooperation on the very next move.

DAVID LAX & JAMES SEBENIUS, THE MANAGER AS NEGOTIATOR: BARGAINING FOR COOPERATION AND MUTUAL GAIN

29–35 (1986).

That negotiation includes cooperation and competition, common and conflicting interests, is nothing new. In fact, it is typically understood that these elements are both present and can be disentangled. Deep down, however, some people believe that the elements of conflict are illusory, that meaningful communication will erase any such unfortunate misperceptions. Others see mainly competition and take the cooperative pieces to be minimal.

Some overtly acknowledge the reality of each aspect but direct all their attention to one of them and wish, pretend, or act as if the other does not exist. Still others hold to a more balanced view that accepts both elements as significant but seeks to treat them separately. In this chapter, we argue that *all* these approaches are flawed.

A deeper analysis shows that the competitive and cooperative elements are inextricably entwined. In practice, they cannot be separated. This bonding is fundamentally important to the analysis, structuring, and conduct of negotiation. There is a central, inescapable tension between cooperative moves to create value jointly and competitive moves to gain individual advantage. This tension affects virtually all tactical and strategic choice. Analysts must come to grips with it; negotiators must manage it. Neither denial nor discomfort will make it disappear.

. . .

Negotiators and analysts tend to fall into two groups that are guided by warring conceptions of the bargaining process. In the left-hand corner are the "value creators" and in the right-hand corner are the "value claimers."

Value creators tend to believe that, above all, successful negotiators must be inventive and cooperative enough to devise an agreement that yields considerable gain to each party, relative to no-agreement possibilities. Some speak about the need for replacing the "win-lose" image of negotiation with "win-win" negotiation, from which all parties presumably derive great value....

Roger Fisher and Bill Ury give an example that concerns the difficult Egyptian–Israeli negotiations over where to draw a boundary in the Sinai. This appeared to be an absolutely classic example of zero-sum bargaining, in which each square mile lost to one party was the other side's gain. For years the negotiations proceeded inconclusively with proposed boundary lines drawn and redrawn on innumerable maps. On probing the real interests of the two sides, however, Egypt was found to care a great deal about sovereignty over the Sinai while Israel was heavily concerned with its security. As such, a creative solution could be devised to "unbundle" these different interests and give to each what it valued most. In the Sinai, this involved creating a demilitarized zone under the Egyptian flag. This had the effect of giving Egypt "sovereignty" and Israel "security." This situation exemplifies extremely common tendencies to assume that negotiators' interests are in direct opposition, a conviction that can sometimes be corrected by communicating, sharing information, and inventing solutions.

. . .

Value claimers, on the other hand, tend to see this drive for joint gain as naive and weak-minded. For them, negotiation is hard, tough bargaining. The object of negotiation is to convince the other guy that he wants what you have to offer much more than you want what he has; moreover, you have all the time in the world while he is up against pressing deadlines. To "win" at negotiating—and thus make the other fellow "lose"—one must start high, concede slowly, exaggerate the value of concessions, minimize the benefits of the other's concessions, conceal information, argue forcefully on behalf of principles that imply favorable settlements, make commitments to accept only highly favorable agreements, and be willing to outwait the other fellow.

The hardest of bargainers will threaten to walk away or to retaliate harshly if their one-sided demands are not met; they may ridicule, attack, and intimidate their *adversaries*. For example, Lewis Glucksman, once the volatile head of trading activities at Lehman Brothers, the large investment banking firm, employed the hardest sort of bargaining tactics in his bid to wrest control of Lehman from then-Chairman Peter G. Peterson after being elevated to co-CEO status with Peterson. As co-CEO, Glucksman abruptly demanded full control of the firm, making a thinly veiled threat that unless his demands were met, he would provoke civil war at Lehman and take the entire profitable trading department elsewhere. When Peterson and others desperately sought less damaging accommodation, Glucksman conveyed the impression that "his feet were set in cement," even if that meant the destruction of the firm. (Ultimately, Peterson left with a substantial money settlement and Glucksman presided briefly over a shaken Lehman that was soon sold at a bargain price to American Express.)

At the heart of this adversarial approach is an image of a negotiation with a winner and a loser: "We are dividing a pie of fixed size and every slice I give to you is a slice I do not get; thus, I need to *claim* as much of the value as possible by giving you as little as possible."

. . .

Both of these images of negotiation are incomplete and inadequate. Value creating and value claiming are linked parts of negotiation. Both processes are present. No matter how much creative problem solving enlarges the pie, it must still be divided; value that has been created must be claimed. And, if the pie is not enlarged, there will be less to divide; there is more value to be claimed if one has helped create it first. An essential tension in negotiation exists between cooperative moves to create value and competitive moves to claim it.

. . .

The tension between cooperative moves to create value and competitive moves to claim it is greatly exacerbated by the interaction of the tactics used either to create or claim value.

First, tactics for claiming value (which we will call "claiming tactics") can impede its creation. Exaggerating the value of concessions and minimizing the benefit of others' concessions presents a distorted picture of one's relative preferences; thus, mutually beneficial trades may not be discovered. Making threats or commitments to highly favorable outcomes surely impedes hearing and understanding others' interests. Concealing information may also cause one to leave joint gains on the table. In fact, excessive use of tactics for claiming value may well sour the parties' relationship and reduce the trust between them. Such tactics may also evoke a variety of unhelpful interests. Conflict may escalate and make joint prospects less appealing and settlement less likely.

Second, approaches to creating value are vulnerable to tactics for claiming value. Revealing information about one's relative preferences is risky. . . .

The information that a negotiator would accept position A in return for a favorable resolution on a second issue can be exploited: "So, you'll accept A. Good, Now, let's move on to discuss the merits of the second issue." The willingness to make a new, creative offer can often be taken as a sign that its proposer is able and willing to make further concessions. Thus, such offers sometimes remain undisclosed. Even purely shared interests can be held hostage in exchange for concessions on other issues. Though a divorcing husband and wife may both prefer giving the wife custody of the child, the husband may "suddenly" develop strong parental instincts to extract concessions on alimony in return for giving the wife custody.

In tactical choices, each negotiator thus has reasons not to be open and cooperative. Each also has apparent incentives to try to claim value. Moves to claim value thus tend to drive out moves to create it. Yet, if both choose to claim value, by being dishonest or less than forthcoming about preferences, beliefs, or minimum requirements, they may miss mutually beneficial terms for agreement.

Indeed, the structure of many bargaining situations suggests that negotiators will tend to leave joint gains on the table or even reach impasses when mutually acceptable agreements are available.

THOMAS A. BASS, FORGIVENESS MATH: MATHEMATICAL GAMES EXPLAIN THE EVOLUTIONARY EXISTENCE OF COOPERATIVE BEHAVIOR

14(5) Discover 62, 62–67 (1993).

Nice guys do not always finish last. In fact, they sometimes finish first. And now we have scientific evidence to prove it, thanks to the work of two Austrian mathematicians who have discovered the value of forgiveness. Or at least they've discovered how forgiveness might have come into being in our dog-eat-dog world.

"Generosity pays off under conditions of uncertainty. You should not be too tolerant, but not too intolerant, either," says Karl Sigmund, a 47-year-old mathematician at the University of Vienna. "Never forget a good turn, but try occasionally to forgive a bad one. We benefit from cultivating a keen sense of gratitude dosed with a small amount of generosity."

[After summarizing Robert Axelrod's classic computer tournament, the author continues:] In 1980 Axelrod came up with a different kind of competition. He wanted to use computers to simulate natural selection by modeling ecological encounters in nature. Participants in this ecological tournament formed a population that altered with each repetition of the game. The strategies that got the most points during Round One, for instance, would be rewarded with offspring: two or three other versions of themselves, all of which would participate in the next round. In this way one can build up entire populations of strategic cooperators or defectors. During successive rounds, winning strategies multiplied while less successful rivals died out.

This is the tournament that first got Karl Sigmund interested in the prisoner's dilemma. Sigmund had been working on theoretical chemistry at the University of Vienna, studying the hypercycle, a system of self-reproducing molecules that might hold clues to how life evolved on Earth. "I got very excited when I found the prisoner's dilemma had meaning in evolutionary biology," says Sigmund. He got so excited, in fact, that he switched from studying self-replicating molecules to studying models of animal behavior.

"For a mathematician," says Sigmund, "whether you study molecules or the behavior of animals doesn't matter. It all reduces to the same differential equations. Mathematically this is really one field: the population dynamics of self-replicating entities. They can be RNA molecules or reproductive strategies or animals preying on each other or parasites or whatever. Success determines the composition of the field, and the composition determines success. It is not easy to predict where this may lead."

Sigmund watched with interest as Axelrod played his ecological tournament out to the thousandth round. Again, Tit for Tat was the winner. "At first glance this may appear to be paradoxical, but of course it isn't," says Sigmund. When thrown into a hornet's nest of inveterate defectors, a single Tit for Tat will do less well than the meanies, because it loses out on the first round before switching into tough-guy mode. But when playing itself or other nice strategies, Tit for Tat will do significantly better than such hard-liners as Always Defect, which can't get more than one point per interaction with itself. "The moral is that Tit for Tatters do best when they start interacting in clusters or families," Sigmund says. "Kinship facilitates cooperation." In a mixture of Always Defect and Tit for Tat, even if only a small percentage of the population is using the nice policy, that policy will start reproducing itself and quickly take over the game.

Even as Tit for Tat was racking up one success after another, it was clear to Axelrod and Sigmund that the strategy had a fatal flaw. "It has no tolerance for errors," says Sigmund. "While computer programs interact flawlessly, humans and other animals certainly do not. In biological or human interactions, it is clear that sometimes the wires get crossed and you make a mistake about the identity of someone. You meet a friend and, not recognizing him, you defect. This is the Achilles' heel of Tit for Tat, which is particularly vulnerable against itself."

A realistic version of Tit for Tat against Tit for Tat can fall into endless cycles of retaliation. Since all it knows how to do is strike back at defectors, one scrambled signal will send Tit for Tat spiraling into vendettas that make the Hatfields and the McCoys look tame by comparison. The average payoff for Tit for Tat drops by 25 percent if you introduce only a few such mistakes into the tournament. "This is a terrible performance," Sigmund says, noting that a random strategy (unthinkingly defecting or cooperating in each round with equal probability) will do just as well.

"The obvious way to break up this vicious cycle of grim retaliation consists in being ready, on occasion, to let bygones be bygones. We can even compute the optimal measure of forgiveness," says Sigmund. The Viennese Golden Mean—the extra dose of generosity that makes for the best of all strategies in a less-than-perfect world—is contained in the following rule: Always meet cooperation with cooperation, and when facing defection, cooperate on average one out of every three times. The strategy that embodies this rule is called Generous Tit for Tat.

The merits of Generous Tit for Tat were already known in the early 1980s, when a Swedish scientist named Per Molander computed the benefits of generosity in a world where pure Tit for Tat could sometimes make a mistake—like Oedipus meeting his father. Molander arrived at the figure of one-third through repeated rounds of trial and error. Molander's finding does not mean that you should turn the other cheek to every third blow. Obviously it would be a big mistake to let your opponent know exactly when you were going to be nice. The number is just an average.

· · ·

Realizing how important mistakes can be to the prisoner's dilemma, Sigmund and Nowak started playing the game with what are called stochastic strategies. Stochastic means "random," and strategies such as these—Generous Tit for Tat being one of them—allow for reacting to one's opponent with a degree of flexibility.

"We had been experimenting with games where everyone was playing the same strategy and watching what would happen when a small minority came in and started playing something else," says Sigmund. "Would they spread or be wiped out? Later we got the idea, why not try out our model with 100 different strategies, chosen at random to be more or less tolerant, more or less forgiving? Some would forgive one out of two times, some one out of five, and so on. And some, of course, would never forgive."

· · ·

After two black weeks of watching meanies invade their tournament, Nowak and Sigmund accidentally stumbled on the key to evolving cooperation. They noticed the game took a radically different turn with one small alteration. If a dose of Tit for Tat—just enough to establish a tiny enclave, a dose as small as one percent of the population—was added to the game at the start, then it flipped directions. "Generous Tit for Tat is not strong enough to organize this emergence of cooperation," says Sigmund. "What one needs is a kind of police force, a minority that helps by its very strictness to effect this move but that does not ultimately prove the best.

"If you don't have Tit for Tat but some other strategy, it cannot do it. It must be a very strict retaliator. But then after you have the switch toward cooperation, it is not Tit for Tat that profits. Its frequency goes up, but then it yields to Generous Tit for Tat. Tit for Tat is not the aim of evolution, but it makes it possible. It is a kind of pivot.

"For 100 generations the Always Defect strategy dominates the population with what looks like inescapable ferocity; it looks so bad you almost give up hope. A beleaguered minority of Tit for Tat survives on the edge of extinction. But when the suckers are nearly wiped out and the exploiters have no one left to exploit, the game reverses direction. The retaliators spring back to life. The exploiters suffer crippling reverses." There was great pleasure, Sigmund recalls, in watching the Always Defectors weaken and then die out.

ROBERT H. FRANK, THOMAS GILOVICH, AND DENNIS T. REGAN, DOES STUDYING ECONOMICS INHIBIT COOPERATION?

7 J.Econ.Perspectives 159–71 (1993).

From the perspective of many economists, motives other than self-interest are peripheral to the main thrust of human endeavor, and we indulge them at our peril. In Gordon Tullock's (1976) words (as quoted by Mansbridge, 1990, p. 12), "the average human being is about 95 percent selfish in the narrow sense of the term."

In this paper we investigate whether exposure to the self-interest model commonly used in economics alters the extent to which people behave in self-interested ways.

. . .

ECONOMISTS AND THE PRISONER'S DILEMMA

. . .

We conducted a prisoner's dilemma experiment involving both economics majors and nonmajors. All groups were given an extensive briefing on the prisoner's dilemma at the start of the experiment and each subject was required to complete a questionnaire at the end to verify that he or she had indeed understood the consequences of different combinations of choices; in addition, many of our subjects were students recruited from courses in which the prisoner's dilemma is an item on the syllabus. Our subjects met in groups of three and each was told that he or she would play the game once only with each of the other two subjects. The payoff matrix . . . was the same for each play of the game. Subjects were told that the games would be played for real money, and that confidentiality would be maintained so that none of the players would learn how their partners had responded in any play of the game.

Following a period in which subjects were given an opportunity to get to know one another, each subject was taken to a separate room and asked to fill out a form indicating a response (cooperate or defect) to each of the other two players in the group. After the subjects had filled out their forms, the results were tallied and the payments disbursed. Each subject received a single payment that was the sum of three separate amounts: the payoff from the game with the first partner; the payoff from the game with the second partner; and a term that was drawn at random from a large list of positive and negative values. None of these three elements could be observed separately, only their sum. The purpose of this procedure was to prevent subjects from inferring both individual and group patterns of choice. Thus, unlike earlier prisoner's dilemma experiments, ours did not enable the subject to infer what happened even when each (or neither) of the other players defected.

. . .

For the sample as a whole there were a total of 267 games, which means a total of 534 choices between cooperation and defection. For these choices, the defection rate for economics majors was 60.4 percent, as compared to only

38.8 percent for nonmajors. This pattern of differences strongly supports the hypothesis that economics majors are more likely than nonmajors to behave self-interestedly ($p < .005$).

One possible explanation for the observed differences between economics students and others is that economics students are more likely to be male, and males have lower cooperation rates. To control for possible influences of sex, age, and experimental condition, we performed the ordinary least squares regression. . . .

Consistent with a variety of other findings on sex differences in cooperation, we estimate that, other factors the same, the probability of a male defecting is almost 0.24 higher than the corresponding probability for a female. But even after controlling for the influence of gender, we see that the probability of an economics major defecting is almost 0.17 higher than the corresponding probability for a nonmajor.

. . .

As part of the exit questionnaire that tested understanding of the payoffs associated with different combinations of choices, we also asked subjects to state reasons for their choices. We hypothesized that economists would be more inclined to construe the objective of the game in self-interested terms, and therefore more likely to refer exclusively to features of the game itself, while noneconomists would be more open to alternative ways of interpreting the game, and would refer more often to their feelings about their partners, aspects of human nature, and so on. Indeed, among the sample of economics students, 31 percent referred only to features of the game itself in explaining their chosen strategies, compared with only 17 percent of the noneconomists. The probability of obtaining such divergent responses by chance is less than .05.

. . . Recalling our earlier finding that defection rates for the sample as a whole fall steadily between the freshman and senior years, the question is thus whether defection rates fall to the same degree over time for economists as for noneconomists. We found that the pattern of falling defection rates holds more strongly for noneconomics majors than for economics majors in the no-promises subsample. For noneconomics underclassmen in this group (freshmen and sophomores), the defection rate is 53.7 percent, compared to only 40.2 percent for upperclassmen. By contrast, the trend toward lower defection rates is virtually absent from economics majors in the no-promises subsample (73.7 percent for underclassmen, 70.0 percent for upperclassmen). In other words, students generally show a pronounced tendency toward more cooperative behavior with movement toward graduation, but this trend is conspicuously absent for economics majors.

Naturally, we are in no position to say whether the trend for noneconomists reflects something about the content of noneconomics courses. But the fact that this trend is not present for economists is at least consistent with the hypothesis that training in economics plays some causal role in the lower observed cooperation rates of economists.

. . .

Should we be concerned that economics training may inhibit cooperation? Some might respond that while society would benefit if more people cooperated in social dilemmas, economists cannot be faulted for pointing out the unpleasant truth that self-interest dictates defection. One difficulty with this response is that it may be wrong. Several researchers have recently suggested that the ultimate victims of noncooperative behavior may be the very people who practice it. . . .

In an ever more interdependent world, social cooperation has become increasingly important—and yet increasingly fragile. With an eye toward both the social good and the well-being of their own students, economists may wish to stress a broader view of human motivation in their teaching.

PETER PASSELL, THE LAW AS THE FREE MARKET'S ROGUE: HOSTAGE TO THE PRISONER'S DILEMMA

The New York Times, March 25, 1994, at B–18.

KATE: For someone who has nothing nice to say about lawyers, you certainly have enough of them around.

GARFINKLE: You have to. They're like nuclear warheads. They have theirs, so you need yours, but ... they're only good in their silos.

> —"Other People's Money,"
> Jerry Sterner

Looking for a new reason to blame lawyers for it all? Economists are at your service.

One recent study documented a strong negative link between the proportion of law graduates in a country's work force and its rate of economic growth. Another estimates that litigation between companies reduces their combined stock value, on average, by 1 percent—real money in a world of multibillion-dollar corporations.

But as many a learned counsel would be happy to point out, there is a seeming contradiction in economists' distaste for lawyers. Modern economics is built on the rock of competition and free choice. If lawyers, who are certainly competitive, can find willing customers for their services, where do economists get off second-guessing the market?

Not to worry, lawyer-bashers. Two seasoned practitioners of the dismal science, Profs. Orley Ashenfelter of Princeton and David Bloom of Columbia, have at least come up with an explanation. Competitive markets do sometimes fail to produce efficient outcomes, they note. And they believe that the market for legal services fails in a particularly perverse and fascinating way, known in the jargon of the mathematical theory of games as "the prisoner's dilemma."

. . .

Take Smith and Jones, who disagree about the ownership of $100,000 worth of property. They can settle the dispute very cheaply by splitting the difference or by asking a neutral party to arbitrate. Alternatively, either can hire a lawyer for $10,000 to represent him in a formal proceeding.

Jones believes that by hiring counsel while Smith does not, he can improve his chances of winning by at least enough to make his $10,000 expenditure worthwhile. Likewise for Smith. On the other hand, if both hire lawyers the value of legal representation is neutralized, and the total size of the pie to be split between the two parties is reduced to $80,000.

So one might expect that Smith and Jones would cooperate—that is, that the incentives offered each of them by the free market would lead them to minimize the collective cost of settling their dispute. What makes the prisoner's dilemma so compelling and so frustrating is that noncooperative behavior dominates cooperative behavior in spite of the certain knowledge that the process will burn $20,000 in legal fees.

· · ·

And it is here that Professors Ashenfelter and Bloom strike their blow against the bar, offering evidence that noncooperation pays—that the likely payoff in hiring a lawyer does exceed the cost.

In a yet-to-be-published paper entitled "Lawyers as Agents of the Devil," the two economists looked first at public-employee wage disputes from 1981 to 1984 in New Jersey, where arbitrators, rather than splitting the difference, were required to choose one of the disputants' final offers. By the estimates of Professors Ashenfelter and Bloom, expert representation sufficiently increased the probability of winning to make it worthwhile to hire a lawyer.

They also examined the outcomes of 755 union grievance proceedings in Pennsylvania in which arbitrators decided whether employers had the right to discharge workers. Here, they assumed that the loss of a coveted union job cut an average worker's future earning power by 10 percent, and calculated that the improved chances of keeping that job by retaining a lawyer was worth at the very least $5,000—far more than the cost of representation. Similar results were found in a study by the Rand Corporation Institute for Civil Justice involving debt-collection, personal-injury and breach-of-contract cases resolved through arbitration in Pittsburgh.

· · ·

In any event, economists may not have the last word on the games that lawyers and their clients are compelled to play. Douglas Baird, director of the law-and-economics program at the University of Chicago Law School, contends that the "traditional prisoner's dilemma ends badly only because the prisoners aren't able to communicate or to hold the other to an agreement." And, he asserts, those conditions do not typically apply to legal disputes.

Profs. Ronald Gilson of Stanford Law School and Robert Mnookin of Harvard Law School press the point further in an article soon to be published in the Columbia Law Review. They argue that if parties to a dispute believed that they stood to gain collectively from cooperation, and if each was in a position to neutralize the advantage of trickery by the other, would not cooperation become the dominant strategy?

By the same token, they believe that lawyers themselves often have strong incentive to signal a willingness to cooperate. Since many clients prefer to hire lawyers who are disinclined to no-holds-barred warfare (providing the other side does the same), it would pay many lawyers to establish reputations as peacemakers. And indeed they note that the divorce bar is clearly divided between "gladiators" out for blood and "peacemakers" who seek amicable resolution.

But if the free market is inclined to reward lawyers who use low-cost strategies, why has there been an escalation in civil litigation in recent decades? One reason, Professor Mnookin argues, is that as the legal profession has grown, it has become harder for lawyers to establish a clear reputation as peacemakers among other lawyers and potential clients.

Another is that commercial law has become more complex, offering more ways for an advocate to hide his intentions and fail to honor the spirit of an interim agreement. This "noise" in the legal system is often so loud, Professor Mnookin suggests, that it is easy to misinterpret the other side's strategy. And a very noisy case may lead to the classic prisoner's dilemma, in which neither party can risk a cooperative stance lest he be tagged as the sucker.

While the two economists see lawyers as the problem, Professor Mnookin views them as the potential solution. He wants to make it easier for lawyers to establish and sustain professional reputations as reliable peacemakers—for example, by letting them more simply withdraw from cases in which clients pressure them to act uncooperatively. And he imagines the establishment of "cooperative boutiques," laws firms that would handle only cases in which all parties signaled their interest in cooperation.

The big question here is whether lawyers as a whole have the will or the way to reduce the demand for their services. And Professor Tullock is plainly skeptical. How, he wonders, could the bar cotton to reforms that would cause "many lawyers to become vacuum cleaner salesmen?"

RONALD J. GILSON & ROBERT H. MNOOKIN, DISPUTING THROUGH AGENTS: COOPERATION AND CONFLICT BETWEEN LAWYERS IN LITIGATION

94 Colum.L.Rev. 509, 534–40 (1994).

Viewing the perceived deterioration in the conduct of commercial litigation through the lens of the prisoner's dilemma suggests two explanations for the increase in contentiousness: a change in the character of the litigation itself; and the impact of growth in the size of the legal community upon the formation and maintenance of reputations for cooperation.

1. THE CHANGING PAYOFF STRUCTURE IN LITIGATION

Two conclusions about the character of large commercial litigation have emerged in recent years, one empirical and relating to its frequency, the second subjective and relating to its conduct. Recent studies have documented a dramatic increase in the amount of commercial litigation after 1970. A nationwide study of federal court contract cases found that the annual number of filings, after remaining at a relatively constant level of about 14,000 during the 1960s, began rising in the 1970s and reached an annual rate of over 47,000 by 1986. Similarly, a study of breach of contract filings in the Southern District of New York (Manhattan)—the federal trial court with what is likely the largest commercial caseload in the country and certainly the court with the largest commercial bar—found that contracts cases increased from an average of some 391 cases per year during the 1960s to an average of 1272 cases per year during the period 1973 through 1979, with some years exceeding 1400 cases. At the same time, the involvement of large New York law firms in these cases increased substantially.

Over the same period, commercial litigators attested to the increasingly uncivil conduct of civil litigation. The phenomenon of discovery abuse was the most obvious manifestation. Over-reaching requests for production were met with dogged resistance to any but perfunctory compliance, and the liberal discovery contemplated by the Federal Rules of Civil Procedure—which aimed to eliminate surprise and facilitate a resolution of the merits based on full information—led instead to trench warfare. Motion and counter-motion, each accompanied by requests for sanctions, created multiple satellite litigation that pushed the merits into the background.

The prisoner's dilemma heuristic suggests a possible link between the empirical fact of increased commercial litigation and the subjective fact that litigation behavior has become significantly more contentious. Recall that in order for lawyers to allow clients credibly to precommit to a cooperative solution the payoffs in the lawsuit must take the form of a prisoner's dilemma: mutual cooperation must have a bigger payoff for each player than mutual defection. If some commercial litigation has payoffs in which one party does not gain from mutual cooperation, such litigation would suffer from defections and be more conflictual. One or both parties would choose gladiators in the pre-litigation game even if that party knew the result would be that the other party would respond in kind.

At least some of the increase in commercial litigation stems from lawsuits in which there were no gains from cooperation. In his study of New York commercial litigation, William Nelson notes that during the 1970s the statutory prejudgment interest rate—the amount a defendant would have to pay a plaintiff on a damage award from the date the damage was suffered to the date of judgment—was no higher than 6%. In contrast, the market rate of interest over the 1974–1980 period ranged from 10.5% at the end of 1974 to 21.5% at the end of 1980, a spread over the statutory rate ranging from 4.5% to 15.5%. Now consider the payoff to a litigation game in which one player owes the other money. As the interest rate spread increases, it becomes more likely that the defendant's dominant strategy will be noncooperation because the gains from the spread outweigh the transaction costs of conflict: the more conflictual the litigation, the longer the process takes, and the longer the defendant earns the interest rate spread. Indeed, in this game the debtor's best outcome is not the "sucker's payoff" in which the debtor acts noncooperatively and the creditor cooperatively, but "thermonuclear war" in which both sides play noncooperatively—the more conflict, the longer the delay.

This example suggests that the payoff structure of commercial litigation is hardly immutable, and change may well affect the frequency of cooperation. Changes in economic conditions or the rules concerning prejudgment interest can affect the payoff structure of commercial litigation. Some jurisdictions now have rules imposing market-level prejudgment interest in some disputes, and it is plain that, as legal fees have increased and interest rates have fallen, there may be fewer disputes in which delay so clearly serves one party's interest. Thus, it may be no coincidence that large corporations became much more interested in Alternative Dispute Resolution (ADR) in the 1980s when interest rates were falling and legal costs were increasing.

. . .

2. THE SIZE OF THE LEGAL COMMUNITY AND REPUTATIONS FOR COOPERATION

Central to the potential for lawyers to facilitate a cooperative solution to a prisoner's dilemma litigation game is an effective reputation market for lawyers. Lawyers must be able to earn and maintain observable reputations for cooperation, and lawyers must be able to observe breaches of reputation by opposing counsel and have an interest in reporting these breaches. There is reason to believe that the enormous growth in size of the large law firms that provide legal representation in most substantial commercial litigation has undermined the effectiveness of the reputation market.

The first step in the analysis is to recognize the extraordinary growth of large law firms. In the late 1950s, only 38 law firms had more than 50 lawyers. By 1985, 508 firms had reached that size. Fewer than a dozen firms exceeded 100 lawyers in 1960; by 1986, there were 251 such firms. In 1968, the largest law firm had 169 lawyers; in 1993 the largest firm had 1662 lawyers and 184 firms were larger than the 1968 leader.

Now consider how lawyers might develop a reputation for cooperation. Suppose that the primary vehicle of reputation formation is a lawyer's relations with other lawyers, who then communicate that reputation to the client community. As discussed earlier, this is a plausible assumption given that cooperation in litigation is not a bright-line concept; because litigation is inherently competitive, a reputation for cooperation will be based on the more ephemeral concept of not being *too* conflictual. This type of standard requires that a lawyer apply it in the first instance.

In this setting, repeated experience with the same lawyers facilitates the formation of a cooperative reputation because competing lawyers are able to factor out the noise associated with the lawyer's conduct in any particular matter. The number of times that one lawyer has the experience of litigating against another lawyer in the community is a function of the size of the community—the smaller the community, the easier it is for lawyers to learn about the predilections of their adversaries toward cooperation.

These circumstances are sufficient to predict a secular trend of decreased reputations for cooperation among law firm lawyers in a rapidly growing legal community. Lawyers will perceive members of the older generation of lawyers as having a reputation for cooperation, their reputations having been developed in a less populated environment. In this environment, leading litigators in a community dealt with each other every day. In contrast, the succeeding generations of lawyers would have found it much more difficult to develop reputations for cooperation because the continued growth of the legal community decreased their opportunity to have had sufficient dealings with a large enough segment of the bar to have developed one. In these circumstances, if a lawyer cannot develop a reputation for cooperation, then the dominant career strategy is noncooperation—to be a gladiator. Thus, with the passage of time, as the older lawyers retire and are replaced by younger lawyers, the legal community becomes dominated by lawyers with a noncooperative style and conflict in litigation increases over time.

To be sure, most lawyers do not identify themselves as bombers or gladiators. Rather, they describe their personal strategy as flexible, either cooperator or gladiator, depending on how the other side plays. In effect, the picture is of a population of tit-for-tat lawyers: each cooperates until the other side defects and then retaliates. Wrapping oneself in the cloak of tit-for-tat does have a powerful rhetorical effect. Not only is blame for observed conflict placed on the other lawyer—retaliation comes only after the other side defects—but it also carries a strong claim of effectiveness. In Robert Axelrod's now classic tournament, tit-for-tat proved the most successful strategy for playing a repeated prisoner's dilemma game.

The puzzle, then, is to explain what generates all the litigation conflict. If litigators generally claim that they always cooperate unless the other side defects, who is left to defect first? The problem is that the effectiveness of the tit-for-tat strategy depends on a particular characteristic of the environment in which the game is played. As typically stated (and as was the case in Axelrod's tournament), the tit-for-tat strategy assumes that each player has perfect information about the other player's actions. That is, each player knows with certainty whether the other player has cooperated or defected. In contrast, when one player may mistake the character of the other player's actions, tit-for-tat leads not to cooperation, but to continuing gladiatorial defection. Suppose one player misinterprets her opponent's action as defection when her opponent actually meant to cooperate. Tit-for-tat dictates following the opponent's move on all moves after the first. Thus, cooperation ends after the misinterpretation. One player defects, mistakenly thinking her opponent had done so, and her opponent then follows suit, the mistake "echoing" back and forth as the players simply repeat the initial mistake.

Thus, the information structure of the litigation game can explain the presence of significant conflict in litigation even though most lawyers claim to play tit-for-tat. Litigation is quite "noisy." Clearly identifying whether the other side has cooperated or defected in a competitive environment where cooperation is defined as being not *too* conflictual, is often quite difficult.

Chapter 3

DISTRIBUTIVE BARGAINING— COMPETITIVE MOVES TO CLAIM VALUE

The last chapter explored the contours of the mixed motive exchange symbolized by the Prisoner's Dilemma. The readings suggested that competitive and collaborative bargaining strategies are each legitimate and are interconnected: They do not exist in isolation from one another. The effective negotiator must be sufficiently flexible to know how to select the appropriate strategy at each opportunity during the negotiation process. Remembering the lessons of tit-for-tat ensures against exploitation in each bargaining context.

It is difficult to understand how to employ the intertwined strategies of collaboration and competition, however, without artificially separating them for a time and studying them independently. The present chapter begins this process by identifying the characteristics of a negotiation strategy designed to **claim** value by obtaining the largest possible share of whatever resources are available for distribution. The next chapter explores how to use strategies designed to **create** value by expanding the range of available options for agreement. The skilled negotiator knows how to use the **predictability** of the distributive strategies and how to capture the **creativity** of the more collaborative ones.

We have all experienced the rich benefits, and the painful downsides, of using competitive strategies to gain a bargaining advantage. On many occasions people attempt to obtain as much value as possible from their negotiating opposite, and perceive that they can obtain this value only if the opposite foregoes it. This strategy is called **distributive bargaining** because the negotiators distribute a single medium of exchange or "pool of value," frequently money. Habitués of garage sales and swap meets, visitors to Third World souks, and attorneys settling casualty litigation all must be experts in competitive negotiating techniques. This is particularly true for those of us whose natural instincts lie away from the push and pull of aggressive tactics. While some people may prefer a more collaborative negotiating environment, effective negotiators forswear using distributive bargaining only at their peril. In fact, whenever we decide to advance our own interests though the opposite may lose, we dance to the rhythms of competitive bargaining.

Elmtree House, developed by Howard Raiffa, illustrates how we commonly use distributive bargaining strategies to help put deals together. The story highlights many of the assumptions made and the tactics used to gain a bargaining advantage when there is only one resource to distribute, in this case the money necessary to complete a real estate transaction. Raiffa's more detailed explanation of the process in later chapters of *The Art and Science of Negotiation* is well worth extensive study.

Next, Donald Gifford's excerpt offers us a compact primer to the theoretical framework of the competitive negotiation strategy. Gifford shows that many of the moves made in the Elmtree House negotiation were grounded on a sound theoretical foundation. Like the other strategies we will discuss, competitive efforts to claim value by distributive bargaining have a predictable structure and rhythm. By understanding this predictable "dance" of the distributive strategy, and the tactics frequently used to obtain a bargaining advantage, we can negotiate more effectively when the context calls for it.

Much of the predictability of the distributive strategy stems from the negotiator's use of tactics to obtain a bargaining advantage. Tactics are psychological maneuvers designed to influence negotiating opposites to view their own position as less powerful or our position as more powerful than would otherwise be the case. Competitive negotiators use tactics for one reason: Unless effectively countered, they work! The numbers of available tactics are legion; they include silence; anger; misrepresentation; lack of authority; the "good cop, bad cop" scenario; time pressure; ultimatums; insults; refusal to make concessions; flattery. The list is all but endless. We explore the use of tactics in this chapter.

Influential early authors focused largely on developing skills in the use of tactics. Representative of this genre is the reading from Michael Meltsner and Philip Schrag. Their tantalizing prescriptive advice is aimed at lawyers representing Legal Services clients before government agencies, who frequently find themselves in an undesirable power position vis-a-vis their bargaining opposites.

More recent assessments of competitive strategies build upon this earlier work on hard bargaining. First, Howard Raiffa amplifies the lessons of Elmtree House to show the predictability of the distributive strategy. Once the parties hear the music, and the "dance" of reciprocal concessions begins, we can make a number of empirical observations about the use of these concessions as a strategy for reaching an advantageous agreement. Next, Charles Craver suggests that practical negotiators commonly employ variations of some tried-and-true tactics to attain their objectives. Finally, distributive bargaining tactics have also been analyzed using game theoretic modeling and other social sciences research methods. One of the most powerful competitive techniques is to make a commitment to a particular position. David Lax and James Sebenius demonstrate that commitments to certain results can influence negotiations dramatically; and if they are not deployed effectively, their influence may be disadvantageous. This chapter concludes with a short case study. Gary Lowenthal recounts how then-Vice President Spiro Agnew used a commitment to a position to gain a decided advantage in his negotiation of a *nolo contendere* plea.

Readings

1. Howard Raiffa, The Art & Science of Negotiation 35–43 (1982).

2. Donald Gifford, *A Context–Based Theory of Strategy Selection in Legal Negotiation,* 46 Ohio St.L.J. 41, 48–52 (1985).

3. Michael Meltsner & Philip Schrag, *Negotiating Tactics for Legal Services Lawyers,* 7 Clearinghouse Review 259–62 (1973).

4. Howard Raiffa, The Art and Science of Negotiation 47–50 (1982).

5. Charles Craver, *Negotiation Techniques: How to Keep Br'er Rabbit Out of the Brier Patch,* Trial 65, 67–74 (June 1988).

6. David Lax & James Sebenius, The Manager as Negotiator: Bargaining for Cooperation and Competitive Gain 123–30 (1986).

7. Gary Lowenthal, *A General Theory of Negotiation Process, Strategy and Behavior,* 31 U.Kan.L.Rev. 69, 76–77 (1982).

8. For Further Reading

   a. Robert J. Condlin, *Cases on Both Sides: Patterns of Argument in Legal Dispute–Negotiation,* 44 Md.L.Rev. 65 (1985).

   b. Herb Cohen, You Can Negotiate Anything (1980).

   c. Jules Coleman, *Negating Negotiation Avoidance Techniques,* 34 The Practical Lawyer 83–95 (1988).

   d. Roger Dawson, You Can Get Anything You Want (But You Have to Do More Than Ask) (1985).

   e. Daniel Druckman, *Determinants of Compromising Behavior In Negotiation: A Meta–Analysis,* 38 J. Conflict Res. 507 (1994).

   f. Chester Karrass, The Negotiating Game (1970).

   g. Leonard Koren & Peter Goodman, The Haggler's Handbook: One Hour to Negotiating Power (1991).

   h. Herbert Kritzer, Let's Make a Deal (1991).

   i. Carrie Menkel–Meadow, Review Essay, *Legal Negotiation: A Study of Strategies in Search of a Theory,* 1983 Am.Bar Found. Res.J. 905.

   j. Gerald Nierenberg, Fundamentals of Negotiating (1974).

   k. Dean Pruitt, Negotiation Behavior (1981).

   l. Linda L. Putnam, *Challenging the Assumptions of Traditional Approaches to Negotiation,* 10 Negot.J. 337 (1994).

   m. Jeswald W. Salacuse & Jeffrey Z. Rubin, *Your Place or Mine? Site Location and Negotiation,* 6 Negot.J. 5 (1990).

   n. Deborah L. Shapiro & Robert J. Bies, *Threats, Bluffs, and Disclaimers in Negotiations,* 60 Org.Beh. & Human Dec.Proc. 14 (1994).

HOWARD RAIFFA, THE ART & SCIENCE OF NEGOTIATION
35–45 (1982).

The following case study is mostly make-believe; one might speak of it as an "armchair" case. It involves a colleague of mine—I'll call him Steve—who, as a professor of business, was quite knowledgeable about finance but not a practitioner of the art and science of negotiation.

Steve was on the governing board of Elmtree House, a halfway house for young men and women ages eighteen to twenty-five who needed the support of a sympathetic group and professional guidance to ease their transition from mental institutions back to society. Many of the residents had had nervous breakdowns, or were borderline schizophrenics, or were recovering from unfortunate experiences with drugs. Located on the outskirts of Boston in the industrial city of Somerville, Elmtree House accommodated about twenty residents. The neighborhood was in a transition stage; some said that it would deteriorate further, others that it was on the way up. In any case, it did not provide an ideal recuperative setting because of its agitated atmosphere. Although the house was small and quite run down, the lot itself was extensive, consisting of a full acre of ground. Its once-magnificent stand of elm trees had succumbed to disease.

The governing board, through a subcommittee, had once investigated the possibility of moving Elmtree from Somerville to a quieter, semiresidential community. Other suitable houses were located in the nearby cities of Brookline, Medford, and Allston, but the financial aspects were prohibitive and the idea of moving was reluctantly dropped.

Some months later, a Mr. Wilson approached Elmtree's director, Mrs. Peters, who lived in the house with her husband and child. Wilson indicated that his firm, a combined architectural and developmental contractor, might be interested in buying the Elmtree property. This was out of the blue. No public announcement had ever been made that Elmtree House was interested in a move. Mrs. Peters responded that the thought had never occurred to her, but that if the price were right, the governing board might just consider it. Wilson gave Mrs. Peters his card and said that he would like to pursue the topic further if there were a chance for a deal.

The governing board asked Steve to follow up on this promising lead.

. . .

During the next twelve days, Steve did a number of things. First, he tried to ascertain Elmtree's *reservation price* or walkaway price—that is, the minimum price that Elmtree House, the seller, could accept. The reservation price was difficult to determine, since it depended on the availability of alternative sites to relocate. Steve learned that of the other sites that had previously been located, the one in Brookline was no longer available but the other two, in Medford and in Allston, were still possibilities—for the right price. Steve talked with the owners of those sites and found out that the Medford property could be had for about $175,000 and the Allston property for about $235,000.

Steve decided that Elmtree House would need at least $220,000 before a move to Medford could be undertaken and that it would need $275,000 to justify a move to Allston. These figures took into account the cost of moving, minor repairs, insurance, and a small sum for risk aversion. The Allston site (needing $275,000) was much better than the Medford site (needing $220,000), which in turn was better than the site at Elmtree. So Steve decided that his reservation price would be $220,000. He would take nothing less, and hope to get more—possibly enough more to justify the Allston alternative. This bit of research took about six hours, or a couple of evenings' work.

Meanwhile Steve's wife, Mary, contacted several realtors looking for alternate properties. There were a few nibbles, but nothing definite turned up.

What next?

Steve next investigated what Elmtree House would bring if sold on the open market. By examining the sale prices of houses in the vicinity and by talking to local realtors and real estate experts, he learned that the Elmtree property was probably worth only about $125,000. He felt that if sold without Wilson in the picture, the house would go for between $110,000 and $145,000 (with probability one-half), and it was just as likely to go below $110,000 as above $145,000. How disappointing! This took another four hours of research time.

. . .

As of two days before the start of real negotiations, Steve would have bet even money that Wilson's *RP* lay in the interval from $250,000 (the lower quartile) to $475,000 (the upper quartile).

. . .

What should be Steve's opening gambit? Who should start the bidding first? If Wilson insisted that Steve make the first offer, what should that be? If Wilson opened with *x* thousand dollars, what should Steve's counteroffer be? How far could this be planned in advance? Were there any obvious traps to be avoided?

Steve and I felt that our probabilistic assessment of Wilson's *RP* was so broad that it would be easy to make a mistake by having our first offer fall below his true reservation price. But if we started with a wildly high request like $900,000—way over what we would settle for—it might sour the atmosphere.

Steve decided to try to get Wilson to move first; if that did not work and if he were forced to make the first offer, he would use the round figure of $750,000, but he would try to make that offer appear very flexible and soft. Steve thought about opening with an offer of $400,000 and holding firm for a while, but we felt there was a 40 percent chance that this amount would be below Wilson's *RP*. If Wilson moved first, Steve would not allow him to dwell on his offer but would quickly try to get away from that psychologically low anchor point by promptly retorting with a counteroffer of, say, $750,000.

I told Steve that once two offers are on the table—one for each party—the final point of agreement could reasonably be predicted to fall midway between those two extremes. So if Wilson offered $200,000 and if Steve came back with $400,000, a reasonable bet would be a settlement of $300,000—provided, of course, that that midway figure fell within the potential zone of agreement, the range between Steve's (the seller's) true *RP* and Wilson's (the buyer's) true *RP*. For starters, Steve thought that it would be nice if he could get $350,000 from Wilson, but, of course, Steve realized that his own *RP* was still $220,000.

.   .   .

As it turned out, the first round of negotiations was, in Steve's eyes, a disaster, and afterward he wasn't even sure that there would be a second round. Mrs. Peters performed admirably, but to no avail; it seemed unlikely that Wilson would raise his offer to Elmtree's reservation price. After preliminary pleasantries and some posturing, Wilson said, "Tell me the bare minimum you would accept from us, and I'll see if I can throw in something extra." Steve expected that gambit, and instead of outright misrepresentation he responded, "Why don't you tell us the very maximum that you are willing to pay, and we'll see if we can shave off a bit." Luckily, Wilson was amused at that response. He finally made his opening offer at $125,000, but first bolstered it with a lot of facts about what other property was selling for in that section of Somerville. Steve immediately responded that Elmtree House could always sell their property for more money than Wilson was offering, and that they did not have the faintest intention of moving. They would consider moving only if they could relocate in a much more tranquil environment where real estate values were high. Steve claimed that the trouble of moving could be justified only by a sale price of about $600,000, and Mrs. Peters concurred. Steve chose that $600,000 figure keeping in mind that the mid-point between $150,000 and $600,000 was above his aspiration level of $350,000. Wilson retorted that prices like that were out of the question. The two sides jockeyed around a bit and decided to break off, with hints that they might each do a bit more homework.

.   .   .

Two days later, however, Steve received a call from Wilson, who said that his conscience was bothering him. He had had a dream about Mrs. Peters and the social good she was bringing to this world, and this had persuaded him that, even though it did not make business sense, he should increase his offer to $250,000. Steve could not contain himself and blurted out his first mistake: "Now that's more like it!" But then he regained his composure and said that he thought that he could get Elmtree's board to come down to $475,000. They agreed to meet again in a couple of days for what would hopefully be a final round of bargaining.

Following this phone conversation with Wilson, Steve told me that he had inadvertently led Wilson to believe that his $250,000 offer would suffice; but Steve also felt that his offer of $475,000 was coming close to Wilson's *RP*, because this seemed to be the only reason for Wilson's reference to a "final round of bargaining." We talked further about strategy and we revised some probabilistic assessments.

Over the next two days there was more jockeying between the two sides, and Wilson successively yielded from $250,000 to $275,000 to $290,000 and finally to a *firm last offer* of $300,000, whereas Steve went from $475,000 to $425,000 to $400,000, and then—painfully—when Wilson sat fixedly at $300,-000, inched down to $350,000. Steve finally broke off by saying that he would have to contact key members of the governing board to see if he could possibly break the $350,000 barrier.

. . .

The next day Steve called Wilson and explained to him that the members of Elmtree's board were divided about accepting $300,000 (that was actually true). "Would it be possible for your company to yield a bit and do, for free, the equivalent of $30,000 or $40,000 worth of repair work on Elmtree's new property if our deal with you goes through? In that case, we could go with the $300,000 offer." Wilson responded that he was delighted that the board was smart enough to accept his magnanimous offer of $300,000. Steve was speechless. Wilson then explained that his company had a firm policy not to entangle itself with side deals involving free contract work. He didn't blame Steve for trying, but his suggestion was out of the question.

"Well then," Steve responded, "it would surely help us if your company could make a tax-free gift to Elmtree House of, say, $40,000, for Elmtree's Financial Aid Fund for needy residents."

"Now that's an idea! Forty grand is too high, but I'll ask our lawyers if we can contribute twenty grand."

"Twenty-five?"

"Okay—twenty-five."

It turned out that for legal reasons Wilson's company paid a straight $325,000 to Elmtree House, but Wilson had succeeded in finding a good face-saving reason for breaking his "firm last offer" of $300,000.

DONALD GIFFORD, A CONTEXT–BASED THEORY OF STRATEGY SELECTION IN LEGAL NEGOTIATION

46 Ohio St.L.Rev. 41, 48–52 (1985).

THE COMPETITIVE STRATEGY

The competitive negotiator tries to maximize the benefits for his client by convincing his opponent to settle for less than she otherwise would have at the outset of the negotiation process. The basic premise underlying the competitive strategy is that all gains for one's own client are obtained at the expense of the opposing party. The strategy aims to convince the opposing party that her settlement alternative is not as advantageous as she previously thought. Competitive tactics are designed to lessen the opponent's confidence in her case, thereby inducing her to settle for less than she originally asked. The competitive negotiator moves "psychologically against the other person," with behavior designed to unnerve the opponent. Competitive negotiators expect similar behavior from their opponents and therefore mistrust them. In undermining their opponents' confidence, competitive negotiators employ a strategy which often includes the following tactics:

1. a high initial demand;

2. limited disclosure of information regarding facts and one's own preferences;

3. few and small concessions;

4. threats and arguments; and

5. apparent commitment to positions during the negotiating process.

A negotiator who utilizes the competitive strategy begins with a high initial demand. Empirical research repeatedly demonstrates a significant positive relationship between a negotiator's original demand and his payoff. A high initial demand conceals the negotiator's minimum settlement point and allows the negotiator to grant concessions during the negotiating process and still achieve a favorable result. The negotiator's opening position may also include a false issue—a demand that the negotiator does not really care about, but one that can be traded for concessions from the opponent during the negotiation. Generally, the more that the negotiator insists upon a particular demand early in the negotiation, the larger the concession that ultimately will be obtained from the opponent in exchange for dropping that demand. In addition, the opponent may have evaluated the negotiator's case more favorably than the negotiator has; a high demand protects the negotiator from quickly agreeing to a less favorable settlement than one which he might later obtain. If the demand is high but credible, the opponent's response to the demand may also educate the negotiator about how the opponent evaluates her own case.

The competitive negotiator selectively and strategically shares information with his opponent. He does not disclose the least favorable terms to which his client would agree, that is, his minimum reservation point. He prefers to obtain an even more favorable settlement in excess of his reservation point. If the negotiator reveals his reservation point too quickly, the opponent has no incentive to offer anything more than the reservation price. Therefore, the competitive negotiator carefully hides not only his reservation point, but also any information which would allow the opponent to determine his true reservation point. For example, in a criminal case, the prosecutor might conceal from the defense attorney information regarding her caseload, her familiarity with the case, her own vacation plans, and the attitude of the victim toward the case. Conversely, the competitive negotiator selectively discloses information which strengthens his case and which undermines the opponent's case. The competitive negotiator should also pursue tactics that glean information about his opponent's reservation price, his opponent's attitude toward the case, and specific facts about the case.

The competitive strategy of negotiations mandates that the party make as few concessions as possible. If a concession must be made, it should be as small as possible. The competitive negotiator makes concessions reluctantly, because concessions may weaken one's position through both "position loss" and "image loss." Position loss occurs because in most negotiations a norm exists against withdrawing a concession. Further, an early concession results in an opportunity loss for something that might have been extracted in exchange for the concession later in the negotiation process. Image loss occurs because after a concession, the opponent perceives that the negotiator is flexible; in the opponent's mind this may suggest that further concessions can be obtained. Obviously, however, concessions are generally an inevitable part of the negotiating process. Concessions made by a negotiator build an expectation of reciprocity and lead to further concessions by the opponent which bring the parties closer to agreement. Granting concessions prevents premature deadlock and impasse and maintains goodwill with the adversary. This may be necessary to complete the negotiations or to foster a continued cooperative venture in the future. When possible, the competitive negotiator seeks to create the illusion in his opponent's eye that he is making a concession without diminishing his own satisfaction. This is done by either conceding on an issue the negotiator does not care about or appearing to make a concession without really making one.

The competitive negotiator obviously strives to force his opponent into making as many and as large concessions as possible while he makes few concessions, small in degree. To force concessions from his opponent, he employs both arguments and threats. In negotiations, arguments are communications intended to persuade the opponent to draw logical inferences from known data. For example, a plaintiff's attorney might describe a favorable eyewitness account of a collision and ask the defense counsel to infer the probability that her client will be found liable. Arguments should suggest to the opponent that her case is weaker than she previously thought and, therefore, that she should make new concessions. A threat, on the other hand, is a communication intended to inform the opponent that unless she agrees to a settlement acceptable to the negotiator, the negotiator or his client will act to the opponent's detriment. For example, a union negotiator might threaten that the union will strike if management refuses to make wage concessions.

The competitive negotiator not only uses offensive tactics to force concessions from his opponent, but he also makes as few concessions as possible. The competitive negotiator ignores both arguments and threats, believing that this is the best response. When the negotiator must make a concession, the competitive strategist suggests that the negotiator give the opponent a "positional commitment," a reason why he is not conceding more. Without such a positional commitment, according to the competitive strategist, the opponent will perceive the grant of a concession as a weakness and will expect further concessions. The negotiator's resolve to concede nothing more can be substantiated by linking the concession to a principle, to the negotiator's personal reputation, or to a threat of ending negotiations.

To the extent that the success of a negotiation strategy is measured by the payoff in a single negotiation involving the division of limited resources between two parties, studies of simulated negotiations suggest that the competitive strategy yields better results than other strategies for the negotiator. However, the competitive strategy suffers severe disadvantages. The likelihood of impasse is much greater for negotiators who employ the competitive strategy than for those who use other approaches. Competitive tactics engender tension and mistrust between the parties, which can give the appearance that the parties are farther apart than they really are. These negative attitudes may carry over into matters other than the current negotiation and may make continuing relationships difficult.

MICHAEL MELTSNER AND PHILIP G. SCHRAG, NEGOTIATING TACTICS FOR LEGAL SERVICES LAWYERS

7 Clearinghouse Review 259, 259–63 (1973).

This article catalogues several successful negotiating tactics. Of course, not every tactic described is appropriate for every negotiation; the use of each depends on the particular case and especially upon the perceived relative strengths of the parties during the bargaining process. In general, a party who appears to himself and to his adversary to be strongly desirous of negotiations is less able to use the more powerful tactics set forth. Even the attorney who must negotiate from a position of perceived weakness should be familiar with the tactics that may be used against him, so that he may defend himself as best he can.

This list of tactics is not intended to endorse the *propriety* of every one of them, but there can be no doubt of their *efficacy* in appropriate situations. All of these techniques are commonly used by lawyers, and the attorney who chooses to abjure one because it is ethically dubious should at least learn to recognize and to understand the device so that he can defend against it. The more "tricky" of these ploys are used most commonly in urban centers, where lawyers are not likely to be negotiating repeatedly with the same adverse attorneys who will eventually recognize their favorite tactics. Lawyers who have to deal with each other in case after case are more likely to conduct an open, straightforward discussion than those who may never negotiate with each other again.

1. Preparatory Tactics

1. *Arrange to Negotiate on Your Own Turf*

Whenever possible, insist that the meeting be held in your office or in another setting where you will feel more comfortable than your adversary, and where he will be at a psychological disadvantage because he has had to come to you. . . .

Some neighborhood poverty lawyers who negotiate with attorneys for banks, realty corporations, and other large firms have added a new twist to the "home base" tactic by attempting to maneuver their adversaries into entering the ghetto, sometimes for the first time in their lives. Their fears for their physical safety and their shock at viewing local housing conditions may reduce their bargaining effectiveness.

Negotiating in your own office has some specific practical advantages as well. If agreement is reached, it gives you the option of calling in your secretary and dictating a memorandum of agreement on the spot; you may not desire to do this, but the option is *yours*. You save traveling time and impose its cost on your adversary. And you have the opportunity, seconds after the meeting has been completed, to dictate a precise memorandum to your files relating the detailed information your adversary disclosed during the session.

2. *Balance or Slightly Outnumber the Other Side*

In a bargaining session where two negotiate against one, or three against two, the side with fewer representatives is usually at a disadvantage in that it will tire more readily and will be less able to control the flow of discussion. . . .

3. *Time the Negotiations to Advantage*

When one side wants to get the discussion over with quickly, it usually loses.... Some lawyers make it a point to schedule negotiations with government attorneys at 4:00 p.m., on the assumption that civil service lawyers expect to go home at 5:00 p.m. and will bargain much more quickly and carelessly at that hour than they would in the morning. Similarly, a lawyer who is not used to working on weekends will probably negotiate more poorly on a Saturday or Sunday than during the week.

4. *Know the Facts Thoroughly*

. . .

5. *Lock Yourself In*

This is a risky but powerful prenegotiation tactic and should be used only with the greatest care. In cases that have attracted public attention, an attorney can increase his bargaining power by announcing publicly a position from which he will not retreat so that his adversary knows that he will lose face if he does in fact retreat. Then the attorney can convincingly say that aspect of his position is nonnegotiable. Attorneys who use this tactic sometimes have their bluff called, and may, in fact, have to make a concession and then explain the retreat to their clients.

6. *Designate One Of Your Demands a "Precondition"*

If the other side wants to talk (*e.g.,* if it requested the negotiations), a lawyer can often improve the chances of a favorable outcome by calling one of his demands a "precondition" to negotiations....

II. INITIAL TACTICS

7. *When It Is in Your Interest, Make the Other Side Tender the First Offer*

The party making the first offer suffers the disadvantage of conceding that it really wants to settle. Furthermore, it may make an offer that actually concedes more than the other side thought it could get at the end of the negotiating process. The attorney who receives such a surprising offer will declare his shock that so little is being tendered, and will demand much more. One surprisingly successful technique for evoking the first offer is to remain silent. Few people can tolerate more than a few seconds of silence during a negotiation; most feel compelled to say something to break the ice....

8. *Make Your First Demand Very High*

Outrageously unreasonable demands become more justifiable after substantial discussion. Even if an initially high demand is rejected, it makes a subsequent demand that is almost as high appear to be a more reasonable compromise. The negotiator who opens with a reasonable compromise is likely to be pushed to a worse settlement than he could have obtained by harder bargaining. Nevertheless, some demands are too outrageous to make. They will encourage your adversary to believe that you are not seriously interested in bargaining despite your protestations to the contrary.

9. *Place Your Major Demands at the Beginning of the Agenda*

There seem to be "honeymoon" periods, in which negotiators make compromises more freely, at the outset of negotiations and at their conclusion.

By forcing your adversary to deal at the outset, when he wants most to compromise, with the items of greatest interest to you, or at the end, when he has invested many hours or weeks of time in negotiating and wants a return on his investment, you can improve your client's position.

10. Make the Other Side Make the First Compromise

There is a psychological advantage in benefitting from the first concession. Studies indicate that losers generally make the first concessions in negotiating a dispute.

III. TACTICS GENERALLY

11. Use Two Negotiators Who Play Different Roles

. . .

12. Invoke Law or Justice

To a surprising extent, lawyers are impressed with the citation of authority, and laymen tend to be overwhelmed by a reference to a case or statute. . . . If the law is not on your side, avoid using it. Instead, invoke more general principles of justice, or whatever other kind of authority (e.g., public pressure) seems to support your position.

13. Be Tough—Especially Against a Patsy

. . .

14. Appear Irrational Where It Seems Helpful

This is a dangerous but often successful tactic. An adversary who is himself an expert negotiator can be thrown off base considerably by a lawyer who does not seem to play the same game, for example, one who seems to behave irrationally. Premier Nikita Krushchev significantly increased the deterrent power of the relatively small Soviet nuclear force by banging his shoe on the table at the United Nations in 1960; he gave the impression of being somewhat imbalanced—a man who might unleash nuclear weapons upon even a slight provocation.

15. Raise Some of Your Demands as the Negotiations Progress

The conventional model of negotiation contemplates both sides lowering their demands until a compromise is finally reached. But the highly successful negotiator backtracks; he raises one of his demands for every two concessions he makes and occasionally reopens for further discussion topics that everyone thought had been settled and laid aside. This tactic not only reduces the aggregate concession he makes, but it makes the other side want to finish the negotiation quickly before he stiffens his position any more or retracts the concessions he had made. The party who desires to finish quickly has two strikes against him.

16. Claim That You Do Not Have Authority to Compromise

. . . The freshman negotiator sometimes makes the mistake of trying to impress the other side with his authority; the expert modestly explains that he has very little authority, and that his client is adamant. . . .

17. *Clear the Agreement With Your Client Before Signing It*

Before you reach final agreement, you will want to consult with your client. Checking with the client is not only an obligation that you owe to him, it is an important bargaining tactic. It enables you to delay the proceedings while you check, and it gives you a chance to consider any errors you might have made before you sign.

IV. POST-NEGOTIATION TACTICS

18. *Make Your Adversary Feel Good*

Never gloat over the terms of a settlement. Not only is such behavior boorish, but it may provoke an adversary to reopen negotiations or to adopt a different and stronger negotiating posture the next time you deal with him. If you can do so with candor, feel free to tell opposing counsel what a hard bargain he drove and what a good job he did for his client. If you meet an adversary and his client together, tell the client what a good job his lawyer did for him....

19. *After Agreement has Been Reached, Have Your Client Reject It and Raise His Demands*

This is the most ethically dubious of the tactics listed, but there will be occasions where a lawyer will have to defend against it or even employ it. After laboring for hours, days, or weeks to work out a settlement, a negotiator is likely to be dismayed by the prospect of the agreement falling through. As a result, his adversary may be able to obtain last minute concessions. Such a strategy can boomerang; it may so anger an adversary that he simply refuses to bargain, even though bargaining is still in his interest, or he may fight fire with fire by increasing his own demands.

20. *Promptly Reduce The Agreement to Writing Yourself*

... Reduction of terms to writing is an effective means of discovering whether there is actual agreement. Not only is the written instrument evidence of the agreement, but the formulation of its terms will tend to govern the conduct of the parties in the future. Quite often the terms that have been agreed upon will be subject to differing interpretations, some of which favor your side, some of which favor your adversary's side. You should, therefore, volunteer to undertake the labor of drafting the agreement. By doing so, you can choose language which reflects your interpretation of the terms agreed upon.

HOWARD RAIFFA, THE ART & SCIENCE OF NEGOTIATION
47–50 (1982).

A simple laboratory bargaining problem can be introduced with less than one page of confidential instructions to the seller and buyer. The context is the sale of a used car, the Streaker, and the setting is dated to justify a seller's reservation price of $300 and a buyer's reservation price of $550. The instructions to each give only the vaguest of hints about the other person's *RP*. The challenge for a buyer is to get a good deal for herself, and she will be judged in terms of how well she has done in comparison to other buyers in an identical situation; the seller is judged similarly, in comparison to other sellers. This is like a duplicate bridge scoring system.

Players who put themselves in the role of one or the other of these negotiators will naturally ask a number of questions. What analyses should be done? What bargaining ploys seem to work? Should I open first with an offer? If I open first, how extreme should I be? Am I better off giving a reasonable value that would yield me a respectable surplus and remaining firm, or should I start with a more extreme value and pace my concessions with those of the other party? What is a reasonable pattern of concessions? Our data indicate that in this situation most pairs of negotiators come to an agreement.

A typical pattern of concessions is depicted in Figure 3, where s_1, b_1, s_2, b_2, and so on represent the prices successively proposed by the seller and buyer. I call this pattern "the negotiation dance." The seller might open with a value of \$700 (s_1 in the figure); the buyer retorts with $b_1 = 250; then in succession comes $s_2 = 500 (breaking the buyer's RP), $b_2 = 300 (breaking the seller's RP), $s_3 = 450, $b_3 = 400, and a final-contract price of $x^* = 425. Would x^* be higher if s_1 were \$900 instead of \$700? If so, why not make $s_1 = $2,000$?

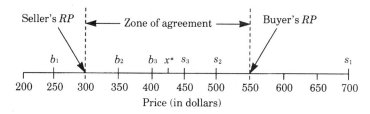

Figure 3. The negotiation dance (x^* = final-contract price).

Our data yielded a number of interesting findings. First, the final contracts ranged over the entire zone of agreement, from \$300 to \$550. A sprinkling (less than 1 percent) of cases were settled out of the zone of agreement for a value less than \$300 or more than \$550; the subjects in these cases misinterpreted the directions. In some cases, but surprisingly few (around 3 percent), agreement was never achieved.

Second, the average of the final contracts was \$415 with a standard deviation of 52, indicating a surprising spread of outcomes. The average opening offer of the sellers was \$525 (standard deviation of 116); the average opening offer of the buyers was \$261 (standard deviation 112).

Third, the Boulware strategy of making a reasonable opening and remaining firm works sometimes, but more often than not it antagonizes the other party, and many of the no-agreements resulted from this strategy. Advice: don't embarrass your bargaining partner by forcing him or her to make all the concessions.

Fourth, once two offers are on the table (s_1 and b_1), the best prediction of the final contract is the midpoint, $(s_1 + b_1)/2$—provided that the midpoint falls within the zone of agreement. If the midpoint falls outside this zone, then it's hard to predict where the final contract will fall. It is not true that x^* will be near the reservation price that is closer to the midpoint. The reason is that the concessions will have to be lopsided, and it's hard to predict the consequences. Thus, if $b_1 = \$250$ and $s_1 = \$2,000$, with the midpoint being $\$1,125$, the seller is going to be forced to make huge concessions and $x *$ might end up closer to $\$300$ than to $\$550$.

Fifth, from a linear regression analysis it appears that if the buyer's opening bid is held constant, then on the average adding $\$100$ to the opening bid of the seller nets an increase of about $\$28$ to the final contract. If the seller's opening bid is held constant, then on the average subtracting $\$100$ from the opening bid of the buyer nets a decrease of about $\$15$ from the final contract.

With one group of 70 subjects I ran a variation of the Streaker experiments with some fascinating but inconclusive results. In the variation, the instructions to the buyers were the same: as in the original experiments, they still had a reservation price of $\$550$. But the instructions to the sellers were altered: they still had to get at least $\$300$, but they were told not to try to get as much as possible because of the desirability of later amicable relationships with the buyers. The sellers were told that they would receive a maximum score if they could sell the car for $\$500$ and that every dollar above $\$500$ would detract from their score; a sale of x dollars above $\$500$ would yield them the same satisfaction as x dollars below $\$500$. Thus, for example, a score of $\$525$ would be equivalent to a score of $\$475$. Of course, the buyers were not aware of these confidential instructions to the sellers.

Surprisingly, the sellers did better playing this variation with benevolent intentions toward the buyer than they did with aggressive intentions to squeeze out as much as possible. In the variation, the average price for the car was $\$457$ instead of $\$415$. One reason for this might have been that in the original version, the sellers were told only to get more than $\$300$ and they did not have any target figure. In the variation, they were told that the best achievable value was $\$500$ and this became a target value. Indeed, the sellers' opening offers averaged higher in the variation than in the original exercise ($\$592$ versus $\$525$). In the variation, the sellers came down faster from high values (above $\$500$) but they became more reluctant to reduce their prices as they pierced their $\$500$ aspiration level, thus making it seem to the buyers that they were approaching their reservation values.

Some sellers said that they felt some qualms when they let themselves be bargained back from $\$600$ to $\$500$, knowing that this was the direction in which they wanted to move. Some sellers told the buyers that they thought $\$500$ was the fair price and that they did not want to get a higher value; but the buyers they were bargaining with tended not to believe them, and these sellers on the average hurt themselves.

CHARLES B. CRAVER, NEGOTIATION TECHNIQUES: HOW TO KEEP BR'ER RABBIT OUT OF THE BRIER PATCH
Trial 65, 67–74 (June 1988).

Practicing lawyers negotiate constantly—with their partners, associates, legal assistants, and secretaries, with prospective clients and actual clients, and with opposing parties on behalf of clients. Although practitioners tend to use their negotiation skills more often than their other lawyering talents, few have had formal education about the negotiation process.

The process consists of three formal phases:

—The information phase, where each party endeavors to learn as much about the other side's circumstances and objectives as possible;

—the competitive phase, where negotiators try to obtain beneficial terms for their respective clients; and

—the cooperative phase, where if multiple-item transactions are involved, parties may often enhance their joint interests.

. . .

The Competitive Phase

Once the information phase ends, the focus usually changes from what the opposing party hopes to achieve to what each negotiator must get for his client. Negotiators no longer ask questions about each other's circumstances; they articulate their own side's demands.

"Principled" Offers and Concessions

Negotiators should develop a rational basis for each item included in their opening positions. This provides the other party with some understanding of the reasons underlying their demands, and it helps to provide the person making those demands with confidence in the positions. Successful negotiators establish high, but rational, objectives and explain their entitlement to these goals.

When negotiators need to change their position, they should use "principled" concessions. They need to provide opponents with a rational explanation for modifications of their position.

For example, a lawyer demanding $100,000 for an injured plaintiff might indicate willingness to accept $90,000 by saying that there is a 10 percent chance that the plaintiff might lose at trial or a good probability that the jury in a comparative-negligence jurisdiction will find that the plaintiff was 10 percent negligent. This lets the other party know why the change is being made, and it helps to keep the person at the $90,000 level until he is ready to use a "principled" concession to further reduce the demand.

. . .

Threats and Promises

Almost all legal negotiations involve use of overt or at least implicit threats. Threats show recalcitrant parties that the cost of disagreeing with offers will transcend the cost of acquiescence. Some negotiators try to avoid use of formal "threats," preferring less-challenging "warnings." These negotiators simply caution opponents about the consequences of their unwillingness to accept a mutual resolution.

If threats are to be effective, they must be believable. A credible threat is one that is reasonably proportionate to the action it is intended to deter—seemingly insignificant threats tend to be ignored, while large ones tend to be dismissed. Negotiators should never issue threats unless they are prepared to carry them out, since their failure to do so will undermine their credibility.

Instead of using negative threats that indicate what consequences will result if the opposing party does not alter its position, negotiators should consider affirmative promises that indicate their willingness to change their position simultaneously with the other party. The classic affirmative promise—the "split-the-difference" approach—has been used by most negotiators to conclude a transaction. One side promises to move halfway if only the other side will do the same.

Affirmative promises are more effective than negative threats at inducing position changes, since the first indicates that the requested position change will be reciprocated. A negative threat merely suggests dire consequences if the other side does not alter its position. They are more of an affront to an opponent than affirmative promises, and, as a result, are more disruptive of the negotiation process.

. . .

Limited Authority

Many advocates like to indicate during the preliminary stages that they do not have final authority from their client about the matter in dispute. They use this technique to reserve the right to check with their client before any tentative agreement can bind their side.

The advantage of a limited-authority approach—whether actual or fabricated—is that it permits the party using it to obtain a psychological commitment to settlement from opponents authorized to make binding commitments. The unbound bargainers can then seek beneficial modifications of the negotiated terms based on "unexpected" client demands. Since their opponents do not want to let such seemingly insignificant items negate the success achieved during the prior negotiations, they often accept the alterations.

Bargainers who meet opponents who initially say they lack the authority to bind their clients may find it advantageous to say that they also lack final authority. This will permit them to "check" with their own absent principal before making any final commitment.

A few unscrupulous negotiators will agree to a final accord with what appears to be complete authority. They later approach their opponent with apparent embarrassment and explain that they did not really have this authority. They say that their principal will require one or two modifications before accepting the other terms of the agreement. Since the unsuspecting opponent and his client are now committed to a final settlement, they agree to the concessions.

Negotiators who suspect that an adversary might use this technique may wish to select—at the apparent conclusion of their transaction—the one or two items they would most like to have modified in their favor. When their opponent requests changes, they can indicate how relieved they are about this, because their own client is dissatisfied. Then they can offer to exchange their items for those their adversary seeks. It is fascinating to see how quickly the opponent will now insist on honoring the initial accord.

The limited-authority situation must be distinguished from the one where an opponent begins a negotiation with no authority. This adversary hopes to get several concessions as a prerequisite to negotiations with a negotiator with real authority.

Negotiators should avoid dealing with a no-authority person, since he is trying to induce them to bargain with themselves. When they give their opening position, the no-authority negotiator will say that it is unacceptable. If they are careless, they will alter their stance to placate the no-authority participant. Before they realize what they have done, they will have made concessions before the other side has entered the process.

. . .

Boulwareism

This technique gets its name from Lemuel Boulware, former Vice President for Labor Relations at General Electric. Boulware was not enamored of traditional "auction" bargaining, which involves using extreme initial positions, making time-consuming concessions, and achieving a final agreement like the one the parties knew from the outset they would reach. He decided to determine ahead of time what GE was willing to commit to wage and benefit increases and then formulate a complete "best-offer-first" package. He presented this to union negotiators on a "take-it-or-leave-it" basis unless the union could show that GE had made some miscalculation or that changed circumstances had intervened.

Boulwareism is now associated with best-offer-first or take-it-or-leave-it bargaining. Insurance company adjusters occasionally try to establish reputations as people who will make one firm, fair offer for each case. If plaintiff does not accept that proposal, they plan to go to trial.

Negotiators should be hesitant to adopt Boulwareism. The offeror effectively tells the other party that he knows what is best for both sides. Few lawyers are willing to accord such respect to the view of opposing counsel.

Boulwareism deprives the opponent of the opportunity to participate meaningfully in the negotiation process. A plaintiff who might have been willing to settle a dispute for $50,000 may not be willing to accept a take-it-or-leave-it first offer of $50,000. The plaintiff wants to explore the case through the information phase and to exhibit his negotiating skill during the competitive phase. When the process has been completed, he wants to feel that his ability influenced the final outcome.

Negotiators presented with take-it-or-leave-it offers should not automatically reject them simply because of the paternalistic way in which they have been extended. They must evaluate the amount being proposed. If it is reasonable, they should accept it. Lawyers should not permit their own negative reaction to an approach preclude the consummation of a fair arrangement for their clients.

. . .

Belly–Up

Some negotiators act like wolves in sheepskin. They initially say they lack negotiating ability and legal perspicuity in a disingenuous effort to evoke sympathy and to lure unsuspecting adversaries into a false sense of security. These negotiators "acknowledge" the superior competence of those with whom they interact and say that they will place themselves in the hands of their fair and proficient opponent.

Negotiators who encounter a belly-up bargainer tend to alter their initial position. Instead of opening with the tough "principled" offer they had planned to use, they modify it in favor of their pathetic adversary, who praises them for their reasonableness, but suggests that his client deserves additional assistance. They then endeavor to demonstrate their ability to satisfy those needs. The belly-up participant says the new offer is a substantial improvement, but suggests the need for further accommodation. By the time the transaction is finished, the belly-up bargainer has obtained everything he wants. Not only are his opponents virtually naked, but they feel gratified at having assisted such an inept bargainer.

Belly-up bargainers are the most difficult to deal with, since they effectively refuse to participate in the process. They ask their opponent to permit them to forgo traditional auction bargaining due to their professed inability to negotiate. They want their reasonable adversary to do all the work.

Negotiators who encounter them must force them to participate and never allow them to alter their planned strategy and concede everything in an effort to form a solution acceptable to such pathetic souls. When belly-up negotiators characterize initial offers as unacceptable, opponents should make them respond with definitive offers. True belly-up negotiators often find it very painful to state and defend the positions they espouse.

Passive–Aggressive Behavior

Instead of directly challenging opponents' proposals, passive-aggressive negotiators use oblique, but highly aggressive, forms of passive resistance. They show up late for a scheduled session and forget to bring important documents. When they agree to write up the agreed-upon terms, they fail to do so.

Those who deal with a passive-aggressive opponent must recognize the hostility represented by the behavior and try to seize control. They should get extra copies of important documents just in case their opponent forgets to bring them. They should always prepare a draft of any agreement. Once passive-aggressive negotiators are presented with such a fait accompli, they usually execute the proffered agreement.

DAVID LAX & JAMES SEBENIUS, THE MANAGER AS NEGOTIATOR: BARGAINING FOR COOPERATION AND COMPETITIVE GAIN
123–30 (1986).

[C]onsider two equally senior law partners trying to decide which one gets the prestigious corner office overlooking the bay. Either Cadwalader or Botts will get the office if they can agree, but if they cannot, it will go to Stimson, an annoyingly aggressive junior partner. Because both senior partners want to maintain the traditional privileges and rewards for seniority and performance and because both detest Stimson, each prefers that either one take the office rather than let it fall to the upstart.... Because Cadwalader is a litigator and Botts is a tax man, they have no other real involvement and thus neither has a means to compensate the other for not taking the office. For either senior partner, successfully claiming value means getting the office for himself.

· · ·

THE COMMITMENT

Such a distributive bargain can be "won" by the side that first commits credibly and irreversibly to a preferred settlement.

One bargainer commits to a point in the bargaining range by imposing large costs on herself for accepting settlements less attractive than this point. If these costs would make accepting any lesser settlement worse than her current alternatives, the other bargainer is stuck: he confronts a preordained choice between accepting the commitment point—which at least is in the bargaining set—or taking his own, less desirable alternative.

For example, suppose that Cadwalader, egged on in a rash moment by fellow litigators, makes a bet in the partners' dining room with a greedy but valued client: if Botts gets the office, Cadwalader will pay the client $50,000. If it bothers Cadwalader more to lose $50,000 than to see Stimson get the office, this bet changes his valuation of the outcomes: now he would rather let the office go to the upstart than agree to give it to Botts. If Botts believes that the client will not let Cadwalader out of the bet, Botts must choose between giving Cadwalader the office and giving it to Stimson. If Botts does not fly into a rage at the way Cadwalader has rigged the situation, and if, on reflection, he really prefers to see the office occupied by one of the senior partners, he has no choice but to agree to give it to Cadwalader.

. . .

But, making such a commitment binding, credible, visible, and irreversible is difficult. First, the claim might not be believed, even if true.... And, such commitments can sometimes be reversed.... Botts might attempt to persuade the client to repudiate his bet with Cadwalader for the health of the law firm and because it inappropriately alters the attorney-client relationship. In general, making commitments stick requires ingenuity and, often, a substantial investment of resources.

Even a successful commitment to a position may not obtain the desired agreement. First, if the negotiators make incompatible commitments from which they cannot back down, they will deadlock. If Botts simultaneously makes a similar agreement with his biggest client, and neither he nor Cadwalader budge, Stimson gets the office. Second, the commitment itself can change how the person on whom it has been sprung values the possible outcomes. For example, if Cadwalader's commitment angers Botts and causes him to crave revenge—by keeping Cadwalader from getting the office—more than the tradition that he originally valued, if Botts would feel publicly shamed by conceding, or if he believes that giving in to such tactics would set an intolerable precedent, Botts may come to prefer no agreement to letting Cadwalader win. If so, Cadwalader's commitment may only have been the first move in a destructive escalation of conflict.

. . .

The artificiality of these examples should not obscure the practical importance of commitments. They are potent tactics in much more complex situations. For example, when a major investor attempted a hostile takeover of a large company, he included an interesting clause in agreements over the money he raised for the takeover: the interest rate he would be required to pay for this money would jump by 1.5 percent if he chose to make a counteroffer higher than his initial offer. Or, consider NATO's decision to put a significant number of American troops on the border of West and East Germany to commit the United States to respond to a Russian invasion of West Germany. Although the NATO forces would be unable to repel an invasion, it would necessarily kill American soldiers and a U.S. administration would incur huge political costs if it did not respond.

.   .   .

Negotiators sometimes threaten drastic consequences if their highly partisan demands are not met. A threat can be understood as a conditional commitment to do something undesirable if the threatened party does not comply. To take a farfetched example, suppose that a mild-mannered accountant threatens to blow up the seller's car if she does not sell it to him for a pittance. Suppose she refuses. What would motivate him to carry out the threat? It would be costly, messy, and dangerous for him and still he would not have the car. He has a serious credibility problem. Contrast his threat with the implied threat of co-CEO Lew Glucksman of Lehman Brothers to provoke internal upheaval and perhaps take the profitable trading operation to another firm if his abrupt demand to run Lehman by himself was not honored. Glucksman, with a reputation for volatile, vindictive, and even irrational actions, conveyed the powerful impression that his feet were "set in concrete"; he left little doubt that the apparent costs of executing his threat were meaningless to him and that he would act. In general, a threat tends to be more effective the more the underlying commitment to carry it out is binding, credible, visible, and irreversible.

.   .   .

Making a commitment risks impasse if the other party becomes incompatibly committed. Moreover, a negotiator usually does not know his counterpart's reservation value. With bad luck, too greedy a commitment may be unacceptable and, if irrevocable, will cause a breakdown.

Not surprisingly, some commitments, especially blunt ones, lead to bargaining explosions. The victim may not like the precedent being set for the style of future dealings. Or conceding to a blunt commitment may involve sufficient loss of face as to be undesirable; the commitment can start a destructive escalation of conflict.

Commitments based on "fair" principles and social norms are likely to be more effective than those made to apparently arbitrary positions. (Like committing to a position, one commits to a principle by imposing costs on oneself for abandoning that principle.) This may be true for reasons beyond any natural appeal of focal points.

A number of studies suggest that when a bargainer attributes his concession to his own weakness and the counterpart's strength, a blowup is likely. The bargainer would lose face or self-esteem by conceding. When this new interest (face) is included, he may find that no agreement, which retains self-esteem, is better than an agreement that seems to sacrifice it. This might well be the case for Botts when Cadwalader makes his bet or when someone stubbornly insists on an apparently arbitrarily chosen $104 settlement without any explanation. In contrast, when the bargainer can attribute the concession to something *outside* the two parties such as a mutually recognized norm, concession may not cause a loss of self-esteem. One might commit to refusing an employee a raise in various ways that do not risk his losing face in the dealing. For example, one may argue that such a raise would set an unacceptable precedent for all other employees in the same job grade or that one's boss would not accept it. Skillful commitments to norms and external standards are more likely to lead to concessions than commitments to more arbitrary points.

GARY LOWENTHAL, A GENERAL THEORY OF NEGOTIATION PROCESS, STRATEGY, AND BEHAVIOR

31 U.Kan.L.Rev. 69, 76–77 (1982).

Rigid commitment to a position at or near an opponent's minimum settlement point, therefore, is a basic tenet of competitive negotiation: As a result, the competitor often will find a means to restrict her flexibility, usually before entering negotiations or early in the bargaining process. The plea bargaining strategy of Vice President Agnew in 1973 illustrates this principle. Federal authorities investigated Agnew for receiving kickbacks from contractors, primarily while he was Governor of the State of Maryland. The Justice Department's overriding concern in plea negotiation was for Agnew to resign the vice-presidency as soon as possible, to avoid an extended constitutional crisis. Other prosecutorial priorities included a public disclosure of the facts uncovered during the investigation, and an in-court admission by Agnew that he was guilty of either bribery or extortion, the two most serious allegations made against him. During initial plea negotiations, which were held secretly, Agnew's lawyers indicated his willingness to resign office, so long as he could plead nolo contendere to a tax evasion charge, with no admission of guilt by the Vice President, and with a promise that he would not be sentenced to jail. Negotiation reached an impasse when the parties could not agree over the need for Agnew to acknowledge his guilt publicly. In addition, the Justice Department would not go on record with a recommendation against incarceration.

Agnew's response to the impasse was to "go public" with a series of pronouncements designed to rally support for his plight. In a well publicized speech, he took emphatic positions on both his innocence and his intentions concerning a possible resignation from office:

> In the past several months I have been living in purgatory. I have found myself the recipient of undefined, unclear, and unattributed accusations that have surfaced in the largest and most widely circulated organs of our communications media. *I want to say at this point—clearly and unequivocally—I am innocent of the charges against me* . . . . (applause)

> I want to make another thing so clear that it cannot be mistaken in the future. Because of these tactics which have been employed against me, because small and fearful men have been frightened into furnishing evidence against me ... *I will not resign if indicted. I will not resign if indicted* . . . . (cheers and wild applause)

Agnew's remarks were, by one account, "an unsubtle variety of public plea bargaining: make me a better deal, or I'll turn your country upside down for you." His public pronouncements of innocence and persecution communicated to his many supporters that he would not back down in a confrontation with the Justice Department. He could not, after committing himself publicly to this posture, make major bargaining concessions without looking like a fool. The Justice Department negotiators were left with the sense that an expeditious resignation of office would not be forthcoming, especially on the prosecutors' terms. Indeed, when negotiations resumed, the prosecution softened its position on the extent of Agnew's public acknowledgement of guilt, and also acquiesced to an agreement calling for no incarceration.

Chapter 4

INTEGRATIVE BARGAINING—
COLLABORATIVE MOVES
TO CREATE VALUE

———

The last chapter described the salient features of distributive bargaining strategies. There are several reasons, however, why these competitive strategies are not the only ones effective negotiators use. Sometimes competitive negotiations lead to impasse, and if the parties are going to find a point of agreement they must escape from the boundaries of the zero-sum game and find other ingredients of exchange. At times this expansion involves linkage of several distributive bargains; at others it means the search for additional items to distribute. Effective negotiators search to expand options and escape impasse.

At other times the relationship between the parties provides the impetus for developing a more cooperative bargaining context. This relationship may have preceded the current negotiation, as with intimates, or with repeat players in a routinized context. Often the process of negotiating itself encourages the development of a more cooperative context, even among people without a prior bargaining history. As the negotiation unfolds, parties may learn enough about one another to stimulate a more collaborative environment. In this climate, they may perceive competitive tactics as less productive than their more temperate counterparts.

In the past decade, writers have focused increasingly upon the structure of more cooperative conflict management techniques designed to create value, frequently labeled **integrative bargaining.** In 1982, Roger Fisher and William Ury drew upon earlier work and wrote the popular *Getting to Yes.* In this book, now available in scores of languages in bookstores throughout the known world, the authors set out a framework for what they call "principled negotiation." Fisher and Ury make several prescriptive suggestions for principled negotiators. They urge negotiators to "separate the people from the problem;" to "focus on interests, not positions;" to "invent options for mutual gain;" and to "insist on objective criteria." Their primary contribution is the notion that interests lie behind the positions that people take on issues. Interests are less tangible and measurable than the issues that frame hard bargaining; and Fisher and Ury argue for focusing on interests. With interest-based bargaining, they assert that the principled negotiator can enhance the quality of settlement and create favorable conditions for a durable agreement. Every serious student of negotiation should read their book.

The selections in this chapter explain the anatomy of integrative bargaining and the ways in which effective negotiators can use its techniques to create value and expand options for resolution. In the first reading, we develop the theoretical framework and justification for using an integrative bargaining process. Donald Gifford continues his succinct description of available bargaining strategies. In the previous chapter Gifford outlined the premises supporting a competitive approach to negotiation. Here, he explains the two related theoretical components of a different pattern of negotiation. Parties can adopt a cooperative strategy designed to preserve a good bargaining relationship. This good relationship might be important not for altruistic reasons, but because it will achieve better and more fair agreements. Parties can also adopt an integrative strategy by focusing on their opposite's underlying interests in the negotiation and by expanding the range of available options for agreement.

This basic structure of integrative bargaining is one that Carrie Menkel–Meadow believes is uniquely designed to meet the parties' needs by solving their problem in its broadest sense. Her classic article remains pivotal to our understanding of the integrative model. The *Getting to Yes* branch of integrative bargaining theory stresses interests and the search for normative objective criteria that facilitate the search for points of agreement. Menkel–Meadow augments this focus by asserting that the parties' underlying needs will provide the fuel for creative settlement. Her "problem solving" approach stresses the desirability of dialogue between lawyer and client, and with one's bargaining opposite, to identify, clarify and prioritize the needs of both parties to a dispute.

Leonard Greenhalgh follows, alerting us to the pitfalls of an overly adversarial bargaining strategy, one in which the ubiquitous metaphor of "winning" may lead to Pyrrhic negotiation outcomes. Next, an excerpt from Dean Pruitt presents several techniques for engaging in integrative bargaining. He introduces the concept of "firm flexibility" to ensure against exploitation when seeking alternative ways of resolving disagreement.

As these excerpts demonstrate, one key to using integrative bargaining effectively is to understand the difference between issues and interests in negotiation. Most people—especially in our culture, and particularly those of us who are legally trained—can identify the issues in their negotiations. Issues are tangible, measurable and concrete. They are items like money, units of time, square footage, particular contract terms, specific amendments to the collective bargaining agreement. Issues set the agenda for bargaining. Once parties take inconsistent positions on the issues involved in their negotiation, the competitive strategies of distributive bargaining are inevitably used to resolve the conflict. Interests, however, allow for a different style of bargaining. While positions are the negotiator's suggested means of resolving particular issues, interests are the deeper ends we seek in bargaining, the motivations for our positions on issues. They are frequently abstract and difficult to measure explicitly, but they are very real to the resolution of the negotiation. Interests include such motivations as financial security, self esteem, a good working relationship, adherence to precedent, fairness, reputation, and saving face. The practical difference between these two terms is much more than merely semantic.

The next reading in this chapter helps us understand how to conduct negotiations as an exercise in understanding and satisfying interests. As Lax and Sebenius point out, the crucial task of integrative bargaining is to identify and focus upon the interests of the parties. Our interests are frequently more expansive than we first understand them to be; they are of numerous types; they can be prioritized to facilitate possible tradeoffs; they are not necessarily inconsistent with the interests of our bargaining opposite; and they are often not constant, varying during the process of negotiation.

Our discussion of cooperative strategies of integrative bargaining concludes with two provocative writings. First, Frans de Waal, a Dutch sociobiologist, raises the possibility that an integrative bargaining approach is not merely an optional strategy, but is a frequently observed phenomenon in all primate interaction, and may have deep psychic or even genetic roots. Finally, we should note that integrative bargaining, even if biologically ordained, is not without its problems in application. Nor is the doctrine of principled negotiation without its critics. In the final selection of this chapter, Robert Condlin outlines some of these criticisms. The effective negotiator must consider these implications when selecting the integrative strategic option.

Readings

1. Donald Gifford, *A Context–Based Theory of Strategy Selection in Legal Negotiation,* 46 Ohio St.L.J. 41, 52–57 (1985).
2. Carrie Menkel–Meadow, *Toward Another View of Legal Negotiation: The Structure of Problem Solving,* 31 UCLA L.Rev. 754, 794–817 (1984).
3. Leonard Greenhalgh, *The Case Against Winning in Negotiations,* 3 Negot.J. 167, 167–73 (1987).
4. Dean Pruitt, *Achieving Integrative Agreements,* in Max Bazerman & Roy Lewicki, eds., Negotiating in Organizations 36–44 (1983).
5. David Lax & James Sebenius, *Interests: The Measure of Negotiation,* 2 Negot.J. 76, 78–91 (1986).
6. Frans de Waal, Peacemaking Among Primates 231–38, 269–71 (1989).
7. Robert J. Condlin, *Bargaining in the Dark: The Normative Incoherence of Lawyer Dispute Bargaining Role,* 51 Md.L.Rev. 1, 26–49 (1992).
8. For Further Reading
   a. Karl Albrecht & Steve Albrecht, Added Value Negotiating (1993).
   b. Max H. Bazerman & Margaret A. Neale, *The Role of Fairness Considerations and Relationships in a Judgmental Perspective of Negotiation, in Barriers to Conflict Resolution* 87 (Kenneth Arrow, *et al,* eds. (1995)).
   c. Robert J. Condlin, *"Cases On Both Sides:" Patterns of Argument in Legal Dispute–Negotiation,* 44 Md.L.Rev. 65 (1985).
   d. Kim P. Corfman & Donald R. Lehman, *The Importance of Others' Welfare in Evaluating Bargaining Outcomes,* 20 J.Consumer Res. 124 (1993).

e. Daniel Druckman, *Determinants of Compromising Behavior In Negotiation: A Meta–Analysis,* 38 J.Conflict Res. 507 (1994).

f. Roger Fisher, William Ury, & Bruce Patton, Getting to Yes: Negotiating Agreement Without Giving In (2nd ed. 1991).

g. Roger Fisher & Scott Brown, Getting Together: Building A Relationship That Gets to Yes (1988).

h. Roger Fisher, *Comment,* 34 J.Leg.Educ. 120 (1984).

i. Roger Fisher, *Beyond Yes,* 1 Negot.J. 67 (1985).

j. Raymond A. Friedman, *Missing Ingredients In Mutual Gains Bargaining Theory,* 10 Negot.J. 265 (1994).

k. Raymond A. Friedman & Debra L. Shapiro, *Deception and Mutual Gains Bargaining: Are They Mutually Exclusive?,* 11 Negot.J. 243 (1995).

l. Donald Gifford, *The Synthesis of Legal Counselling and Nego- tiation Models: Preserving Client–Centered Advocacy in the Negotiating Context,* 34 UCLA L.Rev. 811 (1987).

m. Steven Goldberg, Eric Green & Frank Sander, *Saying You're Sorry,* 3 Negot.J. 221 (1987).

n. Gary Goodpaster, *Rational Decision–Making in Problem– Solving Negotiation: Compromise, Interest–Valuation, and Cognitive Error,* 8 Ohio St.J. on Disp.Res. 299 (1993).

o. Lynn Henderson, *Legality and Empathy,* 85 Mich.L.Rev. 1574 (1987).

p. Patrick Kaufmann, *Commercial Exchange Relationships and the "Negotiator's Dilemma",* 3 Negot.J. 73 (1987).

q. William McCarthy, *The Role of Power and Principle in Get- ting to Yes,* 1 Negot.J. 59 (1985).

r. Elizabeth A. Mannix, Catherine H. Tinsley & Max Bazerman, *Negotiating Over Time: Impediments to Integrative Solutions,* 62 Org.Beh. & Human Dec.Proc. 241 (1995).

s. Carrie Menkel–Meadow, Review Essay, *Legal Negotiation: A Study of Strategies in Search of a Theory,* 1983 A.B.F.Res.J. 905–37.

t. Carrie Menkel–Meadow, *Is Altruism Possible in Lawyering,* 8 Ga.St.U.L.Rev. 385 (1992).

u. Robert Mnookin, *Why Negotiations Fail: An Exploration of Barriers to the Resolution of Conflict,* 8 Ohio St.J. on Disp. Res. 235 (1993).

v. John Murray, *Understanding Competing Theories of Negotia- tion,* 2 Negot.J. 179 (1986).

w. Howard Raiffa, *Post–Settlement Settlements,* 1 Negot.J. 9 (1985).

x. Howard Raiffa, *Mock Pseudo–Negotiations With Surrogate Disputants,* 1 Negot.J. 111 (1985).

y. John Roemer, *The Mismarriage of Bargaining Theory and Distributive Justice,* 97 Ethics 88 (1986).

z. Joshua Stulberg, *Negotiation Concepts and Advocacy Skills: The ADR Challenge,* 48 Albany L.Rev. 719 (1984).

aa. Lawrence Susskind, *Negotiating Better Development Agree- ments,* 3 Negot.J. 11 (1987).

bb. Leigh Thompson, Erika Peterson & Susan E. Brodt, *Team Negotiation: An Examination of Integrative and Distributive Bargaining,* 70 J. Personality and Social Psych. 66 (1996).

cc. William Ury, Getting Past No: Dealing With Difficult People (1991).

dd. James J. White, *The Pros and Cons of "Getting to Yes"*, 34 J.Leg.Educ. 115 (1984).

DONALD GIFFORD, A CONTEXT–BASED THEORY OF STRATEGY SELECTION IN LEGAL NEGOTIATION

46 Ohio St.L.Rev. 41, 52–57 (1985).

THE COOPERATIVE STRATEGY

A view of human nature different than that upon which the competitive strategy is premised, with its emphasis on undermining the confidence of opposing counsel, underlies most collaborative interaction. In everyday events, even when they are deciding how to divide a limited resource between them, two negotiators often seek to reach an agreement which is fair and equitable to both parties and seek to build an interpersonal relationship based on trust. This approach to negotiation can be designated the cooperative strategy. The cooperative negotiator initiates granting concessions in order to create both a moral obligation to reciprocate and a relationship built on trust that is conducive to achieving a fair agreement.

The cooperative negotiator does not view making concessions as a necessity resulting from a weak bargaining position or a loss of confidence in the value of her case. Rather, she values concessions as an affirmative negotiating technique designed to capitalize on the opponent's desire to reach a fair and just agreement and to maintain an accommodative working relationship. Proponents of the cooperative strategy believe that negotiators are motivated not only by individualistic or competitive desires to maximize their own utilities, but also by collectivistic desires to reach a fair solution. Cooperative negotiators assert that the competitive strategy often leads to resentment between the parties and a breakdown of negotiations.

According to Professor Otomar Bartos, an originator of the cooperative strategy, the negotiator should begin negotiations not with a maximalist position, but rather with a more moderate opening bid that is both favorable to him and barely acceptable to the opponent. Once two such opening bids are on the table, the negotiators should determine the midpoint between the two opening bids and regard it as a fair and equitable outcome. External facts, such as how large a responsive concession the negotiator expects from the opponent, whether she is representing a tough constituency that would view large concessions unfavorably, and whether she is under a tight time deadline and wants to expedite the process by making a large concession, affect the size of the negotiator's first concession. According to Professor Bartos, the negotiator should then expect the opponent to reciprocate with a concession of similar size so that the midpoint between the parties' positions remains the same as it was after the realistic opening bids were made. The concessions by the parties are fair, according to Bartos, as long as the parties do not need to revise their initial expectations about the substance of the agreement.

The term cooperative strategy embraces a larger variety of negotiation tactics than Bartos' detailed model. Cooperative strategies include any strategies that aim to develop trust between the parties and that focus on the expectation that the opponent will match concessions ungrudgingly. Endemic to all cooperative strategies is the question of how the negotiator should respond if the opponent does not match her concessions and does not reciprocate her goodwill. The major weakness of the cooperative approach is its vulnerability to exploitation by the competitive negotiator. The cooperative negotiator is severely disadvantaged if her opponent fails to reciprocate her concessions. Cooperative negotiation theorists suggest a variety of responses when concessions are not matched. Professor Bartos recommends that the negotiator "stop making further concessions until the opponent catches up."

Because of its vulnerability to exploitation, the cooperative theory may not initially appear to be a viable alternative to the competitive strategy. As mentioned previously, in tightly controlled experiments with simulated negotiations, the competitive strategy generally produces better results. However, in actual practice, the competitive approach results in more impasses and greater distrust between the parties. Furthermore, most people tend to be cooperative in orientation and trusting of others. Professor Williams found that sixty-five percent of the attorneys he surveyed used a cooperative approach. This, of course, means that in a majority of cases the cooperative negotiator will not be exploited by her opponent, because the opponent also uses a cooperative approach. Most cooperative negotiators probably would not feel comfortable using the competitive negotiators' aggressive tactics, which are designed to undermine the opponent and his case. Nor would they relish living and working in the mistrustful milieu which may result from the use of the competitive strategy.

The Integrative Strategy

Both the competitive and cooperative strategies focus on the opposing positions of the negotiators—each negotiator attempts to achieve as many concessions from the other as possible. These concessions move the negotiations closer to an outcome favorable to the negotiator; however, each concession diminishes the opponent's satisfaction with the potential agreement. Integrative bargaining, on the other hand, attempts to reconcile the parties' interests and thus provides high benefits to both. Integrative bargaining is usually associated with a situation in which the parties' interests are not directly opposed and the benefit of one widget for one party does not necessarily result in the loss of one widget for the opponent. Instead, the parties use a problem-solving approach to invent a solution which satisfies the interests of both parties.

Integrative bargaining recently has received widespread attention as the result of the publication of Professors Roger Fisher and William Ury's popular text, *Getting to Yes: Negotiating Agreement Without Giving In*. Professors Fisher and Ury's negotiation strategy is largely based on integrative bargaining theory, although it goes beyond integrative theory in important ways. The authors call their strategy principled negotiation and identify four basic points to this approach:

People: Separate the people from the problem.

Interests: Focus on interests, not positions.

Options: Generate a variety of possibilities before deciding what to do.

Criteria: Insist that the result be based on some objective standard.

The first point distinguishes integrative bargaining from both cooperative bargaining and competitive bargaining, according to Professors Fisher and Ury. The competitive bargainer believes that his relationship with the opponent is important, because he seeks to change the opponent's position through sheer willpower. The cooperative negotiator builds trust in order to reach a fair agreement. In contrast, Professors Fisher and Ury's principled negotiator attempts to separate the interpersonal relationship between the negotiators from the merits of the problem or conflict.

Professors Fisher and Ury's second and third points are the standard components of integrative bargaining theory. The negotiation dance of concession matching or positioning, which is a part of both competitive and cooperative behavior, often obscures the parties' real interests. A major component of integrative bargaining is the free exchange of information between the negotiators so that each party's motives, goals, and values are understood and appreciated.

Integrative bargaining attempts to locate a solution that satisfies both parties' respective interests. Professor Dean Pruitt, a social psychologist, identifies several types of integrative agreements. The most dramatic integrative solution emerges when the parties "brainstorm" and develop a new option that satisfies the significant needs of both parties. The second type of integrative bargaining is often referred to as "logrolling." In logrolling, each negotiator agrees to make concessions on some issues while his counterpart concedes on other issues; the agreement reconciles the parties' interests to the extent that the parties have different priorities on the issues. For example, a plea bargaining agreement might provide that the defendant will plead guilty to a felony, and the prosecutor will recommend that the defendant receive probation. Defendants are often most concerned with the possibility of imprisonment; the prosecutor, in a particular case, may care more about securing a felony conviction than she does about the defendant's sentence.

Another form of integrative bargaining is described by Professor Pruitt as "cost cutting." A negotiator, in order to reach an agreement, may find ways to diminish the tangible or intangible costs to the opponent when the opponent accepts an agreement that satisfies the negotiator. For example, a management attorney who agrees to the wage demands of a certain type of worker might be concerned that in the future the union will expect similarly generous agreements for other workers. The union negotiator may reassure management that she understands that this wage agreement for certain employees stems from special circumstances, such as historical inequities, and that similar wage concessions should not be expected for other employees.

Several procedures facilitate reaching an integrative agreement. The free exchange of information and brainstorming efforts to invent options for mutual gains were discussed previously. In addition, the possibility of logrolling suggests that disputed issues should be considered simultaneously rather than sequentially. The negotiator should also develop a set of goals and other requirements in order to generate and screen alternative proposals. To the extent that the parties exchange negotiating proposals, the integrative negotiator should try to incorporate into his proposal some element of an opponent's previously suggested solution. Finally, the negotiator should continually alter his own proposal incrementally so he only gradually reduces the level of benefit to be realized by his client. This behavior is referred to by Professor Pruitt as "heuristic trial and error."

Traditional integrative bargaining strategy does not have universal applicability. The strategy is utilized most easily when the parties share a problem-solving orientation, and either an identifiable mutual gain option is available or multiple issues which can be traded off against one another exist. It is less useful when the parties disagree on only a single issue and the parties' interests are inherently opposed. Examples of situations that present direct conflicts include personal injury litigation and plea bargaining.

Professors Fisher and Ury urge the "principled negotiator" to insist upon a result based on objective criteria when the parties' interests seem to directly conflict and no mutually advantageous solution appears to be available. In this situation, they recommend the following steps:

1.   Frame each issue as a joint search for objective criteria.

2.   Reason and be open to reason as to which standards are most appropriate and how they should be applied.

3.   Never yield to pressure, only to principle.

By stressing the desirability of reaching a fair decision, Professors Fisher and Ury appear to be borrowing from the principles of the cooperative strategists, especially from Professor Otomar Bartos. With this addition to traditional integrative bargaining, Professors Fisher and Ury claim to have found an "all-purpose strategy" that can be used in any negotiation regardless of the number of issues, the nature of the issues, or the orientation of the opposing party.

The Strategic Choice Model

The three negotiation strategies outlined above are not mutually exclusive; frequently a negotiator will use more than one strategy in a single negotiation. Some issues in a negotiation may lend themselves to an integrative approach, while others must be resolved through competitive or cooperative bargaining. Furthermore, most negotiations that begin with competitive approaches will culminate prior to agreement with either cooperative or integrative bargaining. Social psychologist Professor Dean Pruitt, in his strategic choice model of negotiation, recognizes that various negotiation strategies will be used in the same negotiation. The strategic choice model suggests that the negotiator must choose between engaging in competitive behavior, making a unilateral concession, and suggesting an integrative proposal at every point in the negotiation process. These alternative tactics correspond closely with the competitive, cooperative, and integrative strategies previously outlined.

CARRIE MENKEL–MEADOW, TOWARD ANOTHER VIEW OF LEGAL NEGOTIATION: THE STRUCTURE OF PROBLEM SOLVING

31 UCLA L.Rev. 754, 794–813 (1984).

TOWARD A MODEL OF PROBLEM SOLVING NEGOTIATION: A THEORY OF NEEDS

Problem solving is an orientation to negotiation which focuses on finding solutions to the parties' sets of underlying needs and objectives. The problem-solving conception subordinates strategies and tactics to the process of identifying possible solutions and therefore allows a broader range of outcomes to negotiation problems.

. . .

The Underlying Principles of Problem Solving:
Meeting Varied and Complementary Needs

Parties to a negotiation typically have underlying needs or objectives—what they hope to achieve, accomplish, and/or be compensated for as a result of the dispute or transaction. Although litigants typically ask for relief in the form of damages, this relief is actually a proxy for more basic needs or objectives. By attempting to uncover those underlying needs, the problem-solving model presents opportunities for discovering greater numbers of and better quality solutions. It offers the possibility of meeting a greater variety of needs both directly and by trading off different needs, rather than forcing a zero-sum battle over a single item.

The principle underlying such an approach is that unearthing a greater number of the actual needs of the parties will create more possible solutions because not all needs will be mutually exclusive. As a corollary, because not all individuals value the same things in the same way, the exploitation of differential or complementary needs will produce a wider variety of solutions which more closely meet the parties' needs.

A few examples may illustrate these points. In personal injury actions courts usually award monetary damages. Plaintiffs, however, commonly want this money for specific purposes. For instance, an individual who has been injured in a car accident may desire compensation for any or all of the following items: past and future medical expenses, rehabilitation and compensation for the cost of rehabilitation, replacement of damaged property such as a car and the costs of such replacement, lost income, compensation for lost time, pain and suffering, the loss of companionship with one's family, friends and fellow employees and employer, lost opportunities to engage in activities which may no longer be possible, such as backpacking or playing basketball with one's children, vindication or acknowledgement of fault by the responsible party, and retribution or punishment of the person who was at fault. In short, the injured person seeks to be returned to the same physical, psychological, social and economic state she was in before the accident occurred. Because this may be impossible, the plaintiff needs money in order to buy back as many of these things as possible.

In the commercial context, a breach of contract for failure to supply goods might involve compensation for the following: the cost of obtaining substitute goods, psychological damage resulting from loss of a steady source of supply, lost sales, loss of goodwill, any disruption in business which may have occurred, having to lay off employees as a result of decreased business, restoration of good business relationships, and retribution or punishment of the defaulting party.

. . .

Some of the parties' needs may not be compensable, directly or indirectly. For example, some injuries may be impossible to fully rehabilitate. A physical disability, a scar, or damage to a personal or business reputation may never be fully eradicated. Thus, the underlying needs produced by these injuries may not be susceptible to full and/or monetary satisfaction. The need to be regarded as totally normal or completely honorable can probably never be met, but the party in a negotiation will be motivated by the desire to satisfy as fully as possible these underlying human needs. Some parties may have a need to get "as much X as possible," such as in demands for money for pain and suffering. This demand simply may represent the best proxy available for satisfying the unsatisfiable desire to be made truly whole—that is to be put back in the position of no accident at all. It also may represent a desire to save for a rainy day or to maximize power, fame or love.

. . .

It is also important to recognize that *both* parties have such needs. For example, in the personal injury case above, the defendant may have the same need for vindication or retribution if he believes he was not responsible for the accident. In addition, the defendant may need to be compensated for his damaged car and injured body. He will also have needs with respect to how much, when and how he may be able to pay the monetary damages because of other uses for the money. A contract breaching defendant may have specific financial needs such as payroll, advertising, purchases of supplies, etc.; defendants are not always simply trying to avoid paying a certain sum of money to plaintiffs. In the commercial case, the defendant may have needs similar to those of the plaintiff: lost income due to the plaintiff's failure to pay on the contract, and, to the extent the plaintiff may seek to terminate the relationship with the defendant, a steady source of future business.

. . .

Understanding that the other party's needs are not necessarily as assumed may present an opportunity for arriving at creative solutions. Traditionally, lawyers approaching negotiations from the adversarial model view the other side as an enemy to be defeated. By examining the underlying needs of the other side, the lawyer may instead see opportunities for solutions that would not have existed before based upon the recognition of different, but not conflicting, preferences.

The Structure of Problem Solving

1. Identifying the Parties' Underlying Needs and Objectives

Unlike the adversarial model which makes assumptions about the parties' desires to maximize individual gain, problem solving begins by attempting to determine the actual needs of particular clients. The problem-solving model seeks to avoid a lawyer who acts for a hypothetical, rather than a real, client by creating a "standardized person to whom he attributes standardized ends."

Ascertaining the client's needs will, of course, begin with the initial interview. This is not the place to review the extensive interview literature, but in thinking ahead to the negotiation which might occur, a lawyer might begin by asking the client such general questions as "how would you like to see this all turn out?" or "what would you like to accomplish here?" before channelling the client's objectives in directions the lawyer knows are legally possible. The client may be the best source of ideas that go beyond what the court or the legal system might commonly permit. Once the client's ideas are brought to the surface, the lawyer can explore the needs they are meant to satisfy, and the legal and non-legal consequences of these and other solutions.

Since so many legal problems are reduced to monetary solutions, consideration of the economic needs and objectives of the client faced with a dispute or transaction is a good place to begin.

. . .

Next the lawyer might consider that with which she is most familiar—the legal issues.

. . .

The negotiator might consider how any solution affects the client's relationship to others.

. . .

The negotiator might also ask the client to consider the personal feelings generated by the dispute or transaction.

. . .

For each of these basic categories of needs the negotiator should also consider how the needs may change over the long run. There may be additional needs which the client has not articulated and which have as yet unrealized consequences. Frequently, some of the latent needs or concerns can be ascertained by simply following up a client's statement of need with an inquiry as to why that item or thing is desired. For each stated need, the lawyer should engage in a systematic inquiry into long and short run consequences and the latent concerns behind those which are manifest.

Ideally, this framework for determining the parties' needs must be considered from both parties' perspectives. At the very least, it should encourage lawyers and clients to consider whether all the potential needs presented by a negotiation have been canvassed.

2. *Creating solutions*

a. *Meeting the Parties' Needs* Having identified the parties' needs one can begin the search for solutions with those that are suggested by the parties or that otherwise directly meet the parties' needs.

. . .

Regardless of how limited the possible solutions may appear to be, they are, in this context, far more likely to satisfy the parties and effectuate a more permanent agreement than would most results achieved in court or in adversarial negotiations.

The needs of the parties, therefore, may serve as a springboard for potential solutions to the problem. By focusing on economic needs the parties may discover ways to cut costs, dovetail short- and long-term interests, or minimize tax consequences. By discovering that they have different values about social needs, for example, time spent with children, they may be able to agree to child custody arrangements. By determining that a client's need to give a gift is more important than the economic consequences something may be given without demanding a trade. And, by ascertaining that the parties value some items differentially, it may be possible to trade or "logroll" one item for another.

. . .

b. Expanding the Resources Available Of course, the parties' needs will not be sufficiently complementary in all cases to permit direct solutions. Needs may conflict or there may be conflict over the materiel required to satisfy the needs. In addition to focusing on the parties' needs as a source of solutions, negotiators can attempt to expand the resources that the parties may eventually have to divide. In essence, this aspect of problem-solving negotiation seeks wherever possible to convert zero-sum games into non-zero-sum or positive-sum games. By expanding resources or the materiel available for division, more of the parties' total set of needs may be satisfied. Indeed, as the literature on legal transactions and the economic efficiency of such transactions makes clear, the parties come together to transact business precisely because their joint action is likely to increase the wealth available to both. To the extent that principles of wealth creation and resource expansion from transactional negotiation can be assimilated to dispute negotiation, the parties to a negotiation have the opportunity to help each other by looking for ways to expand what is available to them.

. . .

The key to finding solutions that are not simply compromises of the original demand is to develop ways of expanding the resources available before division, if division is indeed necessary. The linear conception of negotiation does not serve well in this endeavor. The dilemma of non-zero-sum games is that there is no single, totally optimal solution, although game theorists and economists have tried to locate them in theory and in simulation. In summary, by using substantive strategies such as exploring shared interests, by exploiting value differences in needs, by looking to third parties, by sharing, by aggregating or disaggregating, by neutralizing, by seeking substitute goods, by exploring long- and short-term values, and by using other specific devices a greater number of solutions may be found. In addition, the particular solutions may be better, and the parties may be more likely to have all or a greater number of their total needs satisfied.

c. Just or Fair Solutions For those who seek the most effective or efficient solutions from a utilitarian perspective, it is enough to settle at a point where no party can gain without hurting the other party. This is the best solution that can be reached when all preferences and needs are taken into account. But legal negotiations leave us with two special non-Pareto optimal problems. First, should the zealous advocate pursue a gain for his client that would cause a loss to the other side? Second, when might the negotiator choose to pursue less gain for his client or actually cause his client to suffer some loss so as to benefit or not hurt the other side? In some sense these questions are on opposite sides of the same coin. Without solving either definitively, the problem-solving model of negotiation may provide some avenues of inquiry.

. . .

Regarding the second case, and as part of the first, the following formulation is offered to those who wish to take the evaluation of a problem-solving solution beyond a utilitarian analysis. In considering the acceptability of a particular solution, both lawyer and client might engage in a dialogue about the fairness or justness of their proposals. Putting aside for the moment philosophical debates about the appropriate measures of justness or fairness, lawyer and client might simply ask each other what, if any, detrimental effect their solution has on themselves, the other party, third parties, or the larger society. No current rule requires the lawyer or her client to act on such a dialogue. However, in considering whether the negotiation problem has been solved in a way which meets the underlying objectives of the parties, asking such questions might prevent clients and lawyers from seeking objectives that they ought not or do not want.

LEONARD GREENHALGH, THE CASE AGAINST WINNING IN NEGOTIATIONS

3 Negot.J. 167, 167–73 (1987).

If you pay close attention to the vocabulary people use when discussing negotiations, you'll note that "winning" occurs with striking frequency. People involved in management training offer to teach "winning negotiation tactics." Researchers who identified a paradox experienced by negotiators gave it the intriguing label, "the winner's curse." Other scholars have created their own unwitting paradox by characterizing mutual gain outcomes as "win-win" solutions.

Making a case against "winning" seems heretical, like attacking patriotic ideals or revered institutions. Nevertheless, my aim in this article is to point out that the metaphor of winning is not only inappropriate in most situations, but is actually dangerous when used to characterize negotiations. In a nutshell, winning implies losing, and this dichotomy is inherently zero-sum in nature. The metaphor of winning is appropriate for describing power struggles, but inappropriate for describing other means of resolving apparent conflicts, particularly cooperative solutions such as problem-solving or other forms of integrative bargaining.

Therefore I'd like to argue that scholars and practitioners should scrupulously question—and in most cases, avoid—the notion of winning when thinking about conflicts. Much more than a semantic debate is involved here. The notion of winning is a metaphor that has the power and potential to create tunnel vision, and lead people to visualize conflicts in counterproductive ways. . . .

PREVALENCE OF WIN-LOSE METAPHORS

Because of the prevalence of sports metaphors in the United States and in other Western cultures, winning comes up often as a theme in describing negotiations. Sports metaphors are somewhat interchangeable with military metaphors, as is evident from the prevalence of hybrid metaphors. We speak of war games, the arms race, tennis volleys, shots on goal, knocking out a machine gun emplacement, and designation of players as lines, forwards, captains, guards, and so on. Thus it is not always possible to tell precisely when someone using win-lose metaphors is visualizing sports or war, and harder still to tell what imagery those metaphors evoke in the listener or reader. Either way, the win-lose metaphor is limiting when used uncritically to characterize negotiations....

WINNING AS A MASCULINE METAPHOR

Sports metaphors seem far more prevalent among males than among females. This can be traced to the fact that competitive games play a more prominent role in the early development and socialization of boys than they do in girls. More specifically, boys typically are taught to play games in which the objective is to defeat their playmates (now defined as opponents) and then gloat about the victory—or worse, ridicule the playmates who have lost the game. By contrast, girls tend to choose relationship-oriented games ("Barbie and Ken" doll games or "house"). When they do participate in competitive games, girls are taught to end the game or change the rules if it becomes apparent that the game has stopped being fun for their playmates who are not doing so well. In other words, girls are taught to play games that preserve and enhance the relationship, while boys are taught to preserve and enhance their feelings of self-worth at the *expense* of the relationship.

The vestiges of these childhood experiences are quite prominent in the thought patterns of adult negotiators. Men have a general tendency to think in terms of competing and therefore rely heavily on win-lose metaphors; women, on the other hand, have a general tendency to think in terms of preserving and enhancing relationships, and win-lose metaphors are less salient to them. These differences in general tendencies often parallel the differences in the way the two sexes approach negotiations. In particular, men tend to use negotiation tactics that are shaped by win-lose metaphors— tactics that tend to poison relationships, preclude cooperative solutions to conflicts, and deny them the benefits of long-term reciprocal exchanges.

PITFALLS OF WIN-LOSE METAPHORS

The most obvious disadvantage of win-lose metaphors is their inherent zero-sum quality. Sports contests, like battles, are meant to be won. The common norm is for players to strive to the best of their ability, strength, and stamina to defeat the other player (or team). In fact, to do less is "unsports-manlike"; nobody wants to beat or even be narrowly defeated by a player who wasn't trying very hard. Instead, the losing player is supposed to *escalate* the attack to make the other player's victory as difficult as possible. The emphasis on winning is so heavy that even a tie score is undesirable. In fact, many sports have rules that preclude ties or have mechanisms to eliminate them such as "sudden death overtime." As a result of these connotations, when the sports metaphor is applied to negotiation situations, there is little room for compromise, or even mercy.

Furthermore, the notion of a "win-win solution" in this context makes no sense. The metaphor cannot be stretched to accommodate a win-win outcome without violating the essence of sports contests or military engagements. It seems more advisable to abandon the inescapably zero-sum winning metaphor, therefore, when discussing nonzero-sum outcomes. It is better to talk about mutual advantage, because the focus is on the benefits of cooperation rather than on winning; the latter focus tends to portray the other negotiator as an opponent and implies that the benefit has to come at someone else's expense. Simply, the "win-win" notion, besides being illogical, conjures up all the wrong images . . . .

Winning-oriented sports metaphors have several disadvantages beyond fostering a zero-sum perspective. One of these is the emphasis on rules rather than relationships. In sports contests, it is generally acceptable for players to stretch rules to the limit; the norms tolerate almost any tactic that can be used in pursuit of victory, so long as it doesn't violate explicit rules. Innovations within the rules that give the contestant an advantage make heroes of the rule-benders. . . .

It appears, first of all, that a focus on rules easily can lead to attempts to exploit rather than negotiate fairly. The tactics of the sports-oriented negotiator are constrained by explicit rules rather than being motivated by the good of all the parties involved. In other words, rather than devise creative solutions to mutual problems, negotiators often spend valuable time and energy trying to figure out how much they can get away with. Even worse, ethical considerations tend to become subordinated to the rules applied to the situation; this has a profound impact on trust. . . .

The emphasis on rules that arises from the sports metaphor may have an additional, perhaps even more subtle, negative effect: It may increase a disputant's tendency to litigate rather than mediate a dispute. This tendency occurs because, outside of sports situations, referees (or umpires) are poor models of conflict "resolvers." . . .

Another disadvantage of having one's thinking shaped by sports metaphors is that they induce disputants to focus on the immediate conflict episode rather than take a longer-term perspective. Sports contests are discrete, independent events. Irrespective of who won or lost the last game, the scores are set at zero at the beginning of the next game. Furthermore, sports norms would not permit players to let one team win this week in exchange for reciprocal leniency by the other team the next week. Thus, the history and future of the ongoing relationship between contestants is irrelevant in sports.

When this same short-term perspective is applied to negotiation situations, the conflict becomes much more difficult to deal with than it would be otherwise. Negotiators with a short-term perspective can choose harsh or exploitive tactics without fear of repercussions, because they view any future interaction as "a new game." Likewise, there is nothing to gain in the future from being accommodating in the current interaction, since anything "given up" is perceived as forever lost. From this standpoint, intransigence—and even aggression—is rational. . . .

A final disadvantage of the win-lose metaphor is that it induces negotiators to try to fractionate the other party. The rationale is that if the opposing group can be thrown into disarray, that group is easier to defeat. This strategy is the basis for propaganda campaigns against enemies. For example, after last fall's quasi-summit meeting in Iceland, Soviet General Secretary Mikhail Gorbachev began an energetic media campaign to encourage divisiveness within the U.S. and NATO over the Strategic Defense Initiative.

Fractionating the other party has the advantage of weakening coalitions; however, this practice also may subsequently make the conflict more difficult to resolve, simply because there is no clear leader or unified group that can agree to a comprehensive settlement. The Palestine Liberation Organization, the Organization of Petroleum Exporting Companies, and the Afghan resistance movement are familiar examples of parties to a conflict whose fractionation makes them difficult to negotiate with successfully. What happens is that some subgroups agree to a settlement, while others resist, engaging in passive resistance, subtle sabotage, wildcat strikes, outright defiance, or turning on the subgroups who have agreed.

A Better Metaphor?

What makes the win-lose metaphor particularly insidious in negotiations is its invisibility: It is so innocuous to most people that it goes unnoticed and, therefore, its usefulness and disadvantages are not evaluated. The metaphor is innocuous because it seems superficially compatible with the ways companies compete in the marketplace, but this apparent compatibility is actually spurious. Relationships between people are qualitatively different from relationships between organizations; therefore, people need to assess the metaphor's advantages and limitations for each application. . . .

Metaphors are highly individualized because they must suit an individual's tastes and experiences; some themes, however, are likely to be more helpful than others. For example, synergy—or even symbiosis—is a better theme than competition for visualizing interdependent relationships. Singing a duet is a synergic metaphor: Simon and Garfunkel achieved musical heights neither could achieve alone. Lovemaking is another: Romeo and Juliet gained such benefits from their relationship that neither wanted to live without it. Parenting is a third possible metaphor: Parents may experience considerable difference of opinion concerning how to raise the child, but both must settle on a joint course of action and then continually renegotiate agreements as new situations arise.

Perhaps no one metaphor is ideal for all situations; instead, people probably need to have a repertoire available. Whatever the choice, a scenario for negotiators to avoid is to have only win-lose metaphors available.

DEAN G. PRUITT, ACHIEVING INTEGRATIVE AGREEMENTS

In Max Bazerman & Roy Lewicki, eds., Negotiating in Organizations 36–44 (1983).

There are four main reasons for bargainers (or the mediators assisting them) to seek integrative agreements rather than compromises:

(1) If aspirations are high and both sides are resistant to conceding, it may not be possible to resolve the conflict unless a way can be found to reconcile the two parties' interests.

(2) Integrative agreements are likely to be more stable. Compromises are often unsatisfactory to one or both parties, causing the issue to come up again at a later time.

(3) Because they are mutually rewarding, integrative agreements tend to strengthen the relationship between the parties. This has a number of benefits, including facilitating problem solving in later conflicts.

(4) Integrative agreements ordinarily contribute to the welfare of the broader community of which the two parties are members. For example, a firm will usually benefit as a whole if its departments are able to reconcile their differences creatively.

METHODS FOR ACHIEVING INTEGRATIVE AGREEMENTS

Five methods for achieving integrative agreements will now be described. These are means by which the parties' initially opposing demands can be transformed into alternatives that reconcile their interests. They can be used by one party, both parties working together, or a third party such as a mediator. Each method involves a different way of refocusing the issues under dispute. . . .

The methods will be illustrated by a running example concerning a husband and wife who are trying to decide where to go on a two-week vacation. The husband wants to go to the mountains, his wife to the seashore. They have considered the compromise of spending one week in each location but are hoping for something better. What approach should they take?

Expanding the Pie

Some conflicts hinge on a resource shortage. For example, time, money, space, and automobiles are in short supply but long demand. In such circumstances, integrative agreements can be devised by increasing the available resources. This is called expanding the pie. For example, our married couple might solve their problems by persuading their employers to give them four weeks of vacation so that they can take two in the mountains and two at the seashore. Another example is that of two milk companies vying to be first to unload cans on a platform. The controversy was resolved when somebody thought of widening the platform.

. . .

Expanding the pie requires no analysis of the interests underlying the parties' demands. Hence its information requirements are slim. However, this does not mean that a solution by this method is always easy to find. There may be no resource shortage, or the shortage may not be easy to see or to remedy.

Refocusing questions that can be useful in seeking a solution by pie expansion include: How can both parties get what they want? Does the conflict hinge on a resource shortage? How can the critical resource be expanded?

Nonspecific Compensation

In nonspecific compensation, one party gets what he or she wants and the other is repaid in some unrelated coin. Compensation is nonspecific if it does not deal with the precise costs incurred by the other party. For example, the wife in our example might agree to go to the mountains, even though she finds them boring, if her husband promises her a fur coat. Another example would be giving an employee a bonus for going without dinner.

. . .

Two kinds of information are useful for devising a solution by nonspecific compensation: (a) information about what is valuable to the other party; for example, knowledge that he or she values love, attention, or money; (b) information about how badly the other party is hurting by making concessions. This is useful for devising adequate compensation for these concessions....

Refocusing questions that can help locate a means of compensation include: How much is the other party hurting in conceding to me? What does the other party value that I can supply? How valuable is this to the other party?

Logrolling

Logrolling is possible in complex agendas where several issues are under consideration and the parties have differing priorities among these issues. Each party concedes on low priority issues in exchange for concessions on issues of higher priority to itself. Each gets that part of its demands that it finds most important. For example, suppose that in addition to disagreeing about where to go on vacation, the wife in our example wants to go to a first-class hotel while her husband prefers a tourist home. If accommodations are a high priority issue for the wife and location for the husband, they can reach a fairly integrative solution by agreeing to go to a first-class hotel in the mountains. Logrolling can be viewed as a variant of nonspecific compensation in which both parties instead of one are compensated for making concessions desired by the other.

. . .

Refocusing questions that can be useful for developing solutions by logrolling include: Which issues are of higher and lower priority to myself? Which issues are of higher and lower priority to the other party? Are some of my high-priority issues of low priority to the other party and vice versa?

Cost Cutting

In solutions by cost cutting, one party gets what he or she wants and the other's costs are reduced or eliminated. The result is high joint benefit, not because the first party has changed his or her demands but because the second party suffers less. For instance, suppose that the husband in our example dislikes the beach because of the hustle and bustle. He may be quite willing to go there on vacation if his costs are cut by renting a house with a quiet inner courtyard where he can read while his wife goes out among the crowds.

. . .

Refocusing questions for developing solutions by cost cutting include: What costs are posed for the other party by our proposal? How can these costs be mitigated or eliminated?

Bridging

In bridging, neither party achieves its initial demands but a new option is devised that satisfies the most important interests underlying these demands. For example, suppose that the husband in our vacation example is mainly interested in fishing and hunting and the wife in swimming and sunbathing. Their interests might be bridged by finding an inland resort with a lake and a beach that is close to woods and streams. Follett gives another homely example of two women reading in a library room. One wanted to open the window for ventilation, the other to keep it closed so as not to catch cold. The ultimate solution involved opening a window in the next room, which satisfied both the need for fresh air and the need to avoid a draft.

Bridging typically involves a reformulation of the issue(s) based on an analysis of the underlying interests on both sides. For example, a critical turning point in our vacation example is likely to come when the initial formulation, "Shall we go to the mountains or the seashore?" is replaced by "Where can we find fishing, hunting, swimming, and sunbathing?" This new formulation becomes the basis for a search model which is employed in an effort to locate a novel alternative. The process of reformulation can be done by either or both parties or by a third party who is trying to help.

People who seek to develop solutions by bridging need information about the nature of the two parties' interests and their priorities among these interests. Priority information is useful because it is rare to find a solution, like opening the window in the next room of the library, that bridges all of the two parties' interests. More often, higher-priority interests are served while lower-priority interests are discarded. For example, the wife who agrees to go to an inland lake may have foregone the lesser value of smelling the sea air and the husband may have foregone his preference for spectacular mountain vistas.

. . .

Refocusing questions that can be raised in search of a solution by bridging include: What are the two parties' basic interests? What are their priorities among these interests? How can the two sets of high-priority interests be reconciled?

. . .

The Nature of Problem Solving

Bargainers are sometimes able to "luck into" a highly integrative agreement as, for example, when prior creative activity has produced a good standard solution. But more often they, or some third party working with them, must engage in problem solving, that is, must seek a new option that better satisfies both parties' interests than those currently available. The more vigorous is this problem solving, the more integrative is the final agreement likely to be, up to the limits imposed by the integrative potential.

Problem solving takes a variety of forms. For example, one can raise refocusing questions of the kind described earlier or seek and provide information about priorities and interests. (When both parties provide such information, it is called *information exchange*). An important aspect of problem solving is openness to new alternatives, that is, a willingness to seek them oneself and give them serious consideration when suggested by the opponent or some third party.

In seeking new alternatives, it is necessary to adopt a policy of *firm flexibility*. One must be *firm* with respect to one's *ends* (i.e., one's interests), giving them up only if they are clearly unobtainable. Otherwise the solution will be one-sided in favor of the other party rather than represent a true integration of the two parties' needs. Yet one must also be *flexible* with respect to the *means* to these ends, continually seeking new alternatives until a mutually acceptable one can be found.

An example of firm flexibility can be seen in actions taken by President John F. Kennedy in 1961 during the second Berlin crisis. The Russians, led by Premier Nikita Khrushchev, had been trying to end American occupation of West Berlin by threatening to sign a separate peace treaty with East Germany and buzzing planes in the Berlin Corridor. Recognizing that some concessions had to be made, Kennedy "decided to be firm on essentials but negotiate on nonessentials". In a speech on July 25, he announced three fundamental principles that ensured the integrity and continued American occupation of West Berlin. The firmness of these principles was underscored by a pledge to defend them by force and a concomitant military buildup. Yet Kennedy also indicated flexibility and a concern about Russian priorities by calling for negotiations to remove "actual irritants" to the Soviet Union and its allies. Two results were achieved: the building of the Berlin Wall, which can be viewed as a bridging solution that solved the problem of population loss from East Germany without disturbing American rights in West Berlin, and eventual negotiations that put these rights clearly in writing.

DAVID LAX & JAMES SEBENIUS, INTERESTS: THE MEASURE OF NEGOTIATION

2 Negot. J. 76, 78–91 (1986).

It should be clear that negotiators may have many kinds of interests: money and financial security, a particular conception of the public interest, the quality of products, enhancing a reputation as a skilled bargainer, maintaining a working relationship, precedents, and so on. However, one distinction—between intrinsic and instrumental interests—can provide an economical way to capture some important qualities of interests, call negotiators' attention to often-overlooked, sometimes subtle interests, and lead to improved agreements.

One's interest in an issue is *instrumental* if favorable terms on the issue are valued because of their effect on subsequent dealings. One's interest in an issue is *intrinsic* if one values favorable terms of settlement on the issue independent of any subsequent dealings. Thus, a divorcing parent's interest in gaining custody of his or her child, the farmer's interest in water rights, or a country's interest in secure borders can usefully be thought of as intrinsic interests. Such interests need not have any obvious or agreed-upon economic value. For example, Charles, a 60–year–old venture capitalist, was negotiating the dissolution of a strikingly successful technology partnership with Marie, a young, somewhat standoffish woman whom he had brought on as a partner two years before. At first Charles bargained very hard over the financial terms because he viewed them as indicating who had really contributed important ideas and skills to the venture's success. When Marie belatedly acknowledged her genuine respect for his ideas and contributions, Charles became much less demanding on the financial issues. In this instance, it happened that the venture capitalist also had a strong intrinsic interest in psychic gratification from acknowledgement of his role as mentor and father-figure.

Most issues affect both intrinsic and instrumental interests. Dealings with a subordinate who wants to hire an assistant can arouse an intrinsic interest in the overall size of the budget as well as a concern with the perceived precedent the hiring will set in the eyes of the subordinate's peers— an instrumental interest. Recognizing the distinction may lead to improved agreements; the subordinate who can create a justifiable device to prevent decisions about his or her staff support from setting precedents may well receive authorization to hire a new assistant.

One of the main reasons we focus on the intrinsic-instrumental distinction is for the light it sheds on three often-misunderstood aspects of negotiation: interests in the process, in relationships, and in principles.

"Process" Interests—Intrinsic and Instrumental. Analysts often assume that negotiators evaluate agreements by measuring the value obtained from the outcome. Yet, negotiators may care about the *process* of bargaining as well. Even with no prospect of further interaction, some would prefer a negotiated outcome reached by pleasant, cooperative discussion to the same outcome reached by abusive, threat-filled dealings. Others might even derive value from a strident process that gives them the satisfied feeling of having extracted something from their opponents. Either way, negotiators can have intrinsic interests in the character of the negotiation process itself.

Beyond such intrinsic valuation, an unpleasant process can dramatically affect future dealings; the supplier who is berated and threatened may be unresponsive when cooperation at a later point would help. Indeed, negotiators often have strong instrumental interests in building trust and confidence early in the negotiation process in order to facilitate jointly beneficial agreements.

"Relationship" Interests—Intrinsic and Instrumental. Negotiators often stress the value of their relationships; this interest sometimes achieves an almost transcendent status. For example, Fisher and Ury say that "every negotiator has two kinds of interests: in the substance and in the relationship." Many negotiators derive intrinsic value from developing or furthering a pleasant relationship. Moreover, when repeated dealings are likely, most negotiators perceive the instrumental value of developing an effective working relationship. . . .

. . .

Interest in "Principles"—Intrinsic and Instrumental. Negotiators may discover shared norms or principles relevant to their bargaining problem. Such norms may include equal division, more complex distributive judgments, historical or ethical rationales, objective or accepted standards, as well as notions that simply seem fair or are represented as such. Acting in accord with such a norm or principle may be of intrinsic interest to one or more of the parties; for example, a settlement of $532—arrived at in accord with the mutually acknowledged principle that each party should be paid in proportion to time worked—may be valued quite differently than the same dollar figure reached by haggling. Of course an acknowledged norm need not be an absolute value in a negotiation: it may be partly or fully traded off against other interests.

. . .

The principles that guide agreement in the first of many related disputes may set a powerful precedent. Thus, negotiators may work hard to settle the first dispute on the basis of principles that they believe will yield favorable outcomes in subsequent disputes. They may take a loss with respect to intrinsic interests in the first negotiation in order to satisfy their instrumental interests in the principles used to guide the agreement.

In short, with many less tangible interests—such as process, relationships, or fairness—a negotiator should ask why they are valued. Distinguishing between their instrumental and intrinsic components can help. But even with these components sorted out, how can a negotiator go about assessing their "relative importance?" More generally, what logic guides setting priorities among conflicting interests?

THINKING ABOUT TRADEOFFS

Listing one's own interests as well as a best guess at those of other parties is certainly useful. But difficult questions tend to arise in negotiations that force one to make sacrifices on some interests in order to gain on others: How much of a trade is desirable? In buying a seller-financed house, how should Ralph evaluate higher purchase prices compared to lower mortgage interest rates? How much more should a manufacturer be willing to pay for the next quality grade of components? How much should a sales manager trade on price for the prospects of a better relationship? How much should a manager be willing to give up on substance to secure a favorable precedent?

Thinking about tradeoffs is often excruciatingly difficult and badly done. Yet, whether or not negotiators choose to ponder priorities, they effectively make tradeoffs by their choices and agreements in negotiation.

. . .

... [C]onsider Joan, a plaintiff crippled in a car accident who wishes to negotiate an out-of-court settlement with an insurance company that is better than her alternative of a full court trial. Suppose that, only taking trial uncertainties and legal fees into account, Joan would be willing to accept a settlement of $300,000. But this analysis leaves her uncomfortable. The trial would cause her great anxiety, and her analysis so far does not take this anxiety into account. How should she consider the anxiety factor in her preparation for negotiation? Perhaps she should lower her minimum requirements, but by how much? How can she even think about this?

After several anxious, inconclusive struggles with this assessment, a friend asks Joan to imagine the anxiety she would feel during a trial. The friend then asks her to imagine that a pharmacist offered to *sell* her a magic potion that would completely eliminate the feeling of anxiety from court proceedings. What would be the most she would pay for the potion before the trial? Would she pay $10? "That's silly. Of course." Would she pay $100? "Sure." $100,000? "Certainly not, that's one-third of my minimum settlement!" What about $50,000? "Probably not." $1,000? "I think so." $10,000? "Well, that's a tough one. But, if push came to shove, the trial would be an awful experience. So probably yes." $25,000? "Maybe not, but I'm not sure." ... And so on.

We want to stress our opinion that the important point in making such assessments is not quantitative precision. An absolutely precise cutoff would seem artificial. What is important is to get a sense of the order of magnitude of the value Joan places on avoiding anxiety. Here we see that she would pay between $10,000 and $25,000 or a little more to eliminate the anxiety. Thus, she should be willing to reduce her minimum settlement requirements by that amount because a negotiated settlement would avoid the anxiety. She should, of course, strive for more, but she can feel more comfortable knowing that her minimum requirements now roughly reflect her interest in avoiding trial anxiety.

· · ·

In some instances, concerns with precedent, prestige, anxiety, reputation, and similar interests loom large; negotiators focus on them and, because such interests are difficult to weigh, feel paralyzed with respect to their choices as a negotiator. After fretting inconclusively, the negotiators may ask themselves how much they would be willing to pay to have the prestige conferred upon them by other means. They might discover that they value the prestige possibilities little relative to possible substantive gains. Or, by similar analytical introspection, they might discover that they would be willing to pay only a small sum to avoid an undesirable precedent. In such cases, the negotiators would have learned a great deal.... In other instances, interests in precedent or reputation overwhelm the possible improvements in substantive outcome.... In other instances, simple self-assessment may suggest that the monetary and nonmonetary issues are roughly comparable concerns or that the monetary aspects predominate.

· · ·

General Lessons for Assessing Interests

The most important lessons from this kind of assessment are those that help one think more clearly about the qualitative judgments that negotiators implicitly make all the time. Such evaluations are often made with respect to nominal issues rather than directly on underlying interests....

When thinking about how well different packages satisfy her interests, the negotiator may discover reformulations that align more closely with her interests. If some of these "new" issues are easier to grant, they may form the basis for a better agreement.

During the process, the negotiator may learn about and change her perceptions about how well different positions on the issues serve her interests. As she learns, the relative importance of the increments on the issues may shift. If so, she should modify her assessments.

In contrast to the apparent crispness of the issues, interests are often vaguer. There may be no apparent scale with which to measure, for example, precedent or organizational status. Yet, the same logic that is useful for making issue tradeoffs can apply to assuring the relative impact of interests. The generic steps are as follows:

- Identify the interests that may be at stake.

- For each interest, imagine the possible packages that serve it best and worst; for example, imagine the range of precedents that might follow from the negotiation. This roughly defines the *increment*.

- ... the importance of each interest depends on the relative importance of its *increment* compared to those of the other interests; how does the gain from the worst to the best possible precedent compare with the gain from the worst to the best possible monetary outcome?

The currency of negotiation generally involves *positions* on *issues* but the results are measured by how well underlying *interests* are furthered. As such, it is helpful to shuttle constantly between often abstract interests and more specific issues, both to check for consistency and to keep real concerns uppermost in mind.

Assessing the Interests of Others

Finally, it goes almost without saying that negotiators should constantly assess their counterparts' interests and preferences. Obviously, careful listening and clear communication help this process. Uninvolved third parties can render insights not suspected by partisans wrapped up in the negotiation. And some negotiators find that, as part of preparing for the process, actually playing the other party's role can offer deepened perspectives. In various management programs at Harvard, for example, senior industrialists have been assigned the parts of environmentalists and vice versa. To simulate arms talks, high-level U.S. military officers and diplomats have been assigned to play Russian negotiators in intensive simulations. Palestinians and Israelis have had to swap places. After some initial discomfort and reluctance, the most common reaction of participants in these exercises is surprise at how greatly ... role-playing enhances their understanding of each side's interests, of why others may seem intransigent, and of unexpected possibilities for agreement.

Beyond various ways of trying to put oneself in the other's shoes, assessment of another's interests may be improved by investigating:

- Their past behavior in related settings, both in style and substance.

- Their training and professional affiliation: engineers and financial analysts will often have quite different modes of perception and approaches to potential conflict from, say, lawyers and insurance adjusters.

- Their organizational position and affiliation. Those in the production department will often see long, predictable manufacturing runs as the company's dominant interest while marketers will opt for individual tailoring to customer specs and deep inventories for rapid deliveries. This is but one example of the old and wise expression "where you stand depends on where you sit."

- Whom they admire, whose advice carries weight, and to whom they tend to defer on the kind of issues at stake.

In the end, interests are bound up with psychology and culture. Some settings breed rivalry; others esteem the group. Some people are altruists; others sociopaths. To some, ego looms large; to others, substance is all. Airport bookstore wisdom names Jungle Fighters, Appeasers, Win–Winners, and Win–Losers. Professionals diagnose personality Types A and B and victims of cathected libido. Others have developed such classes, sometimes wisely, but for now we stress that *perceived* interests matter, that perceptions are subjective. Thus, to assess interests is to probe psyches.

PRESCRIPTIVE SUMMARY

As a summary for analysts and practitioners, we have converted the main observations of this paper into the following prescriptive checklist:

Assessing Which Interests Are At Stake

- Beyond the obvious tangible interests that may be affected by issues to be discussed, consider subtler interests in reputation, precedent, relationships, strategy, fairness, and the like.

- Distinguish underlying interests from the issues under discussion and the positions taken on them.

- Distinguish between intrinsic and instrumental reasons for valuing interests, especially some of the subtler ones.

- In seeking to understand other's interests, remember that interests depend on perceptions, that perceptions are subjective, and thus that to assess interests is to probe psyches. This process can be aided by clear communication, the advice of third parties, role-playing, and taking into account past behavior, training, professional affiliation, and organizational position, as well as those to whom the other defers.

- Keep in mind that interests and issues can change on purpose or accidentally as the parties learn, events occur, or certain tactics are employed.

Assessing Tradeoffs

- Tradeoffs are as important to interests as proportions are to recipes.

- To assess tradeoffs among intangible interests, it is sometimes helpful to imagine services one could buy otherwise to satisfy the same interests.

- To assess tradeoffs among issues:

____ Specify the worst and best possible outcomes on each issue to define the possible increments.
____ Compare the increments by thinking hard about underlying interests and which increments are most valued.
____ Break the increments into smaller pieces and similarly compare their relative evaluation.
____ Change assessments with learning about how different positions on the issues affect interests.
____ Assess interest tradeoffs using the same logic.

When to Focus on Interests and When on Issues

- Focus the negotiation on interests to enhance creativity and break impasses by reformulating issues to align better with underlying interests.

- Focus the negotiation on positions, issues, or a narrower set of interests when underlying conflicts of ideology make agreement difficult or when a restricted focus is more advantageous for claiming value.

Negotiation is a process of potentially opportunistic interaction in which two or more parties with some conflicting interests seek to do better by jointly decided action than they could otherwise. The alternatives to negotiated agreement or what the parties could do alone define the threshold of value that any agreement must exceed. The potential of negotiation is bounded only by the quality of agreement that can be devised. But, for evaluating alternatives and creating agreements, interests are the measure and raw material of negotiation.

FRANS DE WAAL, PEACEMAKING AMONG PRIMATES
231–38, 269–71 (1989).

Three boys were interrogated at an Amsterdam police station after having drawn suspicion on themselves by spending more money than is normal for ten-year-olds. The youths admitted that they had found a wallet containing five thousand-guilder notes, but they had in their possession only a little over two thousand guilders. Where had the rest of the money gone? The answer made headlines. The boys had thrown two of the five bills into one of the city's age-old canals—their solution to the indivisibility of five by three. This is a dramatic illustration of how much people value good relationships.

I should qualify this. We value good relationships only to a point. The three boys must have been close friends. If one of them had been an outsider—new to the neighborhood, for example—an entirely different division might have been arranged. Who cares about an outsider, unless he is a very tough fellow? The goal of conflict settlement is not peace per se; it is the maintenance of relationships of proven value. This value is a highly variable item, not only across relationships but also across time within a particular relationship. Thus, a married couple who have successfully reconciled thousands of conflicts may nevertheless reach a point where it does not seem worthwhile to go through the same ritual again. They will increasingly place self-interest above marital harmony.

One compelling goal of people is to have relationships that work to their own advantage. If this occurs in perfect harmony, fine. If it requires coercion and threats, followed by soothing remarks, often this is fine too. Even if one party exerts constant pressure, we stay in the relationship as long as we need it. We do everything possible to keep our social network operative, not necessarily with the most agreeable methods. Some of the best relationships are riddled with squabbles, in that the two parties fluctuate between reinforcing their bond and getting the best possible deal from it. It is comparable to the way a drawbridge serves two kinds of traffic. Keeping the bridge down causes a jam-up of boats in the canal; keeping the bridge open brings auto traffic to a halt. Just as a drawbridge can never stay in one position, relationships continually go through ups and downs to ensure that issues do not remain unresolved and that hurt feelings are mended.

While aggression is part of each and every human relationship, social scientists treat it as an inherently evil behavior. "Aggression is arguably the most serious of human problems" is a typical opening sentence of books on the topic (this particular one is by Jeffrey Goldstein). Authors support such a statement by a review of derailed aggression and all the misery it causes. I am certainly not of the opinion that aggression is unqualifiedly good—I have seen my share of blood and injuries—but I would prefer that scientists take a more encompassing look. Beyond the excesses of murder, rape, and child abuse, there is an entire spectrum, including the everyday hostilities with which we are in fact quite comfortable. Rather than start with the assumption that aggression shapes our lives in a negative manner only, we would be wiser to leave all options open, including the possibility of constructive outcomes of conflict. . . .

I recently asked a world-renowned American psychologist, who specializes in human aggression, what he knew about reconciliation. Not only did he have no information on the subject, but he looked at me as if the word were new to him. I do, of course, speak with an accent, but this was not the problem. He reflected on my remarks, yet the concept had evidently never taken center stage in his thinking. His interest turned to irritation when I suggested that conflicts are inevitable among people and that aggression has such a long evolutionary history that it is logical to expect powerful coping mechanisms. He did not see what evolution had to do with it and argued that the most important goal is to understand and remove the causes of aggressive behavior.

To view aggression exclusively as an ugly, maladaptive trait requires that buffering mechanisms be ignored. If a mother monkey slaps her infant, then immediately embraces and consoles it, she has in one breath taught her child whatever she deemed necessary and demonstrated her continuing affection. The effect on the mother-child relationship is not necessarily what we think. For example, rhesus mothers, who are quite severe with their young, develop lifelong bonds with their daughters. Chimpanzee mothers, who hardly ever punish their offspring, rarely develop close-knit matrilines; most daughters migrate to other communities. If aggression were our sole criterion, we might call rhesus mothers "bad" and chimpanzee mothers "good." The judgment would be reversed if bonding were our favorite measure. And what if we preferred the loose bonds of chimpanzees over the close but strictly hierarchical ties of rhesus monkeys? The more we reflect on these issues, the less sense moral categories begin to make. . . .

Our human societies are structured by the interplay between antagonism and attraction. Disappearance of the former is more than an unrealistic wish, it is a misguided one. No one would want to live in the sort of society that would result, as it would lack differentiation among individuals. A school of herrings is a good example of an aggregation predominantly based on attraction: the fish move together without any problems, but they have no social organization to speak of. If certain species, such as humans, reach a high degree of social differentiation, role division, and cooperation, this occurs because the cohesive tendency is counteracted by internal conflict. Individuals delineate their social positions in competition with others. We cannot have it both ways: a world in which each individual attains his or her own identity, and a world without clashing individual interests.

. . .

Monkeys and apes adapt their behavior to circumstances, achieving great sophistication in conflict resolution. They may not hold preliminary negotiations about the shape of the table at which the parties will meet, or set up so-called proximity talks with a go-between for delegations in different rooms, yet chimpanzees know what mediation is. In the Arnhem colony it is not uncommon for a female to break the ice between adult males who, after a fight, stay close to each other but seem unable to reopen communication. Avoiding eye contact, the two males play the familiar game of glancing over when the other looks away. A female may approach one male, briefly groom or touch him, and walk over to the other with the first male following closely. This way he need not face his adversary. When the female sits down next to the second male, both groom her. Only a small shift is necessary for them to groom each other after the female has walked off. That the mediator knows what she is doing is clear from the way she looks over her shoulder and waits for a male who is reluctant to follow. She may even go back and tug at his arm.

Although I have never observed conflict mediation among macaques, this is not necessarily because of a lack of social awareness in these monkeys. Once the second-ranking rhesus male, Hulk, chased one of the younger males, Tom. Immediately afterward, Tom's mother approached Hulk to groom him. While she was doing so, Tom came closer and closer until he sat less than a meter behind the two. As soon as his mother noticed him, she stepped aside and looked away. She left the scene when her son took her place against Hulk's back. We have witnessed a number of similar situations, in which monkeys made room for contact between former opponents. These observations warn that the mediation skills of chimpanzees and humans may not be totally without antecedent. Our monkeylike ancestors may already have possessed an important prerequisite—the ability to recognize and facilitate reconciliation attempts between others.

. . .

CONCLUSION

The message of this book is at odds with that of some biologists, who have one-sidedly emphasized the aggressive nature of our species and the ruthless struggle within the animal kingdom. Ever since Darwin, the biological spotlight has been on the outcome of competition—who wins, who loses. When social animals are involved, this is a dreadful simplification. Antagonists do more than estimate their chances of winning before they engage in a fight: they also take into account how much they need their opponent. The contested resource often is simply not worth putting a valuable relationship at risk. And if aggression does occur, both parties may hurry to repair the damage. Victory is rarely absolute among interdependent competitors, whether animal or human.

Jean–Jacques Rousseau believed that there is no evil in the human heart, that all the ills of humanity began with civilization. Yet aggression is one of a large number of human behavioral characteristics that cross the boundaries of language, culture, race, even species: it cannot be fully understood without taking the biological component into account. This book has, I trust, demonstrated that appropriate countermeasures evolved along with aggressive behavior, and that both humans and other primates apply these measures with great skill. The basic pattern is that two conflicting individuals or parties become friends again. The process sounds simple enough, yet it is one of the most complex transitions we can go through.

Forgiveness is not, as some people seem to believe, a mysterious and sublime idea that we owe to a few millennia of Judeo–Christianity. It did not originate in the minds of people and cannot therefore be appropriated by an ideology or a religion. The fact that monkeys, apes, and humans all engage in reconciliation behavior means that it is probably over thirty million years old, preceding the evolutionary divergence of these primates. The alternative explanation, that this behavior appeared independently in each species, is highly "uneconomical," for it requires as many theories as there are species. Scientists normally dismiss uneconomical explanations unless there is strong evidence against the more elegant unified theory. Because no such evidence exists in this instance, reconciliation behavior must be seen as a shared heritage of the primate order. Our species has many conciliatory gestures and contact patterns in common with the apes (stretching out a hand, smiling, kissing, embracing, and so on). Language and culture merely add a degree of subtlety and variation to human peacemaking strategies.

ROBERT J. CONDLIN, BARGAINING IN THE DARK: THE NORMATIVE INCOHERENCE OF LAWYER DISPUTE BARGAINING ROLE

51 Md.L.Rev. 1, 23–33 (1992).

PRINCIPLED BARGAINING

. . .

The concept of principled bargaining has great analytical power and appeal. It builds on the idea of "legal astuteness," identified, but not elaborated upon, in the theory of cordial bargaining, and in the process adds an important normative dimension to the idea of cooperation. Being cooperative now means adhering to authoritative substantive norms—legal, moral, and political—which form the backdrop of dispute settlement and make its outcomes legitimate and fair. It is no longer enough that bargainers be cordial, predictable, and nice; they must do justice as well. This normative addition transforms bargaining theory from a theory of strategy and manners to one also of morality and politics, and in so doing, helps justify bargaining's place in the system of adjudicatory justice.

While a major advance, therefore, principled bargaining is not without its difficulties, as one of its leading proponents has acknowledged. A few representative illustrations will show how this is so. To begin with, principled bargaining's starting point, that "conflict lies not in objective reality, but in people's heads," is often just wrong. It is also incongruous with the theory's heavy reliance on the possibility of principled resolutions. Not all beliefs and values can be measured against each other, or against some common denominator (or principle). Bargainers who disagree are not invariably confused or mistaken about what they believe or want; sometimes their beliefs and wants are grounded in irreconcilable notions of entitlement, and interpretive or communicative skill will not make these conflicts go away. If principled bargaining theory claimed only that communication can distort meaning and create the appearance of conflict when none is present, that it can produce "cognitive conflict," and then argued that cognitive conflict should be avoided whenever possible, few would disagree. These points are not news, however, and are hardly worth the fanfare with which the theory of principled bargaining has been announced and advanced. Instead, principled bargaining seems committed to the stronger claims that substantive differences are most often illusory, and simultaneously that they can be resolved by objective criteria. These stronger claims are what make principled bargaining interesting, but they are also what make it suspect.

Apart from its grounding on a suspect premise, principled bargaining also has weaknesses in each of its core principles. For example, in discussing the importance of separating the people from the problem, the leading proponents of principled bargaining recommend both that bargainers identify with the other side ("see the situation as the other side sees it"), and that they manipulate the other side when it is possible to do so. "Manipulate" is my characterization but it seems fair. For example, a principled bargainer is encouraged to "devot[e] substantial time to working out the practical arrangements" of concessions so as to provide the other bargainer "with an impressive achievement and a real incentive to reach agreement on other issues." Drag out concession-making, in other words, even when one is ready to concede, so that the other side will think it has accomplished more than it has and be correspondingly grateful. This may be instrumentally useful advice, but it encourages bargainers to be strategically inauthentic, and it seems slightly out of place in a bargaining method based on mutual cooperation and empathic identification with the other side. Following the dictates of principled bargaining is not always easy, in part, because the theory is not always clear about whether it is a genuine alternative to discredited positional bargaining, or a set of more sophisticated techniques for operating successfully within the positional mode.

Similarly, the advice to focus on interests rather than positions is based on an unargued premise, that the two are different in some significant sense, which is convincing to proponents of principled bargaining for reasons that ordinary language seems not to explain. In bargaining, all statements of interest are not very thinly disguised statements of position (i.e., that the interest must be provided for by some explicit term in the agreement), and statements of position are inarticulate but usually discernible statements of interest (i.e., that the money or whatever else is being discussed is desired for some particular reason or reasons—to feel vindicated, be made whole, take revenge, or the like). It simply is not possible for conversation of any sophistication to be about just one or the other. Principled bargaining implicitly admits this impossibility when it acknowledges that bargaining ultimately must involve the discussion of and agreement on settlement terms (positions), and describes a range of rhetorical and psychological techniques designed to help in this process. Given this acknowledgment, it is perhaps a bit disingenuous to suggest that "focusing on interests not positions" will make bargaining more productive.

. . .

Principled bargaining's third foundational rule, the directive to invent options for mutual gain by expanding the bargaining pie and looking for shared and dovetailing interests, is often a helpful guide in resolving particular disputes, but of more limited use in constructing a general theory of bargaining. Bargainers sometimes get locked into unnecessarily zero-sum conceptions of their situations, and see conflicts where none exist, and when this happens, it can help to redefine issues, clarify goals, and expand the pie. Conceptually, however, this is not bargaining. Bargaining begins at the point where differences must be reconciled, accommodated, or compromised. It is not the same as individual bargainer interest clarification (i.e., learning), and is not needed when interest clarification will suffice. Inventing options for mutual gain is about avoiding the need to bargain, an important practical topic, but of limited significance in the theoretical task of explaining bargaining.

Finally, and most interestingly, there are weaknesses in the most controversial part of principled bargaining theory: its insistence on the use of "objective criteria" for determining outcome. "Objective" is an emotionally evocative term, with positive associations for most, but it is ambiguous in an important sense, which the theory of principled bargaining trades on, but does not discuss. Objective can mean neutral or nonpartisan, in the sense of treating each side's interests equally. Flipping a coin or splitting the difference is objective in this sense. Or it can mean fair and legitimate, in the sense of respecting recognized entitlements of the parties, and reconciling conflicts between them through the use of principles, procedures, and substantive norms that are accepted as authoritative. Neutrality and fairness are not always the same, however, as it is possible to be both neutral and unfair, and fair but biased. The theory of principled bargaining does not say so directly, and there may be some waffling, but its suggested examples of objective criteria, such as splitting techniques that divide pots into rough equivalents, consensus community practices, or the parties' past behavior, seem based on an understanding of objectivity as neutrality. Like "neutral" mechanisms generally, however, such criteria have a strong bias in favor of status quo distributions, and the status quo is not always fair, particularly to those who reasonably reject existing definitions of worth, received distributions of resources and power, consensus procedures, or the wisdom of past behavior, their own included. Principled bargaining cannot simply assume that neutral principles will be fair, and if it intends to stand on this proposition, then it must argue for it, directly and at length.

A second problem with objective criteria, as principled bargaining acknowledges, is that often there will be more than one objective criterion (by whatever definition) available to settle a dispute. In choosing among them, principled bargainers are told to look for second level criteria, or metacriteria, that will tell one which is the appropriate first level norm. But principled bargaining does not explain why it is reasonable to expect the problem of more than one criterion to go away at the appellate level, or in other words, why it is reasonable to expect to find only one meta-criterion. Thus, in the end, principled bargaining falls into the familiar formalist trap of the infinite rule regress. Principled bargainers are also encouraged to discover appropriate criteria by referring to norms they have used in similar circumstances in the past. If each side comes from a different "tradition" and has done different things, however, or if one or the other now reasonably believes that its past behavior was in error, the theory of principled bargaining does not help. Suggesting that bargainers act like judges rather than advocates is also not useful, unless one is willing to suppose, as few are, that in most disputes there is only one right decision for a judge to make.

Chapter 5

MOVING BETWEEN AND BEYOND THE STRATEGIES—DEVELOPING ALTERNATIVES AND CHANGING THE GAME

This chapter closes the first section of these readings by considering two skills all effective negotiators should possess. The first is the negotiator's ability to alter the bargaining pattern that is being used once negotiations have commenced. In Chapter Two, we saw that the Generous Tit-for-Tat strategy, based on contemporary Prisoner's Dilemma research, encourages effective negotiators to be flexible and to move between distributive and integrative strategies as the context warrants. Likewise, Fisher and Ury suggested in *Getting to Yes* that good bargainers practice "negotiation jujitsu" to convert competitive processes to principled ones. The assumptions of this body of work are that negotiators can influence strategy selection, and that integrative solutions will best meet the parties' interests.

In practice, this advice proves difficult to follow. The first selections in this chapter suggest how to make good strategy selection decisions, and when appropriate, how to encourage the opposite to adopt a more cooperative approach to bargaining. An excerpt from Donald Gifford focuses on how to determine whether to adopt a competitive or noncompetitive bargaining strategy. He explains the factors that should inform an effective negotiator's internal strategy selection conversation. Robert Condlin then helps explain why negotiators attempting to resolve disputes have such trouble adopting integrative strategies. The last selection in this section is from William Ury's marvelously titled *Getting Past No*. Here, in the context of a hostage negotiation, Ury explains how an effective negotiator can make even the most hard-nosed opposite responsive to the strategy of "breakthrough negotiation."

The second skill, closing out the readings in this chapter, is the ability to determine when some alternative to the current negotiation is preferable to continued bargaining. Effective negotiators need to know when there is insufficient value in a negotiation at the current settlement point, or when negotiations have led to impasse or some other impediment to agreement. The honing of this skill requires us to look both inside and outside the terms of the present negotiation. Knowing about one's Best Alternative To A Negotiated Agreement, colloquially termed one's BATNA, and having external alternatives well developed, both enhances our power to effect a good outcome in **this** bargain and provides a benchmark for knowing when **another** process is preferable to what we can obtain in the present deal.

Knowing how to calculate the external "bottom line" converts this concept from being a tactic of veiled threat into a helpful tripwire signaling when we should look elsewhere for agreement. The next selection, by Lax and Sebenius, explains why it is important to develop alternatives to the current negotiation, and how power increases when we know to leave the present bargaining context and pursue our alternatives. Finally, Donald Gifford returns to discuss how lawyers can work with their clients to determine the minimum reservation point in settling a claim.

Readings

1. Donald Gifford, *A Context–Based Theory of Strategy Selection in Legal Negotiation,* 46 Ohio St.L.J. 41, 58–71 (1985).

2. Robert J. Condlin, *Bargaining in the Dark: The Normative Incoherence of Lawyer Dispute Bargaining Role,* 51 Md.L.Rev. 1, 7–11 (1992).

3. William Ury, Getting Past No: Dealing With Difficult People 137–46 (1991).

4. David Lax & James Sebenius, *The Power of Alternatives or the Limits to Negotiation,* 1 Negot.J. 163 (1985).

5. Donald Gifford, Legal Negotiation: Theory and Applications 50–54 (1989).

6. For Further Reading

   a. Bryan Downie, *When Negotiations Fail: Causes of Breakdown and Tactics for Breaking the Stalemate,* 7 Negot.J. 175 (1991).

   b. Roger Fisher, William Ury & Bruce Patton, Getting To Yes: Reaching Agreement Without Giving In (2d ed. 1991).

   c. Roger Fisher & Scott Brown, Getting Together: Building a Relationship that Gets to Yes (1988).

   d. David Lax & James Sebenius, The Manager As Negotiator: Bargaining for Cooperation and Competitive Gain (1986).

   e. Robert H. Mnookin, Scott R. Peppet & Andrew S. Tulumello, *The Tension Between Empathy and Assertiveness,* 12 Negot.J. 217 (1996).

   f. Robin L. Pinkley, Margaret A. Neale & Rebecca J. Bennett, *The Impact of Alternatives to Settlement in Dyadic Negotiation,* 57 Org.Beh. & Hum.Dec.Proc. 97 (1994).

   g. Richard Walton & Robert McKersie, A Behavioral Theory of Labor Negotiations (1965).

   h. Sally B. White & Margaret A. Neale, *Reservation Price, Resistance Point and BATNA's: Determining the Parameters of Acceptable Negotiated Outcomes,* 7 Negot.J. 379 (1991).

   i. H. Peyton Young, ed., Negotiation Analysis (1991).

DONALD GIFFORD, A CONTEXT–BASED THEORY OF STRATEGY SELECTION IN LEGAL NEGOTIATION

46 Ohio St.L.J. 41, 58–71 (1985).

1. THE OPPONENT'S NEGOTIATION STRATEGY

The single most important factor to consider in choosing between a competitive and noncompetitive strategy is the opponent's likely negotiating strategy. To be successful, the cooperative and integrative approaches require that both the negotiator and her opponent adopt the same strategy. Thus, a negotiator who is paired against a competitive opponent should not adopt a cooperative strategy, because her cooperative tactics will be exploited. Instead of reciprocating the cooperative negotiator's concessions, the competitive opponent will interpret the concessions as a sign of weakness and will grant fewer concessions. The cooperative negotiator loses both position and image in this situation and moves no closer to agreement. The cooperative strategy succeeds only if the opponent reciprocates and makes concessions. Although the integrative strategy is somewhat less vulnerable to exploitation by a competitive negotiator than the cooperative approach, it also requires an exchange of information and a responsiveness to the other negotiator's interests and needs; these tactics may be exploited by the competitive negotiator who will refuse to exchange information and respond to the adversary's needs.

. . . Predictions about which strategy an opponent will employ can be gleaned from at least four sources:

(1) *The Opponent's Early Strategy in the Instant Negotiation* . . . .

(2) *The Opponent's Strategy in Past Negotiations* . . . .

(3) *The Strategy of Similarly Situated Negotiators* . . . .

(4) *The Negotiator's Favored Strategy if She Were in the Opponent's Position* . . . .

2. RELATIVE BARGAINING POWER

The second factor the negotiator should consider in choosing a negotiation strategy is the relative power of the negotiator and the opponent. Power can be defined as the capacity to influence the opponent. The critical factor in negotiations is not power itself, but rather the opponent's perception of power. A negotiator's power results from the negative consequences she can inflict on an opponent if an agreement is not reached and from the benefits that the negotiator can bestow on an opponent if a settlement is achieved.

The extent of a negotiator's power over an opponent depends largely on the alternatives available to the opponent if an agreement is not reached. If not reaching an agreement produces severe consequences for the opponent, then the negotiator has great leverage to dictate the terms of an agreement. Conversely, if the opponent has other viable options if attempts at an agreement fail, a negotiator has relatively little power . . . .

When a negotiator's power is greater than that of her opponent, she may choose either a competitive or a noncompetitive strategy. A negotiator with a viable alternative to a negotiated agreement is exposed to minimal risk if she chooses the competitive strategy, despite the increased risk of settlement impasse. In addition, threats made by a powerful negotiator who uses a competitive strategy will be perceived as more credible and will more likely lead to concessions by an opponent than would threats by a weaker negotiator.

The less powerful negotiator has two options available: (1) she can attempt to increase her own power and decrease that of her opponent, or (2) she can pursue a noncompetitive strategy.

. . .

3. FUTURE DEALINGS WITH THE OPPONENT

The third important factor to consider in choosing a negotiating strategy is the likelihood of future interaction with the opposing party. When a relationship between the parties will likely continue, a noncompetitive approach is recommended, because the competitive strategy often generates distrust and ill will. These negative feelings may harm the negotiator in future dealings with the opponent....

4. THE ATTITUDE OF THE NEGOTIATOR'S CLIENT

The choice of the best negotiating strategy may also depend on whether a negotiator is representing himself or a client. As previously noted, the formal norms governing the practice of law provide that the client establish certain parameters for the choice of a negotiation strategy. Beyond this, the attorney's desire to maintain rapport with an adversarial client often necessitates the adoption of a competitive strategy. Visibly competitive tactics may convince a client otherwise not inclined to trust his attorney that his attorney is representing his interests and is not "selling out" to the opponent. In simulated negotiations, social scientists have found that representatives who are accountable to constituents are more likely to be tough and to use competitive tactics.

5. PRESSURE TO REACH AGREEMENT

Various kinds of pressure to reach an agreement may also affect the choice of the most appropriate negotiation strategy. Clients often desire an early conclusion to negotiations for a number of reasons: they may need settlement proceeds immediately, desire to minimize legal fees and other expenses resulting from prolonged negotiations, and want to minimize the psychological strain associated with continued conflict. Pressure to reach an agreement also results from imminent trial deadlines and judicial attempts to settle cases. Finally, expeditious settlement is often a necessity for attorneys who have heavy caseloads, such as urban prosecutors and public defenders. Pressure to settle a case quickly, from whatever source, suggests using a noncompetitive strategy, and usually a cooperative strategy as opposed to an integrative one. Social scientists' research shows that time pressures result in lower demands, faster concessions, and lower aspiration levels....

6. THE STAGE OF THE NEGOTIATION

In most negotiations, not just those in which considerable pressure to reach agreement is felt, the negotiator's choice of strategic moves may depend on the stage of the negotiation. The possibility of changing strategies during a negotiation previously was described as feasible under the strategic choice model. Competitive strategic moves serve important functions early in the negotiation.   They suggest to the opponent that the negotiator will not concede easily and also help to convince the client that the negotiator is working vigorously on his behalf.   In order for the negotiators to reach an agreement and conclude the negotiations, however, at least one of the parties must make a noncompetitive move: either one or both parties must make concessions or devise an integrative solution.

7.   THE NEGOTIATOR'S PERSONALITY

Although the negotiator's personality should not dictate her choice of negotiation strategy, personality inevitably affects the ability of the negotiator to implement a particular strategy.   Therefore, a negotiator must consider her own personality when choosing a strategy.   Research demonstrates that negotiators who exhibit personality traits such as authoritarianism, high self-esteem, risk aversion, and strong internal control are more likely to choose a competitive approach; presumably these same traits increase the likelihood that a negotiator will be effective in employing a competitive strategy and in undermining the opponent's belief in his own position.   Conversely, cognitive complexity (intelligence), and passivity, which Professor Gerald Williams refers to as "a clear tendency to be a milquetoast," are personality traits identified with persons who typically pursue a noncompetitive approach.   A person who is able to develop trust and good working relationships and who is able to persuade is likely to be effective as a cooperative negotiator.

8.   NEGOTIATION NORMS

Finally, the norms associated with a negotiation strongly affect the choice of a negotiation strategy.   These norms include both formal rules governing professional conduct and informal but generally accepted conventions of the negotiation context.   For example, Professor Gerald Williams' survey of Phoenix lawyers suggests that the mere threat of filing a lawsuit in a commercial or real property dispute is regarded as a "heavy-handed" tactic, likely to incur the wrath of the opponent and be counterproductive.   The informal norm in these disputes, therefore, suggests the use of a noncompetitive strategy.   On the other hand, personal injury specialists regard a desire to settle a case either prior to filing a lawsuit or perhaps even more than a few months before trial as a dangerously noncompetitive tactic likely to lead to exploitation by the predominantly competitive negotiators in that environment.   The relative acceptance of competitive and noncompetitive strategies may also depend on the geographic area in which an attorney practices.   More generally, Professor Williams' survey of the negotiating traits of lawyers suggests two very important conclusions about negotiations in the legal context: lawyers use predominantly noncompetitive strategies, and they expect opposing counsel to reciprocate.

ROBERT J. CONDLIN, BARGAINING IN THE DARK: THE NORMATIVE INCOHERENCE OF LAWYER DISPUTE BARGAINING ROLE
51 Md.L.Rev. 1, 7–11 (1992).

Dispute bargaining is almost created by strategy, undertaken in the first instance not because it is intrinsically worthwhile, aesthetically pleasing, important to personal development, or the naturally best way for people to interact, but because it is an instrumentally effective method for settling conflicting claims to limited resources, opportunities, and the like. It is not an essential human activity, and it probably would not exist, at least not pervasively, in a world without scarcity. Instead, it is a socially constructed process in which participants manipulate a complex web of interpretive, advocative, and trading practices in order to put individual objectives in their best possible light and increase the likelihood that they will be realized. It takes its form in the first instance from a process of reasoning backwards instrumentally from such objectives. Strategy is not all of bargaining, of course, but it is an inescapable, irreducible part, the core out of which the process's moral, political, and social issues emerge, and from which they take their own special character and shape. A bargainer has no choice but to be strategic, other than the choice not to bargain at all, and this reality acts as a backdrop to all understanding of lawyer bargaining behavior and role.

In this world of strategic interaction, uncertainty, thought of as incomplete and imperfect information about the factors a rational actor should take into account in deciding how to proceed, is dispute settlement's most salient attribute. Parties come to bargaining with diverse and not always compatible expectations about outcome, and often incommensurable beliefs about the legitimacy of their respective positions. While they know in advance that such incompatibility and incommensurability are possible, they do not know in any particular case to what extent they are present. When they enter a negotiation, therefore, bargainers do not know for certain whether they will be friends or enemies, focused on questions of efficiency or fairness, able to work together or locked intractably in combat. As a result, they must approach the negotiation prepared for all of the above.

Uncertainty results in part from the fact that in law, and in life generally, there are competing conceptions of the good, and thus no necessary consensus on how a dispute ought to be resolved, or even on the principles on which a resolution could be grounded. Not everyone believes, for example, that property rights count for as much as personal rights (or even that rights discourse is the best framework for resolving questions of resource distribution), that all values can be expressed in terms of some common denominator such as money, that proceeding forward efficiently is more important than determining responsibility for present states of affairs, that properly promulgated laws are necessarily valid, or that procedural justice is the same as justice simpliciter. Parties starting from such diverse premises often reach different conclusions about what result a bargaining interaction ought to produce, and with good reason. The effect is that bargainers usually cannot say with precision at the beginning of a negotiation what their counterparts will accept to settle the dispute. They can make predictions, and these often will come close, particularly if their past dealings involved similar disputes or were long standing. But they cannot be exact in these predictions or do more than specify a range of possible outcomes. If it were otherwise, there would be no need to bargain. Each would offer the minimum the other would take, because to offer more would be to make a gift and not a bargain.

Uncertainty is exacerbated by the fact that bargainers must make statements and describe intentions in their clients' best light, and therefore, in the strongest credible terms that the most generous or compliant (hypothetical) adversary might accept. Consequently, what is said in bargaining is usually an exaggerated version of what is meant, and known to be so. Yet, bargainers need to know whether particular adversaries are the most generous, or of what generosity consists in a given case. Therefore, they must learn during the course of the bargaining interaction what their counterparts truly believe and would be willing to do, and to do this they must interpret actions and statements of the other side as much for what they reveal as for what they say. In such a world, communication itself is another source of uncertainty. Every disclosure is viewed as (and is) potentially a concession, every argument potentially a provocation, and every proposal potentially a gift. In speaking at all, then, bargainers understandably will be cautious and circumspect, revealing as little and defending as much as possible until the other's intentions are known. While this is only prudent—one does not bare the throat until it is clear that it will not be cut—the effect is to make communication more difficult. Suspicion increases, candor diminishes, and indirect and self-protective methods of expression replace open and straightforward ones.

Uncertainty is also increased by the recursiveness of the bargaining dynamic. In the process of trying to dope out, influence, and trade favorably with one another, the state of mind each bargainer tries to understand has as one of its properties the fact that it is also trying to understand the other. Bargaining is thus a process of mutually assessed mutual assessment, in which each party makes moves that carry fateful implications and that must be chosen in light of one's thoughts about the other's thoughts about oneself, and so on. Such information is unknowable in any final sense, of course, because it changes at the moment it becomes known, by virtue of the fact that it is known. Bargainers can make assumptions about what their counterparts believe, about what they (the bargainers) believe, about what the others believe, and so on, but to the extent that they try to understand these beliefs finally, they will inevitably be trapped in an outguessing regress....

... Dispute bargainers must and do learn to trust, of course, for without trust bargainers could not settle disputes. But this is an instrumental understanding of trust, as predictability, or the capacity to know when others will honor their commitments, and trust as predictability does not do much to soften the cautiousness and suspicion that is built into the structure of the bargaining conversation or to change bargaining's distinctive and identifying character as strategic interaction.

Calling dispute settlement strategic does not diminish the importance of the moral and political dimensions of choosing a bargaining approach. It is often more important to be candid or fair than to be instrumentally successful. Nor does it resolve the question of how to behave when settling disputes. There are different and often contradictory strategies for achieving bargaining objectives, ranging from the most cooperative and mutual on the one end, to the most competitive and individualistic on the other, and similarly different ways of defining the hierarchy of bargaining goals so that anything from obtaining the maximum share of the bargaining pot to preserving working relationships with other bargainers and principals could be at the top. To see dispute settlement as strategic, however, is to see it as bargainers see it, to recognize what drives it, and to understand the way in which questions about it, even moral and political questions, must be framed....

In short, the lack of perfect information about adversary wants and needs, the possibility of competing conceptions of the good, the practice of a "best lights" discourse, recursiveness, and ordinary prudence combine to cause dispute bargainers to approach a bargaining relationship cautiously and to communicate strategically. . . .

WILLIAM URY, GETTING PAST NO: DEALING WITH DIFFICULT PEOPLE

137–46 (1991).

There is a story of a man who left seventeen camels to his three sons. He left half the camels to his eldest son, a third to his middle son, and a ninth to his youngest. The three set to dividing up their inheritance but couldn't negotiate a solution—because seventeen could not be divided by two or three or nine. The sons finally consulted a wise old woman. After pondering the problem, the old woman said, "See what happens if you take *my* camel." So then the sons had eighteen camels. The eldest son took his half—that was nine. The middle son took his third—that was six. And the youngest son took his ninth—that was two. Nine and six and two made seventeen. They had one camel left over. They gave it back to the wise old woman.

Like the seventeen camels, your negotiations will often seem intractable. Like the wise old woman, you will need to step back from the negotiation, look at the problem from a fresh angle, and find an eighteenth camel.

Breakthrough negotiation is such an eighteenth camel. It can help you reach agreement in negotiations that at first seem impossible. The challenge is to get past the usual obstacles: your own natural reaction, your opponent's negative emotions, his hardball tactics, his unsatisfied interests, and his belief that he can win through the exercise of power.

Consider how all five steps of the breakthrough strategy were applied in one of the most difficult situations imaginable: a hostage negotiation with an armed criminal.

A HOSTAGE NEGOTIATION

On Thursday morning, October 14, 1982, scores of police converged on the nation's second-largest medical facility, Kings County Hospital in Brooklyn, New York. A convicted armed robber named Larry Van Dyke was holed up in a basement locker room with five hospital employees. Van Dyke, who had just had a cast removed from a broken arm, had seized a gun from a corrections officer, shot and wounded him, and tried to escape. Cornered by police, Van Dyke had taken hostages. Almost immediately he had let one person go, instructing him to tell police: "I want out of here or I'm going to start killing people."

A decade earlier the police would probably have handled such an incident by using force. "In the old, old days," a police captain recalled, "we'd surround the place, give the guy the bullhorn, fire the tear gas, put on some type of flak jacket, and engage the guy in a firefight."

But instead of fighting, the police decided to talk. Detective Lieutenant Robert J. Louden, a trained hostage negotiator, began a conversation with Van Dyke by shouting through the closed locker-room door: "How ya doin'?

My name's Bob and I'm here to see what's going on. I'm here to help sort this out and help us get out of this mess. What's your name?"

Van Dyke replied, "My name's Larry Van Dyke and I've got a whole roomful of people. I've got nothing to lose. I'm not going back to jail. You've got thirty minutes to give me my freedom."

Louden did not reject the demand or the deadline, but reframed them instead as aspirations: "I'll see what I can do. I'll look into it for you and get back to you as soon as I can. As you know, these things take time. It's not a decision I can make. In the meantime, is there anything *I* can get for you?" Louden was trying to refocus Van Dyke's attention on what was achievable.

As Louden was talking, a backup negotiator stood behind him. The backup's job was to prompt Louden with questions, pass him messages, and make sure he kept his emotional balance. It was Louden's way of going to the balcony.

Van Dyke warned that if the police tried an assault, he would kill the hostages. Louden assured him that no one was going to hurt him. "You don't know how we operate," the detective said. "In ten years no one's ever been hurt. We don't storm doors. It's not like TV." Van Dyke's lawyer counseled his client: "Larry, no one is going to hurt you. In three hundred cases, the hostage negotiation unit has never hurt anyone."

Van Dyke threatened to break out of the room with his hostages. Louden told him: "Larry, you're better off staying in. You've got us locked out and we've got you locked in. We've got plenty of people out here. We don't want to use force, but we will if we need to. You're smart. You know how the game is played. Let's see if we can work this out."

Louden asked open-ended questions to find out what Van Dyke was thinking and what he wanted: "How did you get into this mess? How can we sort it out?" Van Dyke started complaining about corruption and abuse in the state prison system. Louden listened sympathetically, saying, "I understand how you feel," "I've heard similar things from others," and "Because you've raised it, we may be able to launch an investigation into the corruption." He was trying to build rapport with Van Dyke, acknowledging his points and agreeing where possible; in effect, Louden stepped to Van Dyke's side.

Van Dyke demanded to talk to Bella English, a reporter from the *Daily News* whose writing he admired. Louden agreed to help find her and persuaded Van Dyke to accept a field telephone to make communication easier.

Step by step, the detective made progress. Bella English was flown to the site in a police helicopter. "We want you to go on the phone," Louden told her, "but please don't use negative words like 'hostage' or 'jail.'"

English introduced herself to Van Dyke and asked him why he wanted to talk to her. "Because you're a fair reporter," he replied. He told her that he faced a prison sentence of twenty-five years to life on robbery charges. Coached by Louden, English tried to reassure Van Dyke that this was not necessarily so. Shortly thereafter, Van Dyke agreed to let one hostage go as soon as he received pillows, blankets, and coffee. At 4:15 P.M., the hostage emerged.

Four hours later Van Dyke agreed to let another hostage go if radio station WOR allowed English to broadcast his gripes about prison conditions. A few minutes after the broadcast, Van Dyke released the second hostage. "That was real good," Van Dyke told English. "You just saved a life." "No," English replied, "*you* just saved a life."

Van Dyke then agreed to free a third hostage if WABC–TV broadcast a live message during the eleven o'clock evening news. The station complied, at the Police Department's request. On the air, the freed hostage conveyed a message of love from Van Dyke to his wife and said no one would be hurt, "as long as the police didn't provoke anything."

Shortly after midnight, however, Van Dyke's mood changed. The police heard him threatening a hostage: "Old man, get on your knees. I got a gun to his head here. I don't want to hurt anybody but if they treat me ridiculous, I'll act ridiculous." Van Dyke tried to fix the blame on Louden. "This ain't going quick enough. I'm going to kill these people and it will be your fault."

But Louden deflected the blame: "Bullshit, Larry. We're here to help. We're all in this together. But if you do that, it's not us. It's you. Now let's see if we can work this out." Louden constantly sought to redirect attention back to the problem.

On Friday morning, tensions rose. Van Dyke had asked for the morning newspapers, but became angry when he saw reports that he had been accused of informing on fellow inmates. "They blew it!" he screamed in rage. "They said I snitched on inmates and guards. Guards, correct. Inmates, no." He said he had been forced by prison guards to entrap other guards in drug deals, and claimed he would be killed if he was returned to state custody.

Louden tried to calm Van Dyke, addressing his basic need for security: "I know you're not an informant. Whoever gave that statement was wrong. All the media can hear me saying that. Let me see if I can work it so you don't have to go back to a *state* pen."

Louden contacted federal and state correction officials to explore whether Van Dyke could be transferred to a federal penitentiary. The tension began to dissipate when Mike Borum, a deputy state correction commissioner, came to tell Van Dyke that he would try to arrange a transfer. Van Dyke told his cousin, a corrections officer who had been brought to the scene: "I'm thinking of surrendering. They offered me a good deal." Louden had built Van Dyke a golden bridge to retreat across.

Van Dyke agreed to release a fourth hostage if WABC–TV and WINS radio agreed to broadcast the release live, and also let Van Dyke tell his side of the story. On the air he complained about state prison conditions: "I have been beat up, I have been set up."

Four hours later Van Dyke became morose, insisting he didn't want to return to jail. He told Louden: "I've got nothing to lose. We're going to play Russian roulette." Louden tried to reassure him and talked soothingly to him through the night.

Early Saturday morning Van Dyke finally agreed to release the final hostage in return for press coverage and Borum's public promise of a transfer. At eight o'clock Louden was able to report to Van Dyke that Borum was making his statement on WABC–TV. Twenty-five minutes later the last hostage was released. At eight-thirty, Van Dyke came out to surrender. He was granted his request to talk with the press. "I'm not a madman," he said. "I'm a man that was trying to get freedom.... I got caught. I'm here." Then police took him away to the Metropolitan Correction Center, a federal detention center in lower Manhattan.

After forty-seven hours, one of the longest and most dramatic hostage incidents in New York City history was over. "Personally, I couldn't have held out much longer," said Louden, hoarse and weary.

The outcome was a victory for the police, who were able to win the release of hostages, prevent bloodshed, and take the criminal back into custody. Louden said that he and other members of his team had finally persuaded Van Dyke to give up by "trying to build trust and confidence, trying to establish that we could treat each other as human beings and help each other out of this okay."

Van Dyke didn't win his freedom, but he won a public promise to be transferred to a federal prison. After he surrendered, Van Dyke gave police the highest compliment they could have hoped for: "They shot straight with me," he said.

Just as the best general never has to fight, so the police never had to use force. They used their power not to attack Van Dyke, but to contain him and educate him that his best alternative lay in surrendering peacefully. They brought him to his senses, not his knees.

The Five Steps of Breakthrough Negotiation

Whether you are negotiating with a hostage-taker, your boss, or your teenager, the basic principles remain the same. In summary, the five steps of breakthrough negotiation are:

1. Go to the Balcony. The first step is to control your own behavior. When your opponent says no or launches an attack, you may be stunned into giving in or counterattacking. So, suspend your reaction by naming the game. Then buy yourself time to think. Use the time to figure out your interests and your BATNA. Throughout the negotiation, keep your eyes on the prize. Instead of getting mad or getting even, focus on getting what you want. In short, go to the balcony.

2. Step to Their Side. Before you can negotiate, you must create a favorable climate. You need to defuse your opponent's anger, fear, and suspicions. He expects you to attack or to resist. So do the opposite: Listen to him, acknowledge his point, and agree with him wherever you can. Acknowledge his authority and competence, too. Disarm him by stepping to his side.

3. Don't Reject ... Reframe. The next step is to change the game. Instead of rejecting your opponent's position—which usually only reinforces it—direct his attention to the problem of meeting each side's interests. Take whatever he says and reframe it as an attempt to deal with the problem. Ask problem-solving questions, such as "Why is it that you want that?" or "What would you do if you were in my shoes?" or "What if we were to ...?" Rather than trying to teach him yourself, let the problem be his teacher. Reframe his tactics, too: Go around stone walls, deflect attacks, and expose tricks. To change the game, change the frame.

4. Build Them a Golden Bridge. At last you're ready to negotiate. Your opponent, however, may stall, not yet convinced of the benefits of agreement. You may be tempted to push and insist, but this will probably lead him to harden and resist. Instead, do the opposite—draw him in the direction you would like him to go. Think of yourself as a mediator. Involve him in the process, incorporating his ideas. Try to identify and satisfy his unmet interests, particularly his basic human needs. Help him save face and make the outcome appear as a victory for him. Go slow to go fast. In sum, make it easy for him to say yes by building him a golden bridge.

5. Bring Them to Their Senses, Not Their Knees. If your opponent still resists and thinks he can win without negotiating, you must educate him to the contrary. You must make it hard for him to say no. You could use threats and force, but these often backfire; if you push him into a corner, he will likely lash out, throwing even more resources into the fight against you. Instead, educate him about the costs of not agreeing. Ask reality-testing questions, warn rather than threaten, and demonstrate your BATNA. Use it only if necessary and minimize his resistance by exercising restraint and reassuring him that your goal is mutual satisfaction, not victory. Make sure he knows the golden bridge is always open. In short, use power to bring him to his senses, not his knees.

The breakthrough strategy requires you to resist normal human temptations and do the opposite of what you usually feel like doing. It requires you to suspend your reaction when you feel like striking back, to listen when you feel like talking back, to ask questions when you feel like telling your opponent the answers, to bridge your differences when you feel like pushing for your way, and to educate when you feel like escalating.

At every turn the strategy calls on you to choose the path of indirection. You break through by going around your opponent's resistance, approaching him from the side, acting contrary to his expectations. The theme throughout the strategy is to treat your opponent with respect—not as an object to be pushed, but as a person to be persuaded. Rather than trying to change his mind by direct pressure, you change the environment in which he makes decisions. You let him draw his own conclusions and make his own choice. *Your goal is not to win over him but to win him over.*

From Adversaries to Partners

It takes two to tangle but it takes only one to begin the process of untangling a knotty situation. It is within your power to transform your most difficult negotiations. During the American Civil War, Abraham Lincoln made a speech in which he referred sympathetically to the Southern rebels. An elderly lady, a staunch Unionist, upbraided him for speaking kindly of his enemies when he ought to be thinking of destroying them. His reply was classic: "Why, madam," Lincoln answered, "do I not destroy my enemies when I make them my friends?"

The breakthrough strategy is designed to do precisely that—to destroy your adversary by making him your partner in problem-solving negotiation.

DAVID A. LAX AND JAMES K. SEBENIUS, THE POWER OF ALTERNATIVES OR THE LIMITS TO NEGOTIATION

1 Negot.J. 163, 163–77 (1985).

If one characterizes negotiation as an interactive process by which two or more people seek jointly or cooperatively to do better than they could otherwise, then the "otherwise" becomes crucial. The parties' best alternatives without agreement imply the *limits* to any agreement. For each side, the basic test of any proposed joint agreement is whether it offers higher subjective worth than that side's best course of action absent agreement. Thus, moves "away from the table" to shape the parties' alternatives to agreement may be as or more important than tactics employed "at the table." Actions of the first type delimit the range of possible agreements; those of the second type influence which point in the range may be chosen. The strategic arsenal from which moves of the second type are drawn includes actions that improve alternatives to the negotiation at hand: for example, searching for a better price or another supplier, cultivating a friendly merger partner in response to hostile takeover negotiations, or preparing an invasion should talks fail to yield a preferable outcome.

By stressing that the desirability of negotiated agreement derives from its possible superiority to individual action, we emphasize our view that negotiation is a *means* of doing better cooperatively than would be possible otherwise.

As such, potential negotiated agreements should be evaluated as competitors to other possibilities for furthering desired ends. This focus helps determine whether to negotiate at all, whether to continue the process, whether to accept a proposal, and whether an agreement, once reached, will be secure.

1. ALTERNATIVES IN THEORY

Many theorists take for granted that if bargaining is inconclusive, the parties fall back to their best alternatives.... Yet relatively little attention is given to the strategic aspects of alternatives or to negotiators' complex moves to shape, protect, and improve them. Generally, analysts take the strategy (*including* any search for better alternatives) to be employed in case of no agreement as a given or sort of benchmark for the study of subsequent bargaining. This approach often carries the implication that the alternatives, like the parties or the issues, form an unchangeable part of a bargain's specification. By this reasoning, admitting moves that affect alternatives and then discovering that the negotiation changes amounts to analytic sleight of hand.

Many circumstances, however, can justify treating alternatives as subject to change during the negotiation, thereby overcoming the theorist's potential objection.... In view of this dynamic relationship between bargaining "inside" and searching "outside," fully rational participants may continually contemplate altering their choice of tactics, including the possibility of a reactivated or intensified search for better alternatives. In general, resources such as effort, time, or money should go toward affecting alternatives or generating new ones until the expected improvement in the value of the negotiated outcome from expending additional resources just equals the cost of doing so.

Like the commitment, the threat, and the promise, the alternative can fundamentally affect the bargaining process. Highlighting it as such, however, risks a negative emphasis, for in concentrating on the *limits* of negotiation, the *potential* is ignored. Many techniques and principles exist to help invent and improve joint arrangements that each side would value more than its best alternative. After all, the main point of negotiating lies in the possibility of gains from cooperation. But alternatives—by implying the limits, reservation prices, or bottom lines—provide the standards against which to measure potential agreements.

. . .

2. PRESCRIPTIONS AND PROPOSITIONS

To counter this common tendency, we have argued that analysts and practitioners should complement their customary focus on the bargaining process with scrutiny of moves intended favorably to alter the bargaining range itself. Lurking barely below the surface of the preceding discussion has been a general prescription that can be easily summarized: Realize the potential of alternatives to agreement.

. . .

A. *Evaluating Alternatives to Agreement*

. . .

If careful evaluation of the sides' alternatives is the first part of realizing their potential, a good negotiator will often consider improving his or her alternatives. The 1971 Maltese–British negotiations over renewed base rights provide an instructive example. Britain had enjoyed the use of a Maltese naval base and had extended its use to other NATO countries. Nevertheless, advances in ship design and warfare methods rendered the Maltese bases of considerably less importance than in earlier years. To obtain much-improved base rental terms, however, the Maltese made highly visible overtures to the Soviet Union about locating one of their bases in Malta. They also approached Libya and other Arab states for large assistance payments in return for Malta's neutrality. At a simple level, this increased the attractiveness of Malta's alternatives to negotiated agreement with the British. But the same moves made Britain's alternatives to agreement with Malta considerably worse. As *The Times* of London noted, "What is important . . . is not that [the facilities] are badly needed in an age of nuclear war but that they should not on the other hand be possessed by Russia." Not only did these actions put pressure directly on Britain, but NATO anxiety, which the Maltese carefully cultivated, served indirectly to increase the pressure. Beyond vastly increased base rentals from Britain, other NATO members ultimately agreed to provide supplemental aid to Malta. Without passing judgment on the questionable prudential or moral implications of such tactics, especially in the longer run, it is worth highlighting the fact that the Maltese actions to improve their own alternatives and worsen those of their negotiating counterparts considerably improved their bargaining position.

. . .

If negotiation is seen as a *means* of doing better by joint action than would be possible otherwise, it should not be surprising that nonnegotiation courses of action will sometimes prove to be the superior means. . . .

In a more strident vein, President Reagan's early dealings with professional air traffic controllers over their contract was resolved when the president fired them all and activated a contingency plan to run the nation's air traffic control system. From Reagan's perspective, decisive, noncooperative action not only settled the air traffic situation but sent strong signals for moderation to other public employee unions and enhanced the president's reputation for toughness. Again, this case suggests a "failure" of negotiation that at least for one participant offered a superior alternative to any negotiable agreement.

Our first prescription, therefore, is to evaluate all sides' alternatives, to consider steps to improve them, and, when negotiated possibilities are distinctly inferior—having carefully accounted for effects on relationships and future linked dealings—to take the best alternative course of action.

B. Anticipate Inflated Perceptions of Alternatives

A negotiator's evaluation of alternatives is inherently subjective and, thus, depends on perceptions. Analysts and practitioners should, therefore, be sensitive to different possible perceptions of the same alternative. In an experiment at Harvard, the findings of which have been replicated in many contexts with students and executives, players were given detailed information about the history of an out-of-court negotiation over insurance claims arising from a personal injury case. They were not told whether the negotiators settled or if the case went to court. Each player was assigned to the role of either the insurance company or the defendant. After reading the case file, the players were privately asked to give their true probability estimates that the plaintiff would win the case and, given a win, the expected amount of the ultimate judgment. Systematically, those assigned the role of the plaintiff estimated the chances of winning and the expected amount of winning as much higher than those assigned the role of the insurance company defendant. Players who were not assigned a role prior to reading the case gave private estimates that generally fell between those of the advocates for each position. Similar results have been found in cases involving the worth of a company that is up for sale. Even given identical business information, balance sheets, income statements, and the like, those assigned to buy the company typically rate its true value as low, while those assigned to sell it give much higher best estimates. Neutral observers ranked the potential someplace in between.

These results, in combination with many other negotiation experiences, suggest that advocates tend to overestimate the attractiveness of their alternatives to negotiated agreement. If each side has an inflated expectation of its alternatives, no zone of possible agreement for negotiation may exist. Awareness of this common bias dictates a conscious attempt to be more realistic about one's own case, not to "believe one's own line" too much, and to be aware and seek to alter counterparts' estimates of their alternatives.

.   .   .

C. *Understand the Link between Alternatives and So–Called "Power"*

Because improvement in perceptions of one's alternatives implies a favorable change in the bargaining range, the ability to affect alternatives—and perceptions of them—lies at the root of many conceptions of bargaining "power." The tight complementarity of alternatives and the negotiation process as well as the relation of alternatives to concepts of power are perfectly clear in a variety of settings. Suppose the boss orders an ethically questionable action. Contrast the resulting situation of the employee who can generate a good outside job offer with that of the one who cannot. Consider how the presence of marketable skills can likewise change a wife's approach to negotiating the end of a bad marriage. What comes of the onerous claims of the neighborhood bully when his reliably protective older brother is drafted?

. . .

Tactical Skill.

Bargaining tactics are often held to be potent. As noted above, however, the best alternative decisively limits the *range* in which they are applicable. The would-be house buyer who psychoanalyzes the seller, details the dwelling's flaws, and makes a low offer is wasting time if the seller can elicit a better price elsewhere.

. . .

It is commonly asserted that the party who "cares more" about the issues at stake in a negotiation is at a disadvantage and that this "greater" interest can be exploited.

. . .

The Ability to Commit.

. . . One commits to a point in the bargaining range by imposing large costs upon oneself for accepting settlements less attractive than the specified point. If these conditional costs render lesser settlements unacceptable relative to one's current alternatives, one's counterpart faces a preordained choice between accepting either the point in the bargaining range or a less desirable alternative. A commitment, therefore, functions by restricting the bargaining range in a way that favors the committing party.

There is a complementarity between strategic moves to commit and strategic moves to improve one's alternative. Improving one's alternative also restricts the bargaining range in a favorable way, but by a different mechanism: it changes the standard of acceptability to which possible settlements are compared. Committing, by contrast, changes the agreement possibilities relative to a fixed standard of acceptability. To accept less than one's improved alternative is to forgo an attainable benefit. To accept less than the point to which one has committed is to incur a self-imposed cost.

. . .

Commitments and strategic improvements in alternatives are thus somewhat complementary tactics. Bargainers must expend resources to employ either. But successful commitments are risky because they are difficult to make credible, binding, visible, and irreversible. Negotiators often do not know the limits of the mutually acceptable bargaining range. Thus a commitment to a favorable point involves the additional risk of falling outside the true range. A better alternative, however, does not incur this liability. Moreover, one's commitment is vulnerable both to the other side's prior commitment and to an improvement in its alternative. An improvement in one's alternative, though, cannot be superseded by prior or subsequent commitments. A threat, of course, may hold the possibility of degrading the opponent's original or even improved alternatives. A negotiator's choice among tactics should reflect these considerations.

Ability to Inflict Harm.

The ability to inflict harm or withhold benefits is a classical bargaining lever. Of course, "the offer that can't be refused" and a nation's threat of economic or military sanctions can both be understood as functioning through alternatives to agreement, specifically, worsening those of the other side if acquiescence is not forthcoming.

. . .

Dependence on the Other Party.

A dependent relationship, such as that of child and parents, of worker and boss, or of colony and colonial power, is often thought to imply the bargaining weakness of the dependent party. Dependence increases as agreement (which *depends* on the other side) yields greater benefits relative to the value of independent alternatives.

. . .

Willingness to Take Risks or Incur Costs.

These qualities, often loudly proclaimed, can be directly translated into the language of alternatives. The more risk-prone and cost-insensitive a bargainer is, the more attractive a risky, costly alternative to a proffered deal becomes. The subjective utility of no agreement is key to the role of alternatives. Risk and cost attitudes are merely part of the utility yardstick by which a bargainer evaluates potential outcomes and portrays them to the other negotiators.

"Power" is a notoriously slippery concept. Yet a number of common notions of bargaining power—tactical skill, intensity of preference, ability to commit, dependence, and risk-proneness—are all intimately related to alternatives. When ambiguous statements about power can be reduced to precise statements about alternatives, we prefer to speak directly in terms of alternatives. A bargainer's quest for power should often start with alternatives.

D. *Focus on Alternatives to Continuing Agreement*

Thus far, advice has concerned alternatives to negotiated agreement before and during the negotiation. Quite frequently, however, once an agreement is hammered out, its terms may not be secure. One or the other party may renege on or demand a revision of the terms. Sometimes such a demand is quite predictable. Consider the case of a multinational mining company negotiating with a country over digging a mine. Before the project has commenced, the company's alternative to agreement with the host is to take its business elsewhere. The country may have only a limited number of weaker contenders for the deposit. Yet once terms are agreed upon and the company has sunk hundreds of millions of dollars into the mine, its alternative to continuing agreement is to leave, now an expensive and losing proposition. With the construction of the mine, however, the country's alternatives to continuing the agreement may have shifted dramatically. Pressure for renegotiation may be expected to mount.

In fact, the structure of this situation is so common that Raymond Vernon has dubbed such mineral agreements "obsolescing bargains," and other analysts have investigated the general properties of these so-called insecure contracts. An insecure contract is an agreement in which one party's incentives to abide by the terms are reduced after the other party has made an irrevocable first move in accord with the agreement. Equivalently, each party's alternative to negotiated agreement changes in a predictable way over the life of the contract.

. . .

E. Manipulate Alternatives to Influence Decentralized Bargaining

Our final proposition concerns the role of alternatives in shaping a network of negotiations to be carried on by others. Quite frequently the rules or structures imposed by others will heavily condition decentralized bargaining. For example, in professional sports a large number of individual negotiations take place between players and teams. Under some league-players' union contracts, players are bound to one team and may not negotiate with others; thus, a player has *no* alternatives (except for nonsports occupations). Predictably, this "reserve clause" system tilts the balance in favor of teams. At the other end of the rules spectrum, players may have the right to negotiate with *all* teams and play for the highest bidder. Under this "free agency" rule, the players have *many* alternatives and, not surprisingly, player salaries tend to be much higher. Between free agency and the reserve clause lie many intermediate options that specify the player's alternatives in more balanced ways. For example, one rule would specify that, if agreement is not reached with a designated team, the player must sit out for a year, without salary or experience, before entering unrestricted free agent status. Another set of rules might allow the player free negotiations but with a limited number of teams. The important point in this example is that the structure of rules governing a large number of decentralized bargains affects those bargains directly through the alternatives available to the parties.

DONALD GIFFORD, LEGAL NEGOTIATION: THEORY AND APPLICATION
50–54 (1989).

The most important aspect of determining the client's interests in the negotiation is to ascertain what alternatives the client has to a negotiated agreement and, perhaps, what negotiated agreement is least advantageous, yet acceptable, from his viewpoint. The least advantageous settlement acceptable to the client, or the "bottom line," is referred to as the client's *minimum disposition*. The advantage of determining a *minimum disposition* in advance of the negotiation is that a quantified "bottom line" prevents both the client and the negotiator from being "swept away" during the negotiation process. Without an explicit *minimum disposition,* a lawyer occasionally accepts a bad deal for her client because she becomes anxious or is persuaded by the other party's assertions during bargaining.

Determining the client's *minimum disposition* in advance of the negotiation, however, may be both unrealistic and undesirable. Any consideration of a "bottom line" prior to the negotiation requires an understanding of both the alternatives to settlement and the likely settlement outcome. At this early stage, though, the information available to lawyer and client usually is incomplete: lawyers typically begin negotiating prior to completing their own investigation of facts, legal research and discovery. In addition, the lawyer is unaware at this stage of how the other side views the case and of additional facts and information that will be gleaned from the other party during the negotiation process. The lawyer, therefore, should make disclaimers about the adequacy of her information during her counseling sessions with the client concerning alternatives. These same factors suggest that any *minimum disposition* determined by the client at this time be regarded as flexible and subject to change as the negotiation continues.

Fisher and Ury, leading proponents of problem-solving bargaining, suggest two additional reasons why a client should not set a "bottom line" prior to bargaining. First, the bottom line is likely to be set too high. Before hearing from the other party, and at a time when uncertainty prevails, it is very easy for the client and the attorney to assess the client's situation through "rose-colored glasses." There is a natural tendency among most people, including lawyers, to defer bad news as long as possible; one reason is that lawyers may believe that good news assists client relations. After all, the other party's unwillingness to fulfill the client's expectations always can be blamed on "unreasonableness." If a rigid *minimum disposition* is set too high, according to Fisher and Ury, the client may subsequently decide to reject a negotiated settlement that meets his interests.

In addition, as with the adoption of a fixed negotiation position, a specific *minimum disposition* inhibits *problem-solving* bargaining. . . .

Regardless of whether a lawyer believes that on balance it is good negotiation practice to establish a *minimum disposition,* she should review with the client his alternatives to the negotiated agreement and determine his "Best Alternative to a Negotiated Agreement" or "BATNA." Fisher and Ury use this term to represent the option available to the client that best satisfies his interests if the negotiation is unsuccessful; they suggest that the client's BATNA be the standard against which any negotiated agreement be measured. In many cases, the client's explicit awareness of his BATNA prevents him from being too optimistic about his prospects if negotiation deadlock occurs. In other cases, it prevents the client from being overly pessimistic and thus entering into an agreement that is not as satisfactory to him as an available alternative.

One of the most valuable types of expertise that the experienced lawyer brings to her professional relationship with her client is knowledge and inventiveness about possible alternatives to the negotiated agreement. . . . [I]f a client is interested in purchasing a small chain of nursing homes, he will be interested in knowing the purchase price of comparable businesses which have sold recently, and what other investment opportunities may be available to him. In many instances, the client will know more about the alternatives than anyone else, and sometimes he will have his own professional investment counselors or accountants to rely upon. In other situations, however, depending upon the nature of the relationship agreed upon by the lawyer and the client, the lawyer also might be expected to provide advice of this kind. If the lawyer is not aware of the necessary information from her own professional experience and background, she needs to research her client's alternatives by consulting with other appropriate professionals. . . .

Regardless of whether the lawyer and client decide upon a rigid *minimum disposition* figure prior to negotiation, or only evaluate the client's Best Alternative to a Negotiated Agreement, each serves as a check on the negotiator. Many lawyers also establish a negotiation *target*. The *target* is set at some level above the *minimum disposition* acceptable to the client, and provides a higher level of satisfaction to the client than an agreement that achieves only the client's *minimum disposition*. Interestingly, the empirical work of Karass suggests that negotiators who have "higher targets" or greater aspirations achieve more for their clients in negotiations than others. In addition, a negotiation *target* can serve as a "tripwire" in a negotiation; when the negotiator makes a proposal on an issue that is less advantageous than the negotiation target, she knows the bargaining is approaching her client's minimum requirements.

The lawyer should also evaluate the other party's alternatives to the negotiated agreement. It is useful to the lawyer to understand the other party's probable BATNA for prediction of eventual agreement and detection of bluffing. Understanding the other party's interests also assists the lawyer in her efforts to use *problem-solving* methods.

In summary, prior to the negotiation the lawyer and client dyad should discuss the client's interests, the chosen negotiation strategy's implications for the client, and alternatives to a negotiated agreement for both the client and the other party. The balance of the prenegotiation planning conference depends upon whether the issues to be negotiated have *integrative* potential or are predominantly *distributive* ones, and upon whether the lawyer intends to use *competitive, cooperative,* or *problem-solving* tactics, or a mixture of strategies.

*

Section II

Negotiation as a Behavioral Process of Interpersonal Communication

As demonstrated in the previous section, most negotiations have predictable patterns and structures. The emphasis in Section One was on describing what people **do** when they bargain. Contemporary empirical scholarship provided the roadmap for understanding effective strategy selection. We explored how bargainers can avoid exploitation and can make decisions to optimize the opportunity to get what they want and need from the transaction.

This does not mean, however, that negotiators with similar information and bargaining strategies will reach similar outcomes. To the contrary, both quantitative empirical data and the qualitative observations of a generation of trainers suggests that the negotiator's personality and behavioral characteristics are vitally connected to bargaining outcomes. The readings of this section highlight some of the themes relevant to the role of behavior and personality in negotiating. Our focus is not so much on what people **do** but on who they **are**; and how who they are affects effective negotiation results.

Chapter 6

NEGOTIATION AS A BEHAVIORAL PHENOMENON

In this chapter's provocative introductory reading, Leonard Greenhalgh considers the implications of the relationship that develops as parties negotiate on the outcome of their bargaining. He challenges the assumption that negotiation behavior is adequately explained by individual value maximization theories. To Greenhalgh, the parties' developing personal relationship determines how negotiations proceed as much as does their effort to maximize utility. He believes bargainers come to the process with a guiding metaphor that defines their bargaining relationship. They make commitments to the relationship that relate to these animating metaphors, and make strategic decisions based in part upon their prior exchange history, either positive or negative. Their bargaining relationship is further influenced by role definition, and by their assessment of the probable duration of the bargaining relationship. Value maximization theories do not account adequately for the critical influence of trust between bargainers on the perceived value of any outcome.

The remaining readings in this chapter explore some intriguing avenues of research into the personal ingredients of effective negotiation. If Greenhalgh is correct, and relationships influence negotiation outcomes as much as economic rationality, then how does an effective negotiator build a good relationship? Roger Fisher and Wayne Davis recount six interpersonal communication traits that can enhance negotiation effectiveness, and outline prescriptive suggestions for how to develop and practice them. Not surprisingly, the authors produce a catalogue that emphasizes Fisher's predisposition for "principled" or integrative attributes.

One additional critical point remains. If personal relationships materially influence bargaining outcomes, and parties can develop skills to foster good bargaining relationships, what explains why negotiators frequently find themselves adrift in irrationality as they attempt to reach agreement? The next three writings help us develop explanations.

Robert Mnookin begins the conversation by cataloguing four of the barriers that may constrain negotiated agreements. His observations have broad application when third party mediators work to help bargainers overcome these barriers. Next, in an excerpt from an influential research symposium on the study of negotiation, Max Bazerman looks more specifically at the cognitive barriers to agreement that Mnookin identified. Bazerman suggests how errors in judgment lead to ineffective outcomes, and how we can build a prescriptive theory to "eliminate these deficiencies from the negotiator's cognitive repertoire." His description of framing behavior is especially useful, and is considered at length.

In the final reading in this chapter, Gary Goodpaster looks at the "cognitive illusions" that can lead to irrational negotiation behavior. His inventory of potential impediments to rational bargaining, and the examples he chooses to illustrate them, can help to reduce the prospect of making strategic errors because of unnoticed or misunderstood psychological phenomena such as issue framing, focal anchoring, efforts to recoup sunk costs and the need to save face.

Readings

1. Leonard Greenhalgh, *Relationships in Negotiations,* 3 Negot.J. 235, 235–43 (1987).
2. Roger Fisher & Wayne H. Davis, *Six Basic Interpersonal Skills for a Negotiator's Repertoire,* 3 Negot.J. 117, 117–22 (1987).
3. Robert H. Mnookin, *Why Negotiations Fail: An Exploration of the Barriers to the Resolution of Conflict,* 8 Ohio St.J. on Disp.Resol. 235, 235–47 (1993).
4. Max H. Bazerman, *Negotiator Judgment,* 27 Am.Beh.Scientist 211, 211–24 (1985).
5. Gary Goodpaster, Negotiation and Mediation: A Guide to Negotiation and Negotiated Dispute Resolution 123–35 (1997) (also in 8 Ohio St.J. on Disp. Resol. 299, 344–59 (1993).
6. For Further Reading
    a. Max H. Bazerman, Judgment in Managerial Decision Making (1994).
    b. Max H. Bazerman & Margaret A. Neale, Negotiating Rationally (1992).
    c. David Binder, Paul Bergman & Susan C. Price, Lawyers as Counselors: A Client–Centered Approach (1991).
    d. John W. Cooley, *The Geometries of Situation and Emotions and the Calculus of Change in Negotiation and Mediation,* 29 Valparaiso U.L.Rev. 1 (1994).
    e. Daniel Druckman, ed., Negotiations: Social–Psychological Perspectives (1977).
    f. Roger Fisher & Scott Brown, Getting Together: Building a Relationship That Gets to Yes (1988).
    g. Robert H. Frank, Passions Within Reason: The Strategic Role of the Emotions (1988).
    h. Roderick W. Gilkey & Leonard Greenhalgh, *The Role of Personality in Successful Negotiating,* 2 Negot.J. 245 (1986).
    i. Daniel Kahneman & Amos Tversky, *Prospect Theory: An Analysis of Decision Under Risk,* 47 Econometrica 263 (1979).
    j. Daniel Kahneman, *Reference Points, Anchors, Norms and Mixed Feelings,* 51 Org.Beh. & Hum.Dec.Proc. 296 (1992).
    k. Daniel Kahneman & Amos Tversky, *Conflict Resolution: A Psychological Perspective,* in Barriers to Conflict Resolution (Kenneth Arrow, *et al.,* eds. (1995)).
    l. Roderick M. Kramer & David M. Messick, eds., Negotiations as a Social Process (1995).

m. Gary Lowenthal, *A General Theory of Negotiation Process, Strategy, and Behavior,* 31 U.Kansas L.Rev. 69 (1982).

n. John Murray, *Considering a Negotiator's View of the Court Process,* 2 J. on Disp.Res. 223 (1987).

o. Margaret A. Neale & Max H. Bazerman, *The Effects of Framing and Negotiator Overconfidence on Bargaining Behaviors,* 28 Acad.Mgmt.J. 34 (1985).

p. Margaret A. Neale & Max H. Bazerman, Cognition and Rationality in Negotiation (1991).

q. Linda Putnam & Michael E. Roloff, eds., Communication and Negotiation (1992).

r. Howard Raiffa, *Analytical Barriers,* in Barriers to Conflict Resolution (Kenneth Arrow, *et al.,* eds. (1995)).

s. Douglas Rosenthal, Lawyer and Client: Who's In Charge? (1974).

t. Lee Ross & Constance Stillinger, *Barriers to Conflict Resolution,* 7 Negot.J. 389 (1991).

u. Lee Ross, *Reactive Devaluation in Negotiation and Conflict Resolution,* in Barriers to Conflict Resolution (Kenneth Arrow, *et al.,* eds. (1995)).

v. Leigh Thompson, Kathleen L. Valley & Roderick M. Kramer, *The Bittersweet Feeling of Success: An Examination of Social Perception in Negotiation,* 31 J.Exper.Social Psych. 467 (1995).

w. Amos Tversky & Daniel Kahneman, *The Framing of Decisions and the Rationality of Choice,* 211 Science 453 (1981).

x. William Ury, Getting Past No: Dealing With Difficult People (1991).

y. Richard Walton, Managing Conflict: Interpersonal Dialogue and Third–Party Roles (2d ed. 1987).

z. Andrew Watson, *Mediation and Negotiation: Learning to Deal with Psychological Responses,* 18 J. of Law Reform 293 (1985).

aa. H. Peyton Young, ed., Negotiation Analysis (1992).

LEONARD GREENHALGH, RELATIONSHIPS IN NEGOTIATIONS

3 Negot.J. 235–43 (1987).

Soviet General Secretary Mikhail Gorbachev startled President Reagan in September 1986 by inviting him to meet face-to-face in Iceland. The reported basis of Gorbachev's appeal was his exasperation with the Soviet and American bureaucracies that had been conducting arms control negotiations. Gorbachev urged that the two heads of state personally involve themselves in the process to make some progress toward agreement. Reagan, who is described by the press as a "believer in personal diplomacy," was intrigued, and accepted the opportunity.

The subsequent results of the Iceland summit aside, this dramatic turn of events in the *process* of negotiation between the superpowers highlights an aspect of negotiations that has yet to be fully explored—the relationship that evolves between negotiators or other key decisionmakers. This paper observes that the theories that guide our thinking about negotiation give too much attention to short-term economic rationality—negotiators' striving to maximize the benefit of a transaction—and not enough to what relationships are and how they affect negotiations.

. . .

Relationships need to be understood better by theorists, researchers and practitioners. A starting point in the quest for understanding is to consider what, exactly, *is* a relationship. Negotiators experience a relationship as some sort of bond between the parties, a sense of interconnectedness. The experience bond is associated with how they define the relationship, what they see to be their specific role in it, and the time horizon they take into account when dealing with each other. These facets of relationships are obviously not independent of each other, but each is worth considering separately because each has implications for the adequacy of the existing theories of negotiation.

A relationship is subjectively experienced. Therefore the nature of the relationship depends on each negotiator's somewhat idiosyncratic view of the bond between the parties. Three factors affect this view: how negotiators visualize their interdependence, the type of commitment the negotiator has made to the other party, and the degree of indebtedness he or she feels.

Visualizing Interdependence. Interdependence is an abstract concept. Negotiators think about interdependence by visualizing something less abstract. The tangible imagery they use is known as a guiding metaphor. The choice of metaphor can make a big difference in a negotiator's definition of the relationship because different metaphors have different implications for the negotiator's sense of duty, concern for the other party's interests, obligations, and expectations.

Suppose the negotiator thinks about the interaction with the other party as a chess game. This metaphor implies that the objective is to outwit the opponent by deceiving, trapping, and then overwhelming him or her. In this scenario, the other party is viewed as a ruthless competitor who is constantly plotting ways to undermine, dominate, and if possible, eliminate the negotiator. Many scholars have noted, usually uncritically, that this metaphor dominates thinking about international relations.

A common alternative metaphor is to view the negotiation as a debate in which the person making the best argument wins. The implications of this imagery are that the negotiator's objective is to make the best case for his or her interests, try to refute rather than accommodate the other party's case, then let an external judge decide who won. People using this metaphor are likely to see litigation as an obvious mechanism for dealing with disputes.

A third metaphor many negotiators use is to visualize the parties as if they were a family unit in which they both make contributions for the good of the unit, help to solve the problems facing it, and value their membership in the unit for its own sake, not just from the tangible benefits that can be gained from interacting with the other party.

It should be obvious that the negotiator's choice of guiding metaphors is crucial. Because it affects how they define the relationship, the chosen metaphor determines how negotiators behave toward the other party and what behavior is elicited in response.

Commitments. The relationship as defined by negotiators is not only shaped by guiding metaphors, but is also the result of commitments to the other party. Negotiators can be more or less committed to the relationship. Furthermore, the scope of the commitment may range from specific actions to general end-states, and commitments may be independent of interests. Some examples will illustrate the diverse forms commitments can take.

Whether there is more or less commitment to a relationship can often be seen in the way couples negotiate when they experience marital strains. In such cases, the degree of commitment to the relationship is usually reflected in the sacrifices each party will make to save the marriage. When companies become "couples" of sorts—by means of mergers and acquisitions—each party can likewise be more or less committed to the relationship. A low-commitment intercorporate relationship may be evident after a hostile takeover, when the acquiring company strips the acquired company of its cash, fires people and makes other short-term cuts in expenses to give the acquired company favorable financial ratios, then resells it. (This scenario, I realize, sounds more like corporate rape than corporate marriage, but it does illustrate a low-commitment relationship.) In contrast, the acquisition may be a friendly one that accomplishes vertical integration for both companies and thereby meets complementary needs. Both parties in this case are likely to be more highly committed to the relationship.

In addition to the variability one would expect in the intensity of the commitment, there is considerable variability in its scope. A limited-scope commitment would be to a specific action. The negotiator promises to do something—say, to sell spare parts at cost—and becomes committed to do it even if the agreement is not legally enforceable and is contrary to the negotiator's interests. This type of commitment is narrowest in scope when the negotiator does no less, and no more, than the specific action promised. Broader in scope would be a commitment to achieve a certain end-state; for example, to provide an R & D group with the resources necessary to develop a new technology. Such a commitment would be broad in scope because the nature and amount of resources needed by the R & D group are unlikely to be known in advance.

Since the notion of commitment to a relationship is so important in understanding the broad range of negotiated solutions to disputes, it is amazing that almost nothing has been written about this topic. Commitment provides a perspective that is quite different from the way most economists, social psychologists, and legal researchers focus on negotiations. First, a lack of commitment can make administering a labor contract or verifying a nuclear disarmament treaty a nightmare; and even when enforcement is feasible, practitioners strongly prefer high-intensity, high-scope commitment. Second, commitment explains economically irrational behavior whereby people often make and honor agreements even when doing so has negative utility.

Third, the notion of commitment to a relationship limits the usefulness of the "best alternative to a negotiated agreement" (BATNA) concept. Inherent in the BATNA idea is the assumption that negotiators will walk away from an agreement if there is a higher-utility alternative outside the relationship. This concept, in my opinion, assumes that either the parties' commitment to the relationship is zero, or that the parties factor in the cost of sacrificing the relationship when assessing the utility of offers. Both assumptions seem unrealistic when applied to day-to-day negotiations in the real world.

Imagine, for instance, a dispute between a woman and her husband. He wants her companionship in social and leisure events, but she is too busy with her medical practice. The BATNA concept assumes the husband will seriously consider meeting his social needs outside the marriage when evaluating her counteroffers. Examples involving others with whom one frequently negotiates show similar shortcomings of the BATNA concept—for example, negotiations with one's boss, children, key customers, social organizations, and any other entity to which one has a strong, ongoing relationship.

Indebtedness. Negotiators' feelings of indebtedness toward the other party have an effect beyond the way the relationship is visualized and the negotiator's commitment to it.

Psychologists and sociologists who have evolved the Exchange Theory point of view have noted that in ongoing relationships, as contrasted with brief encounters, there is a sense of cumulative, mutual indebtedness that bonds the parties together. One person may express this by saying of his negotiating partner, "she has done so much for me over the years." The social bonding that results from such a complex, mutually-beneficial exchange relationship can result in a "we" feeling that deemphasizes self-interest and zero-sum thinking, and is the cause of concessionary behavior that might be considered economically irrational.

The history of exchange between the parties may, of course, have negative rather than positive consequences for the parties' definition of the relationship. Conflict escalation occurs when one party perceives an imbalance in hostile acts. This principle is internalized at an early age. For instance, the child engaged in a playground fight might say, "You kicked me and pulled my hair; all I did was bite you." Both children know the conflict is unstable in the two-for-one scenario. The one child feels the need to slap the other, and the other child may well acquiesce to it in order to restore the balance of exchange.

The equal harm principle is preserved in the thinking of adults, such that the history of negative exchange may also be a crucial factor in shaping how negotiators conceive of the relationship. In extreme cases of long-term mutual hostility, the relationship may be poisoned to the point of precluding the resolution of specific disputes through negotiation. As examples, the conflicts in Northern Ireland and the Middle East may be unresolvable through negotiation as a result of their long histories of negative exchange. This enmity happens in social units smaller than cultures. Representatives of rival corporations, or of union and management within a corporation, can experience similar levels of bitterness and hostility. Families can get into feuds with other families. And individuals can become sworn enemies for life. Irrespective of the size of the party involved, the result is apparent economic irrationality, in that the parties engage in self-defeating behavior in order to deny benefits to the other party.

Whether positive or negative, the history of exchange—along with anticipated future exchange—needs to be taken into account in a comprehensive theory of negotiation. The theory should recognize that the objective value or harm of a negotiator's actions is less important than how these actions are subjectively *experienced* by the other party.

In the case of positive exchange, the raw utility of benefits received would be modified by the receiving party's attributions of why the benefits were given. For example, if the giver is perceived to have had no choice, such as when a pay raise is given to a subordinate because Congress increased the minimum wage, then the receiver of the benefit may feel no obligation to reciprocate the benefit. Similarly, a favor that represents a big sacrifice for one person incurs a greater obligation than does the same favor from someone who could supply it with little sacrifice.

. . .

NEGOTIATORS' EXPERIENCED ROLES

The preceding section explored various facets of how negotiators define the terms of their relationship with the other party. This section explores how they define their own roles in the interaction. Negotiators primarily take on one of three possible roles: a principal negotiating for his or her own interests; a representative of some constituency who is negotiating for the constituency's interests; or some other social role not immediately relevant to the economic consequences of the transaction—such as a friend, watchdog, devil's advocate, authority figure, reference group member, expert, or the like. Role posture can have a strong effect on the experienced relationship.

The vast majority of research on negotiations involves interactions between principals. When one or both negotiators are acting as representatives of some constituency whose interests are at stake, the dynamics of the transaction—and the relationship—become more complex. Scholars, most notably Richard Walton and Robert McKersie, have described the complexities involved in negotiating as a representative. However, comparatively little empirical research has been done to explore systematically the dynamics of transactions between and among representatives—and even less on the dynamics of relationships between and among representatives.

. . .

Roles other than principal or representative can produce different dynamics in the transaction, and may shape the relationship. Suppose Joe is negotiating with Sue, a long-time friend, over the price of some antique furniture she wants to buy. Joe can either deal with Sue in her role as friend or essentially treat their friendship as irrelevant in the transaction and negotiate "at arms length." In the arms-length case, he would be dealing with her in her role as principal, and the outcome of their negotiation would presumably be determined largely by its economic rationality. Alternatively, Joe can deal with Sue primarily in her role as friend, in which case the outcome would be influenced by their history of exchange, commitment to the relationship, and other factors less relevant to economic rationality than to the relationship itself.

. . .

Assumed role is important in negotiations because it shapes how negotiators experience the relationship. The farther the experienced role gets from the principal role, the more that models of bargaining based on the economic rationality of the transaction have to be modified to maintain their explanatory power.

A Negotiator's Time Horizon

The third major factor that influences relationships is the time horizon that is salient to the negotiator. A transaction can be viewed by the negotiator as a single episode or as just one event in a long-term series of interactions. These alternative viewpoints make a big difference in how the negotiation unfolds and in the type of model needed to understand the negotiation.

An episodic view occurs when negotiators treat the immediate transaction as a one-time deal (irrespective of whether they in fact will go on interacting with the other party). From this perspective, the past and future of the relationship are not considered. Negotiators whose definition of the situation is strongly shaped by sports metaphors tend to see transactions as "games" in which anything that happened in previous "games" is irrelevant. Thus, an episodic view precludes a negotiator from feeling indebted to the other party, and even close friends may find the rich and complex history of exchange disregarded. Because the future is also irrelevant (next time, it's a "new game") in the context of an episodic view, negotiators choose tactics without fear of repercussions, and negotiations may degenerate into competitive decisionmaking aimed at maximizing self-interest, or worse, beating the opponent even if this does not maximize self-interest.

The perspective is quite different when negotiators keep the long-term relationship in focus. In addition to taking into consideration the history of exchange and showing restraint in their choice of tactics, negotiators with this view experience less urgency to maximize their gain in the current transaction. Their generosity in this dispute will obligate the other party to reciprocate in the next dispute, therefore their concessions are viewed as investments rather than unrecoverable losses.

Trust in Relationships

The preceding discussion explored various dimensions of relationships. All of these are important because they influence a negotiator's summary assessment of the relationship. This assessment is made not only in terms of the benefit (or "utility") to be derived from the relationship, but also in terms of *trust*.

The bargaining theory available to us does not do justice to the importance of trust. In the majority of studies, the trust variable is accommodated, if at all, simply as a predictive factor used to discount the expected value of various outcomes obtainable from the other party. Thus, the theory might hold that a negotiator would be indifferent between a low-expectation, high-value outcome and a high-expectation, low-value outcome. Indeed, laboratory simulations can be staged in such a tightly constrained manner that negotiators will make choices that support such theories, but these studies do not seem to go far in enriching our understanding of trust and its role in negotiations.

In real-world negotiations, trust is a much richer concept. In practical terms, trust involves the extent to which a negotiator honors commitments, norms, and principles of fairness. Trust applies bilaterally (or multilaterally in the case of multiparty negotiations): there is the extent to which a negotiator is willing to live up to the trust placed in him or her, and the negotiator's trust in the other party.

Trust embodies a negotiator's summary judgments about the nature and strength of the relationship. It is affected by—and in turn, affects—all of the facets of relationships discussed above. Trust is what Gorbachev and Reagan needed to establish in the Iceland meeting. Without it, verification becomes of paramount concern in the arms control agreement they both sought, and both sides need to impose surveillance requirements the other cannot tolerate. Trust is also precisely what makes a Japanese contract viable.

A negotiator's trust in the other party arises from his or her assessment of how the other party conceives of the relationship in terms of commitment, experienced role, indebtedness, and perceived interdependence. Negotiators are therefore vigilant in seeking clues to the other party's trustworthiness during interactions. In fact, a large part of "getting to know" or "developing rapport with" the other party involves developing trust and learning the limits of the other party's trustworthiness.

Trust is a vitally important factor in real-world negotiations. And, as with commitment, negotiation theory and research literature pays little attention to this crucial factor.

Until we develop more comprehensive theories, we must remain keenly aware of the limitations of thinking about negotiations in terms of the economics of the immediate transaction, rather than in terms of how that transaction fits into the broader relationship between the parties.

ROGER FISHER AND WAYNE H. DAVIS, SIX BASIC INTERPERSONAL SKILLS FOR A NEGOTIATOR'S REPERTOIRE

3 Negot.J. 117, 117–22 (1987).

There is an infinite range and variety in interpersonal skills. Many of these skills can be seen as attractive opposites, such as being independent and being cooperative, or being pragmatic and being imaginative, or being controlled and being expressive. We would like to be good at both but tend to be stronger in one than the other.

These desirable qualities can be visualized as lying on the circumference of a circle, so that becoming more skillful is seen as extending our skills in all directions. Improving our skills can then be recognized not as correcting a fault (such as "I am too flexible"), but rather as becoming more skillful at its attractive opposite (e.g., "I want to become better at being firm when that is appropriate.").

To broaden one's repertoire, it may help to think of these qualities as falling into six basic categories of interpersonal skills in which each effective negotiator enjoys some competence and confidence. We have tentatively identified these as follows:

- expressing strong feelings appropriately;
- remaining rational in the face of strong feelings;
- being assertive within a negotiation without damaging the relationship;

- improving a relationship without damage to a particular negotiation;

- speaking clearly in ways that promote listening; and

- inquiring and listening effectively.

In use, these skills are often closely associated with each other, but in developing the skills and in practicing them it helps to focus on them one at a time. The following checklist can be used as a guide for negotiators who wish to develop a strong, well-balanced repertoire.

EXPRESSING STRONG FEELINGS APPROPRIATELY

. . .

- *Recognize feelings.* A negotiator needs to recognize that feelings are a natural human phenomenon. They exist. There is nothing wrong with *having* emotions, although *expressing* them in particular ways may be costly or counterproductive.

- *Be aware.* It is a wise practice to become *aware* of the emotions—both our own and those of the other side—that are involved in any given negotiation. It appears to be true that if we suppress or deny our own feelings, we are likely to be unaware of the feelings of those with whom we are dealing. Before we can safely and appropriately express our feelings, we need to become aware of them, and to acknowledge them consciously.

In general, when some feeling inside seems to be growing larger and out of control, naming or identifying that feeling internally will, by itself, tend to reduce the feeling, make it more life-size, and help bring it under control.

- *Develop a range of expression.* When it comes to communicating feelings to someone else, it is well to recognize that there is a spectrum of ways to do so, ranging from talking rationally about them, through increasing the emotional content of verbal and nonverbal communication, to letting the emotions take charge.

. . .

- *Relate tone to substance.* Too often we fail to relate the emotional content of a communication to the substantive issue being discussed. It is far easier to be assertive—and certainly more effective—if we have something sensible to assert. Key to an effective communication of feeling is likely to be some well-prepared substantive content that identifies the purpose of the communication, justifies the feeling, and enlists its expression in the furtherance of that purpose.

REMAINING RATIONAL IN THE FACE OF STRONG FEELINGS

. . .

There are several different ways to deal effectively with displays of strong emotion in negotiation. Depending on the circumstances, any one of the following suggestions should prove useful:

- *Acknowledge their feelings.* When others begin to heighten the emotive content of their speech, they may not be fully aware of the feelings growing inside them. If we acknowledge that they *may* (don't attribute!) be feeling a certain way, that will usually help them to become more aware and in control of their feelings, and give us enough distance so that we don't react.

- *Step above the fray.* When the discussion turns so emotional that rational discussion seems pointless, we might withdraw from the discussion long enough for us and others to regain some composure. State frankly our reasons for withdrawing, and couple that with a commitment to return.

- *Step aside; let their emotions hit the problem.* If they're expressing an emotion, encourage them to express it fully and completely—so they can feel that they've "got it all out."

- *Separate the causes of their feelings from the substantive problem, and deal with them in parallel.* Once feelings have been fully expressed and acknowledged, it may be appropriate to analyze what engendered the feelings and take steps to alleviate those causes.

- *Be purposive.* At the outset, consciously consider and decide on the purpose of the negotiation. Then, when emotions run too strong, we can ask the parties to question whether or not the direction of the discussion serves the agreed-upon purposes of the meeting.

BEING ASSERTIVE WITHOUT DAMAGING THE RELATIONSHIP

.   .   .

With or without increasing the emotional content of our expressions, it is possible to be assertive without damage to a relationship. The suggested general strategy is:

- *Disentangle relationship issues from substantive ones and work on them in parallel.* Although substantive disagreements can make a working relationship more difficult, and although a good working relationship can make it easier to reach agreement, the process of dealing with differences is usefully treated as a subject quite distinct and separate from the content and extent of those differences.

- *Be "soft on the people."* Avoid personal judgments. Acknowledge some merit in what the other side has said or done. Be open, polite, courteous, and considerate.

- *Have something to assert.* Know the *purpose* of the session in terms of some product that it is reasonable to expect. Focus on one or two points that we would like to communicate forcefully, such as: the strength of our BATNA (Best Alternative to a Negotiated Agreement); the necessity of meeting some interest of ours; or our adherence to a particular standard of legitimacy unless and until we are convinced that some other standard is at least equally fair.

- *Be firm and open.* Be prepared to remain firm as long as that appears to us to make sense on the substance of the negotiation. At the same time, be open—both in words and thought—to alternative views that are truly persuasive.

IMPROVING A RELATIONSHIP WITHOUT DAMAGE TO A PARTICULAR NEGOTIATION

. . .

- *Good relations help reach good outcomes.* It is important to recognize that relationship-building moves tend to strengthen rather than weaken our chances for achieving a good agreement.

- *Acknowledge merit in something they have done.* It is almost always possible to find something meritorious that the other side has done— perhaps in an area apart from what is being negotiated. By acknowledging that, we can communicate that we recognize and respect their worth as people.

- *Acknowledge a need on our part.* Relationships tend to be stronger when there is some interdependence: both sides feel and recognize their need or reliance on the other side in order to achieve mutually-desired ends.

- *Take steps outside the negotiation to improve the relationship.* We can concentrate our relationship-building actions in temporally-discrete segments of the negotiation, or when we are physically away from the table.

SPEAKING CLEARLY IN WAYS THAT PROMOTE LISTENING

. . .

- *Speak for yourself.* Phrase statements about their behavior, motives, statements, etc. in first-person terms of our perceptions and feelings. They may deny the accusation, "You're a bigot!" They can't deny the statement, "I'm feeling discriminated against."

- *Avoid attribution and check assumptions.* Recognize when we make assumptions about their thoughts, feelings, motives, and so on, and try to verify those assumptions with the other side before acting on them. Inquire about their understanding of the background issues or information.

- *Use short, clear statements.* The longer any statement we make, the more they will edit it so they can respond. The more important our message is, the more succinct it should be. If the message is complex, break it down into small parts and confirm their understanding of each segment.

- *Ask them to repeat back what we've said.* In effect, encourage them to be active listeners by asking them to confirm in their own words what they've heard us say.

ACTIVELY INQUIRING AND LISTENING

. . .

- *Explicitly allocate time to listen and understand the other side.* Set portions of the agenda for them to explain their interests and ideas. That helps to put us into a "listening mode." An added benefit of this practice is that it establishes a precedent for reciprocal treatment of us by them.

- *Separate understanding their arguments from judging and responding to them.* Make sure that their full argument has been stated, and that we understand it before trying to respond.

- *Repeat back their statements in our own words.*

- *Inquire actively about the reasoning behind their statements.* Even if we repeat back what they said, often they haven't said all they were thinking. There will be some implicit reasoning or logic underlying their statements. It's helpful to ask them to make that reasoning explicit, and then to repeat back their explanation.

ROBERT H. MNOOKIN, WHY NEGOTIATIONS FAIL: AN EXPLORATION OF BARRIERS TO THE RESOLUTION OF CONFLICT

8 Ohio St.J. on Disp.Res. 235, 235–47 (1993).

Conflict is inevitable, but efficient and fair resolution is not. Conflicts can persist even though there may be any number of possible resolutions that would better serve the interests of the parties—the recent history of ethnic and religious strife in Lebanon, Israel, Cyprus, and Yugoslavia serves as a reminder of this. In our everyday personal and professional lives, we have all witnessed disputes where the absence of a resolution imposes substantial and avoidable costs on all parties. Moreover, many resolutions that are achieved—whether through negotiation or imposition—conspicuously fail to satisfy the economist's criterion of Pareto efficiency. Let me offer a few examples where, at least with the benefit of hindsight, it is easy to identify alternative resolutions that might have left both parties better off.

. . .

A conflict between Eastern Airlines and its unions represents a conspicuous example of a lose-lose outcome. In 1986, Frank Lorenzo took over Eastern, then the eighth largest American airline, with over 42,000 employees and about 1,000 daily flights to seventy cities. For the next three years, Lorenzo, considered a union buster by organized labor, pressed the airline's unions for various concessions, and laid off workers to reduce costs. The unions retaliated in a variety of ways, including a public relations campaign suggesting Eastern's airplanes were being improperly maintained because Lorenzo was inappropriately cutting costs. In March 1989, labor-management skirmishes turned into all-out war. Eastern's machinists went on strike, and the pilots and flight attendants initially joined in. The ensuing "no holds barred" battle between Lorenzo and the machinists led to losses on both sides.

Soon after the strike began, to put pressure on the unions and to avoid creditor claims, Eastern's management filed for bankruptcy, hired permanent replacements for the strikers, and began to sell off assets. While the pilots and flight attendants held out only a few months, the machinists union persisted in its strike, determined to get rid of Lorenzo at whatever cost. In one sense, they succeeded, for in 1990 the bankruptcy court forced Lorenzo to relinquish control of Eastern. It turned out to be a pyrrhic victory for the union, however, for on January 18, 1991, Eastern Airlines permanently shut down operations.

The titanic struggle between Texaco and Pennzoil over Getty Oil provides another example of a bargaining failure, although of a somewhat more subtle sort. Here, both corporations survived, with a clear winner and loser; Texaco paid Pennzoil $3 billion in cash to end the dispute in 1988. The parties reached settlement, however, only after a year-long bankruptcy proceeding for Texaco and protracted legal wrangling in various courts. While the dispute dragged on, the combined equity value of the two companies was reduced by some $3.4 billion. A settlement *before* Texaco filed for bankruptcy would have used up fewer social resources and would have been more valuable to the shareholders of both companies than the resolution created by the bankruptcy court about a year later.

. . .

On her death bed, Gertrude Stein was asked by Alice B. Toklas, "What is the answer? What is the answer?" After a long silence, Stein responded: "No, what is the question?" Examples like these, and I am sure you could add many more of your own, suggest a central question for those of us concerned with dispute resolution: Why is it that under circumstances where there are resolutions that better serve disputants, negotiations often fail to achieve efficient resolutions? In other words, what are the barriers to the negotiated resolution of conflict?

. . .

A. STRATEGIC BARRIERS

The first barrier to the negotiated resolution of conflict is inherent in a central characteristic of negotiation. Negotiation can be metaphorically compared to making a pie and then dividing it up. The process of conflict resolution affects both the size of the pie, and who gets what size slice.

The disputants' behavior may affect the size of the pie in a variety of ways. On the one hand, spending on avoidable legal fees and other process costs shrinks the pie. On the other hand, negotiators can together "create value" and make the pie bigger by discovering resolutions in which each party contributes special complementary skills that can be combined in a synergistic way, or by exploiting differences in relative preferences that permit trades that make both parties better off. Books like "Getting to Yes" and proponents of "win-win negotiation" emphasize the potential benefits of collaborative problem-solving approaches to negotiation which allow parties to maximize the size of the pie.

Negotiation also involves issues concerning the distribution of benefits, and, with respect to pure distribution, both parties cannot be made better off at the same time. Given a pie of fixed size, a larger slice for you means a smaller one for me.

Because bargaining typically entails both efficiency issues (that is, how big the pie can be made) and distributive issues (that is, who gets what size slice), negotiation involves an inherent tension—one that David Lax and James Sebenius have dubbed the "negotiator's dilemma." In order to create value, it is critically important that options be created in light of both parties' underlying interests and preferences. This suggests the importance of openness and disclosure, so that a variety of options can be analyzed and compared from the perspectives of all concerned. However, when it comes to the distributive aspects of bargaining, full disclosure—particularly if unreciprocated by the other side—can often lead to outcomes in which the more open party receives a comparatively smaller slice. To put it another way, unreciprocated approaches to creating value leave their maker vulnerable to claiming tactics. On the other hand, focusing on the distributive aspects of bargaining can often lead to unnecessary deadlocks and, more fundamentally, a failure to discover options or alternatives that make both sides better off.

. . .

Strategic behavior—which may be rational for a self-interested party concerned with maximizing the size of his or her own slice—can often lead to inefficient outcomes. Those subjected to claiming tactics often respond in kind, and the net result typically is to push up the cost of the dispute resolution process.... Parties may be tempted to engage in strategic behavior, hoping to get more. Often all they do is shrink the size of the pie. Those experienced in the civil litigation process see this all the time. One or both sides often attempt to use pre-trial discovery as leverage to force the other side into agreeing to a more favorable settlement. Often the net result, however, is simply that both sides spend unnecessary money on the dispute resolution process.

B. THE PRINCIPAL/AGENT PROBLEM

The second barrier is suggested by recent work relating to transaction cost economics, and is sometimes called the "principal/agent" problem. Notwithstanding the jargon, the basic idea is familiar. The basic problem is that the incentives for an agent (whether it be a lawyer, employee, or officer) negotiating on behalf of a party to a dispute may induce behavior that fails to serve the interests of the principal itself. The relevant research suggests that it is no simple matter—whether by contract or custom—to align perfectly the incentives for an agent with the interests of the principal. This divergence may act as a barrier to efficient resolution of conflict.

Litigation is fraught with principal/agent problems. In civil litigation, for example—particularly where the lawyers on both sides are being paid by the hour—there is very little incentive for the opposing lawyers to cooperate, particularly if the clients have the capacity to pay for trench warfare and are angry to boot. Commentators have suggested that this is one reason many cases settle on the courthouse steps, and not before: for the lawyers, a late settlement may avoid the possible embarrassment of an extreme outcome, while at the same time providing substantial fees.

C. COGNITIVE BARRIERS

The third barrier is a by-product of the way the human mind processes information, deals with risks and uncertainties, and makes inferences and judgments. Research by cognitive psychologists during the last fifteen years suggests several ways in which human reasoning often departs from that suggested by theories of rational judgment and decision making. Daniel Kahneman and Amos Tversky have done research on a number of cognitive biases that are relevant to negotiation. I would like to focus on two aspects of their work: those relating to loss aversion and framing effects.

Suppose everyone attending this evening's lecture is offered the following happy choice: At the end of my lecture you can exit at the north end of the hall or the south end. If you choose the north exit, you will be handed an envelope in which there will be a crisp new twenty dollar bill. Instead, if you choose the south exit, you will be given a sealed envelope randomly pulled from a bin. One quarter of these envelopes contain a $100 bill, but three quarters are empty. In other words, you can have a sure gain of $20 if you go out the north door, or you can instead gamble by choosing the south door where you will have a 25% chance of winning $100 and a 75% chance of winning nothing. Which would you choose? A great deal of experimental work suggests that the overwhelming majority of you would choose the sure gain of $20, even though the "expected value" of the second alternative, $25, is slightly more. This is a well known phenomenon called "risk aversion." The principle is that most people will take a sure thing over a gamble, even where the gamble may have a somewhat higher "expected" payoff.

Daniel Kahneman and Amos Tversky have advanced our understanding of behavior under uncertainty with a remarkable discovery. They suggest that, in order to avoid what would otherwise be a sure loss, many people will gamble, even if the expected loss from the gamble is larger.

Loss aversion can act as a cognitive barrier to the negotiated resolution of conflict for a variety of reasons. For example, both sides may fight on in a dispute in the hope that they may avoid any losses, even though the continuation of the dispute involves a gamble in which the loss may end up being far greater. Loss aversion may explain Lyndon Johnson's decision, in 1965, to commit additional troops to Vietnam as an attempt to avoid the sure loss attendant to withdrawal, and as a gamble that there might be some way in the future to avoid any loss at all. Similarly, negotiators may, in some circumstances, be adverse to offering a concession in circumstances where they view the concession as a sure loss. Indeed, the notion of rights or entitlements may be associated with a more extreme form of loss aversion that Kahneman and Tversky call "enhanced loss aversion," because losses "compounded by outrage are much less acceptable than losses that are caused by misfortune or by legitimate actions of others."

One of the most striking features of loss aversion is that whether something is viewed as a gain or loss—and what kind of gain or loss it is considered—depends upon a reference point, and the choice of a reference point is sometimes manipulable.

. . .

The purpose of the hypotheticals is to suggest that whether or not an event is framed as a loss can often affect behavior. This powerful idea concerning "framing" has important implications for the resolution of disputes to which I will return later.

D. "REACTIVE DEVALUATION" OF COMPROMISES AND CONCESSIONS

The final barrier I wish to discuss is "reactive devaluation," and is an example of a social/psychological barrier that arises from the dynamics of the negotiation process and the inferences that negotiators draw from their interactions. My Stanford colleague, psychology Professor Lee Ross, and his students have done experimental work to suggest that, especially between adversaries, when one side offers a particular concession or proposes a particular exchange of compromises, the other side may diminish the attractiveness of that offer or proposed exchange simply because it originated with a perceived opponent. The basic notion is a familiar one, especially for lawyers. How often have you had a client indicate to you in the midst of litigation, "If only we could settle this case for $7,000. I'd love to put this whole matter behind me." Lo and behold, the next day, the other side's attorney calls and offers to settle for $7,000. You excitedly call your client and say, "Guess what—the other side has just offered to settle this case for $7,000." You expect to hear jubilation on the other end of the phone, but instead there is silence. Finally, your client says, "Obviously they must know something we don't know. If $7,000 is a good settlement for them, it can't be a good settlement for us."

Both in laboratory and field settings, Ross and his colleagues have marshalled interesting evidence for "reactive devaluation." They have demonstrated both that a given compromise proposal is rated less positively when proposed by someone on the other side than when proposed by a neutral or an ally. They also demonstrated that a concession that is actually offered is rated lower than a concession that is withheld, and that a compromise is rated less highly after it has been put on the table by the other side than it was beforehand.

. . .

Ross has described a range of cognitive and motivational processes that may account for the reactive devaluation phenomenon. Whatever its roots, reactive devaluation certainly can act as a barrier to the efficient resolution of conflict. It suggests that the exchange of proposed concessions and compromises between adversaries can be very problematic. When one side unilaterally offers a concession that it believes the other side should value and the other side reacts by devaluing the offer, this can obviously make resolution difficult. The recipient of a unilateral concession is apt to believe that her adversary has given up nothing of real value and may therefore resist any notion that she should offer something of real value in exchange. On the other hand, the failure to respond may simply confirm the suspicions of the original offeror, who will believe that her adversary is proceeding in bad faith and is being strategic.

MAX H. BAZERMAN, NEGOTIATOR JUDGMENT: A CRITICAL LOOK AT THE RATIONALITY ASSUMPTION

27 Am.Beh.Sci. 211, 211–24 (1985).

Prescriptive strategies focus on how negotiators should behave to maximize their utility. If followed, prescriptive approaches should increase the performance of negotiators. However, it is argued here that a number of systematic judgmental deficiencies impede individuals from implementing prescriptive strategies optimally. Specifically, the behavioral decision theory literature has proposed a number of cognitive limitations that inhibit our ability to follow prescriptive advice.

Negotiator judgment can be improved first by describing the ways in which negotiators deviate from rationality, and then by prescribing a strategy for eliminating these deficiencies from the negotiator's cognitive repertoire.

Eliminating these deficiencies from negotiator judgment allows the negotiator to come closer to following the advice of prescriptive research. Thus the two approaches are complementary rather than competing.

The core of this article describes five specific deviations from rationality that affect negotiator judgment. It then specifies how biased decision processes differ from prescriptive analyses of negotiator behavior, prescribes how negotiators can be trained to eliminate deviations from rationality, and shows how this research can be integrated with prescriptive research.

THE FRAMING OF NEGOTIATOR JUDGMENT

Consider the following two scenarios:

> You are a wholesaler of refrigerators. Corporate policy does not allow any flexibility in pricing. However, flexibility does exist in the expenses you can incur (shipping, financing terms, etc.), which have a direct effect on the profitability of the transaction. These expenses can all be costed out in dollar-value terms. You are negotiating a $10,000 sale. The buyer wants you to pay $2,000 in expenses. You want to pay less. When you negotiate the transaction, do you try to minimize your expenses (reduce these losses from the $2,000 figure) or maximize net price—price less expenses (increase the net price from the $8,000 figure)?

> You bought your house in 1977 for $60,000. You currently have the house on the market for $109,900, with a real target of $100,000 (your estimation of the true market value). An offer comes in for $90,000. Does this offer represent a $30,000 gain in comparison with the original purchase price, or a $10,000 loss in comparison with your current target?

The answer to the question posed in each scenario is "Both." Each is a "Is the cup half full or half empty?" situation. From a normative perspective, and based on our intuition, the difference in the two points of view is irrelevant. Recently, however, Kahneman and Tversky have suggested that important differences exist in how individuals respond to questions framed in terms of losses versus gains. This difference is critical in describing negotiator behavior.

Tversky and Kahneman (1981) presented the following problem to a group of subjects:

> The U.S. is preparing for the outbreak of an unusual Asian disease which is expected to kill 600 people. Two alternative programs are being considered. Which would you favor?

> 1. If Program A is adopted, 200 will be saved.

> 2. If Program B is adopted, there is a one-third probability that all will be saved and a two-thirds probability that none will be saved.

Of 158 respondents, 76% chose Program A, while only 24% chose Program B. The prospect of being able to save 200 lives for certain was valued more highly by most of the subjects than a risky prospect of equal expected value. Thus, most subjects were risk-averse.

A second group of subjects received the same cover story and the following two choices:

> 1. If Program A is adopted, 400 people will die.

2. If Program B is adopted, there is a one-third probability that no one will die and a two-thirds probability that 600 people will die.

Out of the 169 respondents in the second group, only 13% chose Program A, while 87% chose Program B. The prospects of 400 people dying was less acceptable to most of the subjects than a two-thirds probability that 600 would die. Thus, most subjects given these alternatives were risk-seeking.

Careful examination of two problems finds them to be *objectively* identical. However, changing the description of outcomes from lives saved (gains) to lives lost (losses) was sufficient to shift the majority of subjects from a risk-averse to a risk-seeking orientation. This result is inconsistent with utility theory, which predicts the same response when objectively identical problems are presented. These well-replicated findings, however, are consistent with Kahneman and Tversky's (1979) prospect theory, which predicts risk-averse behavior when individuals are evaluating gains and risk-seeking behavior when individuals are evaluating losses.

To exemplify the importance of "framing" to negotiation, consider the following labor-management situation suggested by Bazerman and Neale (1983): The union claims it needs a raise to $12 per hour, and that anything less would represent a loss given current inflation. Management argues that it cannot pay more than $10 per hour, and that anything more would impose an unacceptable loss. What if each side had the choice of settling for $11 per hour (a certain settlement) or going to binding arbitration (a risky settlement)? Since each side is viewing the conflict in terms of what it has to lose, following Tversky and Kahneman's findings, each side is predicted to be risk-seeking and unwilling to take the certain settlement. Changing the frame of the situation to a positive one, however, results in a very different predicted outcome: If the union views anything above $10 per hour as a gain, and management views anything under $12 per hour as a gain, then risk-aversion will dominate and a negotiated settlement will be likely. Using an example conceptually similar to the above scenario, Neale and Bazerman (1983) found that negotiators with positive frames are significantly more concessionary and successful than their negative counterparts.

. . .

Many prescriptive approaches to negotiation (Raiffa, 1982) lead negotiators to evaluate their risk preferences as part of their prescriptive analysis. However, a negotiator's strategic choice is likely to be affected inappropriately by the negotiator's frame—nominal dollar gain versus real dollar loss, net profit or expenses away from gross profit, and so on. In evaluating their risk preferences, negotiators need to be aware of the influence of positive versus negative frames; otherwise, their decision may reflect this cognitive distortion more than their actual preferences.

What determines whether a negotiator will have a positive or negative frame? The answer lies in the selection of a perceptual anchor. Consider the anchors available to a union negotiator in simply negotiating a wage: (1) last year's wage, (2) management's initial offer, (3) the union's estimate of management's resistance point, (4) the union's resistance point, or (5) your bargaining position, which has been announced publicly to your constituency. As the anchor moves from 1 to 5, what is a modest *gain* in comparison to last year's wage is a *loss* in comparison to the publicly specified goals. As the anchor changes from 1 to 5, the union negotiator moves from a positive frame to a negative frame. For example, if workers are currently making $10 per hour and demanding an increase of $2 per hour, a proposed increase of $1 per hour can be viewed as a $1 per hour gain in comparison to last year's wage (Anchor 1) or a loss of $1 per hour in comparison to the goals of the union's constituency (Anchor 5). In order to avoid the adverse effects of framing, the negotiator should be aware of his or her frame and examine the context from alternative frames.

In addition to thinking about how frames affect the primary negotiator, framing has important implications for the tactics negotiators can use. The framing effect suggests that in order to induce concessionary behavior from an opponent, a negotiator should always create anchors that lead the opposition to a positive frame and negotiate in terms of what the other side has to gain. In addition, the negotiator should make it salient to the opposition that it is in a risky situation where a sure gain is possible.

The Mythical Fixed-Pie of Negotiations

Integrative agreements are nonobvious solutions to conflict that reconcile the parties' interests and yield a higher joint benefit than a simple compromise could create. To illustrate, consider the compromise between two sisters who fought over an orange. The two sisters agreed to split the orange in half, allowing one sister to use her portion for juice and the other sister to use the peel of her half for a cake. The two parties in this conflict overlooked the *integrative* agreement of giving one sister all the juice and the other sister all the peel.

. . .

The fixed-pie assumption of the distributive model represents a fundamental bias in human judgment. That is, negotiators have a systematic intuitive bias that distorts their behavior: They assume that their interests directly conflict with the other party's interests. The fundamental assumption of a fixed-pie probably results from a competitive society that creates the belief in a win-lose situation. This win-lose orientation is manifested objectively in our society in athletic competition, admission to academic programs, industrial promotion systems, and so on. Individuals tend to generalize from these objective win-lose situations and apply their experience to situations that are not objectively fixed-pies. Faced with a mixed-motive situation requiring both cooperation and competition, it is the competitive aspect that becomes salient—resulting in a win-lose orientation and a distributive approach to bargaining. This in turn results in the development of a strategy for obtaining the largest share possible of the perceived fixed-pie. Such a focus inhibits the creativity and problem-solving necessary for the development of integrative solutions.

. . .

The above arguments suggest that while some fixed-pies exist objectively, most resolutions depend on finding favorable trade-offs between negotiators, trade-offs that necessitate eliminating our intuitive fixed-pie assumptions. Winkelgren (1974) suggests that we often limit our finding creative solutions by making false assumptions. The fixed-pie perception is a fundamentally false assumption that hinders finding creative (integrative) solutions. A fundamental task in training negotiators lies in identifying and eliminating this false assumption, and institutionalizing the creative process of integrative bargaining.

The analytical development of integrative solutions is central to most prescriptive frameworks. However, most prescriptive approaches assume a negotiator will follow the prescription, unaffected by his or her intuitive strategies for negotiation. In contrast, this article argues that an individual fully versed in the prescriptive writing on negotiation may fall back on past intuitive fixed-pie strategies when faced with a potentially integrative problem. Why? The fixed-pie assumption is an institutionalized part of most negotiators' intuitive repertoire. Until this fundamental aspect of the negotiator's cognitive repertoire is altered, the bias will impede the individual's ability to implement the prescriptive recommendations.

· · ·

The Nonrational Escalation of Conflict

Consider the following situation:

It is 1981. PATCO (The Professional Air Traffic Controllers Organization) decides to strike to obtain a set of concessions from the U.S. government. It is willing to "invest" the temporary loss of pay during the strike in order to obtain concessions. No government concessions result or appear to be forthcoming. PATCO is faced with the option of backing off and returning to work under the former arrangement or increasing its commitment to the strike to try to force the concessions it desires.

In this example, PATCO has committed resources to a course of action. It is then faced with escalating that commitment or backing out of the conflict. This example illustrates a decision problem that occurs in a variety of conflicts in which an actor can become trapped into a costly course of action. The escalation of commitment to a failing course of action has become a topic of interest among decision researchers. [S]tudies indicate that individuals, groups, and organizations who make decisions that do not lead to expected positive results tend nonrationally to commit added resources to a previously chosen course of action. These researchers would have predicted that PATCO was far more likely to persist in its course of action than a rational analysis would have dictated.

It is easy to see the process of nonrational escalation of commitment unfold in a number of actual conflict situations. The negotiation process commonly leads both sides initially to make extreme demands. The negotiation literature predicts that if negotiators become committed to their initial public statements, they will nonrationally adopt a nonconcessionary stance. Further, if both sides incur losses as a result of a lack of agreement (e.g., a strike), their commitment to their positions is expected to increase, and their willingness to change to a different course of action (i.e., compromise) is expected to decrease. The more a negotiator believes there is "too much invested to quit," the more likely he or she is to be intransigent.

An understanding of escalation can be very helpful to a negotiator in understanding the behavior of the opponent. When will the other party really hold out? The escalation literature predicts that the other side will really hold out when it has "too much invested" in its position to give in. This suggests that there are systematic clues as to when you can threaten your opponent and win, and when the threat will receive an active response, due to your opponent's prior public commitment to a course of action. Strategically, then, a negotiator should avoid inducing the opponent to make statements or to behave in any way that would create the illusion of having invested too much to quit.

Descriptive research on the nonrational escalation of commitment can be integrated with prescriptive approaches to negotiation. Prescriptive approaches provide strategies for deciding whether or not to continue a conflict. The escalation literature, however, suggests that many of the inputs required by the prescriptive approach (e.g., What is the likelihood that the other side will give in? What are the costs of continuing the conflict?) are likely to be biased in favor of escalating the conflict. In order to use a prescriptive approach optimally, we need to understand and change the nonrational tendency of negotiators to escalate commitment to an existing conflict.

Negotiator Overconfidence

Consider the following scenario:

You are an advisor to a major-league baseball player. In baseball, a system exists for the resolution of compensation conflicts that calls for a player and a team who do not agree to submit final offers to an arbitrator. Using final offer arbitration, the arbitrator must accept one position or the other, not a compromise. Thus, the challenge for each side is to come just a little closer to the arbitrator's perception of the appropriate compensation package than the opposition. In this case, your best intuitive estimate of the final offer that the team will submit is a package worth $200,000 per year. You believe that an appropriate wage is $400,000 per year but estimate the arbitrator's opinion to be $300,000 per year. What final offer do you propose?

This scenario represents a common cognitive trap for negotiators. Individuals are systematically overconfident in estimating the position of a neutral third party and in estimating the likelihood that a third party will accept their position. In the baseball example, if the arbitrator's true assessment of the appropriate wage is $250,000, and you believe it to be $300,000, you are likely to submit an inappropriately high offer and overestimate the likelihood that the offer will be accepted. Consequently, the overconfidence bias is likely to lead the advisor to believe that less compromise is necessary than a more objective analysis would suggest.

Research demonstrates that negotiators tend to be overconfident that their positions will prevail if they do not "give in." Neale and Bazerman (1983b; Bazerman and Neale, 1982) show that negotiators consistently overestimate the probability, under final offer arbitration, that their final offer will be accepted. That is, while only 50% of all final offers can be accepted, the average subject estimated that there was a much higher probability that his or her offer would be accepted. If we consider a final offer as a judgment as to how much compromise is necessary to win the arbitration, it is easy to argue that when a negotiator is overconfident that a particular position will be accepted, the incentive to compromise is reduced. If a more accurate assessment is made, the negotiator is likely to be more uncertain and uncomfortable about the probability of success. One strategy to reduce this uncertainty is to compromise further.

. . .

Training negotiators to recognize the cognitive patterns of over confidence should include the realization that over confidence is most likely to occur when a party's knowledge is limited. Most of us follow the intuitive cognitive rule: "When in doubt, be over confident." This suggests that negotiators should be aware of the benefits of obtaining objective assessments of worth from a *neutral* party, realizing that this neutral assessment is likely to be systematically closer to the other party's position than the negotiator would have predicted intuitively.

THE WINNER'S CURSE

Imagine that you are in a foreign country. You meet a merchant who is selling a very attractive gem. You have bought a few gems in your life but are far from being an expert. After some discussion, you make the merchant an offer that you believe (but are uncertain) is on the low side. He quickly accepts, and the transaction is completed. How do you feel? Most people would feel uneasy with the purchase after the quick acceptance. Yet, why would you voluntarily make an offer that you would not want accepted?

The key feature of the "winner's curse" in the bargaining context is that one side has much better information than the other side. Though we are all familiar with the slogan "buyer beware," our intuition seems to have difficulty putting this idea into practice when asymmetric information exists. Most people realize that when they buy a commodity they know little about, their uncertainty increases. The evidence presented here indicates that against an informed opponent, their expected return from the transaction may decrease dramatically. Practically, the evidence suggests that people undervalue the importance of accurate information in making transactions. They undervalue a mechanic's evaluation of a used car, a house inspector's assessment of a house, or an independent jeweler's assessment of a coveted gem. Thus, the knowledgeable gem merchant will accept your offer selectively, taking the offer when the gem is probably worth less than your estimate. To protect yourself, you need to develop or borrow the expertise to balance the quality of information.

GARY GOODPASTER, NEGOTIATION AND MEDIATION: A GUIDE TO NEGOTIATION AND NEGOTIATED DISPUTE RESOLUTION

123–35 (1997).

Notwithstanding the fullest understanding and the most careful planning and preparation, efforts to undertake problem-solving bargaining can go awry. This is because the parties do not take into account some of the ways in which humans tend to make decisions in uncertain situations. Researchers studying human problem solving and decision making observe that human beings possess "bounded" rationality. Humans make choices based on a simplified mental model of a real situation. We unconsciously use judgmental strategies to make decisions when asked to take risks or when interpreting ambiguous or otherwise unclear information. In certain circumstances, these cognitive strategies, sometimes called judgmental heuristics or cognitive illusions, can even cause us to make objectively inconsistent or irrational choices. While useful and efficient, shortcuts enable us to draw conclusions about situations without consciously analyzing them. These strategies can lead to misjudgment and erroneous decisions.

. . .

REFERENCE POINTS

There appear to be two phases in common decision-making. The first is a simplification or "editing" phase, where the decision maker engages in a preliminary analysis of the decision situation in order to simplify it. The second is an evaluation phase, where the decision maker decides which of the "edited" choices is the best.

Editing involves coding possible choices and assessing gains or losses with respect to a defined reference point. For example, if I am considering taking a new job, I will most likely take the characteristics of my present job as a reference point. These will help me compare the new job and make a decision about whether to accept a new position. I will take my current salary, benefits, duties, and so on, as givens and attempt to figure out how the new job may better or worsen those items.

Obviously, if we make judgments by reference to a defined point, what that point is and how we define it are quite important. In a negotiation, a party's overall decision reference point is its reservation price, that is, whatever it feels it must minimally obtain in order to agree at all. In interest-based bargaining, a party establishes that point for itself by figuring out its best alternatives to a negotiated agreement.

A.   Framing

People tend to adopt their status quo, whatever that may be in what is at issue, as a reference point for their decision making. What people value, positively or negatively, are changes in their wealth or welfare from their defined reference point.

However a party establishes its reference point for assessing negotiation offers, what is important to understand is that it may be possible to induce a party to change its judgmental reference point. If a party changes its reference point, it will, out of necessity, perceive its decision situation differently. This is what occurs when an interest-based negotiator negotiates with a positional bargainer and persuades the latter to look at the situation from the point of view of his interests rather than his positions. Consequently, it is possible to shape the decisions people are likely to make by inducing them to consider their decision from a different reference point.

In simpler terms, the way parties state a problem affects the way they approach and resolve it. The way negotiators define and view issues affects the way they bargain and the concession and settlement decisions they make. Issue-framing therefore can affect negotiation results, and there are a variety of factors that negotiators should take into account in framing their negotiations.

1. Risks of loss or gain

For most people, losses loom larger than gains. We are generally more willing to gamble to prevent or minimize losses than to secure or maximize gains. Put otherwise, people are loss-averse; that is, inclined to protect their current position and willing to take risks to prevent losses. They will not, however, take similar risks to secure gains. People are risk-positive or even risk-seeking in taking action to prevent a loss, but risk-averse in taking action to secure a gain.

We can even expand these propositions somewhat. Persons presented with a choice between a certain small gain and a possible larger gain also tend to act conservatively, taking the small gain and not gambling for the larger. On the other hand, where people see the situation as a choice between a small sure loss and a larger possible loss, they will gamble to avoid the smaller loss. Consider the following example.

Choose between:

a. a sure gain of $3000;

b. an 80 percent chance of winning $4000 and a 20 percent chance of winning nothing.

In this situation, most people choose alternative *a*. Consider, however, the following example.

Choose between:

a. a sure loss of $3000;

b. an 80 percent chance of losing $4000 and a 20 percent chance of losing nothing.

Most people choose alternative *b*. In other words, people will take risks to try to prevent a loss, but will not take equal risks to try to secure a gain.

. . .

The way one frames an issue, therefore, affects the decision made. In a negotiation, framing the issue, especially as it bears on risk, can affect both the character of the bargaining and negotiation results. Negotiating parties risk nonagreement by the positions they take and maintain. If the parties are some distance apart, there will be no agreement unless one or both concede to close the gap. In this situation, refusing to concede or conceding too little constitute risky behavior. Making concessions, by contrast, moves toward securing an agreement and is therefore an attempt to avoid the risk of no agreement. Consequently, a party that views a negotiation as an effort to minimize losses is more likely to engage in hard-bargaining (risky behavior) than a party focused on potential negotiation gains.

If all parties to a negotiation look upon it as an opportunity to maximize gains, they will all make concessions and come to agreement more easily and productively. Indeed, this is part of the theory of problem-solving bargaining. If a negotiator frames the negotiation as an opportunity to secure a gain or prevent a loss, she presents choices in a way most likely to encourage the other side to make concessions.

On the other hand, if a negotiator attempts to hard-bargain, she may do so by framing her own position in the negotiation as an effort to prevent losses. With a risk-positive frame, she will be less likely to make concessions and perhaps more likely to get them. Similarly a negotiator seeking to get as much gain as possible from a negotiation may frame her own situation negatively, as an effort to minimize losses. At the same time she might attempt to persuade the other side to view its situation positively, as an opportunity to secure gains. This analysis counsels the problem-solving negotiator that she must determine the other party's negotiation frame, and, if necessary, seek to change it from a risk-positive to a risk-averse frame. It becomes apparent that understanding how parties frame a negotiation choice, and understanding how to reframe it are essential to effective problem-solving negotiation.

2. Anchoring and adjustment

When people are uncertain, it is possible to center their attention on a particular point merely by mentioning it. Then, when asked to make a decision, the person, once focused, unconsciously uses that point as a reference point for their decision. In other words, decision-makers adjust their decision up or down from the noticed reference point. Focusing a person's attention on a certain point tethers or anchors his judgment to the vicinity of the point.

This psychological phenomenon, appropriately called anchoring, is easiest to demonstrate through estimation exercises. For example, experimenters asked subjects to estimate what percentage of countries in the United Nations were African. Before making the estimate, however, experimenters asked the subjects to state whether the percentage was greater or less than a number chosen by spinning a wheel having the numbers 1 through 100 on it. Unknown to the subjects, who supposed the number selection was by chance, the experimenters rigged the wheel to stop at 10 or 65. The subjects who saw the 10 made an average estimate that the percentage of African countries was 25 percent. Those who saw 65 made an average estimate of 45 percent. Obviously, seeing the 10 and the 65 influenced the later estimates of the subjects, even though they believed that chance determined the numbers they saw.

This experiment, and others like it, make it clear that it is possible to affect people's judgments through using an anchor. Once focused on a point or alternative, people confine their search for solutions within an area centered on the focus. People use the focus as a reference point for judgment, and adjust from there.

. . .

3. Attribution error

In the United States, most people, when observing someone making a choice, attribute the choice to the actor's character or disposition. In other words, most people operate from the unconscious premise that people behave as they do because of their dispositions. The actor, however, usually explains his choice by reference to the immediate situation, that is, the factors he thought he faced causing him to choose one way rather than another.

I once observed a classroom during a lecture-discussion. During the lecture, several women students raised their hands, but the professor did not call on them. At last, he did call on a male student who had raised his hand. A female student then challenged him, asserting that he was obviously sexist as he had not earlier called on women students. The professor, while taken aback, responded, "Well, perhaps. You will have to judge, but I really wasn't ready to take questions or comments earlier. I wanted first to cover some more material." Clearly, the female critic attributed the professor's behavior to his character or disposition, while he attributed it to the situation.

Attributing a person's action to his disposition could be a correct assessment, but could also be wrong. It will almost certainly be wrong from the actor's viewpoint, and the actor is not likely to be responsive to assessments, offers, or suggestions not salient to his own perception of the situation.

It is easy to imagine how different observer and actor perceptions of this kind could affect negotiators' judgments about one another. If each negotiator, observing the other, attributes the other's choices to disposition rather than to the situation, each may draw conclusions, and make predictions, which may be incorrect. One might think, for example, that because the other side was very resistant to one's proposals, it was basically competitive. To counter, one might bargain competitively as well. This could be mistaken, however, for it could be that the other negotiator was simply responding to the way the proposals were framed as he perceived them to bear on his interests.

"[Persons] tend to simplify their decision task by ignoring the *contingent decision processes* of competitive others. They assume the other side will act in a certain way, rather than realizing that the opponent's behavior is contingent on a variety of factors." Attributing behavior to disposition simplifies judgment, but leads to misunderstandings that impede or distort judgment. To avoid such errors of understanding, the negotiator must attempt to enter the other side's "problem space," that is, to see the negotiation issues and situation as the other side sees them. The negotiator, rather than offering his own positions and rationales, needs to elicit talk. He needs to get a good sense of the other side's values, preferences, concerns and interests, the pressures it feels, the aspirations it has, and so on.

. . .

7. "Sunken" costs

Suppose you have purchased an expensive ticket to a musical production, let's say at a cost of $100. On the evening you had planned to go and see it, you feel tired and think, "Golly, I wish I hadn't bought that ticket. I'd much rather stay home tonight than go to the theater." Should you go to the theater or stay home? Would you stay home if you could get your $100 back? Should you treat your ticket purchase as an investment you do not want to waste, or should you conclude that the money you paid for the ticket is gone, *whatever you do*?

Money you have already paid out, or investments of any kind that you have made, which you will lose no matter what you do are called sunk costs. If you actually prefer to stay home rather than go to the theater, but you go to the theater anyway, you are doing something that you don't want to do in order to avoid a loss that you will have in any case. You invest more, or impose additional costs on yourself, in order to feel that your prior expenditure has not been in vain, has not been wasted. But, while it is rational to base a decision on future consequences, it is irrational to base it on past events you cannot change. It is irrational to act merely to honor sunk costs, that is, to let a past investment govern a future choice simply in order to feel that you have gotten something for your investment. In other words, sunk costs, by themselves, do not provide a rational justification for incurring additional costs or maintaining a course of action.

. . .

The irrational inclination to honor sunk costs may arise in negotiations in a variety of ways. One might, for example, try to conclude a deal, rather than look elsewhere, because of the time, effort, and resources expended in the negotiation so far. But such costs are not necessarily an appropriate focus of negotiation decision making. Instead one should focus on the future consequences of the deal and the other alternatives one has, including all associated costs.

In a similar way, a concern with sunk costs might incline a negotiator to hard-bargain rather than problem-solve. If a party focuses on losses as a reference point, he will take risks, including risks of non-agreement, to avoid suffering the loss. If it were possible to persuade the party to think of the loss as sunk costs, however, it would be easier to focus on how a possible agreement would affect its interests in the future. A company sues an architect for an allegedly flawed building design that the company has spent $500,000 to correct. The suit, which is not by any means a sure winner, will cost the company $250,000 to pursue through trial, including all attorney fees, discovery and expert witness costs, and lost staff time. In negotiations with the architect and her insurer, should the company hold out for $500,000 because that is how much it is out of pocket? Clearly, the company should base its decision making solely on the probabilities of winning its suit. If they are good, it should perhaps press for maximum recovery; if not, it should settle for what it can get, notwithstanding the losses it will be unable to recoup.

In summary, rational decisions are based on an assessment of future possibilities and probabilities. The past is relevant only insofar as it provides information about possible and probable futures. Rational decision-making demands the abandonment of sunk costs, unless such abandonment creates problems outweighing the benefits of abandonment.

8. Saving face and "giving" face

How one addresses the question of saving face is not so obvious. Saving face involves finding some interpretation of the situation, including losses, that permits a party to feel, or credibly claim, that it acted or decided justifiably. In other words that what it did was not senseless, but instead had meaning.

. . .

When caught in a spiraling conflict, a party wishing to cut its losses and get out often needs to find an satisfactory interpretation of its withdrawal. It needs an interpretation that justifies its whole course of conduct to that point rather than making it appear senseless, foolish, cowardly, or weak. This is particularly true where the party must explain itself to a constituency or some public. There is simply a need to avoid or blunt belittling criticism.

Saving face is important in successfully concluding some conflicts and negotiations. Indeed, it is so important that negotiators need not only be sensitive to it, but also willing to "give face." By giving face, I mean helping the other party to make face-saving claims about the course of the negotiations and the results achieved. One can do this by constructing some agreed upon, dignifying, justifying, public description of the parties' activities, and agreements or nonagreements. Alternatively, a negotiator can give the other side something it can publicly use to assert that it did not come away from the negotiation defeated, empty-handed, nor in any way taken nor humiliated.

Chapter 7

POWER IN NEGOTIATION—ACTUAL AND PERCEIVED

Power for the negotiator has the same resonance as money for the materialist; the sense that more of it is always useful. It comes as no surprise that those who bargain with more power tend to achieve superior outcomes to those who perceive themselves in the weaker position. Morton Deutch defined power in negotiation as "the possibility of imposing one's will upon the behavior of other persons." But just what, exactly, are the ingredients of negotiation power?

Surprisingly, given its centrality to the bargaining process, what constitutes power in negotiation and how power differentials affect outcome is still a matter of some dispute. There is even disagreement whether power in negotiation is a static or dynamic phenomenon. Can power be marshalled during bargaining to achieve better results, or is one's power in negotiation fixed by the bargaining context and the parties' relationships, and only loosely amenable to manipulation?

Much of the existing theoretical work is found in the sociological and psychological literature. Scholarship in this subject reflects each author's preferred social theory of how to categorize the constituent elements of a person's bargaining power. We will discuss three of the best known categorization schemes.

One pioneering attempt at a taxonomy of power in negotiation was published over thirty-five years ago by the psychologist Bertram Raven and his colleague John French. This model approaches negotiation as a structured interpersonal process. In the first reading in this chapter, Raven looks back at the six ingredients of the Power/Interaction Model they first described. Raven reminisces on how their notions of power in human interaction evolved, and how they and others have augmented their early research implications during the intervening years.

Edward Lawler is another prolific analyst of power in negotiation. As a sociologist, he sees bargaining power as a phenomenon flowing from "the interests of the positions occupied by the parties, rather than [from interpersonal] characteristics of the parties per se." In our second reading, Lawler suggests how power in bargaining affects tactical choice. His conclusions, derived from a "Power–Dependence" model, help us understand the impact of actual or perceived bargaining power on participants' selection of competitive or cooperative negotiation strategies.

Our final model of power in bargaining comes from Roger Fisher. Fisher has long been concerned with understanding competitive and cooperative negotiation strategies. His co-authored *Getting to Yes* has animated much discussion in this field for the past fifteen years, and was a focus of much of our discussion of integrative bargaining in Chapter Four. In the third reading in this chapter, Fisher responds to critics who suggest that the "Principled Negotiation" model he developed in that book gives insufficient emphasis to notions of bargaining power. As befits the lawyer, he moves us from the descriptive to the prescriptive, viewing power in negotiation as a dynamic element that parties can marshal to enhance the elegance of their outcomes. His observations about the potency—and the risks—of making negative commitments are particularly salient.

The reading that concludes this chapter presents a case study in how to analyze the power available to negotiators. William Felstiner and Austin Sarat are two social scientists who are among our best researchers of the lawyering process. In this reading, they challenge the conventional wisdom which holds that the power relationship between lawyer and client "is one of professional dominance and lay passivity...." Using the divorce lawyer's office as their research forum, Felstiner and Sarat give us a deeper and more dynamic understanding of how to assess power in professional practice.

Readings

1. Bertram H. Raven, *The Bases of Power: Origins and Recent Developments,* 49 J. Social Issues 227, 232–37 (1993).
2. Edward J. Lawler, *Power Processes in Bargaining,* 33 Sociol.Q. 17, 17–26 (1992).
3. Roger Fisher, *Negotiating Power: Getting and Using Influence,* 27 Am.Behav.Scientist 149, 150–64 (1983).
4. William L. Felstiner & Austin Sarat, *Enactments of Power: Negotiating Reality and Responsibility in Lawyer–Client Interactions,* 77 Cornell L.Rev. 1447, 1459–66 (1992).
5. For Further Reading
   a. Samuel B. Bacharach & Edward J. Lawler, Bargaining: Power, Tactics and Outcomes (1981).
   b. Samuel B. Bacharach & Edward J. Lawler, *Power Dependence and Power Paradoxes in Bargaining,* 2 Negot.J. 167 (1986).
   c. Max H. Bazerman, *Getting to Yes Six Years Later,* Nat.Inst. of Disp.Res., Dispute Resolution Forum (May 1987).
   d. Herb Cohen, You Can Negotiate Anything (1980).
   e. Karen S. Cook, Richard M. Emerson, Mary R. Gillmore & Toshio Yamagishi, *The Distribution of Power in Exchange Networks: Theory and Experimental Results,* 89 Am.J.Soc. 275 (1983).
   f. Robert Cooter & Stephen Marks (with Robert Mnookin), *Bargaining in the Shadow of the Law: A Testable Model of Strategic Behavior,* 11 J. of Leg.Studies 225 (1982).
   g. Robert A. Dahl, *The Concept of Power,* 2 Behav.Sci. 201 (1957).
   h. Morton Deutch, The Resolution of Conflicts: Constructive and Destructive Processes (1973).

Readings

    i.   Richard M. Emerson, *Power–Dependence Relationships,* 27 Am.Sociol.Rev. 31 (1962).

    j.   Roger Fisher & Scott Brown, Getting Together: Building a Relationship that Gets to Yes (1988).

    k.   Roger Fisher, *Beyond Yes,* 1 Negot.J. 67 (1985).

    l.   John R.P. French, Jr. & Bertram H. Raven, *The Bases of Social Power,* in Studies in Social Power (D. Cartwright, ed., (1959)).

    m. John Kenneth Galbraith, The Anatomy of Power (1983).

    n.   Stephen B. Goldberg & Jeanne M. Brett, *Getting, Spending— and Losing—Power in Dispute System Design,* 7 Negot.J. 119 (1991).

    o.   Leonard Greenhalgh, Scott A. Neslin & Roderick W. Gilkey, *The Effects of Negotiator Preferences, Situational Power and Negotiator Personality on Outcomes of Business Negotiations,* 28 Acad. of Mgmt.J. 9 (1985).

    p.   Paula Johnson, *Women and Power: Toward a Theory of Effectiveness,* 32 J. of Social Issues 99 (1976).

    q.   Elizabeth A. Mannix, Leigh L. Thompson & Max H. Bazerman, *Negotiation in Small Groups,* 74 J. of Appl.Psych. 508 (1989).

    r.   Bernard Mayer, *The Dynamics of Power in Mediation and Negotiation,* 16 Med.Q. 75 (1987).

    s.   Lord William McCarthy, *The Role of Power and Politics in Getting to Yes,* 1 Negot.J. 59 (1985).

    t.   Linda D. Molm, *The Structure and Use of Power: A Comparison of Reward and Punishment Power,* 51 Soc.Psych.Q. 108 (1988).

    u.   Linda D. Molm, *Gender, Power, and Legitimation: A Test of Three Theories,* 91 Am.J.Sociol. 1356 (1986).

    v.   Margaret A. Neale & Max H. Bazerman, Cognition and Rationality in Negotiation (1991).

    w. Martin Patchen, *Strategies for Eliciting Cooperation from an Adversary,* 31 J.Confl.Res. 164 (1985).

    x.   Robin L. Pinkley, Margaret A. Neale & Rebecca J. Bennett, *The Impact of Alternatives to Settlement in Dyadic Negotiation,* 57 Org.Beh. & Hum.Dec.Proc. 97 (1994).

    y.   Dean G. Pruitt, Negotiation Behavior (1981).

    z.   Bertram H. Raven & Arie W. Kruglanski, *Conflict and Power* in The Structure of Conflict 69 (Paul Swingle, ed. (1970)).

   aa. Jeffrey Z. Rubin & William I. Zartman, *Asymetrical Negotiations: Some Survey Results That May Surprise,* 11 Negot.J. 349 (1995).

   bb. Laurie R. Weingart, Elaine B. Hyder & Michael J. Prietula, *Knowledge Matters: The Effect of Tactical Descriptions on Negotiation Behavior and Outcome,* 70 J. of Personality and Social Psych. 1205 (1996).

BERTRAM H. RAVEN, THE BASES OF POWER: ORIGINS AND RECENT DEVELOPMENTS

49 J.Soc.Issues 227, 232–37 (1993).

CONCEPTUALIZING THE BASES OF POWER

Jack French and I began to meet regularly to discuss the development of a general theory of social power. We defined social power as "potential influence," which we should note was very similar to Lewin's—"the possibility of inducing forces." Our approach, then, was to examine what sorts of resources a person might have to draw upon to exercise influence.

. . .

We then discerned that there were two important dimensions that determine the form of influence or compliance: (a) social dependence and (b) the importance of surveillance. We could readily think of examples in which one person, an influencing agent, could convince another with clear logic, argument, or information—where, let us say, a supervisor would give his/her subordinates good reasons why a change in behavior might lead to greater productivity. Even though it was initially the communication from the agent that would produce the change, that change would become *socially independent*—the target of influence would completely accept (i.e., internalize) the change, and the agent would become inconsequential. We called that *informational influence.*

. . .

The threat of punishment would lead to change that continued to be socially dependent upon the agent, but surveillance was important for such influence to be effective. For example, the supervisor says, "Do the job this way or you will be demoted." In its potential, then, we referred to such a resource as *coercive power.* But wouldn't there be a similar situation if the agent promised some sort of reward, an increase in pay or privileges in exchange for compliance? *Reward power,* then, would also be socially dependent, with surveillance important in order for its effects to continue.

So now we had two bases of power, *coercive* and *reward,* in which the change was socially dependent and where surveillance was important, and one, *information,* which was socially independent and where surveillance was unimportant. Could we conceive of bases of power in which surveillance was *un*important, but where resulting changes were still socially dependent? We soon thought of three additional bases of power which would have such consequences: *legitimate power* (what others have called "position power"), *expert power,* and *referent power.* The concept of "legitimate power" came from Max Weber: "After all, I am your supervisor, and you should feel some obligation to do what I ask." *Expert power* has a long and distinguished history in research on opinion and attitude change: "Even if I may not explain the reasons to you, you must know that, after all, I know what is the best thing to do in such circumstances." The concept of *referent power* came from ... Merton (1957), though we could also see it in operation in many of the studies of group norms described earlier. The target of influence in such a case would comply because of a sense of identification with the influencing agent, or a desire for such an identification. The influencing agent then serves as a model by which the target evaluates his/her behavior and beliefs.

. . .

FURTHER DIFFERENTIATION AND ELABORATION

In the years that followed, the bases of social power model has developed substantially, benefiting from research and theoretical developments in various related fields—cognitive social psychology, attitude and attitude change, and organizational psychology. Though we still believe that most social influence can be understood in terms of the six bases of power, some of these bases have been elaborated and further differentiated.

Coercive power and reward power: Personal forms. Going beyond tangible rewards and real physical threats, we have had to recognize that personal approval from someone whom we like can result in quite powerful reward power; and rejection or disapproval from someone whom we really like can serve as a basis for powerful coercive power. There is some indication that the more personal forms, which have sometimes been called "attraction power," are more likely to be associated with women than with men.

Legitimate power: Reciprocity, equity, and dependence. We have had to go beyond the legitimate power that comes from one's formal position and recognize other forms of legitimate power that may be more subtle, which draw on social norms such as (a) the legitimate power of *reciprocity* ("I did that for you, so you should feel obliged to do this for me"); (b) *equity* ("I have worked hard and suffered, so I have a right to ask you to do something to make up for it"), and (c) *responsibility* or *dependence*, a norm saying that we have some obligation to help others who cannot help themselves and who are dependent upon us. (This form of legitimate power has sometimes been referred to as the "power of the powerless.")

Expert power and referent power: Positive and negative forms. Both of these bases of power were originally examined only in their positive forms: A subordinate may do what his/her supervisor asks because he/she feels that the supervisor knows best, or because the supervisor is someone admirable and desirable—who knows, the subordinate may aspire to be a supervisor some day. But it has been observed that sometimes we may do exactly the *opposite* of what the influencing agent does or desires that we do. [What Hovland, Janis, and Kelley called the "boomerang effect."] Why? Perhaps we recognize the expertise of the influencers, but distrust them and assume they are using their superior knowledge for their own best interests, not ours. Or perhaps we see the agent as someone whom we dislike, someone from whom we would prefer to *dis*identify ourselves. Thus we incorporated into our system the concept of *negative* expert power and *negative* referent power.

Informational power: Direct and indirect. Informational power, or persuasion, is based on the information, or logical argument, that the influencing agent could present to the target in order to implement change. However, information can sometimes be more effective if it is presented indirectly. The early research on the effectiveness of "overheard" communications, as compared to direct communications, would seem to bear this out.

... There is quite a difference between an influencing agent directly telling a target what s/he wants and why, vs. doing so through hints and suggestions. Johnson found that women were especially likely to use the indirect forms of information, men more likely to use direct information. Indirect information seems especially useful when a person in what is considered a low-power position attempts to influence someone in a superior position. Thus Stein notes that nurses who may feel that they have a useful suggestion in the treatment of a patient will tend to avoid direct informational influence, and will instead use an indirect approach such as "This medication seemed helpful, doctor, for the patient down the hall who had a similar problem." The more direct form of information (e.g., "Doctor, this other medication, you must know, will be less likely to affect the patient's blood pressure, and would be much better, since he has a heart problem") might not only be less effective, but could result in disastrous interpersonal problems.

NONVOLITIONAL METHODS OF INFLUENCE: FORCE AND MANIPULATION

While it appears that most influence strategies can be analyzed in terms of various combinations of the six bases of power and their variants, we must recognize that there are other means of influence that would not fit so directly. Two such devices are *force* and *manipulation*. All of the other bases of power involve volition on the part of the target—the target can decide whether to comply or accept punishment, to refuse and forgo rewards, to go against the advice of an expert or against the logic of the information, etc. *Force* is defined as a form of induced change in a target that occurs without the target's volition. It includes the use of physical restraints (as in a psychiatric ward) or compulsion without choice—what is often referred to as "brute force." The agent of change may treat the target as if the target is no more than a physical object. We see it in an uncooperative psychiatric patient, who, not responding to various other influence attempts, is physically strapped to his/her bed. Or in the parent who, after nicely asking the child to stop playing in the street, forcibly picks up and locks the child in a room. The term is perhaps most obviously applied in "forcible rape." It is, again, the lack of volition that distinguishes force from coercion (as well as other forms of influence), though the *threat* of force may be used to establish coercive power.

Manipulation is a form of influence in which the influencing agent succeeds in changing a target by first changing some other aspect of the target or his/her environment. In *ecological* or *environmental manipulation* the environment itself is changed so as to either facilitate or inhibit some form of behavior. One can influence a driver to use a seat belt by designing the car so that it cannot be started unless the seat belt is fastened. Or one can keep uncooperative neighbors from trespassing over one's property by erecting a high barbed wire fence. There are other forms of manipulation as well, such as influencing the target's behavior in such a way that he/she is unable to engage in another form of behavior that the agent wishes to prevent. You can manipulate a traveling companion to stop whistling by engaging him/her in active and continuous conversation. Force and manipulation do not fit easily into our power taxonomy since they are characterized by a lack of volition on the part of the target. However, we include them here for completeness.

EDWARD J. LAWLER, POWER PROCESSES IN BARGAINING
33 Sociol.Q. 17, 17–26 (1992).

The basic issue is: How does power in relationships affect parties' use of conciliatory and hostile tactics in bargaining?

. . .

APPROACH TO POWER

In a rather confusing history within both the larger sociological literature on power as well as bargaining literature, power has been conceptualized in three primary ways: (1) as a potential or capability to influence the opponent; (2) as a process in which tactical actions—whether effective or not—seek to influence an opponent; and (3) as a result or outcome of an influence process, that is, as actual or realized power. These emphases actually constitute three complementary facets of power processes, each important to understanding bargaining.

Elaborating other social exchange formulations, we conceptualize power capability, power use, and actual power as distinct moments of a power process. In any power process, therefore, parties have some capability to affect each other's outcomes, an option to use that capability, and an uncertain probability of success. Using social exchange theory, power capabilities are based on the social structure in which the relationship of parties is embedded, a variety of specific tactical actions can use power, and successful use produces actual or realized power at a given point in time. For example, unions negotiating with management have some structurally based capability to apply leverage (e.g., workers difficult to replace, a sizeable strike fund), make tactical decisions about whether and how to use such capability, and achieve variable degrees of influence through such tactics.

These rather sharp distinctions between power capability, power-use, and actual or realized power raise a number of questions, such as: When do actors use their power capability? If used, what tactical form does power-use take? When does use of a power capability produce actual power or influence? Are there conditions where a structural power capability itself—without power-use (i.e., action)—produces actual influence? These are important theoretical questions.

$\cdots$

A Basic Theoretical Contrast

The nonzero-sum implications of power dependence theory lead Bacharach and Lawler to propose a distinction between the "total power" *in the relationship* and the "relative power" of the parties in that relationship. The unit of analysis is the single relation or dyad. Total power refers to the sum of each party's absolute power (i.e., Pab + Pba); relative power refers to the power difference or ratio of each party's absolute power (i.e., Pab/[Pab + Pba]). Given equal power, shifts upward or downward in total power involve proportional changes in the degree of mutual dependence or what Emerson (1972) terms "relational cohesion" and Molm (1987, 1989) terms "average power." Shifts in relative power entail either a redistribution of existing power in the relationship or an unequal distribution of changes in total power.

Importantly, relative and total power can change in a variety of interesting and somewhat independent ways. If two nations over time become the exclusive providers of valued commodities, the total power in the relationship grows without changing relative power, as long as the net growth of each party's absolute power is equal. By the same token, if actors in a close relationship each develop their own set of friends, total power—and, hence, relational cohesion—declines without necessarily changing their relative power. However, if only one person develops a set of friends, both total and relative power change, though in this case all of the change in total power would be an artifact of the change in relative power.

. . .

The nonzero-sum conception of power leads us to distinguish between tactics that use an existing power capability (*power-use tactics*) and those that can change the power relationship in an ongoing struggle (*power-change tactics*) such as between labor and management, divisions in an organization, or particular nations. A threat to leave the relationship exemplifies a "power-use" tactic, while the development of alternative relationships exemplifies a "power-change" tactic (upon which future threats-to-leave might be based). Power-use tactics deal with the immediate conflict of interest parties face in explicit bargaining, while power-change tactics essentially prepare for future conflicts in addition to possibly dealing with the immediate one. Our theorizing bears on both types, but has focused on power-use tactics.

Two major classes of power-use tactics are relevant to explicit bargaining: conciliatory and hostile. The former are positive acts, communicating a willingness to coordinate or collaborate; the latter are negative acts, communicating an inclination toward competition, intimidation, and resistance. In explicit bargaining, concession-making (i.e., concession tactics) is a major form of conciliation, and levying damage (i.e., damage tactics) a major form of hostility. Conciliatory tactics attempt to produce mutual accommodation, and hostile tactics attempt to pressure or force opponent concessions.

POWER CAPABILITY AND POWER-USE

Our major concern is the impact of power capability on power-use as defined above. In this section, we address two questions suggested by the distinction between relative and total power. First, how does the total power in a relationship affect the use of conciliatory and hostile tactics in bargaining? Second, how does relative power (i.e., equal vs. unequal) affect use of conciliatory and hostile tactics? Two core propositions offer broad answers to these questions:

    1. *Total Power Proposition:* Given equal power between two parties in bargaining, higher levels of total power in the relationship decrease hostility and increase conciliation.

    2. *Relative Power Proposition:* Given each party has a "significant" amount of absolute power, a relationship with unequal power produces more hostility and less conciliation than a relationship with equal power.

These core propositions capture and integrate the broadest implications of two distinct branches of theoretical and empirical work, one on *power dependence* and one on *punitive power*. These branches are fully complementary but differ in the structural form of power analyzed (i.e., dependence vs. punitive or coercive), the type of costs power-use inflicts on the opponent (i.e., opportunity costs vs. retaliation costs), the primary dependent variable (conciliation vs. hostility), and the explanatory framework (power dependence theory vs. bilateral deterrence theory). Below we elaborate the connection of these propositions to work on power dependence and bilateral deterrence processes.

The total power proposition is implicit in Emerson's power dependence theory and also some theorizing on deterrence in international relations. In power dependence terms, total power constitutes the level of mutual dependence or "relational cohesion" in the relationship. It suggests that higher total power or mutual dependence increases opportunity costs of leaving the relationship or concluding the bargaining without an agreement. Higher total power essentially raises the stake in reaching a reasonable conclusion. Bargaining in relationships with high, rather than low, total power, therefore, should be more cooperative, take less time, and produce more agreements.

A second tradition, found in one part of the deterrence literature on international relations, also supports this idea—namely, the literature that deals with the control over violence in a bilateral power relationship over time. The maintenance of large power capabilities to forestall hostile action is what Morgan terms "general deterrence." If two parties develop and maintain high levels of coercive power (i.e., capability to damage each other), each ostensibly uses that capability less because of a fear of retaliation. Together, power dependence and bilateral deterrence literatures suggest that the primary reason high total power produces less power use is the type of costs attached to power use—opportunity costs in the case of power dependence versus retaliation costs in the case of deterrence.

. . .

Turning to relative power, the core proposition suggests that unequal power relationships are less stable in bargaining. One reason is dissensus over the legitimacy of the power differences or whether and how such differences should affect the negotiated solution. In an unequal power relationship, the disadvantaged party may resist agreements that reflect their power position, while the advantaged party may hold out for precisely those that provide them a payoff proportional to their power advantage. Some common features of explicit bargaining should accentuate the tendency of unequal power to foster instability. For example, the "mutual consent" should create pressures toward equality and provide the lower-power party a readymade rationale for contesting a close connection between power inequalities and bargaining outcomes. Furthermore, given intergroup bargaining, constituents of the higher-power party will likely form expectations about the ultimate agreement and exert pressure that reflects their interests. In other words, when conflict occurs in a relationship with unequal power *and explicit bargaining develops,* the legitimacy of power differences will likely come under dispute, complicating the agenda.

ROGER FISHER, NEGOTIATING POWER: GETTING AND USING INFLUENCE

27 Am.Beh.Sci. 149, 150–64 (1983).

If I have negotiating power, I have the ability to affect favorably someone else's decision. This being so, one can argue that my power depends upon someone else's perception of my strength, so it is what they *think* that matters, not what I actually have. The other side may be as much influenced by a row of cardboard tanks as by a battalion of real tanks. One can then say that negotiating power is all a matter of perception.

A general who commands a real tank battalion, however, is in a far stronger position than one in charge of a row of cardboard tanks. A false impression of power is extremely vulnerable, capable of being destroyed by a word. In order to avoid focusing our attention on how to deceive other people, it seems best at the outset to identify what constitutes "real" negotiating power—an ability to influence the decisions of others assuming they know the truth. We can then go on to recognize that, in addition, it will be possible at times to influence others through deception, through creating an illusion of power. Even for that purpose, we will need to know what illusion we wish to create. If we are bluffing, what are we bluffing about?

· · ·

Categories of Power

My ability to exert influence depends upon the combined total of a number of different factors. As a first approximation, the following six kinds of power appear to provide useful categories for generating prescriptive advice:

(1) The power of skill and knowledge

(2) The power of a good relationship

(3) The power of a good alternative to negotiating

(4) The power of an elegant solution

(5) The power of legitimacy

(6) The power of commitment

Here is a checklist for would-be negotiators of what they can do in advance of any particular negotiation to enhance their negotiating power. The sequence in which these elements of power are listed is also important.

1. The Power of Skill and Knowledge

All things being equal, a skilled negotiator is better able to influence the decision of others than is an unskilled negotiator. Strong evidence suggests that negotiating skills can be both learned and taught.

· · ·

Knowledge also is power. Some knowledge is general and of use in many negotiations, such as familiarity with a wide range of procedural options and awareness of national negotiating styles and cultural differences. A repertoire of examples, precedents, and illustrations can also add to one's persuasive abilities.

Knowledge relevant to a particular negotiation in which one is about to engage is even more powerful. The more information one can gather about the parties and issues in an upcoming negotiation, the stronger one's entering posture. The following categories of knowledge, for example, are likely to strengthen one's ability to exert influence:

Knowledge about the people involved....

Knowledge about the interests involved....

Knowledge about the facts....

2. The Power of a Good Relationship

The better a working relationship I establish in advance with those with whom I will be negotiating, the more powerful I am. A good working relationship does not necessarily imply approval of each other's conduct, though mutual respect and even mutual affection—when it exists—may help. The two most critical elements of a working relationship are, first, trust, and second, the ability to communicate easily and effectively.

Trust. Although I am likely to focus my attention in a given negotiation on the question of whether or not I can trust those on the other side, my power depends upon whether they can trust me. If over time I have been able to establish a well-deserved reputation for candor, honesty, integrity, and commitment to any promise I make, my capacity to exert influence is significantly enhanced.

Communication. The negotiation process is one of communication. If I am trying to persuade some people to change their minds, I want to know where their minds are; otherwise, I am shooting in the dark. If my messages are going to have their intended impact, they need to be understood as I would have them understood. At best, interpersonal communication is difficult and often generates misunderstanding. When the parties see each other as adversaries, the risk of miscommunication and misunderstanding is greatly increased. The longer two people have known each other, and the more broadly and deeply each understands the point of view and context from which the other is operating, the more likely they can communicate with each other easily and with a minimum of misunderstanding.

. . .

3. The Power of a Good Alternative to Negotiation

To a significant extent, my power in a negotiation depends upon how well I can do for myself if I walk away. In *Getting to YES*, we urge a negotiator to develop and improve his "BATNA"—his Best Alternative To a Negotiated Agreement. One kind of preparation for negotiation that enhances one's negotiating power is to consider the alternatives to reaching agreement with this particular negotiating partner, to select the most promising, and to improve it to the extent possible. This alternative sets a floor. If I follow this practice, every negotiation will lead to a successful outcome in the sense that any result I accept is bound to be better than anything else I could do.

. . .

4. The Power of an Elegant Solution

In any negotiation, there is a melange of shared and conflicting interests. The parties face a problem. One way to influence the other side in a negotiation is to invent a good solution to that problem. The more complex the problem, the more influential an elegant answer. Too often, negotiators battle like litigators in court. Each side advances arguments for a result that would take care of its interests but would do nothing for the other side. The power of a mediator often comes from working out an ingenious solution that reconciles reasonably well the legitimate interests of both sides. Either negotiator has similar power to effect an agreement that takes care of his or her interests by generating an option that also takes care of some or most of the interests on the other side.

A wise negotiator includes in his or her preparatory work the generation of many options designed to meet as well as possible the legitimate interests of both sides. Brainstorming enhances my negotiating power by enhancing the chance that I will be able to devise a solution that amply satisfies my interests and also meets enough of your interests to be acceptable to you.

. . .

5. The Power of Legitimacy

Each of us is subject to being persuaded by becoming convinced that a particular result *ought* to be accepted because it is fair; because the law requires it; because it is consistent with precedent, industry practice, or sound policy considerations; or because it is legitimate as measured by some other objective standard. I can substantially enhance my negotiating power by searching for and developing various objective criteria and potential standards of legitimacy, and by shaping proposed solutions so that they are legitimate in the eyes of the other side.

Every negotiator is both a partisan and one of those who must be persuaded if any agreement is to be reached. To be persuasive, a good negotiator should speak like an advocate who is seeking to convince an able and honest arbitrator, and should listen like such an arbitrator, always open to being persuaded by reason. Being open to persuasion is itself persuasive.

Like a lawyer preparing a case, a negotiator will discover quite a few different principles of fairness for which plausible arguments can be advanced, and often quite a few different ways of interpreting or applying each principle. A tension exists between advancing a highly favorable principle that appears less legitimate to the other side and a less favorable principle that appears more legitimate. Typically, there is a range within which reasonable people could differ. To retain his power, a wise negotiator avoids advancing a proposition that is so extreme that it damages his credibility. He also avoids so locking himself into the first principle he advances that he will lose face in disentangling himself from that principle and moving on to one that has a greater chance of persuading the other side. In advance of this process, a negotiator will want to have researched precedents, expert opinion, and other objective criteria, and to have worked on various theories of what ought to be done, so as to harness the power of legitimacy—a power to which each of us is vulnerable.

6. The Power of Commitment

The five kinds of power previously mentioned can each be enhanced by work undertaken in advance of formal negotiations. The planning of commitments and making arrangements for them can also be undertaken in advance, but making commitments takes place only during what everyone thinks of as negotiation itself.

There are two quite different kinds of commitments—affirmative and negative:

(a) Affirmative commitments

(1) An offer of what I am willing to agree to.

(2) An offer of what, failing agreement, I am willing to do under certain conditions.

(b) Negative commitments

(1) A commitment that I am unwilling to make certain agreements (even though they would be better for me than no agreement).

(2) A commitment or threat that, failing agreement, I will engage in certain negative conduct (even though to do so would be worse for me than a simple absence of agreement).

Every commitment involves a decision. Let's first look at affirmative commitments. An affirmative commitment is a decision about what one is willing to do. It is an offer. Every offer ties the negotiator's hands to some extent. It says, "This, I am willing to do." The offer may expire or later be withdrawn, but while open it carries some persuasive power. It is no longer just an idea or a possibility that the parties are discussing. Like a proposal of marriage or a job offer, it is operational. It says, "I am willing to do this. If you agree, we have a deal."

We have all felt the power of a positive commitment—the power of an invitation. (We are not here concerned with the degree of commitment, or with various techniques for making a constraint more binding, but only with the content of the commitment itself. Advance planning can enhance my power by enabling me to demonstrate convincingly that a commitment is unbreakable. This subject, like all of those concerned with the difference between appearance and reality, is left for another day.) The one who makes the offer takes a risk. If he had waited, he might have gotten better terms. But in exchange for taking that risk, he has increased his chance of affecting the outcome.

. . .

A negative commitment is the most controversial and troublesome element of negotiating power. No doubt, by tying my own hands I may be able to influence you to accept something more favorable to me than you otherwise would. The theory is simple. For almost every potential agreement, there is a range within which each of us is better off having an agreement than walking away. Suppose that you would be willing to pay $75,000 for my house if you had to; but for a price above that figure you would rather buy a different house. The best offer I have received from someone else is $62,000, and I will accept that offer unless you give me a better one. At any price between $62,000 and $75,000 we are both better off than if no agreement is reached. If you offer me $62,100, and so tie your hands by a negative commitment that you cannot raise your offer, presumably, I will accept it since it is better than $62,000. On the other hand, if I can commit myself not to drop the price below $75,000, you presumably will buy the house at that price. This logic may lead us to engage in a battle of negative commitments. Logic suggests that "victory" goes to the one who first and most convincingly ties his own hands at an appropriate figure. Other things being equal, an early and rigid negative commitment at the right point should prove persuasive.

Other things, however, are not likely to be equal.

The earlier I make a negative commitment—the earlier I announce a take-it-or-leave-it position—the less likely I am to have maximized the cumulative total of the various elements of my negotiating power.

The power of knowledge. I probably acted before knowing as much as I could have learned. The longer I postpone making a negative commitment, the more likely I am to know the best proposition to which to commit myself.

The power of a good relationship. Being quick to advance a take-it-or-leave-it position is likely to prejudice a good working relationship and to damage the trust you might otherwise place in what I say. The more quickly I confront you with a rigid position on my part, the more likely I am to make you so angry that you will refuse an agreement you might otherwise accept.

The power of a good alternative. There is a subtle but significant difference between communicating a warning of the course of action that I believe it will be in my interest to take should we fail to reach agreement (my BATNA), and locking myself in to precise terms that you must accept in order to avoid my taking that course of action. Extending a warning is not the same as making a negative commitment.

To make [a] negative commitment at an early stage of the negotiation is likely to reduce the negotiating power of a good BATNA. It shifts the other side's attention from the objective reality of my most attractive alternative to a subjective statement that I won't do things that (except for my having made the commitment) would be in my interest to do. Such negative commitments invite the other side to engage in a contest of will by making commitments that are even more negative, and even more difficult to get out of. Whatever negotiating impact my BATNA may have, it is likely to be lessened by clouding it with negative commitments.

The power of an elegant solution. The early use of a negative commitment reduces the likelihood that the choice being considered by the other side is one that best meets its interests consistent with any given degree of meeting our interests. If we announce early in the negotiation process that we will accept no agreement other than Plan X, Plan X probably takes care of most of our interests. But it is quite likely that Plan X could be improved. With further study and time, it may be possible to modify Plan X so that it serves our interests even better at little or no cost to the interests of the other side.

Second, it may be possible to modify Plan X in ways that make it more attractive to the other side without in any way making it less attractive to us. To do so would not serve merely the other side but would serve us also by making it more likely that the other side will accept a plan that so well serves our interests.

Third, it may be possible to modify Plan X in ways that make it much more attractive to the other side at a cost of making it only slightly less attractive to us. The increase in total benefits and the increased likelihood of quickly reaching agreement may outweigh the modest cost involved.

Premature closure on an option is almost certain to reduce our ability to exert the influence that comes from having an option well crafted to reconcile, to the extent possible, the conflicting interests of the two sides. In multilateral negotiations it is even less likely that an early option will be well designed to take into account the plurality of divergent interests involved.

The power of legitimacy. The most serious damage to negotiating power that results from an early negative commitment is likely to result from its damage to the influence that comes from legitimacy. Legitimacy depends upon both process and substance. As with an arbitrator, the legitimacy of a negotiator's decision depends upon having accorded the other side "due process." The persuasive power of my decision depends in part on my having fully heard your views, your suggestions, and your notions of what is fair before committing myself. And my decision will have increased persuasiveness for you to the extent that I am able to justify it by reference to objective standards of fairness that you have indicated you consider appropriate. That factor, again, urges me to withhold making any negative commitment until I fully understand your views on fairness.

. . .

To make a negative commitment either as to what we will not do or to impose harsh consequences unless the other side reaches agreement with us, without having previously made a firm and clear offer, substantially lessens our ability to exert influence. An offer may not be enough, but a threat is almost certainly not enough unless there is a "yesable" proposition on the table—a clear statement of the action desired and a commitment as to the favorable consequences which would follow.

This analysis of negotiating power suggests that in most cases it is a mistake to attempt to influence the other side by making a negative commitment of any kind at the outset of the negotiations, and that it is a mistake to do so until one has first made the most of every other element of negotiating power.

This analysis also suggests that when as a last resort threats or other negative commitments are used, they should be so formulated as to complement and reinforce other elements of negotiating power, not undercut them. In particular, any statement to the effect that we have finally reached a take-it-or-leave-it position should be made in a way that is consistent with maintaining a good working relationship, and consistent with the concepts of legitimacy with which we are trying to persuade the other side.

WILLIAM L.F. FELSTINER & AUSTIN SARAT, ENACTMENTS OF POWER: NEGOTIATING REALITY AND RESPONSIBILITY IN LAWYER–CLIENT INTERACTIONS

77 Cornell L.Rev. 1447, 1459–66 (1992).

ENACTMENTS OF POWER AND THE NEGOTIATION OF REALITY

In the world of no-fault divorce, the legal process formally has limited functions—dividing assets and future income, fixing custody and visitation, and, occasionally, protecting physical safety and property. Lawyers must understand their client's objectives concerning these issues. But determination of clients' interests is a known quagmire. Clients may not know what they want or may not want what they ought to want. They may change their minds in unpredictable ways, or they may not change their minds when they ought to do so. Clients may be insufficiently self-conscious, or plagued by false consciousness. Moreover, they may find it difficult to distinguish between lawyers who are trying to impose their vision of client needs on clients and lawyers who are trying to get clients to share a vision of those needs that is not controlled by the power of the lawyer's professional position.

. . .

In examining the ongoing and fragile negotiation of reality between lawyers and clients, we focus first on the factors that "distort" reality for lawyers and clients, and then on the strategies and tactics employed to promote particular versions of reality. Clients, of course, have greater difficulty than lawyers in becoming oriented to the world of the legally possible. Some of the difficulty is obvious. Emotionally off-balance, angry, depressed, anxious or agitated, they may have trouble understanding what they are told, believing the information that they get and focusing on the alternatives that are presented to them. They may be impelled to strike at or "pay back" their spouse in ways that are inconsistent with reality and even, by altering the posture of the other side, make their goals more difficult to attain.

Second, clients may expect more of the legal system than it can deliver under even the best of circumstances. Unrealistic expectations may range from saving the marriage to transforming the spouse, but they are most likely to be centered on financial affairs. Clients tend to reason up from needs, rather than down from resources, and they have great difficulty in dealing with the gap between the two. Additionally, clients are slow to realize that many legal entitlements are not self-executing. The judge at the hearing on temporary support may say that the client is entitled to $100 a week, but that does not guarantee that the client will receive anything. Many clients are naive about their own financial needs, and may have to be patiently educated by their lawyers. Some clients have difficulty grasping the limits of what is possible because they cannot believe that the law actually is as it actually is. Finally, clients are slow to understand the costs of achieving their objectives. Vindication, the last dollar of support, meticulous estimates of property value, a neat and precise division of property, a visitation scheme that covers a very wide range of contingencies, and equitable arrangements that govern the future as well as the present may be theoretically possible, but even approximations require extensive services that middle-class clients generally cannot afford.

Lawyers, of course, are less encumbered on the legal side in developing a view of reality in particular cases. Nevertheless, it is not all clear sailing for them. There are, for instance, three kinds of information problems. In order to form a view of the possible they may need to know things that clients sometimes cannot tell them. These include client goals as well as things that clients sometimes will not tell them, such as their feelings. In addition, there are things that clients sometimes try to tell lawyers that lawyers do not recognize or understand. For example, in a case that we previously analyzed at some length, the client could not decide whether she wanted to settle or litigate, and could not make the lawyer understand that she had great difficulty in negotiating a settlement with her spouse because she could not trust him to fulfill any commitments that he made.

Clients are more limited in the resources that they can mobilize to persuade lawyers to accept their view of reality. Their inherent advantage is their knowledge of their spouse and generally superior ability to estimate the spouse's reaction to offers or demands. Lawyers are sensitive to this comparative advantage and often try to exploit it. As one lawyer put it in speaking with one of his clients:

> Let me ask you this, because you know him a lot better. Which do you think he'd be more likely to give a good response to? Something that's in writing, that he needs to respond to in writing, or something oral?

Or, as another stated,

> That's what I'm inclined to do here, unless you're of the opinion you would rather start at sixty-forty. I mean, you know Joan and you know how she would react.

In the latter instance the lawyer is even prepared to alter her favored pattern of negotiation in the face of the client's superior knowledge. For that instant, the social world of the client, rather than the world of law and legal experience, defines the parameters of the reasonable.

In addition to deploying their knowledge of their own social world, clients frequently assert their views, or resist their lawyers through repetition and denial. Lawyers may talk about the unreasonable or the unobtainable, they may predict this or that outcome, but clients need not, and frequently do not, acquiesce. Rather, clients may become quiet or change the subject, only to reintroduce the same topic later. What may seem to the observer to be wasted motion and circularity, may really be a tactic in an ongoing negotiation. Finally, clients on occasion fight back by withholding information, sometimes explicitly, sometimes not. They use this tactic when they want to exclude the lawyer from some field of inquiry, often because they consider an issue out of bounds or would be embarrassed by some disclosure.

The negotiation of reality between lawyer and client is time-consuming and repetitive, yet often incomplete or unclear in its results. Whose definition of reality prevails is often impossible to determine. Even as decisions are made and documents are filed, how those decisions and documents relate to lawyer-client conversations about goals and expectations can be mysterious. It is, however, precisely by attending to this mystery that one can understand enactments of power and tactics of resistance.

Lawyers use an array of strategies to try to persuade their clients to adopt a particular definition of reality. Of course, their knowledge of legal rules and process, and the information that they have about specific players, such as other lawyers, judges and mediators, provide powerful arguments. Unless they have been through the process before, clients' only sources of information about the nature and limits of divorce law are their own lawyer and anecdotes related by their family and friends. In addition to their feel for the legal system and for the *dramatis personae,* lawyers, particularly specialists in family law, benefit from their experiences in prior cases. Having "heard it all before," they frequently interpret the behavior of the spouse and his or her lawyer with some accuracy, looking beyond words and positions articulated to more fundamental concerns.

Still, many divorce lawyers use their knowledge and experience in a manipulative way. The most common technique is to engage in what we call "law talk." Law talk consists of the conversations that lawyers and clients have about the legal system, legal process, rules, hearings, trials, judges, other lawyers and the other lawyer in the case. In general, we have found law talk to be a form of cynical realism through which the legal system and its actors are trashed on various accounts, frequently in an exaggerated fashion. The purpose of this rhetorical style is usually to convince the client that the legal process is risky business, that legal justice is different from social justice, and that clients can only achieve reasonable certainty at a reasonable cost, and maintain some control over a divorce, by negotiating a settlement with the other side.

Even when it takes the form of hyperbole, law talk is not commonly introduced into lawyer-client conversations in an aggressive way. Lawyers often join with their clients' positions and appear, at least initially, to be sympathetic. They introduce their clients to reality by invoking their own understanding of legal norms and their own expectations about what courts would do were they to go before a judge. Clients are told that it does not make sense to "insist on something that is far out of line from what a court would do."

Chapter 8

THE INFLUENCE OF CULTURE ON BARGAINING: GENDER AS A BEHAVIORAL DETERMINANT OF NEGOTIATION STYLE AND STRATEGY

Thus far in this section we have observed that interpersonal communication orientation and skill influences negotiator effectiveness. How well a person utilizes power in bargaining—either actual or perceived power—also influences effectiveness. But such idiosyncratic traits may not be the only behavioral factors affecting the bargaining relationship. Negotiators may exhibit stereotypical behavior patterns characteristic of ethnic, national, age, racial, class or gender influences. A companion volume of materials could—and should—be written about the influence of culture on bargaining. In this chapter, the last in this section, we examine only the barest outlines of this rich and complex theme. Our focus is on the influence of gender on negotiation, the most universally available indicator of cultural differentiation.

It would not be surprising if a person's gender was a significant predictor of negotiation style and strategy selection. For the past thirty years at least, our culture has explored gender role differences in business, personal, social and sexual relationships. We now know much about the impact of gender on personality development. Researchers have also investigated whether gender is a factor in how we choose a predominant bargaining pattern, and whether gender differences have a bearing on potential negotiation success. The readings in this chapter present a framework for assessing the impact of gender on negotiation and describe the results of recent empirical research.

Many of these appraisals of gender influence flow from the work of Carol Gilligan. In the early 1980's, she published *In a Different Voice,* in which she questioned the findings of earlier studies of moral development in children that were premised upon observations and interviews with boys. Her work is based upon research data obtained from girls as well as boys, and articulates a provocative "different voice" of gender-related patterns that are employed when young people are asked to resolve moral dilemmas. Gilligan describes two voices of discourse, a language of justice in outcome and a language of caring for relationship, to symbolize the gender differences she found. The first selection in this chapter involves one of Gilligan's most celebrated contributions, a conversation with Amy and Jake regarding the ethical propriety of several strategies designed to obtain lifesaving medication from a pharmacist.

Gilligan's concept of different voices of communication has direct application to analyzing possible variations in bargaining behavior between men and women. The next two readings show us how. First, Carrie Menkel–Meadow, participating in a discussion with several other people interested in feminist approaches to legal analysis, helps us put the story of Jake and Amy in the context of a lawyer's dispute resolution practice. Then, Deborah Kolb and Gloria Coolidge go further, cataloguing how expected gender differences in bargaining patterns can influence negotiations between men and women. While acknowledging wide variation among individual men and women, they describe four stereotypical differences in the bargaining assumptions of the two genders. Their observations challenge assumptions and prescriptive advice offered by advocates of both positional and interest-based strategies. Kolb and Coolidge conclude with two examples of how insensitivity to alternative gender voices can complicate efforts at effective negotiation.

Finally, we consider whether the theories of alternative voices in negotiation are borne out in practice. The last reading in this chapter is taken from survey research data concerning lawyer's negotiating styles. Several years ago, Gerald Williams conducted a detailed survey of the bargaining styles of attorneys practicing in Phoenix, Arizona. His instrument garnered data from over a hundred lawyers about the behavior patterns of other lawyers with whom they had recently negotiated. Williams and four others reinterpret these data in this reading to assess the role of gender on negotiation strategy selection and on negotiator effectiveness. They test several theories about the relationship between Gilligan's different voices and the strategies of competition and cooperation in bargaining. Their analyses reveal a wealth of useful information, and several surprising results.

Readings

1. Carol Gilligan, In a Different Voice: Psychological Theory and Women's Development 25–32 (1982).

2. Carrie Menkel–Meadow, in *Feminist Discourse, Moral Values and the Law—A Conversation,* 34 Buffalo L.Rev. 11, 50–54 (1985).

3. Deborah M. Kolb & Gloria G. Coolidge, *Her Place at the Table: A Consideration of Gender Issues in Negotiation,* in Negotiation Theory and Practice 261–71 (J. William Breslin & Jeffrey Z. Rubin, eds. (1991)).

4. Lloyd Burton, Larry Farmer, Elizabeth Gee, Lorie Johnson & Gerald Williams, *Feminist Theory, Professional Ethics, and Gender–Related Distinctions in Attorney Negotiating Styles,* 1991 J.Disp.Res. 199, 215–40.

5. For Further Reading

a. Mary F. Belenky, B.M. Clinchy, Nancy R. Goldberger & J.M. Tarule, Women's Ways of Knowing: The Development of Self, Voice and Mind (1986).

b. Benton, *Bargaining Visibility and Attitudes of Male and Female Group Representatives,* 43 J. Personality 661 (1975).

c. Burrell, Donahue & Allen, *Gender–Based Perceptual Biases in Mediation,* 15 Communication Res. 447 (1988).

d. Charles Craver, *The Impact of Gender on Clinical Negotiating Achievement,* 6 Ohio St.J.Disp.Resol. 1 (1990).

e. Kay Deaux, *From Individual Differences to Social Categories: Analysis of a Decade's Research on Gender,* 39 Amer.Psych. 105 (1984).

f. Alice H. Eagley, Sex Differences in Social Behavior: A Social–Role Interpretation (1987).

g. Judith M. Gerson & Kathy Peiss, *Boundaries, Negotiation, Consciousness: Reconceptualizing Gender Relations,* 32 Soc.Probs. 317 (1985).

h. Leonard Greenhalgh & Roderick W. Gilkey, *Our Game, Your Rules: Developing Effective Negotiating Approaches,* in Moore, ed., Not as Far as You Think: The Realities of Working Women (1986).

i. Eva Hoffman, Lost in Translation: A Life in a New Language (1989).

j. Rand Jack & Dana Crowley Jack, *Women Lawyers: Archetype and Alternatives,* in Carol Gilligan, J. Ward & J. Taylor, eds., Mapping the Moral Domain 263 (1988).

k. Robin Lakoff, Language and Woman's Place (1975).

l. Carrie Menkel–Meadow, *Portia in a Different Voice: Speculations on a Women's Lawyering Process,* 1 Berkeley Women's L.J. 39 (1985).

m. Linda D. Molm, *Gender, Power, and Legitimation: A Test of Three Theories,* 91 Am.J.Sociol. 1356 (1986).

n. Sallyanne Payton, *Releasing Excellence: Erasing Gender Zoning From the Legal Mind,* 18 Ind.L.Rev. 629 (1985).

o. Susan Philips, Susan Steele & Christine Tan, eds., Language, Gender and Sex in Comparative Perspective (1987).

p. Dean G. Pruitt, Peter Carnevale, Blythe Forcey & Michael Van Slyck, *Gender Effects in Negotiation: Constituent Surveillance and Contentious Behavior,* 22 J.Exper.Soc.Psych. 264 (1986).

q. Janet Rifkin, *Mediation From a Feminist Perspective: Problems and Promise,* 21 L. & Inequality 2 (1984).

r. Deborah Tannen, You Just Don't Understand: Women and Men in Conversation (1990).

s. Carol Watson, *Gender versus Power as a Predictor of Negotiation Behavior and Outcomes,* 10 Negot.J. 117 (1994).

CAROL GILLIGAN, IN A DIFFERENT VOICE: PSYCHOLOGICAL THEORY AND WOMEN'S DEVELOPMENT

25–32 (1982).

The two children in question, Amy and Jake, were both bright and articulate and, at least in their eleven-year-old aspirations, resisted easy categories of sex-role stereotyping, since Amy aspired to become a scientist while Jake preferred English to math. Yet their moral judgments seem initially to confirm familiar notions about differences between the sexes, suggesting that the edge girls have on moral development during the early school years gives way at puberty with the ascendance of formal logical thought in boys.

The dilemma that these eleven-year-olds were asked to resolve was one in the series devised by Kohlberg to measure moral development in adolescence by presenting a conflict between moral norms and exploring the logic of its resolution. In this particular dilemma, a man named Heinz considers whether or not to steal a drug which he cannot afford to buy in order to save the life of his wife. In the standard format of Kohlberg's interviewing procedure, the description of the dilemma itself—Heinz's predicament, the wife's disease, the druggist's refusal to lower his price—is followed by the question, "Should Heinz steal the drug?" The reasons for and against stealing are then explored through a series of questions that vary and extend the parameters of the dilemma in a way designed to reveal the underlying structure of moral thought.

Jake, at eleven, is clear from the outset that Heinz should steal the drug. Constructing the dilemma, as Kohlberg did, as a conflict between the values of property and life, he discerns the logical priority of life and uses that logic to justify his choice:

> For one thing, a human life is worth more than money, and if the druggist only makes $1,000, he is still going to live, but if Heinz doesn't steal the drug, his wife is going to die. (*Why is life worth more than money?*) Because the druggist can get a thousand dollars later from rich people with cancer, but Heinz can't get his wife again. (*Why not?*) Because people are all different and so you couldn't get Heinz's wife again.

Asked whether Heinz should steal the drug if he does not love his wife, Jake replies that he should, saying that not only is there "a difference between hating and killing," but also, if Heinz were caught, "the judge would probably think it was the right thing to do." Asked about the fact that, in stealing, Heinz would be breaking the law, he says that "the laws have mistakes, and you can't go writing up a law for everything that you can imagine."

Thus, while taking the law into account and recognizing its function in maintaining social order (the judge, Jake says, "should give Heinz the lightest possible sentence"), he also sees the law as man-made and therefore subject to error and change. Yet his judgment that Heinz should steal the drug, like his view of the law as having mistakes, rests on the assumption of agreement, a societal consensus around moral values that allows one to know and expect others to recognize what is "the right thing to do."

Fascinated by the power of logic, this eleven-year-old boy locates truth in math, which, he says, is "the only thing that is totally logical." Considering the moral dilemma to be "sort of like a math problem with humans," he sets it up as an equation and proceeds to work out the solution. Since his solution is rationally derived, he assumes that anyone following reason would arrive at the same conclusion and thus that a judge would also consider stealing to be the right thing for Heinz to do. Yet he is also aware of the limits of logic. Asked whether there is a right answer to moral problems, Jake replies that "there can only be right and wrong in judgment," since the parameters of action are variable and complex. Illustrating how actions undertaken with the best of intentions can eventuate in the most disastrous of consequences, he says, "like if you give an old lady your seat on the trolley, if you are in a trolley crash and that seat goes through the window, it might be that reason that the old lady dies."

In contrast, Amy's response to the dilemma conveys a very different impression, an image of development stunted by a failure of logic, an inability to think for herself. Asked if Heinz should steal the drug, she replies in a way that seems evasive and unsure:

> Well, I don't think so. I think there might be other ways besides stealing it, like if he could borrow the money or make a loan or something, but he really shouldn't steal the drug—but his wife shouldn't die either.

Asked why he should not steal the drug, she considers neither property nor law but rather the effect that theft could have on the relationship between Heinz and his wife:

> If he stole the drug, he might save his wife then, but if he did, he might have to go to jail, and then his wife might get sicker again, and he couldn't get more of the drug, and it might not be good. So, they should really just talk it out and find some other way to make the money.

Seeing in the dilemma not a math problem with humans but a narrative of relationships that extends over time, Amy envisions the wife's continuing need for her husband and the husband's continuing concern for his wife and seeks to respond to the druggist's need in a way that would sustain rather than sever connection. Just as she ties the wife's survival to the preservation of relationships, so she considers the value of the wife's life in a context of relationships, saying that it would be wrong to let her die because, "if she died, it hurts a lot of people and it hurts her." Since Amy's moral judgment is grounded in the belief that, "if somebody has something that would keep somebody alive, then it's not right not to give it to them," she considers the problem in the dilemma to arise not from the druggist's assertion of rights but from his failure of response.

Just as Jake is confident the judge would agree that stealing is the right thing for Heinz to do, so Amy is confident that, "if Heinz and the druggist had talked it out long enough, they could reach something besides stealing." As he considers the law to "have mistakes," so she sees this drama as a mistake, believing that "the world should just share things more and then people wouldn't have to steal." Both children thus recognize the need for agreement but see it as mediated in different ways—he impersonally through systems of logic and law, she personally through communication in relationship. Just as he relies on the conventions of logic to deduce the solution to this dilemma, assuming these conventions to be shared, so she relies on a process of communication, assuming connection and believing that her voice will be heard. Yet while his assumptions about agreement are confirmed by the convergence in logic between his answers and the questions posed, her assumptions are belied by the failure of communication, the interviewer's inability to understand her response.

. . .

Amy is considering not *whether* Heinz should act in this situation ("*should* Heinz steal the drug?") but rather *how* Heinz should act in response to his awareness of his wife's need ("Should Heinz *steal* the drug?").

In this way, these two eleven-year-old children, both highly intelligent and perceptive about life, though in different ways, display different modes of moral understanding, different ways of thinking about conflict and choice. In resolving Heinz's dilemma, Jake relies on theft to avoid confrontation and turns to the law to mediate the dispute. Transposing a hierarchy of power into a hierarchy of values, he defuses a potentially explosive conflict between people by casting it as an impersonal conflict of claims. In this way, he abstracts the moral problem from the interpersonal situation, finding in the logic of fairness an objective way to decide who will win the dispute. But this hierarchical ordering, with its imagery of winning and losing and the potential for violence which it contains, gives way in Amy's construction of the dilemma to a network of connection, a web of relationships that is sustained by a process of communication. With this shift, the moral problem changes from one of unfair domination, the imposition of property over life, to one of unnecessary exclusion, the failure of the druggist to respond to the wife.

CARRIE MENKEL–MEADOW, FEMINIST DISCOURSE, MORAL VALUES, AND THE LAW—A CONVERSATION

34 Buffalo L.Rev. 11, 50–54 (1985).

One of the things that Amy does that might be of interest to law students is typical of a "bad" law student: Amy "fought the hypo." When asked whether or not Heinz should steal the drug, Amy asked a lot of questions about the situation. At fifteen, she is still fighting the hypo. "Look," she says to the researchers, "you have given me a totally silly situation that I do not think really exists in the world. Or if it did, I would know a whole lot more about it." She asks for what has come to be known in academic circles as "a greater feeling for the context." Law students, when faced with hypotheticals that seem to be missing something (perhaps facts about the particular people in the situation, or about the political context in which the case is found, or—to use the legal realist phrase—about what the judge had for breakfast that morning), usually behave the same way Amy did. They feel that the problems are disembodied and disemboweled from the way in which they occur in the world.

. . .

Maybe I have taken too much out of the Amy and Jake problem. It is, nevertheless, an interesting meditation on the legal system because what we see in Jake's description is pretty much how the Heinz dilemma would get solved if it wound up either in court or if the parties attempted to negotiate something between themselves. It was from that work, in looking at how to be a practicing lawyer—in a courtroom, as a negotiator, or as a legal problem solver—that I began to rethink the theory of legal structure. My re-examination could well have been inspired by how Amy looked at the problem.

I should add here that I have noticed, as did Carol in psychology, how many of our conceptions of what the legal system ought to be and ought to do were derived exclusively from male practitioners and male scholars. The law may thus represent an embodiment of Jake's voice, the male voice. As a double footnote, I, like Carol, want to say that although I am speaking of male and female voices, I am simply using those terms as a code for what she observed to exist empirically in those two genders. All of us have elements of both of those voices. Those men who see themselves fitting the description of the female voice should know that that is probably who they are, and vice versa for women. I use that as an easy way to talk about this material, but one that is not necessarily accurate for each one of you individually.

What would the legal system look like if Amy had devised it, either alone or with Jake's help? As I said, Amy might use different forms or different processes. To do this, let's look at the way the Anglo–American court system is in fact structured. We have basically a one-way communication, adverse parties talking to a judge. There may be a witness or, in more complicated form, a jury. But all of this communication is directed at somebody else. There is very little direct communication between the parties. Picking up on Amy's process notion that the parties might talk to each other, we can imagine a structure in which the parties might be asked to sit down and talk about whether the drug should be stolen or financed in some other way. One form that is beginning to emerge, which in some sense is a reaction to this adversary structure, is alternative dispute resolution or mediation.

· · ·

If the parties are not in accord, they will do what most parties do when they are in dispute—they will probably arrive at a solution by negotiation. Typically, a plaintiff and a defendant—Heinz and the druggist—will start arguing with each other. Heinz might say: "I can't pay you anything." The druggist would respond: "I want one hundred dollars." At some point, they will split the difference, settling on paying perhaps half of what the druggist wanted.

What's wrong with that? What's wrong, according to some people, is that it reflects one form of the female voice—it is compromise, it is a combination, it is meeting somewhere in the middle, and it may leave both parties unhappy. What Amy was trying to do was to hold both parties' needs constant and to meet both sets of needs at the same time. Having the parties meet each other's needs does not necessarily result in compromise or accommodation, which is the way in which the female voice is frequently and inaccurately seen—as conciliatory, accommodating, giving up....

A new synergistic solution might emerge simply from having them talk to each other directly about their needs. If we learn to listen to the "Amys" of the world, we might begin to imagine different kinds of constructions and different ways of looking at our legal system in solving our legal problems.

DEBORAH M. KOLB AND GLORIA G. COOLIDGE, HER PLACE AT THE TABLE: A CONSIDERATION OF GENDER ISSUES IN NEGOTIATION

Negotiation Theory and Practice 261–71 (William Breslin & Jeffrey Z. Rubin, Eds. (The Harvard Program on Negotiation Books (1991)).

Our purpose here is to explore the ramifications of feminist theories of development and social organization to the exercise of power and the resolution of conflict in negotiated settings. Based on a review of some of the leading works, we suggest that there are four themes that are most relevant to an understanding of some of the ways that women frame and conduct negotiations. These are:

- a relational view of others;
- an embedded view of agency;
- an understanding of control through empowerment; and
- problem-solving through dialogue.

HER VOICE IN NEGOTIATION

There are at least three reasons why the subject of an alternative voice in negotiation is not closed. First, our experience and those of others suggest that there are significant differences in the ways men and women are likely to approach negotiation and the styles they use in a search for agreement.

Although the research often yields contradictory conclusions (Rubin and Brown, 1975; Deux, 1984; Eagly, 1987; Linn, 1986), in every training situation in which we have been engaged, women come up and ask us to talk about the gender issues. The inference we draw from these interactions is that at least some women experience their gender as a factor in negotiation. The fact that research may not capture this experience may derive from the settings of research (usually the laboratory) and the questions the research poses (which are usually aggregate behavioral indicators). Secondly, there is evidence that in real negotiations (as opposed to simulations), women do not fare that well. In divorce mediation, for example, the settlements women received are inferior economically to those awarded in adjudication (Rifkin, 1984; Pearson and Thoennes, 1988). In queries about salary negotiations, men report higher raises than women (Womack, 1987). If negotiation is a woman's place, we would expect women to excel, not be disadvantaged. There is a third reason why we need to focus on a woman's voice in negotiation: The prescriptions to get to win-win outcomes in negotiation offer ambiguous advice to the negotiator, whether male or female. The advice to focus on interests, not positions, and invent options for mutual gain (Fisher and Ury, 1981) emphasizes the relational dimension of negotiation. There are indications, however, that this advice is quite difficult for many to heed because it runs counter to prevailing cultural norms about the competitive and gaming aspect of negotiation (McCarthy, 1985).

On the other hand, advice to separate people from problems and focus on objective criteria, gives a rationalized and objective cast to negotiation that may be quite different from the subjective and embedded forms of feminine understanding.   Further, in the press to provide prescription, it is the technical and rationalized analysis that increasingly dominates.   Integrative bargaining, or joint-gain negotiation, while acknowledging the importance of empathetic relationships, suggests that the critical skills necessary to implement win-win outcomes are primarily technical and analytic.

Articulating an alternative voice (or voices) becomes increasingly important in an emerging field in which the driving force is toward prescription. These popular theories of negotiation imply that all conflicts are susceptible to similar formulations and that all parties, despite differences in experience and status, can become equally proficient at and achieve the same results, in its application (Northrup and Segall, 1988).   The prescriptive voice of principled or joint gain negotiation, while there is much to applaud in its perspective, has a tendency to drown out alternative ways of seeing and doing things.   We need to consider the structures and contexts in more nuanced ways.   From our perspective we begin with gender and the themes that might comprise an alternative voice.

HER PLACE AT THE TABLE

Styles of Talk

The essence of negotiation is strategic communication.   Parties want to learn about the alternatives available and the priority of interests of the other.   At the same time, they want to communicate in ways that further their own aims, whether it is to elucidate their interests or obfuscate them, depending on strategy (Lax and Sebenius, 1986).   Research on gender in communications suggests that women's distinctive communication style, which serves them well in other contexts, may be a liability in negotiation (Smeltzer and Watson, 1986).

Women speak differently.   Their assertions are qualified through the use of tag questions and modifiers. . . .   [T]he female pattern of communication involves deference, relational thinking in argument, and indirection.   The male pattern typically involves linear or legalistic argument, depersonalization and a more directional style.   While women speak with many qualifiers to show flexibility and an opportunity for discussion, men use confident, self-enhancing terms.   In negotiation, these forms of communication may be read as weakness or lack of clarity and may get in the way of focusing on the real issues in conflict.   Indeed, the women in our class had difficulty putting their wants into words and tended instead to wait for information that was volunteered.

Similarly, women's modes of discourse do not signal influence.   Women's speech is more conforming and less powerful.   Women talk less and are easily interrupted while they, in turn, are less likely to interrupt.   In mixed groups, they adopt a deferential posture and are less likely to openly advocate their positions.   At the same time, there is a proclivity to be too revealing—to talk too much about their attitudes, beliefs, and concerns.

Given that the process of negotiation as it is customarily enacted calls for parties to be clear and communicate directly and authoritatively about their goals, feelings, interests, and problems, a deferential, self-effacing, and qualified style may be a significant detriment. It is also possible that such a stance can also be an asset in projecting a caring and understanding posture. The choice for women is to learn to become more conversant with negotiation skills but also adept in an alternative style of communication at the negotiating table, one that is more congruent with the task.

Expectations at the Table

Existing research is not encouraging. Evidence from research on women in organizations, particularly in management, suggest that it is not so easy for women to act forcefully and competitively without inviting criticism and questions about both her femininity and ability and threatening something of the accustomed social order. When performance in decisionmaking and negotiating tasks is judged equivalent by objective measures, men and women are rated differently by those involved, to the detriment of women. They are seen as less influential and receive less credit for what influence they may have exerted. As mediators they are judged less effective, even when the outcomes they achieved are superior.

At the same time, women are expected to do the emotional work in a group. In negotiation contexts, they often carry the burden for attending to relationships and the emotional needs of those involved. While such a burden might be consistent with a voice she might like to speak in, a woman who has trained herself to negotiate from a different premise might find that these expectations frequently constrain her ability to maneuver for herself or those she represents. Learning how to use their strengths and manage the dual impressions of femininity and strategic resolve are important aspects of negotiating tactics for women.

Relational View of Others

There seem to be two major ways that a relational view of self is potentially manifest in negotiation. The first is the conception a woman has of herself as a party negotiating. She conceives of her interests within a constellation of responsibilities and commitments already made. That is, she is always aware of how her actions in one context impact on other parts of her life and on other people significant to her.

The second implication is that relational ordering in negotiation may be a prerequisite for interaction. Relational ordering means creating a climate in which people can come to know each other, share (or do not share) values, and learn of each other's modes of interacting. Expressions of emotion and feeling and learning how the other experiences the situation are as important, if not more important, than the substance of the discourse. In other words, separating the people from the problem is the problem. Negotiation conducted in a woman's voice would, we predict, start from a different point and run a different course than either a purely principled or purely positional model.

Embedded View of Agency

Women understand events contextually both in terms of their impact on important ongoing relationships and as passing frames in evolving situations which grow out of a past and are still to be shaped in the future. The male imagination stereotypically focuses on individual achievement and is sparked by opportunities for distinctive activity that are bounded by task and structure. This exemplifies a self-contained concept of agency (Bakan, 1966; Sampson, 1988). An embedded form of agency emphasizes the fluidity between the boundaries of self and other (Sampson, 1988). Thus, women are energized by their connections and so interpret and locate activities in a spatial and temporal context in which boundaries between self and others and between the task and its surroundings are overlapping and blurred (Keller, 1985; Sampson, 1988).

If one operates from an embedded view of agency, any negotiation must be understood against the background from which it emerges. That means that there is the expectation that people in negotiation will act in a way that is consistent with their past and future behavior in other contexts. Negotiation is not, therefore, experienced as a separate game with its own set of rules but as part of the extended organization context in which it occurs.

Control Through Empowerment

Power is often conceived as the exertion of control over others through the use of strength, authority or expertise. It is usually defined as the ability to exert influence in order to obtain an outcome on one's own terms (Emerson, 1962). Conceiving of power in this way leads to a dichotomous division between those who are powerful and those who are powerless (Miller, 1982). A model in which power is accrued for oneself at the expense of others may feel alien to some women and/or be seen by others as somehow incongruent with female roles. Anticipating that assertiveness may lead away from connection, women tend to emphasize the needs of the other person so as to allow that other to feel powerful. Her behavior may thus appear to be passive, inactive or depressed.

There is a continuing debate about the place of power in negotiation. Some (e.g., Fisher, 1983) argue that it is possible to mobilize power in ways that contribute to better outcomes, while others suggest such a view denies the economic and political context in which negotiation occurs (McCarthy, 1985; Bazerman, 1987). An empowerment view which allows all parties to speak their interests and incorporates these into agreements that transcend the individualized and personalized notion of acquiring, using, and benefiting from the exercise of power is often dismissed as hopelessly naive. However, it is clear that there are situations (particularly those that involve ongoing and valued relationships) in which mutual empowerment is a much desired end.

Problem Solving Through Dialogue

Dialogue is central to a woman's model of problem solving. It is through communication and interaction with others that problems are framed, considered, and resolved. This kind of communication has specific characteristics that differentiate it from persuasion, argument, and debate.

Women perceive problem-solving to be an interactive process. Just as conflicts build up over time as individuals or groups struggle for future resources or valued positions, women see conflict resolution as evolutionary and collaborative. While it is possible to plan and strategize about one's role prior to an interaction, a woman's strength may be in her ability to adapt and grow as she learns more about situations from involvement.

Problem solving through dialogue in negotiation suggests a special kind of joining and openness in negotiation. In place of a strategic planning model of negotiation, in which considerable effort is devoted to analyzing and second-guessing the possible interests and positions of the other, problem solving through dialogue involves the weaving of collective narratives that reflect newly-emerging understanding. There exists through this kind of interaction the potential for transformed understanding and outcomes. It is a stance of learning about the problem together and is built on the premise that you have a high regard for the other's interest and she has a high regard for yours. Such a framework suggests a rather different structure of negotiation than the "dance" of positions (Raiffa, 1982).

It also suggests a different process from that which is often described as the essence of joint gain negotiation (Fisher and Ury, 1981; Raiffa, 1982; Lax and Sebenius, 1986; Susskind and Cruikshank, 1987). The essence of negotiating for joint gains involves a search for those sets of agreements that satisfy interests which the parties are seen to value differently. The tactics entail the logical identification of these differences and the creative exploration of options which will satisfy them. Implied in this model is a view that goals and interests are relatively fixed and potentially known by the parties. The secret to making agreement lies in designing a process where goals and interests can be discovered and incorporated into an agreement. In problem solving through dialogue, the process is less structured and becomes the vehicle through which goals can emerge from mutual inquiry. The stance of those involved is one of flexibility and adaptiveness (distinguished from control) in response to potential uncertainty (Marshall, 1984). This kind of sensing may lead to transformed understandings of problems and possible solutions.

LLOYD BURTON, LARRY FARMER, ELIZABETH D. GEE, LO-RIE JOHNSON & GERALD WILLIAMS, FEMINIST THEO-RY, PROFESSIONAL ETHICS, AND GENDER–RELATED DISTINCTIONS IN ATTORNEY NEGOTIATING STYLES

1991 J.Disp.Res. 199, 215–40.

A striking characteristic of the literature on negotiation behavior is the persistent tendency to interpret negotiation behavior in terms of variations on two basic models, cooperation and competition, to fear that one (cooperation) is weaker but possibly morally superior, but ultimately to conclude that both models are ethically satisfactory. There is an intriguing parallel in the feminist literature: moral development is discussed in terms of two dominant models as in Gilligan's two modes of moral reasoning, Nodding's conception of the Ethic of Care versus the Ethic of Justice, and Belenky's ways of knowing. There is a fear that one (Care) is weaker, and a fear the other (Justice) may reflect a need for dominance and power, yet ultimately both models are morally acceptable. There is one striking difference, however, between the two bodies of literature. In legal ethics, the morality of a more dominant or power-driven model (competition) is a subject of continuing debate, while in the literature on moral development, the morality of an Ethic of Justice, is held above reproach.

These parallels between Care–Justice and Cooperation–Competition bring us to the question that led the authors to collaborate on this article: Is there possibly a correlation between Care and Cooperation, on one hand, and

Justice and Competition, on the other? Could it be, for example, that Competitive negotiators and theorists are acting in compliance with Gilligan's Ethic of Justice paradigm, while Cooperatives are giving voice to her Ethic of Care? Viewed from this perspective, for example, it may be that Competitive negotiators are motivated by the same ethical impulses that Kohlberg associates with exemplary moral development, suggesting they feel an ethical imperative as well as a strategic advantage in couching disputes in terms of rights and power rather than "interests" (to use Ury, Brett, and Goldberg's construct) and in pressing for unilateral advantage rather than genuinely consensual solutions.

It may be that Cooperative, problem-solving, integrative, unconditionally constructive, "principled" negotiators are more attuned to relationships among the parties, more conscious of the community, and animated by an underlying sense of Care, as contrasted with their more Competitive opposites, who are instead more concerned with case-by-case strategic advantage for their clients. The former may see in the law the potential for individual and social transformation, while the latter will see—and use—the law as sword and shield for the assertion and defense of individual rights.

Those who study or practice negotiation for a living are acutely aware that neither the world nor their own personalities are quite so simple as the Competitive or Cooperative labels imply. Most, by virtue of professional inculcations and life experiences, carry aspects of the Cooperative and the Competitive, the Communitarian and the Libertarian, the Care-giver and the Rights-enforcer. This much is true even without considerations of possible gender-based variations.

The tug-of-war between these divergent Cooperative and Competitive perspectives is, for many, as much a matter of internal dialogue as external debate. It is important to add that both male and female attorneys in the interview research discussed below portray themselves as deeply influenced in practice by Ethic of Care principles. The fact that many females practice Competitive negotiation casts doubt on the assertion that these values and behaviors are either inherently male or female or mutually exclusive.

. . .

ECONOMIC THEORY

Analysis of the Care Hypotheses

Based on Gilligan's construct of women's moral development, we hypothesized that female lawyers would be rated higher on attributes of Care in the Phoenix II survey than male lawyers.

. . .

Ratings of male and female negotiators were quite similar, differing on only four of the fourteen Care variables. More problematically, the four differences were all in the direction of male lawyers being rated as more, rather than less Care-oriented than female lawyers. Thus, male lawyers were rated as more adaptable, less argumentative, more considerate of the needs of the opposing lawyer, and more willing to move from their positions than female lawyers. This result is inconsistent with our hypothesis that females will be more influenced by an ethic of Care than males.

As a further test of the Care hypothesis, rated negotiators were divided into High Care and Low Care groups using a cluster analysis on the fourteen Care variables. Based on the Care hypothesis, one would expect proportionately more female lawyers to cluster into the High Care group and more male lawyers to cluster in the Low Care group.

... [M]ale and female lawyers clustered into the two Care groups in approximately equal proportions. In fact, the proportion of male lawyers in the High Care group turned out to be slightly higher than the proportion of female lawyers in that group. The differences in proportions of male and female attorneys across Care groups do not appear to be statistically significant. In addition to clustering in similar proportions on the Care variables, male and female lawyers in each group also had basically similar rating patterns on all but a few of the 144 variables in the survey.

Analysis of the Justice Hypotheses

Based on Kohlberg's theory of moral development and the feminist critiques asserting it is more reflective of male than female experience, we hypothesized that male lawyers, having been socialized to analyze situations based on "rights" and "justice", would be rated higher on justice attributes in the Phoenix II survey than female lawyers.

. . .

[T]he data provide only modest support for this hypothesis. The ratings of male negotiators on all of the Justice variables consistently tended in the direction of a greater Justice orientation, but only two of the nine differences were statistically significant. In those two comparisons, male lawyers were rated as more "fair-minded" and more "realistic" than the female lawyers. While these two differences were statistically significant, the actual magnitude of the differences between the ratings for male and females is not large. Thus, it is reasonable to conclude that there is no Justice-related difference in the ratings of female and male attorneys or, at best, the result of the analysis of the Justice variables lends only modest support to the hypothesis that males are more Justice-oriented than females.

As a further test the Justice hypothesis, rated negotiators were divided into High Justice and Low Justice groups using a cluster analysis on the nine Justice variables. If the Justice hypothesis is correct, one would expect proportionately more male lawyers to cluster into the High Justice group and more female lawyers to cluster in the Low Justice group.

... [M]ale lawyers clustered into the High Justice group in a slightly higher proportion than female lawyers. While this gives some support to the hypothesis of a greater Justice orientation for male lawyers, it should not escape notice that a substantial number of female lawyers clustered into the High Justice group (57%). Proportionately, nearly as many female lawyers were clustered into the High Justice group as male lawyers. The differences in proportions are not statistically significant. Given the small differences in mean ratings and proportions between the two groups, one must conclude that these results do not provide strong support for the Justice hypothesis.

The two analyses described above point to a conclusion that male and female negotiators in this sample were not perceived to differ on either Care- or Justice-related attributes. Also the data as analyzed do not provide support for either hypothesis as applied to lawyers in the negotiation context. An alternative explanation for the finding of no significant differences in Care and Justice-related attributes between genders is based on the screening and self-selection theories. It may be that women who are more caring choose not to enter law school or the private practice of law and are therefore not represented in our data. In this case, female attorneys practicing law would not be expected to be any different on Care or Justice attributes than their male colleagues.

The Phoenix II questionnaire was not designed to measure Care or Justice, and it is fair to suppose that comparisons of Care and Justice orientations might have been more interesting, and possibly discriminating, if the study had originally been geared to test these hypotheses.

Effectiveness Ratings of the Care and Justice Groups

The Phoenix II research was originally designed to obtain data on attorney negotiating behavior and effectiveness, not the dimensions of Care or Justice. In this section, we use effectiveness ratings contained in the data to compare the negotiating effectiveness of male and female attorneys in the High–Low Care and High–Low Justice groupings. These comparisons ... provided some of the most important findings in the study.

... [The data] shows two important comparisons. The first is the difference in negotiating effectiveness between High Care and Low Care attorneys. For female as well as male groupings, High Care attorneys are rated as significantly more effective as negotiators than their Low Care counterparts. This finding runs counter to the hypothesis that female or male attorneys who are Caring will be perceived as weak. The second compares the comparative negotiating effectiveness of males and females in both groups. Although the numerical effectiveness ratings for males appears slightly higher than for females, a one-way analysis of variance shows there is no difference in negotiating effectiveness between males and females in either group. Not surprisingly, we find ... that male and female High Justice negotiators have significantly higher effectiveness ratings than their Low Justice counterparts. In comparing the effectiveness scores of male and female attorneys, we found that although female ratings appear slightly lower than male, statistically there is no difference between them.

In summary, then, ... three of our most significant findings. First, High Care attorneys, regardless of gender, were rated as significantly more effective as negotiators than Low Care. Second, High Justice attorneys were rated as significantly more effective than Low Justice attorneys. Judging from these statistics, among lawyers, Care and Justice are both rated as positive qualities in the sense that both are directly related to negotiator effectiveness. Third, and most importantly for evaluating the Care/Justice hypotheses and concerns about gender stereotyping, there were no significant differences in effectiveness ratings between male and female attorneys in any of the four groups.

These results suggest that Care, at least in the dimensions measured by our analysis, is not identified with weakness or ineffectiveness in legal negotiations. To this extent, it is probably not necessary for female lawyers to signal non-Care to be considered effective in negotiation. This is further supported by our finding of a strong correlation between Care and the rating female negotiators received on the word "feminine" in the survey. Although this research was not designed to specifically test the signalling hypotheses, and therefore should not be considered the last word on the subject, it is fair to say the findings run counter to the hypothesis that female attorneys should signal "non-care" to be perceived as effective in negotiation.

Another unexpected result is the high proportion of attorneys who clustered into the High category in both Care and Justice: 66% of the males and 55% of the females were High Care; 69% of the males and 57% of the females were High Justice. Especially for males (69% and 66%), but also for females (55% and 57%), it is evident that Care and Justice as measured in this analysis are *not* mutually exclusive categories, but rather are overlapping. About 35% of the male attorneys and 13% of the female obtained High ratings in both Care and Justice. Given that High ratings on Care and Justice are both correlated with greater effectiveness, attorneys who receive low effectiveness ratings may be able to improve their perceived negotiating effectiveness by learning to exhibit more Care and Justice qualities.

. . .

Relationship between Patterns of Cooperation–Competition and Care–Justice

The final hypothesis in relation to the Phoenix II data relates back to the idea that originally motivated the present paper. Based on informal comparisons of the bodies of literature reviewed in this article, the authors had an initial impression there may be a meaningful correspondence between concept of Care as developed in feminist moral and legal theory and the behavior of Cooperative negotiators as reported in Williams.

. . .

. . . 95% of the attorneys in the High Care group were in the Cooperative group of negotiators discovered in the earlier study; the remaining 5% were in the Competitive group. To say the same thing from the point of view of Cooperation, of the 138 Cooperative negotiators identified in the Phoenix II study, 127 were in the High Care group, while 11 were in the Low Care. As to the Low Care category, only 15% were Cooperative negotiators, while 85% were Competitive. Repeating this in terms of Competitive negotiators, of the 69 Competitive negotiators identified in the Phoenix II study, 62 were in the Low Care group, while only 7 were in the High Care. We find, then, an extremely strong correspondence between Care and Cooperative negotiating behaviors, and a similarly strong correspondence between an absence of Care (Low Care) and Competitive negotiating behaviors. Care is directly related to Cooperation and inversely related to Competition in negotiation.

It now becomes important to discover where Justice fits into this picture. In terms of negotiating behavior, is a concern for Justice more likely to manifest itself as Cooperative or Competitive negotiation? . . .

. . . [T]here is a very strong correspondence between High Justice attorneys and the Cooperative pattern of negotiation: of the High Justice attorneys, 92% were identified as Cooperative negotiators in the Phoenix II study, with the remaining 8% identified as Competitive. Or restated in terms of 138 Cooperative attorneys discovered in Phoenix II, 127 were in the High Justice group and only 11 in the Low Justice. Looking then at the Low Justice category, 16% of the Low Justice attorneys were Cooperative, while the remaining 84% were Competitive. Restating this in terms of the Competitive category, of the 69 Competitive negotiators in Phoenix II, 11 were in the High Justice group and 58 were in the Low Justice. Just as there is a strong correspondence between Care and Cooperation, there is a similarly powerful relationship between Justice and Cooperative, and between an absence of Justice (Low Justice) and Competitive or aggressive negotiating behaviors. We find, then, that both Care and Justice are directly related to Cooperation, and both are inversely related to Competition.

This seems to us a remarkable set of findings with implications far richer than we had supposed, or than we can explore fully in this paper. In our discussion of the negotiation hypotheses, we commented on the parallels between the feminist literature and the negotiation literature: both tend to interpret behavior in terms of two predominant patterns (Care–Justice in one; Cooperation–Competition in the other); both also tend to regard one pattern as stronger and the other weaker (Justice and Competition are stronger; Care and Cooperation weaker). We also noted a departure from this parallelism. In the negotiation literature there are recurrent challenges to ethical sufficiency of certain Competitive negotiating practices; we did not find similar challenges to the morality of Justice. Taken together, the findings ... offer an explanation for this departure. In simplest terms, while there is a direct relationship between Care and Cooperation, it does not follow that there is a similar relationship between Justice and Competition. Rather, we found that Justice and Competition (like Care and Competition [sic]) are inversely related. Competitive negotiating behaviors are rated not as an implementation of the Ethic of Justice, but as a departure from Justice. If anything, Justice may be considered as standing in opposition to, and as a possible antidote to, the ethically suspect behaviors of Competition. This helps to explain why the concept of Justice has not been subject to the kinds of attacks in the feminist literature that Competition has in the negotiation literature: Competition is not a manifestation of Justice, but rather a departure from it.

. . .

This suggests that, in the future, the negotiation literature should perhaps shift away from a conception of Care and Justice as opposites and move toward a fuller explanation of both qualities in the negotiation context and an emphasis on ways for women and men to recognize and embody the qualities in their negotiation practices. It also suggests the need for further work on the meaning and appropriateness of Competition or Dominance in negotiation. If Cooperation and effectiveness are able to expropriate Justice, what is left to justify Competition? This is perhaps the most pressing question that remains for the future.

*

Section III

Negotiation as a Communication Process Used Extensively by Lawyers

Lawyers are a distinctive subclass of negotiators. They are members of a profession that exists to act as an intermediary between others involved in activities requiring bargaining. As such, they should be experts in managing the negotiation process. Virtually all transaction planning activities require lawyers to negotiate on behalf of clients. Likewise, over ninety five per cent of all adjudicated disputes are resolved by some process other than courtroom proceedings. Regardless of how much some attorneys may enjoy describing themselves as "litigators," they are at best, as Marc Galanter says, "litigotiators." The truth of the matter is that the overwhelming preponderance of the lawyer's work involves negotiating with others.

Attorneys as a professional class have a number of characteristic attributes that color their approach to the negotiation process. Their role as an agent for their client affects the dynamics of their negotiations. Similarly, their professional training and practice experience give them a distinctive mindset as they bargain with their professional colleagues. This unique professional orientation and role as surrogate negotiator raises a host of perplexing practical and ethical quandaries. The final section in this book of readings addresses the particular context of lawyers as negotiators.

Chapter 9

ATTORNEYS AS NEGOTIATION SURROGATES—THE TENSIONS INHERENT IN THE LAWYER'S PROFESSIONAL ROLE

This short chapter includes readings focusing on the particular difficulties facing bargainers who represent another's interests rather than their own. When we bargain as principal, we are free to adopt any negotiation strategy we feel is effective in the context. We are responsible only to ourselves for the success, failure and implications of our strategic choices. Lawyers represent others in negotiations, however, and consequently bargain with predictable constraints. The strategy they select in bargaining on behalf of a client is itself partially the result of a process negotiation with the client. Because lawyers are frequently employed to resolve conflicts in which two parties are angry, hostile, fearful or mistrustful of the opposite, competitive strategies are overrepresented in the attorney's repertoire.

Lawyers also have an inherent conflict of interest with their clients when they bargain with other lawyers. The client frequently sees only the particular transaction or dispute at hand, and desires the best possible result in this matter alone. For the lawyer, however, professional life is long. A good reputation and working relationship with opposing counsel may create a strain with the client's narrower focus on immediate competitive gain.

Dean Pruitt introduces the idea that representative bargainers occupy a "boundary role" position. They act as intermediaries between conflicting constituents, and customarily display negotiating perceptions and behaviors that are typical of that role. Jeffrey Rubin and Frank Sander speak more specifically about the advantages and disadvantages of using a representative in negotiation. Their observations should influence the negotiation between attorney and client about optimal bargaining personnel. Toward the end of this excerpt, the authors mention possible tensions between attorney and client approaches to negotiation. As representative negotiators, attorneys always have two negotiations occurring simultaneously: One with their bargaining opposite and one with their own client. Frequently, it is the latter

186

negotiation that proves the most difficult. In the next reading, Donald Gifford returns to expand upon the consequences of this tension.

Leonard Riskin also addresses the theme of the professional mask of litigating lawyers. He writes eloquently of the lawyer's psychological mindset in an article advocating expanded use of mediation. His assessment of the constraints of adversarial thinking provokes a broader discussion of the traditional assumptions lawyers make as they attempt to resolve disputes as a surrogate for their clients. Are lawyers adequately equipped to practice more collaborative negotiation strategies, such as integrative bargaining, that are fostered by mediation; or does their standard philosophical map tilt them inevitably toward harder bargaining? This broader discussion occupies us in the next chapter.

Readings

1. Dean Pruitt, Negotiation Behavior 41–45 (1981).

2. Jeffrey Rubin & Frank E.A. Sander, *When Should We Use Agents? Direct vs. Representative Negotiation,* 4 Negot.J. 395–400 (1988).

3. Donald Gifford, *The Synthesis of Legal Counselling and Negotiating Models: Preserving Client–Centered Advocacy in the Negotiation Context,* 34 UCLA L.Rev. 811, 829–39 (1987).

4. Leonard Riskin, *Mediation and Lawyers,* 43 Ohio St.L.J. 29, 43–48 (1982).

5. For Further Reading

   a. Stephen M. Bundy, *Commentary on "Understanding* Pennzoil v. Texaco:" *Rational Bargaining and Agency Problems,* 75 Va. L.Rev. 335 (1989).

   b. Theodore Eisenberg, *Private Ordering Through Negotiation: Dispute Settlement and Rulemaking,* 89 Harv.L.Rev. 637 (1976).

   c. Roger Fisher, *A Code of Negotiation Practice for Lawyers,* 1 Negot.J. 105 (1985).

   d. Ronald J. Gilson & Robert H. Mnookin, *Cooperation and Competition In Negotiation: Can Lawyers Dampen Conflict,* in Barriers to Conflict Resolution 184 (Kenneth Arrow, *et al,* eds. (1995)).

   e. Herbert Kritzer, Let's Make A Deal: Understanding the Negotiation Process in Ordinary Litigation (1991).

   f. Geoffrey Miller, *Some Agency Problems in Settlement,* 16 J.Legal Stud. 189 (1987).

   g. Robert H. Mnookin & Robert B. Wilson, *Rational Bargaining and Market Efficiency: Understanding* Pennzoil v. Texaco, 75 Va.L.Rev. 295 (1989).

   h. John W. Pratt & Richard J. Zeckhauser, Principals and Agents: The Structure of Business (1985).

   i. Douglas Rosenthal, Lawyer and Client: Who's In Charge (1974).

   j. H. Lawrence Ross, Settled Out of Court: The Social Process of Insurance Claims Adjustment (2d ed. 1980).

k. Richard Walton & Robert McKersie, A Behavioral Theory of Labor Negotiations: An Analysis of a Social Interaction System (1965).

DEAN G. PRUITT, NEGOTIATION BEHAVIOR
41–45 (1981).

BARGAINERS AS REPRESENTATIVES

Bargainers often represent other people, who can be called their *constituents*. This is always true when the negotiating party is an organization or nation. Certain individuals become negotiation specialists, with characteristic sets of activities and attitudes.

When negotiators are representatives, we find a complicated communication net, which can be diagrammed schematically as follows:

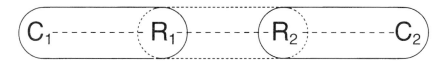

C_1 and C_2 denote the constituents in the two opposing organizations. R_1 and R_2 denote their representatives. The dashed lines denote channels of communication. The ovals at the left and right indicate that a constituent and his or her representative are associated as a group. The middle oval is meant to show that this is often true of the two representatives as well. Because they communicate with one another over a period of time and share similar organizational positions, representatives often develop ties to one another. These ties can contribute to the reconciliation of conflicts that would otherwise be intractable.

This diagram indicates that representatives can be thought of as intermediaries whose job is to reconcile the interests of their own and the opposing organization. They must represent the interests of their constituents to the opposing representative *and* represent the views of the opposing representative to their constituents. For this reason, representatives are said to occupy a *boundary role position*.

Before getting into theory and research on representation, it is necessary to define the term *accountability*. Bargainers are said to be accountable to the extent that their constituents are able to monitor the outcome of the negotiation and reward or punish the bargainers in light of this outcome.

Being a Representative

Most representatives are at least somewhat interested in pleasing their constituents, either because they are accountable to them, like them, or feel responsible for their welfare. Furthermore, experimental evidence indicates that bargainers usually view their constituents as taking a less compromising, more competitive stance than themselves. It follows that bargainers who are representatives will usually be less conciliatory than those who are negotiating on their own behalf. They will concede more slowly, reach fewer agreements, and take more time to reach agreement. This implies that if one bargainer is a representative and the other is not, the representative should ordinarily achieve the larger outcome. However this proposition has not yet been tested.

There is probably some truth to the assumption usually made by representatives that their constituents are tougher than they are. [I have] suggested three reasons why this should be true:

> (1) Representatives often see their role as one of achieving agreement.... (2) Representatives are typically better acquainted than are their constituents with the other party's priorities and hence are more realistic about the difficulty of achieving substantial concessions from the other party.... (3) Representatives have a more intimate relationship with the other party, hence ... they are less likely to take a harsh stance toward the other party's needs.

The evidence that representatives are less compromising than individual bargainers comes from three studies involving both male and female subjects. However, it should be noted that these studies always involved representatives who were uninformed about the wishes of their constituents. In a fourth study information about constituent wishes was provided in some conditions. When the subjects were told that their constituents wanted them to bargain "hard and aggressively," they behaved like uninformed representatives, taking a long time to reach agreement and frequently rejecting the other's demands. When told that their constituents "stressed compromise and cooperation," they behaved like nonrepresentatives, taking less time to reach agreement and rejecting fewer offers. These results have two important implications:

1. The essence of the representative effect is trying to please one's constituent. If the constituent wants conciliatory behavior, representatives are fully as able to concede as bargainers acting on their own. [R]epresentatives are very sensitive to the wishes of their constituents.

2. As indicated earlier, when uninformed about the wishes of their constituents, bargainers tend to view them as uncompromising and competitive, leading the bargainers to make minimal concessions.

. . .

Summary

In the absence of indications to the contrary, representatives tend to view their constituents as desiring a tough, nonconciliatory approach to bargaining of the kind that is produced by a win/lose orientation. Therefore, the more motivated they are to please their constituents, the less conciliatory they will be in their dealings with the other party. It follows that bargainers will ordinarily make larger demands and smaller concessions under the following circumstances: (a) when they are representatives rather than acting on their own, (b) when they are highly accountable to their constituents, especially if they want to continue as group members and feel insecure about their standing in the group, (c) when they have lower status than their constituents, (d) when they are distrusted by their constituents, and (e) (looking only at the studies that show an effect) when the constituents are watching their behavior. That these results involve conformity to the *perceived* wishes of the constituents is suggested by a finding that the effect of being a representative disappears when bargainers are informed that their constituents favor compromise and cooperation.

JEFFREY Z. RUBIN AND FRANK E.A. SANDER, WHEN SHOULD WE USE AGENTS? DIRECT VS. REPRESENTATIVE NEGOTIATION

4 Negot.J. 395–400 (1988).

Although we typically conceive of negotiations occurring directly between two or more principals, often neglected in a thoughtful analysis are the many situations where negotiations take place indirectly, through the use of representatives or surrogates of the principals. A father who speaks to his child's teacher (at the child's request), two lawyers meeting on behalf of their respective clients, the foreign service officers of different nations meeting to negotiate the settlement of a border dispute, a real estate agent informing would-be buyers of the seller's latest offer—each is an instance of negotiation through representatives.

The most obvious effect of using agents—an effect that must be kept in mind in any analysis of representative negotiation—is complication of the transaction.... [I]f we begin with a straightforward negotiation between two individuals, then the addition of two agents transforms this simple one-on-one deal into a complex matrix involving at least four primary negotiations, as well as two subsidiary ones .... In addition, either of the agents may readily serve as a mediator between the client and the other agent or principal. Or the two agents might act as co-mediators between the principals. At a minimum, such a complex structure necessitates effective coordination. Beyond that, this structural complexity has implications—both positive and negative—for representative negotiation in general. Let us now review these respective benefits and liabilities.

EXPERTISE

One of the primary reasons that principals choose to negotiate through agents is that the latter possess expertise that makes agreement—particularly favorable agreement—more likely. This expertise is likely to be of three different stripes:

Substantive Knowledge.

A tax attorney or accountant knows things about the current tax code that make it more likely that negotiations with an IRS auditor will benefit the client as much as possible....

Process Expertise.

Quite apart from the specific expertise they may have in particular content areas, agents may have skill at the negotiation *process*, per se, thereby enhancing the prospects of a favorable agreement. A skillful negotiator— someone who understands how to obtain and reveal information about preferences, who is inventive, resourceful, firm on goals but flexible on means, etc.—is a valuable resource. Wise principals would do well to utilize the services of such skilled negotiators, unless they can find ways of developing such process skills themselves.

Special Influence.

A Washington lobbyist is paid to know the "right" people, to have access to the "corridors of power" that the principals themselves are unlikely to possess. Such "pull" can certainly help immensely, and is yet another form of expertise that agents may possess, although the lure of this "access" often outweighs in promise the special benefits that are confirmed in reality.

. . .

Note also that principals may not always know what expertise they need. Thus, a person who has a dispute that seems headed for the courts may automatically seek out a litigator, not realizing that the vast preponderance of cases are settled by negotiation, requiring very different skills that the litigator may not possess. . . .

DETACHMENT

Another important reason for using an agent to do the actual negotiation is that the principals may be too emotionally entangled in the subject of the dispute. A classic example is divorce. A husband and wife, caught in the throes of a bitter fight over the end of their marriage, may benefit from the "buffering" that agents can provide. . . .

Sometimes, however, it is the *agents* who are too intensely entangled. What is needed then is the detachment and rationality that only the principals can bring to the exchange. For example, lawyers may get too caught up in the adversary game and lose sight of the underlying problem that is dividing the principals (e.g., how to resolve a dispute about the quality of goods delivered as part of a long-term supply contract). The lawyers may be more concerned about who would win in court, while the clients simply want to get their derailed relationship back on track. Hence the thrust of some modern dispute resolution mechanisms (such as the mini-trial) is precisely to take the dispute *out* of the hands of the technicians and give it back to the primary parties.

Note, however, that the very "detachment" we are touting as a virtue of negotiation through agents can also be a liability. For example, in some interpersonal negotiations, apology and reconciliation may be an important ingredient of any resolution. . . . Surrogates who are primarily technicians may not be able to bring to bear these empathic qualities.

TACTICAL FLEXIBILITY

The use of agents allows various gambits to be played out by the principals, in an effort to ratchet as much as possible from the other side. For example, if a seller asserts that the bottom line is $100,000, the buyer can try to haggle, albeit at the risk of losing the deal. If the buyer employs an agent, however, the agent can profess willingness to pay that sum but plead lack of authority, thereby gaining valuable time and opportunity for fuller consideration of the situation together with the principal. . . .

Conversely, an agent may be used in order to push the other side in tough, even obnoxious, fashion, making it possible—in the best tradition of the "good cop/bad cop" ploy—for the client to intercede at last, and seem the essence of sweet reason in comparison with the agent. Or the agent may be used as a "stalking horse," to gather as much information about the adversary as possible, opening the way to proposals by the client that exploit the intelligence gathered.

Note that the tactical flexibility conferred by representative negotiations presupposes a competitive negotiating climate, a zero-sum contest in which each negotiator wishes to outsmart the other....

Where the negotiation is conducted in a problem-solving manner, agents may still be helpful, not because they resort to strategic ruses, but because they can help articulate interests, options, and alternatives. Four heads are clearly better than two, for example, when it comes to brainstorming about possible ways of reconciling the parties' interests.

Offsetting—indeed, typically *more* than offsetting—the three above apparent virtues of representative negotiation are several sources of difficulty. Each is sufficiently important and potentially problematic that we believe caution is necessary before entering into negotiation through agents.

EXTRA "MOVING PARTS"

... [R]epresentative negotiations entail greater structural complexity, additional moving parts in the negotiation machinery that—given a need for expertise, detachment, or tactical flexibility—can help move parties toward a favorable agreement. Additional moving parts, however, can also mean additional expense, in the form of the time required in the finding, evaluating, and engaging of agents, as well as the financial cost of retaining their services. And it can mean additional problems, more things that can go wrong. For instance, a message intended by a client may not be the message transmitted by that client's agent to the other party. Or the message received by that agent from the other party may be very different from the one that that agent (either deliberately or inadvertently) manages to convey to his or her client.

At one level, then, the introduction of additional links in the communication system increases the risk of distortion in the information conveyed back and forth between the principals. Beyond that lies a second difficulty: the possibility that eventually the principals will come to rely so extensively on their respective agents that they no longer communicate directly—even though they could, and even though they might well benefit from doing so....

Yet another potentially problematic implication of this increasingly complex social machinery is that unwanted coalitions may arise that apply undue pressure on individual negotiators....

In sum, the introduction of agents increases the complexity of the social apparatus of negotiation, and in so doing increases the chances of unwanted side effects. A related problem should be briefly noted here: the difficulty of asymmetry, as when an agent negotiates not with another agent but directly with the other principal. In effect, this was the case in 1978 when Egypt's Sadat negotiated with Israel's Begin at Camp David. Sadat considered himself empowered to make binding decisions for Egypt, while—at least partly for tactical purposes—Begin represented himself as ultimately accountable to his cabinet and to the Israeli parliament. While this "mismatched" negotiation between a principal (Sadat) and an agent (Begin) *did* result in agreement (thanks in good measure to President Carter's intercession as a mediator), it was not easy. The asymmetry of role meant that the two sides differed in their readiness to move forward toward an agreement, their ability to be shielded by a representative, and their willingness/ability to guarantee that any agreement reached would "stick."

Different dynamics will characterize the negotiation depending on whether it is between clients, between lawyers, or with both present. If just the clients are there, the dealings will be more direct and forthright, and issues of authority and ratification disappear. With just the lawyers present, there may be less direct factual information, but concomitantly more candor about delicate topics....

PROBLEMS OF "OWNERSHIP" AND CONFLICTING INTERESTS

In theory, it is clear that the principal calls the shots. Imagine, however, an agent who is intent on applying the *Getting to YES* (Fisher and Ury, 1981) approach by searching for objective criteria and a fair outcome. Suppose the client simply wants the best possible outcome, perhaps because it is a one-shot deal not involving a future relationship with the other party. What if the agent (a lawyer, perhaps) *does* care about his future relationship with the other *agent,* and wants to be remembered as a fair and scrupulous bargainer? How *should* this conflict get resolved and how, in the absence of explicit discussion, *will* it be resolved, if at all? Conversely, the client, because of a valuable long-term relationship, may want to maintain good relations with the other side. But if the client simply looks for an agent who is renowned for an ability to pull out all the stops, the client's overall objectives may suffer as the result of an overzealous advocate.

. . .

Differing goals and standards of agent and principal may create conflicting pulls. For example, the buyer's agent may be compensated as a percentage of the purchase price, thus creating an incentive to have the price as high as possible. The buyer, of course, wants the lowest possible price. Similarly, where a lawyer is paid by the hour, there may be an incentive to draw out the negotiation, whereas the client prefers an expeditious negotiation at the lowest possible cost.

. . .

ENCOURAGEMENT OF ARTIFICE AND DUPLICITY

Finally, as already noted, the introduction of agents often seems to invite clients to devise stratagems (with or without these agents) to outwit the other side. Admittedly, there is nothing intrinsic to the presence of representatives that dictates a move in this direction; still, perhaps because of the additional expense incurred, the seductive lure of a "killing" with the help of one's "hired gun," or the introduction of new, sometimes perverse incentives, representative negotiations often seem to instill (or reflect) a more adversarial climate.

. . .

CONCLUSION

It follows from the preceding analysis that, ordinarily, negotiations conducted directly between the principals are preferable to negotiation through representatives. When the principals' relationship is fundamentally cooperative or informed by enlightened self-interest, agents may often be unnecessary; since there is little or no antagonism in the relationship, there is no need for the buffering detachment afforded by agents. Moreover, by negotiating directly, there is reduced risk of miscoordination, misrepresentation, and miscommunication.

On the other hand, representative negotiation *does* have an important and necessary place. When special expertise is required, when tactical flexibility is deemed important and—most importantly—when direct contact is likely to produce confrontation rather than collaboration, agents *can* render an important service.

DONALD G. GIFFORD, THE SYNTHESIS OF LEGAL COUN-SELLING AND NEGOTIATING MODELS: PRESERVING CLIENT–CENTERED ADVOCACY IN THE NEGOTIATION CONTEXT

34 UCLA L.Rev. 811, 829–39 (1987).

COUNSELING AND NEGOTIATION AS CYCLICAL PROCESSES

Uncertainty characterizes the initial counseling encounter between the lawyer and the client prior to the first negotiation session. At this early stage, it usually is not possible to identify all the alternative courses of action available to the client and to assess the costs and benefits of each. With the information at hand, the lawyer frequently cannot predict accurately what course the litigation alternative will follow. More importantly, in a transactional context not involving litigation, or when considering the settlement alternative to litigation, the lawyer can offer at best only an educated guess regarding the other party's response to negotiation proposals or the prospects for a negotiated agreement. The lawyer's understanding of the dispute or transaction increases significantly during the course of the negotiation as his own investigation and the discovery process continues. Further, even when extensive discovery is available, the lawyer learns much about the matter from the other lawyer. Along with increased information about the problem being negotiated, the lawyer also learns what options may be available to her client as a result of the negotiated settlement and how the other party views the subject matter of the negotiations.

Prior to negotiations, the client also is often unable to articulate fully his own goals and preferences. Typically, the client "wants it all" and unrealistically assesses the likely outcomes of both the negotiation and litigation alternatives. The client has not decided how much risk he is willing to assume and which of his multiple objectives is his primary goal in the negotiations. The client is unable to decide these issues until he learns more about the problem from his lawyer's reports of the negotiation sessions.

The subsequent negotiation process usually involves multiple encounters between the negotiating attorneys, either personally or through correspondence, and the attorneys often confer with their respective clients in the intervals between these meetings. . . .

. . . Most legal negotiations . . . are not resolved during a single discrete encounter between the attorneys. Instead, legal negotiations occur over an extended period of time, consist of several exchanges between the attorneys, and are intermixed with meetings between the attorneys and their clients.

Many negotiation contacts are unscheduled, such as an unexpected encounter between lawyers, or an encounter in connection with a different case or transaction, in which a spontaneous, or at least a seemingly unplanned, reference to the negotiation is made.

Negotiations frequently include not only face-to-face encounters, but also written correspondence and telephone conversations. The proposals exchanged through the written and telephonic media are discrete proposals and responses to earlier proposals by the other party. Because transaction costs are lower when the lawyer writes a letter or telephones than when she schedules and attends face-to-face negotiations, these alternate forms of communication likely increase the number of individual exchanges between negotiating attorneys. In many instances, the lawyer consults with her client before writing letters or calling the other lawyer. These alternatives to face-to-face meetings between the attorneys therefore typically increase the effect of client counseling sessions on the negotiation process itself.

. . .

The Boundary-Role Position of Lawyer as Negotiator

As the client's representative in the adversary system, the lawyer represents the client's interests and owes her undivided loyalty to him. In the courtroom context, the focus of the lawyer's obligations is relatively clearly defined except in extreme situations, such as when the client intends to present perjured testimony. When negotiating on behalf of the client, however, the lawyer is drawn in conflicting directions. On one hand, she is obligated professionally to obtain the most favorable settlement possible during the negotiations and not to make binding concessions without the client's authority. On the other hand, ... he must respond to pressures from his negotiating counterparts in negotiations and pursue settlements that are fair and just to both parties. The pressure on the lawyer to accommodate these tensions ... results in part from the expectation of future contact with the other lawyers and in part from the traditions of courtesy and fair play among lawyers.

The responsiveness of the negotiator to both her client and to the other negotiator, and her position as an intermediary between these competing influences, are examples of what social scientists refer to as boundary-role conflict....

The lawyer's role as a moderating influence does not necessarily mean that she is "selling-out" the interests of her client. Professor Eisenberg views the lawyer as an "affiliate" who seeks to reconcile the conflicting interests of the opposing parties in ways that they could not accomplish themselves. According to Eisenberg, by using affiliates in negotiations, an adjudicative element is introduced into the negotiation; negotiators inherently must decide what is a fair and just resolution. Eisenberg also argues that representative negotiation alleviates the anxiety that the disputing parties often experience when they negotiate for themselves. It avoids the embarrassment that would result if either party were required to admit fault personally in order to resolve the conflict. Pruitt, a social psychologist, identifies additional valid reasons why representative negotiators tend to be more compromising than their clients. Professional affiliates understand their role as trying to achieve an agreement, and they also value their continuing relationships with each other. Further, representatives often know more about the other party's negotiating limits, and they therefore have fewer unrealistic illusions about their ability to extract substantial concessions from the other side.

The available experimental data supports the conclusion that negotiators tend to be more compromising than their clients. Negotiators who were observed, monitored, and directed by their clients bargained more competitively and made fewer concessions than negotiators acting independently. Alternatively, representatives who either had no information regarding their clients' bargaining orientation, or were informed that their clients had a cooperative orientation, bargained less competitively. When these results are combined, they confirm that representative negotiators face pressures from both the other negotiator and the client and that when the client exerts no pressure or urges cooperation, the negotiator probably will yield to the other negotiator's influence and bargain cooperatively.

By synthesizing the idea that the attorney as negotiator occupies a boundary-role position with ... recognition of negotiation as a continuing, on-going *cyclical* process, a more sophisticated and realistic portrayal of legal negotiations emerges than under the traditional models of legal negotiation and counseling. The attorney as negotiator typically begins a negotiation with somewhat vague goals and frequently with unrealistic expectations. The negotiator does not ignore the arguments made by the other party's attorney during the negotiation; indeed, effective negotiators consciously use the negotiation session as an opportunity to gain information about the matter being negotiated and about the other side's preferences. The lawyer apprises the client of what she has learned, and these new disclosures often lead the client to change his expectations concerning the negotiation or his preferences as to concessions. The client's reactions to this new information become an important ingredient in the next round of negotiations with the other party. This sequence often will be repeated several times before a negotiation is completed.

LEONARD L. RISKIN, MEDIATION AND LAWYERS
43 Ohio St.L.J. 29, 43–48 (1982).

THE LAWYER'S STANDARD PHILOSOPHICAL MAP

E.F. Schumacher begins his *Guide for the Perplexed* with the following story:

> On a visit to Leningrad some years ago, I consulted a map ... but I could not make it out. From where I stood, I could see several enormous churches, yet there was no trace of them on my map. When finally an interpreter came to help me, he said: "We don't show churches on our maps." Contradicting him, I pointed to one that was very clearly marked. "That is a museum," he said, "not what we call a 'living church.' It is only the 'living churches' we don't show."

> It then occurred to me that this was not the first time I had been given a map which failed to show many things I could see right in front of my eyes. All through school and university I had been given maps of life and knowledge on which there was hardly a trace of many of the things

that I most cared about and that seemed to me to be of the greatest possible importance to the conduct of my life.

The philosophical map employed by most practicing lawyers and law teachers, and displayed to the law student—which I will call the lawyer's standard philosophical map—differs radically from that which a mediator must use. What appears on this map is determined largely by the power of two assumptions about matters that lawyers handle: (1) that disputants are adversaries—*i.e.*, if one wins, the others must lose—and (2) that disputes may be resolved through application, by a third party, of some general rule of law. These assumptions, plainly, are polar opposites of those which underlie mediation: (1) that all parties can benefit through a creative solution to which each agrees; and (2) that the situation is unique and therefore not to be governed by any general principle except to the extent that the parties accept it.

The two assumptions of the lawyer's philosophical map (adversariness of parties and rule-solubility of dispute), along with the real demands of the adversary system and the expectations of many clients, tend to exclude mediation from most lawyers' repertoires. They also blind lawyers to other kinds of information that are essential for a mediator to see, primarily by riveting the lawyers' attention upon things that they must see in order to carry out their functions. The mediator must, for instance, be aware of the many interconnections between and among disputants and others, and of the qualities of these connections; he must be sensitive to emotional needs of all parties and recognize the importance of yearnings for mutual respect, equality, security, and other such non-material interests as may be present.

On the lawyer's standard philosophical map, however, the client's situation is seen atomistically; many links are not printed. The duty to represent the client zealously within the bounds of the law discourages concern with both the opponents' situation and the overall social effect of a given result.

Moreover, on the lawyer's standard philosophical map, quantities are bright and large while qualities appear dimly or not at all. When one party wins, in this vision, usually the other party loses, and, most often, the victory is reduced to a money judgment. This "reduction" of nonmaterial values— such as honor, respect, dignity, security, and love—to amounts of money, can have one of two effects. In some cases, these values are excluded from the decision makers' considerations, and thus from the consciousness of the lawyers, as irrelevant. In others, they are present but transmuted into something else—a justification for money damages. Much like the church that was allowed to appear on the map of Leningrad only because it was a museum, these interests—which may in fact be the principal motivations for a lawsuit—are recognizable in the legal dispute primarily to the extent that they have monetary value or fit into a clause of a rule governing liability.

The rule orientation also determines what appears on the map. The lawyer's standard world view is based upon a cognitive and rational outlook. Lawyers are trained to put people and events into categories that are legally meaningful, to think in terms of rights and duties established by rules, to focus on acts more than persons. This view requires a strong development of cognitive capabilities, which is often attended by the under-cultivation of emotional faculties. This combination of capacities joins with the practice of either reducing most nonmaterial values to amounts of money or sweeping them under the carpet, to restrict many lawyers' abilities to recognize the value of mediation or to serve as mediators.

The lawyer's standard philosophical map is useful primarily where the assumptions upon which it is based—adversariness and amenability to solution by a general rule imposed by a third party—are valid. But when mediation is appropriate, these assumptions do not fit. The problem is that many lawyers, because of their philosophical maps, tend to suppose that these assumptions are germane in nearly any situation that they confront as lawyers. The map, and the litigation paradigm on which it is based, has a power all out of proportion to its utility. Many lawyers, therefore, tend not to recognize mediation as a viable means of reaching a solution; and worse, they see the kinds of unique solutions that mediation can produce as threatening to the best interests of their clients.

"One of the central difficulties of our legal system," says John Ayer, "is its capacity to be deaf to the counsel of ordinary good sense." A law school classroom incident shows how quickly this deafness afflicts students—usually without anyone noticing. Professor Kenney Hegland writes:

> In my first year Contracts class, I wished to review various doctrines we had recently studied. I put the following:
>
> > In a long term installment contract, Seller promises Buyer to deliver widgets at the rate of 1000 a month. The first two deliveries are perfect. However, in the third month Seller delivers only 999 widgets. Buyer becomes so incensed with this that he rejects the delivery, cancels the remaining deliveries and refuses to pay for the widgets already delivered. After stating the problem, I asked "If you were Seller, what would you say?" What I was looking for was a discussion of the various common law theories which would force the buyer to pay for the widgets delivered and those which would throw buyer into breach for cancelling the remaining deliveries. In short, I wanted the class to come up with the legal doctrines which would allow Seller to crush Buyer.
> >
> > After asking the question, I looked around the room for a volunteer. As is so often the case with the first year students, I found that they were all either writing in their notebooks or inspecting their shoes. There was, however, one eager face, that of an eight year old son of one of my students. It seems that he was suffering through Contracts due to his mother's sin of failing to find a sitter. Suddenly he raised his hand. Such behavior, even from an eight year old, must be rewarded.
> >
> > "OK," I said, "What would you say if you were the seller?"
> >
> > "I'd say 'I'm sorry'."

·　·　·

One reason for the dominance of this map is that it may be congruent with the personalities of most lawyers, who may be drawn to the law because of this map and the ability to control that it gives them. There are other reasons, though, for its strength, and some of these impress the map's contours on the minds of even the most conciliatory attorneys. First, it is consistent with the expectations of most clients. Second, it is very often functionally effective in achieving the kinds of results generally expected from a "victory" in the adversary system. Third, it generally redounds to the economic benefit of lawyers, and often of clients. Fourth, it gives the appearance of clarifying the law and making it predictable. Fifth, it accords with widely-shared assumptions that we will achieve the best society by giving individual self-interest full expression.

A final, and dominant, source of the popularity of the standard map is legal education, which is thoroughly pervaded by this vision. Nearly all courses at most law schools are presented from the viewpoint of the practicing attorney who is working in an adversary system of act-oriented rules, a context that he accepts. There is, to be sure, scattered attention to the lawyer as planner, policy maker, and public servant, but ninety percent of what goes on in law school is based upon a model of a lawyer working in or against a background of litigation of disputes that can be resolved by the application of a rule by a third party. The teachers were trained with this model in mind. The students bring a rough image with them; it gets sharpened quickly. This model defines and limits the likely career possibilities envisioned by most law students.

Chapter 10

ATTORNEYS AS BARGAINING SURROGATES: THE UNIQUE CHALLENGES FACING THE NEGOTIATING LITIGATOR

As we saw in the last chapter, attorneys face challenges imposed by their role as the negotiating surrogate for their client. In many ways this role can facilitate effective negotiating; in others it may impede a resolution. This latter difficulty is particularly acute when the lawyer attempts to settle a matter being litigated, a process that Marc Galanter calls "litigotiation." In the words of Samuel Gross and Kent Syverud: "A trial is a failure.... Much of our civil procedure is justified by the desire to promote settlement and avoid trial.... Once in a while, however, the process fails and the case goes to trial." The materials in this chapter underscore the tensions in the lawyer's role when bargaining in the shadow of the court house.

James Freund begins our discussion by outlining the particular pitfalls of settlement advocacy in the shadow of litigation. He has a unique vantage point on this topic, coming from many years on the other side of the practice divide, as an experienced commercial transaction planner at the legendary New York law firm of Skadden, Arps. Next, Donald Gifford walks us through the process by which plaintiff's attorneys settle personal injury cases. He relates the dynamics of this litigation context to the lawyer's roles and strategy selection.

Our next reading, by Gross and Syverud, delves more deeply into questions of strategic case selection for settlement or trial. A rich and sophisticated literature is developing on post-filing case processing. We know empirically that most cases settle, and that there are powerful institutional, economic and interpersonal incentives favoring settlement. What is more difficult to know is why certain cases are tried rather than settled. The authors of this selection first summarize the two principal theories attempting to explain why some cases do not settle, one from a law and economics orientation and the other based on the dynamics of bargaining behavior. They then offer several hypotheses derived from their exhaustive analysis of data from trials of both personal injury claims and commercial disputes. Their conclusions help us understand the context in which lawyers make strategic decisions that may lead either to settlement or courtroom.

In this process of negotiating settlements in the shadow of the courtroom, there are inherent opportunities for conflicts of interest between litigating attorneys and their clients. These conflicts may arise from such factors as the frequently substantial costs of financing litigation; differences in the assessment of the risk of loss; and the impact of the contingent fee agreement. Attorney and client are like allies in warfare. Outwardly they may have an identity of goals and are bound together by professional obligations; yet internally they may have divergent interests and inconsistent long term objectives. The next two readings in this chapter outline methods for minimizing the role conflicts of attorneys. On the prescriptive side, Roger Fisher makes a provocative suggestion: What about negotiation as a specialty? On the regulatory side, Robert Cochran suggests malpractice liability for lawyers who usurp client autonomy to make basic choices about the negotiation strategy they prefer or the type of dispute resolution process they want employed.

This chapter ends with some examples of the perils of representing clients in litigation. First, Leonard Riskin provides insights on what can happen when a court attempts to order the principals to accompany their lawyers to a settlement conference. Secondly, Herbert Kritzer demonstrates how the need for attorneys to obtain their fee upon settlement can affect, and complicate, the search for efficient resolution of litigation for the parties involved. As a case study of this phenomenon, the United States Supreme Court offers a revealing answer to the question: Can the government force plaintiffs' attorneys to waive their statutory fees as a condition of settling a civil rights action?

Readings

1. James Freund, *Bridging Troubled Waters: Negotiating Disputes,* 1985–86 Litigation 43–46.

2. Donald Gifford, *A Context–Based Theory of Strategy Selection in Legal Negotiation,* 46 Ohio St.L.J. 41, 82–88 (1985).

3. Samuel R. Gross & Kent D. Syverud, *Getting to No: A Study of Settlement Negotiations and the Selection of Cases for Trial,* 90 Mich.L.Rev. 319, 320–33; 378–85 (1991).

4. Roger Fisher, *What About Negotiation as a Specialty,* 69 ABA J. 121, 122–24 (1983).

5. Robert Cochran, *Legal Representation and the Next Steps Toward Client Control: Attorney Malpractice for the Failure to Allow the Client to Control Negotiation and Pursue Alternatives to Litigation,* 47 Wash. & Lee L.Rev. 819, 823–24, 853–54, 859–63, 867–68, 876–77 (1990).

6. Leonard Riskin, *The Represented Client in a Settlement Conference: The Lessons of G. Heileman Brewing Co. v. Joseph Oat Corp.,* 69 Wash.U.L.Rev. 1059, 1062–65, 1097–1105 (1991).

7. Herbert Kritzer, *Fee Arrangements and Negotiation,* 21 L. & Soc. Rev. 341, 341–47 (1987).

8. Evans v. Jeff D., 475 U.S. 720, 726–38, 754–59, 106 S.Ct. 1531, 1537–54 (1986).

9. For Further Reading

a. Ian Ayres & Eric Talley, *Solomanic Bargaining: Dividing a Legal Entitlement to Facilitate Cosean Trade,* 104 Yale L.J. 1027 (1995).

b. Wayne D. Brazil, *Effective Approaches to Settlement*: A Handbook for Lawyers and Judges (1988).

c. Lester Brickman, *Contingent Fees Without Contingencies: Hamlet Without the Prince of Denmark,* 37 UCLA L.Rev. 29 (1989).

d. Robert J. Condlin, *"Cases On Both Sides:" Patterns of Argument in Legal Dispute–Negotiation,* 44 Md.L.Rev. 65 (1985).

e. Robert Cooter, Stephen Marks & Robert Mnookin, *Bargaining in the Shadow of the Law: A Testable Model of Strategic Behavior,* 11 J.Legal Stud. 225 (1982).

f. Robert Cooter and Daniel Rubinfeld, *Economic Analysis of Legal Disputes and Their Resolution,* 27 J.Econ.Lit. 1067 (1989).

g. Charles B. Craver, *Negotiation as a Distinct Area of Specialization,* 9 Am.J. of Trial Advocacy 377 (1986).

h. Theodore Eisenberg, *Negotiation, Lawyering and Adjudication: Kritzer on Brokers and Deals,* 19 Law & Soc. Inquiry 275 (1994).

i. Roger Fisher, *A Code of Negotiation Practices for Lawyers,* 1 Negot.J. 105 (1985).

j. Marc Galanter, *Worlds of Deals: Using Negotiation to Teach About Legal Process,* 34 J.Legal Educ. 268 (1986).

k. Marc Galanter, *Why the "Haves" Come Out Ahead: Speculations on the Limits of Legal Change,* 9 Law & Soc.Rev. 95 (1974).

l. Marc Galanter, *Reading the Landscape of Disputes: What We Know and Don't Know (and Think We Know) About Our Allegedly Contentious and Litigious Society,* 31 UCLA L.Rev. 4 (1983).

m. Donald Gifford, *A Context–Based Theory of Strategy Selection in Legal Negotiation,* 46 Ohio State L.J. 41 (1985).

n. Geoffrey C. Hazard, Jr., *Lecture: The Settlement Black Box,* 75 B.U.L.Rev. 1257 (1995).

o. Deborah R. Hensler, *A Glass Half Full, A Glass Half Empty: The Use of Alternative Dispute Resolution in Mass Personal Injury Litigation,* 73 Texas L.Rev. 1587 (1995).

p. Jonathon Hyman, *Trial Advocacy as an Impediment to Wise Negotiation,* 5 Negot.J. 237 (1989).

q. Jonathon Hyman, *Trial Advocacy and Methods of Negotiation: Can Good Trial Advocates be Wise Negotiators?,* 34 UCLA L.Rev. 863 (1987).

r. Herbert Kritzer, The Justice Broker: Lawyers and Ordinary Litigation (1990).

s. Herbert Kritzer, Let's Make a Deal (1991).

t. Russell Korobkin & Chris Guthrie, *Opening Offers and Out-of-Court Settlement: A Little Moderation May Not Go A Long Way,* 10 Ohio St.J. On Disp.Res. 1 (1994).

u. Russell Korobkin & Chris Guthrie, *Psychological Barriers to Litigation Settlement: An Experimental Approach,* 93 Mich. L.Rev. 107 (1994).

v. Craig A. McEwen, *Pursuing Problem–Solving or Predictive Settlement,* 19 Fla.St.L.Rev. 77 (1991).

w. Carrie Menkel–Meadow, *The Transformation of Disputes by Lawyers: What the Dispute Paradigm Does and Does Not Tell Us,* 1985 Mo.J.Disp.Resol. 25.

x. Carrie Menkel–Meadow, *Pursuing Settlements in an Adversary Culture: A Tale of Innovation Co-opted or "The Law of ADR",* 19 Fla.St.L.Rev. 1 (1991).

y. Thomas Miceli & Kathleen Segerson, *Contingent Fees For Lawyers: The Impact of Litigation and Accident Prevention,* 20 J.Legal Stud. 381 (1991).

z. Robert Mnookin & Lewis Kornhauser, *Bargaining in the Shadow of the Law: The Case of Divorce,* 88 Yale L.J. 950 (1979).

aa. John Murray, *Considering a Negotiator's View of the Court Process,* 2 J. on Disp. Resolution 223 (1987).

bb. Kenneth Nolan, *Settlement Negotiations,* 11 Litigation 17 (1985).

cc. Ivan P.L. P'ng, *Strategic Behavior in Suit, Settlement, and Trial,* 14 Bell J. Econ. 539 (1983).

dd. George L. Priest & Benjamin Klein, *The Selection of Disputes for Litigation,* 13 J. Legal Stud. 1 (1984).

ee. George Priest, *Reexamining the Selection Hypothesis,* 14 J. Legal Stud. 225 (1985).

ff. Douglas Rosenthal, Lawyer and Client: Who's in Charge (1978).

gg. Austin Sarat & William Felstiner, *Law and Strategy in the Divorce Lawyer's Office,* 20 Law & Soc.Rev. 93 (1986).

hh. William Simon, *The Ideology of Advocacy: Procedural Justice and Professional Responsibility,* 1978 Wisc.L.Rev. 29.

ii. Linda Stanley & Don Coursey, *Empirical Evidence on the Selection Hypothesis and the Decision to Litigate or Settle,* 19 J.Legal Stud. 145 (1990).

jj. Kent Syverud, *The Duty to Settle,* 76 Va.L.Rev. 1113 (1990).

kk. Peter J. Von Koppen, *Risk Taking in Civil Law Negotiations,* 14 Law & Hum. Beh. 151 (1990).

JAMES FREUND, BRIDGING TROUBLED WATERS: NEGOTIATING DISPUTES
1985–86 Litigation 43–46.

I spend most of my professional hours negotiating mergers and other business deals. Lately, though, I have gotten involved in trying to resolve some commercial disputes, both before and after litigation has begun.

Going in, I thought this would not be too difficult. Cutting up a finite pie seemed a lot easier than pulling together all the pieces of a complicated transaction.

I was dead wrong. Resolving disputes is hard work, in some respects even harder than making a deal. But I found that my experience in putting deals together gave me a fresh perspective on settlement. Here, then, are an outsider's thoughts on how to settle a dispute.

The starting point is the group of difficulties that come from the mere fact of litigation. These include the client's ambivalence, the special problems a litigator faces, the tricky matter of getting talks going, the mood of distrust, and the lack of a problem-solving mentality.

We begin with ambivalence. I was really struck by how ambivalent everyone was, right up to the moment of final settlement, about whether the matter should be settled.

In an acquisition, the prevailing mood is, "Let's get it done." All the pressure drives the parties toward an agreement. The businessmen want the deal done yesterday; the investment bankers sweat over their contingent fees; the lawyers get caught up in the frenzy. The emphasis is on being constructive—finding ways to solve problems and get on with the transaction. A corporate lawyer whose heart is not in it—who tries to delay (or worse, sabotage) an agreement—is anathema. The bogeyman of all concerned is a "busted deal."

But when the parties are at loggerheads in a dispute over a business practice or a broken contract, the mood is entirely different. Often, at least some of the parties or lawyers (invariably those on the other side) prefer that the conflict remain unresolved. Even the party with *more* to gain from a negotiated settlement sometimes seems ambivalent about settling. One minute, he tells you to go ahead and see what you can work out; the next, he has second thoughts and is ready to go back to war.

. . .

The real keys for a lawyer settling a dispute are, first, to overcome his own client's ambivalence and get him committed to a settlement and, second, to persuade his adversary that the proposed resolution is sufficient to give up the fight.

The litigator who is handling the case (assuming it has ripened into a lawsuit) bears a special burden in accomplishing these tasks. Up to now, he has been busy throwing his weight around: alleging total fraud and depredation, seeking trebled recompense, ridiculing his adversary's claims as lacking merit. The litigation papers—with everything larger than life and choking on adverbs (the opponent's argument is characterized as "patently absurd," the simplest contractual phrase is "hopelessly ambiguous")—are enough to send shivers up a corporate lawyer's spine. The litigators tend to be combative types, and their contacts during the lawsuit, sometimes reflecting the emotions of their respective clients, are often of the bristling variety.

To shift abruptly to talking about settlement requires a sizable psychological adjustment. What makes it even more difficult is that the lawyers have no way of knowing whether a settlement will ultimately be reached. The left hand is negotiating while the right prepares to resume the conflict. I think this uncertainty deters trial lawyers from taking positions that imply vulnerability, from swapping meaningful compromises, even from making conciliatory noises, for fear that these concessions will somehow make things more difficult if they have to go back to the mat.

In short, there can be a rigidity in shepherding the litigation that is antithetical to the search for compromise, a search that lies at the core of striking a deal.

The litigator may also have trouble, of a more subtle variety, in his own camp. Clients like their gladiators to be tough, to stand up for them forcefully, and successful litigators often cultivate a hawkish image. So it may be hard for a litigator to prod his client in the direction of settlement.

. . .

In deal-making, most good lawyers start with the attitude that everything is ultimately soluble. All you have to do is reduce what sound like sacred principles to mundane dollars, then throw in a face-saver, and the parties are shaking hands.

Central to this attitude is the sense that the other side's problems are *your* problems, too. If your adversary cannot solve a particular tax issue, for instance, there may be no deal at all. So you have to help the other side to develop a structure that works *for him.*

This attitude of ultimate solubility is conspicuously absent in litigation. The parties' positions always seem irreconcilable—just read the briefs. There is no disposition to solve the other side's problems; everyone is having a hard enough job solving his own.

Still, the crux of accommodation is often to figure out what your adversary's *real* problem is (since he may have been less than forthcoming on this score) and then to come up with a creative solution. But my sense is that litigators, influenced by their clients' huffing and puffing, often do not bother themselves with their adversaries' problems.

. . .

Another problem in settling litigation, as compared with negotiating a deal, is the scarcity of good models on which to rely. In an acquisition, opposing counsel argue over a number of points, but we have a plethora of precedents for how most issues are usually resolved, and these precedents provide sort of a built-in standard of reasonableness. I know what can be yielded—others have done so before me, so my client will not feel too exposed—and, conversely, where I should stand firm.

In contrast, many commercial trials have their own unique facts and dynamics. While analogies may be available and damages measurable within a range, litigators often lack useful benchmarks.

One reason I underestimated the difficulty of dispute resolution is that, in contrast to deal-making, where it is necessary to agree on a large number of points, resolving a dispute often requires agreement on only a single dollar figure. Once the bucks are right, everything else falls into place.

I assumed that fighting over one issue would be easier than trying to sort out dozens of equally important issues. I discovered, though, that the very narrowness of the negotiations makes it *harder* to resolve disputes than to arrange a complex transaction.

. . .

My experience suggests that, at least in some cases, a two-lawyer team—a litigator and a negotiator—has a flexibility of approach that either lawyer alone lacks.

In suggesting this, I intend no disrespect to my litigating colleagues, for whom I have the utmost admiration. In particular, I find no substance in the charge sometimes leveled that litigators do not want to settle because, with all the bravado of their papers, they have talked themselves into thinking that their side of the case is stronger than it really is. In my experience, good litigators—no matter how much they may want to try the case—provide the client with a fair assessment of risks and rewards and recommend settlement if they think that is the appropriate course. Behind all the noise and posturing, they understand what a crapshoot litigation is.

DONALD G. GIFFORD, A CONTEXT–BASED THEORY OF STRATEGY SELECTION IN LEGAL NEGOTIATION
46 Ohio State L.J. 41, 82–88 (1985).

THE PLAINTIFF'S STRATEGY IN PERSONAL INJURY NEGOTIATIONS

The plaintiff's personal injury attorney encounters systemic characteristics different from those encountered by the defense attorney in plea bargaining. These characteristics generally suggest a somewhat different strategy than that recommended for plea bargaining. In particular, the greater bargaining power of the plaintiff's attorney, the greater likelihood that the opponent will use competitive tactics, and the lesser importance of a continuing relationship with the other negotiator may all suggest that a competitive strategy is more advantageous in personal injury negotiations than in plea bargaining. This recommendation assumes a personal injury case of significant value; in the small or medium-sized case, economic reality dictates settlement because the costs of litigation exceed the value of the claim. As a result, negotiations of smaller claims, at least between experienced negotiators, are likely typified by the use of a cooperative strategy and an attempt to find a fair and just value for the claim.

The plaintiff's attorney probably will be negotiating with two different representatives of the defendant's insurance company—the claims adjuster (prior to the filing of a lawsuit) and the attorney hired by the insurance company. Professor H. Laurence Ross, a social scientist who has studied the claims process in great detail, concludes that for these individuals, "organizational pressure would seem to be a more important factor than personality in affecting the outcome of claims." Certain structural characteristics of the claims adjustment process suggest that the claims adjuster's strategy will be competitive; other pressures on the adjuster, however, influence him to adopt a cooperative strategy.

The adjuster will likely begin the negotiations with a competitive strategy. Claims adjusters are trained to settle cases quickly with the claimant for an amount far less than an attorney, once retained, would regard as a fair settlement value. Quite frequently, the claims adjuster begins competitively and argues that if the claimant were to hire an attorney, then the attorney would "take half" and leave the claimant with less than if she were to settle immediately. Even after the claimant hires an attorney, adjusters often test the plaintiff's attorney with competitive tactics to determine whether the attorney, because she is naive, unprepared, or impatient, will settle for less than the fair value of the case. More generally, the adjuster's adversarial orientation causes him to disbelieve the claimant's position until more facts are revealed as a result of discovery and further investigation.

The relationship between the claims adjuster and the insurance company facilitates the use of the competitive strategy, because the adjuster's power to make concessions is limited. His settlement authority frequently is strictly confined; therefore, he cannot reciprocate the concessions made by the plaintiff's counsel without consulting his superiors. In addition, insurance companies may set the reserve on a case unrealistically low so that the plaintiff's demand can be met with the statement that "our reserve is only $15,000." These techniques constitute a competitive tactic known as the "negotiation without authority" ploy. Similarly, while the insurance adjuster conceals his own information, he typically expects the plaintiff's attorney to disclose the fruits of her investigation.

After the plaintiff's attorney demonstrates that she understands the value of the case, the adjuster will probably negotiate cooperatively and yield to the pressure to settle quickly as many cases as possible. As a result, insurance companies pay many questionable claims. In serious cases, "danger value" may be paid, even in the absence of apparent liability, to avoid the risk that a jury might be swayed by sympathy for the severely injured plaintiff and award her a substantial sum. Conversely, in small cases of questionable liability, "nuisance value" is paid because the costs of processing and trying the case exceed the settlement value for the case. In addition, claims adjusters often desire to be fair to injured claimants, even in the absence of clear liability; thus, some minimal payment to an injured plaintiff, when liability is questionable or nonexistent, may nonetheless be a good business practice. The pressure on the claims adjuster to settle cases and his desire to be fair suggest that he will adopt a predominantly cooperative strategy in the later phases of negotiation.

In summary, the conflicting pressures on the insurance adjuster to adopt a competitive strategy or a noncompetitive strategy are generally resolved in two ways. First, the claims adjuster likely will begin with a competitive strategy and become more cooperative as the negotiation progresses. Second, the claims adjuster probably will behave in accordance with the following principle: If cases can be settled inexpensively they should be, but in any event, they should be settled.

Less has been written about the negotiating strategy likely to be used by counsel for the insurance company or the pressures affecting his choice of strategy. The strategy actually used by insurance defense attorneys includes several competitive tactics. Their initial offers are generally quite low. Settlement rarely occurs early in the process; significant offers are often not made until discovery is completed and the parties are figuratively, and often literally, on the courthouse steps. The insurance company's defense attorney also uses delay tactics to press an injured and incapacitated defendant toward early settlement.

As trial approaches, however, the defense attorney's strategy usually becomes cooperative. The defense counsel recognizes that juries tend to overestimate the impartial value of a case because they sympathize with injured plaintiffs and dislike insurance companies. Furthermore, the attorney knows that his client, the insurance company, desires to avoid, if possible, the attorney's fees associated with trial. Finally, the insurance company has a legal obligation to accept any reasonable settlement offer within the policy limits. These reasons suggest that immediately preceding trial, attorneys representing insurance companies are likely to pursue a cooperative strategy and seek a fair and just result.

The second factor that affects the choice of a negotiation strategy, the relative power between the two negotiators, is much different in the personal injury context than in the plea bargaining situation. Usually the personal injury plaintiff has greater negotiating power, but the plaintiff's power varies greatly according to the strength of her case. When the plaintiff's attorney negotiates with the claims adjuster, she has two viable alternatives to a negotiated agreement with the adjuster: further negotiations with the defendant's attorney and trial. On the other hand, the claims adjuster who fails to achieve agreement must report to his superior and explain the failure to close the case and the implicit necessity of paying attorney's fees. All of the previously described pressures on the claims adjuster to settle cases, coupled with the likelihood of a sympathetic jury, increase the plaintiff's attorney's advantage. Of course, if the plaintiff has a weak case that is unlikely to survive a motion for summary judgment or a motion for a directed verdict, then the power advantage is reversed. Generally though, the personal injury attorney's bargaining power advantage over the insurance company suggests that she has the option of choosing between the competitive and cooperative strategies.

Considerations of a possible continuing relationship between the negotiating parties probably is not as important in selecting a negotiation strategy in personal injury negotiations as it is in plea bargaining. In personal injury claims, as in plea bargaining, but unlike labor relations, the parties themselves almost never have a continuing relationship: the accident resulting in the personal injury is a one-time affair. A continuing positive working relationship between the *parties,* which would discourage using a competitive strategy, is not necessary. On the other hand, the plaintiff's personal injury attorney may or may not have continuing contact with a claims adjuster or a defense insurance attorney. To the extent that a continuing relationship is probable, she may want to consider a noncompetitive strategy. However, the degree of continuing contact between a personal injury plaintiff's attorney and the insurance company's defense counsel generally is less than the daily interaction between a prosecutor and a public defender. Therefore, this factor usually will not be as significant in choosing the optimal strategy.

The amount of pressure on the plaintiff's personal injury attorney to settle also varies greatly from case to case. In some cases, the injured client who does not have funds to pay medical bills and living expenses pressures her attorney to settle her claim expeditiously. However, injured plaintiffs usually receive some form of financial assistance such as governmental social welfare benefits, first-party insurance proceeds, or wage continuation plan benefits. These benefits significantly diminish the financial pressure on the plaintiff to settle and make the competitive strategy more viable even though it may delay the receipt of compensation. Judicial pressure to settle during the later stages of personal injury negotiations, however, may dictate the use of a cooperative strategy.

The personal injury attorney is accountable to her client; the need for a harmonious relationship with the client generally influences the negotiator to adopt a competitive strategy during the early phases of negotiations. The plaintiff's attorney is bound by the client's decisions regarding settlement; because personal injury negotiations usually involve a single, easily quantifiable issue and because the client's predominant concern is the easily understood dollar amount of the settlement, she probably will be knowledgeable about, and interested in, the various settlement offers and counteroffers. Most personal injury plaintiffs are likely to have high aspirations; many will remain angry at the defendant who injured them or the deep pocket insurance company that initially made miserly offers because it pursued a competitive strategy. The need to placate her client, therefore, may suggest that the plaintiff's attorney adopt a competitive strategy. Later in the negotiations, especially as trial approaches, plaintiffs frequently become less demanding, and the attorney may change her strategy to a more cooperative approach.

The characteristics of personal injury litigation limit the feasibility of the integrative strategy in most cases. Personal injury negotiation is predominantly a zero-sum negotiation; each dollar the plaintiff gains is a dollar loss to the defendant. Generally, the only significant issue in controversy is the dollar amount of the settlement. The single issue nature of the negotiation prevents the use of logrolling as an integrative technique.

The above analysis suggests that the plaintiff's attorney should use a predominantly competitive strategy in personal injury negotiations. The plaintiff's attorney who adopts a noncompetitive strategy will be severely disadvantaged when negotiating against a claims adjuster or defense attorney who will probably use competitive approaches. Further, the plaintiff's alternatives to a negotiated settlement are more attractive than the criminal defendant's non-negotiation options, so there is less risk in using the competitive strategy in most cases, even if negotiations break down. The lesser possibility of a continuing relationship between the negotiators and the heavier pressure to settle personal injury cases usually will not be sufficiently critical factors to suggest a predominantly cooperative strategy. It is recommended, therefore, that the plaintiff's attorney use a competitive strategy in negotiations with the claims adjuster and in the initial negotiations with opposing counsel. In the final stages of negotiation, the plaintiff's attorney should shift to a cooperative strategy if such a change is suggested by one or more of the following factors:

(1) opposing counsel uses a noncompetitive strategy;

(2) the case is weak and is unlikely to survive the defendant's motion for a directed verdict;

(3) the client's immediate financial situation or other needs exert considerable pressure to settle; or

(4) further competitive tactics will damage a continuing relationship with opposing counsel, to the detriment of the present client and future clients.

The negotiation strategies recommended by personal injury specialists, or observed in actual practice by those who have studied personal injury negotiation, closely mirror the one recommended above, even though personal injury lawyers have not consciously applied the factors identified by social scientists to choose their strategies. These pragmatic tacticians recommend that the personal injury attorney present a high initial demand, employ information gathering tactics in the early phases of negotiation, make threats, make concessions only in response to the opponent's concessions, make only small concessions, and delay settlement until the last possible moment. In other words, real world practitioners recommend using all of the tactics that constitute the competitive strategy. That the competitive strategy is currently the norm in personal injury negotiations provides yet another reason for the personal injury attorney to use this strategy: to use a noncompetitive strategy in a milieu in which attorneys expect the competitive strategy will severely disadvantage the negotiator. That the strategy recommended above is consistent with the recommendations of leading personal injury specialists to use competitive tactics in personal injury litigation also supports the validity of the method outlined in this article for selecting an optimal, effective negotiation strategy in other substantive contexts.

SAMUEL R. GROSS & KENT D. SYVERUD, GETTING TO NO: A STUDY OF SETTLEMENT NEGOTIATIONS AND THE SELECTION OF CASES FOR TRIAL

90 Mich.L.Rev. 319, 320–25, 327–29, 333, 341, 378–85 (1991).

A trial is a failure. Although we celebrate it as the centerpiece of our system of justice, we know that trial is not only an uncommon method of resolving disputes, but a disfavored one. With some notable exceptions, lawyers, judges, and commentators agree that pretrial settlement is almost always cheaper, faster, and better than trial. Much of our civil procedure is justified by the desire to promote settlement and avoid trial. More important, the nature of our civil process drives parties to settle so as to avoid the costs, delays, and uncertainties of trial, and, in many cases, to agree upon terms that are beyond the power or competence of courts to dictate. These are powerful forces, and they produce settlement in a very high proportion of litigated disputes. Once in a while, however, the process fails and a case goes to trial.

Why do these failures occur? One answer is obvious. For every trial, there is at least one person—an attorney, a client, a claims manager—who said "no" to a settlement. Who said no, and why? We asked lawyers and we received a wide range of answers: "The client was stubborn"; "The plaintiff wanted too much"; "We didn't think their case had any merit"; "They just wouldn't pay anything"; "It was a family feud and a matter of pride"; and so on. Everyone seems to agree that these vetoes are not random, but a great deal more is needed to explain why few disputes are tried while the great majority are not.

Over the past decade scholars have developed two major theoretical frameworks that address this question. One holds that a trial represents a failure in parties' *predictions* of the behavior of the court: a trial will occur when the parties make inconsistent and self-serving errors in their estimates of the likely judgment. This theory has been developed primarily in the work of George Priest and Benjamin Klein. A competing view of litigation describes trial as a failure of *bargaining* between the parties, the unintended outcome of strategic ploys that misfire. Among legal scholars, the most prominent exponents of this theory are Robert Mnookin, Lewis Kornhauser,

Robert Cooter, and Stephen Marks. These two views of litigation embody different understandings of the nature of settlements, and they have quite different implications for the composition of the small subset of cases that are selected to go to trial.

The absence of data on pretrial negotiations has handicapped development of this topic. This article is an attempt to begin to correct that problem.

. . .

Both of the existing theoretical frameworks are helpful in describing our findings. Priest and Klein's intuitively appealing model of the selection of cases for trial provides a useful starting point for examining actual litigation. From that starting point we proceed to find strong evidence of strategic bargaining of the sort described by Mnookin, Kornhauser, Cooter, and others—and more than a hint that such bargaining is a major force in determining which cases fail to settle. Neither of the frameworks, however, fully explains the patterns that we observe. On the one hand, several of Priest and Klein's hypotheses—in particular, the claim that the outcomes of trials will gravitate to a fifty percent plaintiff success rate—are inconsistent with actual settlement negotiations and trial outcomes. On the other hand, the formal strategic bargaining models that have been developed lack sufficient detail to explain the remarkably diverse selection patterns that exist in different types of litigation.

Pretrial bargaining and the selection of cases for trial cannot be understood in the abstract. To explain the settlement negotiations and the outcomes in these cases, it is necessary to consider the social and economic context of the litigation, including: (1) the nature of the parties and the relationships between them; (2) their arrangements for paying their attorneys; (3) the existence or absence of insurance to pay the damages and the costs of litigation; and (4) the division of settlement authority between defendants and their insurers. Differences in these variables from one type of case to another help explain conspicuous differences in the pretrial behavior of the parties, and in the judgments they obtain in court.

. . .

TRIAL AND SETTLEMENT THEORIES

A. *Priest and Klein on the Selection of Cases for Trial*

Trials are most likely to occur in close cases. This is a common observation by trial lawyers, and the core assertion of Priest and Klein's influential model of litigation. The model's most influential elements—the "selection hypothesis," which is an attempt to explain why trials occur primarily in close cases, and the "fifty percent implication," which is a specific prediction that follows from the selection hypothesis—are both built around this claim.

The Selection Hypothesis

. . .

The critical step in Priest and Klein's theory is an assumption that the parties' bargaining postures can be determined directly from their assessments of the likely outcome at trial. Building on economic models of litigation developed by Landes, Posner, and Gould, the Priest and Klein model equates a plaintiff's minimum settlement demand with the plaintiff's *estimate* of the expected judgment at trial, *minus* the plaintiff's litigation costs. Similarly, the defendant's maximum settlement offer equals the defendant's *estimate* of the expected judgment at trial, *plus* the defendant's litigation costs.

Priest and Klein assume that the parties will settle whenever the defendant's maximum offer is greater than the plaintiff's minimum demand. Because litigation costs are *added* to the defendant's maximum offer and *subtracted* from the plaintiff's minimum demand, settlement will normally occur. Indeed, if plaintiffs and defendants always agreed in their predictions of trial outcomes, there would be no trials at all. But the parties do not always agree, and their disagreements can lead to very different assessments of the expected judgment. As a result, the plaintiff's minimum demand will sometimes exceed the defendant's maximum offer. In that situation, Priest and Klein assume the parties will not settle. Regardless of the outcome, Priest and Klein tacitly assume that the parties neither bargain nor litigate strategically. The litigants make demands and offers, they settle or try cases, solely because of what they expect the court will do, and not at all because of how they expect opposing parties to respond.

Given these assumptions, Priest and Klein demonstrate that the cases that go to trial will be concentrated among disputes close to the decision standard.... Priest and Klein's selection hypothesis, then, is that tried cases tend to cluster close to the governing decision standard, regardless of the underlying distribution of disputes relative to that standard.

The Fifty Percent Implication

The general prediction of the selection hypothesis—that trials will tend to be close cases—is difficult to confirm or refute. Since it is a comparative assertion (cases tried are closer to the decision standard than cases settled), it requires data on both settlements and trials. Worse, the data would have to quantify a notoriously slippery concept, the weight of evidence on disputed claims. As a result, nobody has made a credible attempt to test the selection hypothesis directly against data from real cases. However, by adding a couple of additional assumptions to this hypothesis, Priest and Klein developed a more specific prediction that is, apparently, quite testable: that plaintiffs will tend to win fifty percent of cases that go to trial, regardless of the proportion of cases in which they would prevail in the underlying distribution of disputes from which trials are selected. To a remarkable extent, this "fifty percent implication," which Priest also describes as the "principal empirical heuristic of the model," has come to overshadow the more general selection effect.

. . .

However limiting its assumptions, the fifty percent hypothesis has the virtue of being easy to remember, and apparently easy to test. It seems that such tests require only information about trial outcomes, which are much more accessible to researchers than settlement negotiations. And tested the fifty percent hypothesis has been, on datasets as diverse as wrongful death cases in Japan, civil rights cases in federal courts, challenges to federal agency decisionmaking, and state court appellate decisions. The tests, however, are often unsatisfying. On the one hand, a finding of a fifty percent success rate is too rarely accompanied by an inquiry into whether the underlying assumptions of the model are actually met. On the other hand, a deviation from a fifty percent rate can almost always be explained as a failure of one or more of these essential assumptions rather than a failure of the hypothesis itself.

B. Bargaining Theory and the Disposition of Litigated Disputes

Pretrial bargaining is strategic. The predicted trial outcome may inform a litigant's strategy, but it cannot determine it, since even a perfect prediction leaves crucial questions unanswered: What fraction or multiple of the expected judgment should the litigant offer, and when? How quickly and in what fashion should she respond to an offer by the other side? Under what circumstances should a party make a sincere offer? An outrageous demand? An insincere threat to go to trial? Despite extensive research, no general theory even claims to describe the optimal settlement strategy. Bargaining remains an art rather than a science.

Bargaining theory has provided an interesting and complex view of the process that leads cases to be tried. The first major statement of that view was presented in Robert Mnookin and Lewis Kornhauser's 1979 article, "Bargaining in the Shadow of Law: The Case of Divorce." The central point of this article is consistent with Priest and Klein's framework: litigants order their private, out-of-court negotiations around the substantive law and procedure that will be applied if the negotiations break down and the court steps out of the shadows to adjudicate the dispute. But Mnookin and Kornhauser also argue that an array of other factors affect negotiating behavior in divorce cases, some of which are largely independent of the expected judgment. These factors include: (1) differences among litigants in how they value monetary and nonmonetary stakes in the litigation; (2) differences in the degree of uncertainty about the outcome, and in the risk aversion of the litigants; (3) the transaction costs and the litigants' ability to bear them; (4) the litigants' feelings toward each other; and (5) strategic behavior.

Much of the work of bargaining theorists has focused on this last factor, strategic behavior. Mnookin and Kornhauser used "strategy" to mean behavior in which litigants *misrepresent* their intentions, desires, or chances of winning in order to obtain an advantage in settlement negotiations. Each party has an *opportunity* to lie because the opponent cannot know the other side's prediction of the outcome at trial, preferences with regard to settlement, or attitudes toward the risk of trial. Each party also has an *incentive* to lie: by lying it may increase its share of the gains from settlement—the trial costs avoided by both plaintiff and defendant.

In a later article Robert Cooter, Stephen Marks, and Robert Mnookin use a broader definition of strategy and attempt to construct a model that identifies those subsets of cases where strategic bargaining behavior is most likely to cause trials. In this model, as under the Priest and Klein framework, it is a necessary condition for settlement that the defendant's expected judgment, plus trial costs, exceeds the plaintiff's expected judgment, minus trial costs. For Cooter, Marks, and Mnookin, however—unlike Priest and Klein—this condition is not sufficient to generate a settlement. Even parties that stand to gain from a settlement must bargain successfully over the distribution of those gains. A litigant's "strategy" consists of the moves she makes to maneuver the opponent into giving her as much of the settlement gains as possible. The array of possible strategies is virtually unlimited.

How does a litigant choose a strategy? At each step in the negotiations she will consider both how the opposing party will react to a possible move and how the court might rule at trial. Thus, a defendant may reject a plaintiff's demand that is better than the outcome the defendant expects at trial, but not as good as the settlement the defendant expects after further negotiations. Such a refusal is a calculated gamble—a judgment that the chance of a more advantageous settlement is worth the risk of a trial with a higher expected cost to the defendant. Trials, according to the model, consist largely of cases where gambles like this did not pay off—where hard bargaining strategies caused negotiations to fail. They can occur even when neither party is unduly optimistic about the judgment.

Cooter, Marks, and Mnookin suggest several ways to test whether it is strategic behavior or optimism about trial results that causes trials. First, strategic behavior is implicated whenever there is a high rate of trials among cases where the outcome is easy to predict (and thus difficult to predict erroneously, whether optimistically or pessimistically). Second, repeat litigants (such as insurance companies) whose opponents are not repeat litigants are more likely to favor hard bargaining strategies, since by doing so they will influence the expectations of future opponents. The model predicts a higher rate of trial in such cases than in cases where repeat litigants sue other repeat litigants. Finally, the model predicts a higher rate of trial under the American rule, where each side pays its own fees, than under the British rule, where the loser pays both sides' fees. If party optimism drove cases to trial, one would expect the opposite to be the case.

These tests all look exclusively to rates of trial relative to settlement for traces of strategic bargaining, rather than to the pattern of demands, offers, and judgments. Unfortunately, none of the tests is as easy to employ as the fifty percent hypothesis. It turns out to be quite difficult to determine which classes of cases have the most predictable outcomes, in part because of the possibility of bias in the subset of cases that go to trial.

· · ·

THE FAILURE OF THE FIFTY PERCENT IMPLICATION

What drives cases to trial? To answer that question, we start with Priest and Klein's analysis of the selection of cases for trial, and particularly with the fifty percent implication. The trials we examined, like the Cook County cases with which Priest and Klein first tested the fifty percent implication, represent only a tiny fraction of the claims that might have gone to trial. Likewise, the overall pattern of outcomes of these cases resembles the Cook County trial outcomes reported by Priest and Klein: 51.4% of all trials resulted in judgments for the plaintiffs, and 48.6% in judgments for defendants. At a glance, our data appear to confirm that, given a low trial rate, plaintiff success in court does approach 50%.

Glances can be misleading. While at first it looks as though these data provide strong support for the fifty percent implication, a closer examination shows that this hypothesis is inconsistent with our observations.... In short, our data, both for the entire set of trials and for the dominant subset of personal injury trials, are even more inconsistent with Priest and Klein's general model as applied to cases with disputed damages than with the simple fifty percent hypothesis.

Why does the fifty percent hypothesis so thoroughly fail to describe these outcomes? One reason, we believe, is that the model on which it is based fails to incorporate important elements of the economic and social structure of litigation.

. . .

CONCLUSION: SOME EMPIRICAL HYPOTHESES

We set out to study settlement negotiations by examining the verdicts in civil jury trials, and the abortive bargaining that preceded those trials. We found that the pattern of trial outcomes varies greatly across categories of cases. By any meaningful measure, plaintiffs lose a strong majority of personal injury trials, but they win most commercial trials. We also found unmistakable evidence of strategic bargaining by civil defendants; the clearest signs of this are the zero-offer cases, trials in which the defendants simply refused to consider negotiated settlements. The proportion of trials that follow zero offers (like the proportion of plaintiff victories) varies considerably from one type of case to another. It is particularly high in medical malpractice cases, apparently because many physician defendants insist on trial in order to obtain vindication.

Given this sort of strategic bargaining by defendants, we have shown that it is in plaintiffs' economic self-interest to pursue many cases that they are likely to lose, as well as those that they expect to win. This will produce a low plaintiff success rate at trial, *if* plaintiffs can afford to act on their economic interests. In general, plaintiffs are able to do so in personal injury cases because their litigation costs are financed by attorneys who work for contingent fees, and because the damages they might collect are guaranteed by the defendants' insurance companies. In commercial cases—where plaintiffs' lawyers are usually paid by the hour, and defendants are usually uninsured—many plaintiffs can only afford to take likely winners to trial. Moreover, judging from their demands, even then they would frequently have settled for less than the award if they had been given an opportunity to do so.

The most general conclusion we can draw from all this is that the main systemic determinants of success at trial and in pretrial bargaining are contextual and relational.

. . .

We face a more complex set of contextual and relational issues when we try to describe the forces that effect success at trial. The litigants' resources make a difference, particularly their wealth. Their conduct is influenced by their relations with outside parties—their desire to preserve or create a reputation, for example, or to discourage future litigation, or to limit (or increase) future settlements. Perhaps the most interesting issues, however, are those that are generated in the interactions between the litigants and their allies.

Few parties approach litigation by themselves. With rare exceptions they need lawyers to represent them; if they are defendants, they usually also need insurers to pay the judgments, if any, and the costs of litigation. A litigant's lawyer, or her insurance company, is an ally in the traditional military sense of the word. They seek the same ultimate outcome, and they are bound to each other by formal mutual obligations. Nonetheless, they may have vastly different resources and power, and their interests and preferences sometimes diverge. Such differences can crop up in the relationship between defendants and defense counsel, but the more common and significant problems concern those allies who play at litigation (at least in part) with their own money: plaintiffs' lawyers (if they are paid on a contingency) and insurers. In both cases, the additional resources that the ally provides are critical to the case, and in both cases the ally's interests will often conflict with those of the party in whose interests it is formally obliged to act.

Several of the patterns that we found in these data suggest general propositions (or, perhaps more accurately, intermediate level propositions) that may be testable. Each of the following assumes that the described circumstance is a change from its opposite, but that otherwise all else remains unchanged.

1. If plaintiffs rather than their attorneys are required to advance trial costs (including attorneys' fees), and to bear the risk of failing to recover those costs, the trial rate will decline and the plaintiffs' success rate at trial will increase.

. . .

2. If one side stands to lose more from a defeat at trial than the other side gains, its success rate at trial will increase and the trial rate will decrease; if one side stands to gain more from a victory at trial than the other side loses, its success rate at trial will increase and the trial rate will increase.

This proposition describes the consequences of unequal stakes in litigation in sufficient detail to predict patterns of outcomes. It is misleading to think of a party's stakes in a trial as a unitary figure—the expected value of the case. Instead, each side attaches separate values to each possible outcome, and their stakes may be unequal (or equal) with respect to victories, or defeats, or both.

The best example of the first sort of inequality is greater risk aversion on the part of plaintiffs. In this context, risk aversion *means* that a loss will harm the affected party more than the monetary value of an equivalent gain. If both sides are equally risk averse then the effects will cancel out, but if one is more so there will be a systematic effect on the outcomes. Plaintiffs are usually individuals; in general, they are more risk averse than the corporations and insurance companies they usually oppose—*if* they have something to lose. Therefore, we find that plaintiffs succeed more often at trials after significant offers (which they must risk losing) than at trials after zero offers. Similarly, plaintiffs succeed more often in commercial trials, where they frequently risk losing the trial costs, than in personal injury cases, where that risk is borne by the less risk-averse plaintiffs' lawyers. On the defense side, this type of asymmetry may operate in some product liability cases, where defendants worry that a judgment at trial may cost them heavily in future claims based on defects in the same product.

The second type of inequality occurs conspicuously in medical malpractice cases. Other researchers have argued that physicians (like manufacturers in product liability cases) face special reputational costs that magnify the harm they suffer from adverse malpractice judgments. In fact the inequality seems to be different: defendants in malpractice cases seem to derive a special nonmonetary value from vindication at trial that is not a cost to the plaintiffs, and that they could not achieve by other means. Accordingly, we found both a high rate of defendant success at trial and a comparatively high trial rate.

3. *If the parties on one side of a set of cases are repeat litigants, their success rate at trial will increase.*

. . .

4. *If defendants are given the authority to veto settlements, but their insurers are required to pay damage awards and the costs of trial, the trial rate will increase and the plaintiffs' success rate at trial will decrease.*

. . .

5. *In cases with high damages, if the defendants have great resources the plaintiffs' success rate at trial will decrease.*

. . .

A great deal of our analysis has focused on the role of insurance companies—as one might expect, given their centrality in American civil litigation. In conclusion, it is useful to say a bit about their primary interests in litigation, in order to provide an overview of some of the problems inherent in any attempt to explain patterns in the outcomes of trials.

One of the startling facts about civil jury trials is that a very small number of verdicts accounts for most of the damages that juries award. In our data, for example, 54% of the damages in personal injury trials were awarded in 3% of the cases. Indeed, 35% of all damages are awarded in just 1% of the cases. These few high judgments inflate the size of the mean judgment in any set of cases far above the median; for example, the mean nonzero negligence judgment in our sample is $208,000, and the median is $58,000.

. . .

For insurance companies, a major goal (if not *the* major goal) in pretrial negotiations must be to avoid huge verdicts. This objective has mischievous consequences that complicate any simple model of the selection of cases for trial. For example, it seems plausible that cases with high stakes will be more likely to go to trial than smaller cases, since the larger the stakes the less (proportionally) the parties stand to gain by saving trial costs. On the other hand, the larger the stakes, the higher the risk of a huge verdict, and the greater the insurer's incentive to offer a settlement that the plaintiff cannot afford to refuse. Similarly, other researchers have plausibly argued that as uncertainty about the outcomes of a set of cases increases, more of them will go to trial, since the parties' predictions will be increasingly likely to diverge. But greater uncertainty also increases the proportion of cases that insurance companies will be anxious to settle because they present the risk of huge verdicts, which ought to decrease the trial rate. Quite likely, different insurers react differently to these competing incentives.

Finally, to the extent that insurance companies do focus on the danger of rare off-scale verdicts, their settlement and trial behavior will be quirky and somewhat unpredictable because they have so few cases to inform their decisions. Economic theories of trial and pretrial bargaining call to mind the standard image of a competitive market: numerous individuals intelligently pursuing independent self-interests. Social reality, as usual, is inconsiderate of global theories. In this case it provides a competing image that is less susceptible to statistical prediction: stragglers picking their way in the dark, trying to avoid an occasional land mine.

ROGER FISHER, WHAT ABOUT NEGOTIATION AS A SPECIALITY

69 ABA J. 121, 122–24 (1983).

Like us, clients are human beings. They react. They get angry. They see their own side of a case more clearly than they do that of others, and they lose perspective. So they retain professional counsel. But how good is the advice we give? Perhaps, just perhaps, one reason there is so much litigation is that clients receive less than optimal advice from us lawyers. Like clients, we lawyers sometimes make mistakes by singlemindedly pursuing the litigation option. Let me suggest some reasons for this attitude.

Although lawyers negotiate every day—with spouse, landlord, colleagues, neighbors, salesmen and children—they often do so poorly. The more serious the disagreement, the less likely we are to engage in joint problem solving. We usually shoot from the hip. Clients would be better served by our persuading opposing counsel today than by our persuading a judge next year, but we usually prepare far less for a negotiation than we would for a trial. Even in professional negotiations, we often attend meetings with no more purpose in mind than to "see what they say." Because we do not have to agree, we treat negotiation as a preliminary and not a final level of action.

In negotiations we are likely to come up with an answer before we fully understand the perceptions and concerns that create the problem. We vacillate between being hard and soft, not knowing which is better. We see no third alternative. We frequently reward the other side's stubbornness by making a concession, forgetting the lessons of Chamberlain and B.F. Skinner that we cannot buy good conduct by yielding to threats. If we respond to outrageous behavior with concessions, we will get more of the behavior we reward.

We often conduct negotiations in ways that are inefficient, exacerbate relations among the parties and produce unwise outcomes.

Another reason so many cases are litigated is that lawyers tend to overestimate the strength of a client's case. There is no doubt that the longer we work on a problem to advance one point of view, the more merit we see in that point of view. We may not be able to persuade a court that our client should prevail, but we always succeed in persuading ourselves. During the two years of arguing cases in the Supreme Court for the solicitor general, I was never on the wrong side—on the side that should have lost. A majority of the Court was sometimes on the wrong side, but not I.

An Experiment

Howard Raiffa of the Harvard Business School conducts an experiment that demonstrates the effect of working on a problem as an advocate. Each student is given an identical set of facts about a business to be sold. Half the students are buyers; half are sellers. The facts encourage each side to make a deal. The only question is price. After studying the facts, each student is asked to write down, privately, his or her estimate of the fair price that would be determined by an impartial appraiser.

This experiment has been done many times with hundreds of students. The average price that buyers think fair is always substantially lower than the average price that sellers think fair. Taking an advocate's point of view does distort our judgment. With both lawyers unduly optimistic, the clients are doomed to litigate far more than they should.

A third factor contributing to the high cost of litigation is the fear by counsel that the first side to propose settlement weakens its negotiating position. Appearing eager to settle is taken as demonstrating a lack of confidence in one's case. Instead, if only to strengthen their hand for future negotiations, both sides concentrate on discovery, preparing for trial and looking tough. Meanwhile, legal fees continue to mount.

The Prescription: Specialization

My suggested answer to all three difficulties is for some lawyers to specialize in negotiation and dispute settlement. The existence of these specialists should improve the quality of the settlement skills offered by the bar and avoid the problems of overoptimism and postponing talks for fear of looking weak.

. . .

The time has come for lawyers to recognize that negotiation is a special field in which it is possible to acquire special competence. Of course, as in litigation, a lot depends on personality and other factors that are impossible to teach. But study, theory and concentrated experience can make a big difference. Lawyers can learn to produce wiser outcomes and to do so more efficiently and amicably.

. . .

The Two-Track Answer

Specialization also provides an answer to the twin problems of overestimating the merits of a client's case and of postponing settlement talks for fear of looking weak. Pursue a two-track approach. Have one lawyer try to settle a case, while a different lawyer pursues litigation.

As believers in the adversary process, lawyers recognize the potential bias in all of us. There is no way in which one lawyer, try as he may, can be counted on to give a judge a properly balanced assessment of the pros and cons. To maximize the chance of a wise decision, the judge needs to hear the case for A from one lawyer and the case for B from another.

For a client, the decision whether to settle or to litigate is of comparable importance. Shouldn't the client also be entitled to the benefits of the adversary process? Isn't a client likely to make a wiser decision if one lawyer presents the case for settlement and a different lawyer the case for litigation?

In any major case a wise client should ask one lawyer to explore the possibilities of settlement and a different lawyer to pursue the litigation option. An expert in negotiation, with full authority to negotiate, subject to client approval, would seek to develop a settlement that could be recommended to the client. With that proposed settlement in hand, the client then could weigh the negotiator's arguments for settlement against his trial counsel's arguments for pursuing litigation. The chance of making a mistaken decision to litigate would be reduced greatly.

This two-track approach also could eliminate that widespread working assumption that the lawyer who is talking settlement must have a weak case. When settlement is being handled by a specialist who never litigates, a proposal to talk settlement is no sign of weakness. On the contrary, a specialist in settling cases has an easy opening: "This case just came into the office. My partner is dying to litigate it and says he is confident of a spectacular victory. My job is to see if I can produce a fair settlement, one that I can persuade our client is better—all things considered—than litigation. Let's see what we can do."

. . .

A TASK FOR EXPERTS

Everyone should know something about putting out fires, and presumably everyone does, but there is a compelling need for professional firefighters. Similarly, all lawyers should know something about negotiation. Most of us should know more than we do. It is high time that we lawyers, whose calling is to serve justice at minimum cost to our clients and to society, should have some members who specialize in the amicable settlement of differences.

ROBERT COCHRAN, LEGAL REPRESENTATION AND THE NEXT STEPS TOWARD CLIENT CONTROL: ATTORNEY MALPRACTICE FOR FAILURE TO ALLOW THE CLIENT TO CONTROL NEGOTIATION AND PURSUE ALTERNATIVES TO LITIGATION

47 Wash. & Lee L.Rev. 819, 823–24, 853–4, 859–63, 867–68, 876–77 (1990).

A difficulty with establishing a rule of client control is identifying what choices the client should make. Even the simplest legal matter involves many choices. In representation concerning a dispute, choices include everything from whether to bring a suit to whether to cite seven or eight cases for a proposition in a memorandum. In representation concerning a business transaction, choices include everything from whether to form a partnership or corporation to what language to use in an employment contract.

This article advocates that courts require lawyers to allow clients to make those choices which a reasonable person, in what the lawyer knows or should know to be the position of the client, would want to make. If a lawyer's failure to allow a client to make such decisions results in a loss to the client, the lawyer should be subject to malpractice liability. Courts should also continue to identify specific choices that as a matter of law are for the client.

It is likely that the next steps in the development of the right of the client to control legal representation will be the recognition of a duty that attorneys allow clients to control the significant decisions during negotiation, in both legal disputes and transactions, and to allow clients to choose to pursue mediation and arbitration as alternatives to litigation. Courts are likely to hold lawyers liable for the failure to allow the client to make these decisions for several reasons.

First, the failure to allow a client to make significant choices during negotiations and to choose mediation or arbitration could cause the client to suffer a significant loss. If a trial or negotiation of a transaction is unsuccessful, and a client, given the opportunity and sufficient information, would have made a different decision that would have benefited the client, the failure of the attorney to allow the client to make that choice has injured the client.

Second, generally, a client can competently make the significant choices that arise in negotiations, and the choice whether to pursue an alternative means of dispute resolution. Unlike some choices that must be made during litigation, the major decisions related to negotiation, mediation, and arbitration generally are not urgent, nor are they so technical that the ordinary client could not make them intelligently.

Third, the imposition of civil liability on an attorney for the failure to allow the client to choose and control alternatives to litigation would build on well established precedents that give the client the right to choose whether to accept an offer of settlement and precedents that give the medical patient the right to be informed about and to choose alternatives to a proposed medical procedure.

Finally, courts and commentators increasingly recognize the value of alternative means of dispute resolution, both because of the great cost of litigation to the legal system and to individuals, and the capacity of alternative means of dispute resolution to foster reconciliation between parties. It is likely that more clients, when informed of the advantages of mediation and arbitration and given the opportunity to choose to pursue them, would do so, and that more disputes would be resolved through these methods.

. . .

NEXT STEPS TOWARD CLIENT CONTROL: THE CLIENT'S RIGHT TO CONTROL
NEGOTIATION AND TO PURSUE ALTERNATIVES TO LITIGATION

... [A]ttorneys should have a duty to allow clients to make those decisions that a reasonable client, in what the attorney knows or should know to be the position of the client, would want to make. However, the right of client control has developed to this point as the right of the client to decide specific issues that arise during representation, and, whether or not courts recognize a broad general right on the part of the client to make significant choices within legal representation, courts should continue to identify specific choices that are for the client.

It is likely that the next steps in the development of a duty to allow clients to control representation will be the recognition of duties to allow the client to make significant decisions concerning negotiation and to allow the client to choose alternatives to litigation. First, during negotiation, in addition to the right to choose to accept or reject a settlement offer, the client should have the right to choose the style and strategy of negotiation, when to make settlement offers, and what to offer. Second, the client should be allowed to choose whether to attempt to resolve disputes through mediation or arbitration. Each of these choices presents potential benefits and risks to clients and clients should be informed of the risks and benefits of each option and allowed to make the choices in light of them.

. . .

What Negotiation Decisions For the Client?

Cases have clearly established that the client has the right to choose whether or not to accept settlement offers from the opposing side, and that clients must approve of settlement offers that their attorneys make. Other decisions during negotiations are also sufficiently important that they should be made by the client.

Assuming that a client wants to attempt to negotiate an agreement or a settlement, a basic question concerning the conduct of the negotiation will be what style and strategy to adopt. The style of negotiation is the interpersonal behavior of the negotiator in dealing with the other side, and may be either competitive or cooperative. Both competitive and cooperative styles of negotiation can be successful. One study found that:

> [E]ffective competitive lawyers are dominating, forceful, attacking, aggressive, ambitious, clever, honest, perceptive, analytical, convincing, and self-controlled. Effective cooperative lawyer-negotiators, on the other hand, were found to be trustworthy, fair, honest, courteous, personable, tactful, sincere, perceptive, reasonable, convincing, and self-controlled.

Though each style can be effective, each carries its own strengths and risks. Competitive bargainers are less likely to give away too much, however a competitive style "generates tension and encourages negotiator mistrust" and creates a greater risk of deadlock. A cooperative style may not yield terms that are as favorable to the client, but a cooperative style reduces the risk of deadlock, requires less negotiation time, and generally produces a higher joint outcome for the parties. The client should have the right to choose the negotiation style.

Whereas the style of negotiation involves the manner of interpersonal behavior with the opponent, the selection of a strategy controls the substantive choices. There are two types of negotiation strategies, adversarial and problem-solving. Whereas an adversarial strategy assumes that there is a given pie to be divided and that any concession to the other side will be a loss to the client, problem-solving negotiation attempts to resolve conflict in a manner that will create a bigger pie and enable both parties to win. Problem-solving negotiators attempt to discover the needs of both of the parties and, together, create solutions that meet those needs. . . .

Adversarial and problem-solving strategies each have potential benefits and risks for the client. Problem-solving negotiation can help both parties if it enables the parties to develop a creative solution that is mutually beneficial. If the parties want to have a continuing relationship, it may be important to each of them that the other benefit from the ultimate resolution of the dispute. However, if the problem is such that the client's only goal is to obtain as much as possible of a pie of a given size, then adversarial bargaining is likely to produce the greater gain. If a party attempts problem-solving and fails to produce a creative solution to the problem, that party may have revealed weaknesses to the other side that will be damaging. The choice of what strategy to employ during negotiation carries with it risks and benefits for the client, and the client should have the right to choose the negotiation strategy.

When to make offers and what offers to make are significant choices during negotiation, especially when the lawyer applies an adversarial negotiation strategy. The closer a party's offer is to a reasonable settlement figure, the more likely it is that a case will be settled, but the less favorable the final settlement figure is likely to be. The party to make the first concession usually does worse in negotiation, and small, infrequent concessions are likely to yield the most favorable results. However, toughness in granting concessions may result in deadlock. Before attorneys make offers, they must obtain client approval, but the right of the client is merely the right to veto any proposed offer. Courts should require lawyers to inform clients of the risks and potential benefits of various offers and allow the client to choose when to make offers, and what offers to make.

The Client's Right to Pursue Alternative Methods of Dispute Resolution

In recent years, there has been a substantial growth in interest in alternative means of dispute resolution. The major alternatives to litigation and negotiation are mediation and arbitration. In mediation, the parties meet with a neutral third party, generally chosen by the parties, who attempts to facilitate the parties' negotiation of a settlement. The mediator helps to facilitate negotiation by helping to define the problem and suggesting options for its resolution. Mediation is like negotiation, in that the parties must reach agreement for there to be a resolution of the dispute. In many cases, agreements worked out by the parties through mediation are subject to the review of counsel before final approval by the parties.

In arbitration, an arbitrator, generally chosen by the parties, conducts a hearing and resolves the dispute. The parties generally are represented by counsel. Arbitration is like litigation in that a third party, the arbitrator, decides how to resolve the dispute. The ground rules of the arbitration generally are created by the agreement of the parties. They determine how many arbitrators there will be, how the arbitrators will be chosen, what rules of evidence will apply, and whether or not the decision may be appealed. Courts have generally upheld agreements to binding arbitration.

There are risks and potential benefits to both mediation and arbitration. An attorney should inform the client of these risks and potential benefits and allow the client to choose whether to pursue these means of dispute resolution.

.   .   .

Mediation, Arbitration, and the Lawyer's Conflict of Interest

The decision whether to adopt mediation or arbitration as a means of dispute resolution should be made by clients, rather than by attorneys, not only because of the risks and potential benefits to the client of each of these methods, but because lawyers are likely to have a conflict of interest over whether to pursue alternative methods of dispute resolution.

As to the decision whether to pursue mediation, an attorney's conflict of interest is likely to be great. Mediation generally is conducted by the parties, without the presence of their attorneys. The attorneys lose work because mediation generally does not require as much attorney time as negotiation or litigation. Attorneys will also have a conflict of interest as to whether to pursue mediation or arbitration if they are not familiar with these processes. If a client wishes to pursue mediation or arbitration and the lawyer is not experienced with these methods of dispute resolution, the lawyer may have to refer the case to another attorney. In light of this risk, lawyers that are not familiar with alternative means of dispute resolution will be tempted to avoid presenting clients with these options.

. . .

The right of the client to control the important decisions during legal representation should be a part of the client's right to autonomy. Client control will generally yield better results for the client, will limit the effect of conflicts of interest that accompany the attorney/client relationship, and will build on the precedent of medical informed consent. Courts should extend the right of client control, both by giving the client the right to control those decisions which a reasonable client, in what the lawyer knows or should know to be the position of the client, would want to control, and by continuing to identify specific choices that, as a matter of law, are for the client.

Whether or not courts adopt a general standard of client control, they should identify the significant choices in negotiation, and the choice whether to pursue mediation or arbitration, as decisions that are for the client. These choices are of great significance to clients and are within the competence of clients. Client control over the decision to use alternative dispute resolution is likely to lead to greater use of mediation and arbitration, a reduction in the load on courts, and more reconciliation among litigants. If clients can show that the failure of the attorney to allow them to control negotiation decisions and to choose mediation or arbitration caused them to suffer loss, courts should allow them a malpractice recovery.

LEONARD L. RISKIN, THE REPRESENTED CLIENT IN A SETTLEMENT CONFERENCE: THE LESSONS OF G. HEILMAN BREWING CO. v. JOSEPH OAT CORP.

69 Wash.U.L.Q. 1059, 1062–65, 1097–1105 (1991).

The relevant part of *G. Heileman Brewing Co.* began in 1984, when a U.S. magistrate in Madison, Wisconsin issued an order that befuddled some of the parties and their lawyers and, on appeal, sharply divided the judges on the Seventh Circuit. The magistrate directed each party and their insurance carriers to send to a settlement conference, in addition to their lawyers, "a representative having full authority to settle the case or to make decisions and grant authority to counsel with respect to all matters that may be reasonably anticipated to come before the conference." National Union Fire Insurance Company of Pittsburgh, the carrier for defendant Joseph Oat Corporation, sent no representative to the key conference. Joseph Oat Corporation, however, did send a representative along with the lawyer the insurance company retained to defend it. The representative was a lawyer, a member of the law firm that generally represented the corporation. He indicated that he had authority to state the position of the corporation: it would make no offer because it believed that if any offer were to be made the insurance carrier was obligated to make it. Interpreting this as a violation of his order, the magistrate sanctioned Joseph Oat Corporation and National, requiring them to pay the expenses, including attorneys fees, the other litigants incurred in attending the conference.

The chief judge of the district court declined to reconsider the order, but a divided three judge panel of the U.S. Court of Appeals for the Seventh Circuit reversed. The full court subsequently withdrew the panel's opinion and upheld the magistrate's order, concluding that a district court, under Federal Rule of Civil Procedure 16 and the court's inherent authority, may order a represented litigant to attend a settlement conference along with his lawyer, and that the magistrate did not abuse his discretion by ordering Oat Corporation to send a representative armed with "full authority to settle the case" or by imposing sanctions on the parties that failed to comply with that order. The six to five vote included five dissenting opinions.

I will not quarrel with either the majority or the dissenters. The majority's conclusion that federal courts have authority to order represented clients to attend a settlement conference was as supportable, based on "narrowly 'legal' considerations," as the contrary conclusion reached in three of the dissenting opinions. In any event, the majority's conclusion now seems firmly entrenched, especially in light of the Civil Justice Reform Act of 1990. That statute, signed by President Bush on December 1, 1990, requires every federal district court to develop a "Civil Justice Expense and Delay Reduction Plan" and provides that such plan may require that "upon notice by the court, representatives of the parties with authority to bind them in settlement discussion *be present or available by telephone* during any settlement conference."

What interests me, then, is not whether the federal courts have this authority, but when, why, and how they should use it. This question is enormously important. Federal courts are experimenting with alternative dispute resolution at dizzying rates, and new legislation makes increased usage likely. The *Heileman* decision, along with the Civil Justice Reform Act of 1990, is likely to encourage judges to compel clients and representatives of organizational litigants armed with settlement authority to attend settlement conferences, along with their lawyers. This practice offers vast possibilities for achieving quicker and sometimes better settlements. It carries equally vast risks. The academic and practice literature, however, has paid remarkably little attention to the questions of when and how to involve clients in such conferences. None of the *Heileman* opinions offers any affirmative guidance. Nor do they elaborate sufficiently on the attributes required of the corporate representative with "full authority to settle."

My aim in this Article is to provide background, along with some modest suggestions, that could assist judges, lawyers, and clients, in determining when and how clients should participate in settlement discussions.

. . .

All the opinions in *Heileman* agree that it is inappropriate for a federal judge to coerce a litigant to settle. Accordingly, they also agree that a federal judge should not order a represented client to attend a settlement conference where such an order would tend to force the litigant to settle in order to avoid the burdens of attendance. Yet the opinions say little about when and for what purposes a judge *should* order such a client or representative to attend a settlement conference.

. . .

Advantages and Disadvantages of Client Attendance in Settlement Conferences

A client's attendance at a settlement conference can take numerous forms. The following continuum describes one aspect of such involvement:

- Client is available by telephone.

- Client waits outside the conference room.

- Client waits outside the conference room part of the time and sits in on the conference part of the time.

- Client sits in on the conference but does not speak, except perhaps to his lawyer.

- Client sits in on the conference and speaks in response to questions from his lawyer or in response to questions from the other lawyer or judge.

- Client sits in on the conference and speaks and ask questions relatively freely.

- Client takes lead in speaking; consults lawyer as needed.

- Client and lawyer meet privately with judge.

- Client meets with judge without lawyers.

- Client meets privately with other client, without lawyers.

Add to these variables differences in attorney-client, client-client, and judge-attorney relationships, differences in the nature of the case, in the type of negotiation conducted, and in the judicial host's interventions, and you have an inkling of the complexity of the idea of client involvement in a settlement conference. Lawyers, judges, and commentators tend to argue about the advantages and disadvantages of client involvement based largely upon unarticulated assumptions about some of these variables.

"Client-Centered" Arguments

One area of debate concerns the effect of the client's participation on the client's own interests. For each potential advantage trumpeted, a corresponding risk or potential disadvantage waits to be sounded:

- The client's presence increases the likelihood that her lawyer will be well prepared. [But: the client's presence may incline some lawyers to posture, to "show off." In addition, the client may become a great bother, interfering with the lawyer's ability to accomplish her or his work.]

- The client's presence can reduce the risk that interests of the lawyer will prevail over those of the client. For instance, a lawyer might recommend for or against a particular settlement because of the lawyer's own financial or professional needs, which could be related to excessive pressure from the judge. [But: the client's presence may remove tactical advantages. For example, often a lawyer will falsely attribute a stubbornness to the client to give the lawyer negotiating strength. In addition, it may be strategically useful to delay consideration of an offer from the other side; this is easier to do with an absent client.]

- The client may be better able to appreciate the value of alternate dispute resolution processes if he hears about them directly from a settlement judge, rather than from his lawyer, who might be unfamiliar with or biased against such processes. [But: the client may too readily succumb to the allure of a "quick fix," thereby giving up the chance of a better result through trial. In addition, the other side may perceive as weakness the client's expression of willingness to try an alternative process.]

- The client could gain respect for the judicial process. [But: if the client is exposed to the realities of settlement conferences he could lose respect for the process and for the impartiality of the judge.]

- The client will feel he has had a chance to tell his story, in his own words, by participating in a settlement conference. [But: to the extent that such a feeling makes it easier for the client to settle, he loses his real day in court.]

- The client can learn much about the strengths and weaknesses of both sides of the case by observing the conduct of the other parties, the lawyers, and the judge; this can soften his attitudes or positions. [But: exposure to the other side's behavior will anger or harden some clients, making settlement more difficult.]

- If the client actually observes the exchange of monetary offers, he can better assess the strength of the other side's commitment to a position; he may notice things the lawyer misses. Although there may be some lawyers who can fully appreciate and convey the nuances of a settlement negotiation, many are vulnerable to misreading, to oversimplifying, and to embracing too-warmly the virtues of their own side's case. [But: the client may misinterpret the events and affect the lawyer's judgment in an erroneous direction or become more difficult to "control."]

- The client's presence permits more rounds of offers and counter-offers. It permits him to act on new information and allows cooperation and momentum to build. In addition, attendance requires the client to pay attention to the case, which, in itself, makes settlement more likely. [But: the client may lose his resolve because of the "crucible effect."]

- The client can clear up miscommunications about facts and interests between lawyers. [But: the client may be too emotionally involved to see the facts clearly.]

- Direct communication between clients can lead to better understanding of each other or of the events that transpired, perhaps even allow a healing of the rift between them. [But: direct communication may cause a flare-up and loss of objectivity. Parties may harden their resolve.]

- The client, because he is more familiar with his situation, may be more able to spot opportunities for problem-solving solutions, which could lead to quicker and more satisfying agreements. [But: the client may give away information about his underlying interests that could leave him vulnerable to exploitation. Moreover, the client will not be sufficiently objective. A lawyer knowledgeable about the client's situation might do a better job of developing problem-solving solutions.]

- Because the client's presence increases the likelihood of a settlement, and a settlement that will be satisfactory to the client, participation likely will result in a savings of time and money for the client. [But: if some of the risks described above materialize, his presence will have caused him to lose time and money.]

- The client would not consider an order to attend a settlement conference as coercive, but rather as an opportunity to participate. [But: the client might react negatively to the coercive nature of the order and be uncooperative.]

These arguments bear two important implications. First, the assertions of both risk and benefit gain strength as the client's actual participation increases. Thus, the client who not only observes the settlement conference, but also talks, may enhance his or her opportunities for developing a problem-solving solution, while simultaneously increasing his or her risks of being exploited, of angering the opponent, or of revealing potentially damaging information....

Second, all the arguments in favor of including the client presume that the client is a competent, reasonably intelligent person with good judgment who will not be pushed into making an agreement. Conversely, the arguments against including the client assume he lacks one or more of these qualities, and that the client's lawyer has them....

Lawyers' and Judges' Perspectives

Although most lawyers apparently believe that the client's presence enhances the prospects for settlement, many judges and lawyers are inclined to exclude clients from active participation in settlement conferences.... These assumptions gain strength from the "lawyer's standard philosophical map" and induce many lawyers and judges to credit the arguments against including clients. Thus, a lawyer may have a reflexive aversion to direct contact between clients because he fears the client may make a damaging disclosure. In turn, this fear may impair the lawyer's ability to imagine opportunities for creative problem solving.

Other, more subtle factors also may incline both lawyers and judges toward excluding clients. The client's presence threatens customary, hierarchial professional practices. It creates a risk, for instance, that the judge's comments could embarrass the lawyer, a risk that could restrict the judge's perception of his freedom to speak with counsel. It also appears to threaten the lawyer-client relationship. Both lawyer and judge may wish to save the time required to explain to the client what is going on. Lawyers also may resent the loss of certain negotiating techniques, such as the "good-cop/bad-cop" routine.

On the other hand, good lawyers and wise settlement judges do not approach settlement discussions woodenly. Many will recognize particular circumstances in which client involvement, even if contrary to their general predilections, is appropriate. This may occur, for example, when the lawyer encounters "client control problems" or when he recognizes that unique characteristics of the case or the client make the client's presence essential.

In addition, the psychological needs of lawyers and judges may be factors in the decision to exclude clients or to suggest, directly or indirectly, that the clients not participate. . . .

. . . The lawyer who wants to maintain the mystique of expertise could feel severely threatened by the presence of a client. The client might interpret his uncertainty as incompetence, or, worse, notice that he is unprepared, that the other lawyer is more clever, or that the judge seems not to respect his opinion. Similarly, some judges might feel discomfort about interfering with lawyer-client relations or the possibility of being challenged, questioned, or evaluated by a client who, not being legally trained, might behave less predictably than the lawyer. In short, the presence of clients may breed anxiety and interfere with the lawyers' and judge's feelings of competence and control. This anxiety may cause an unspoken and, perhaps, unconscious conspiracy between lawyers and judges to exclude clients from all or important parts of settlement conferences.

HERBERT M. KRITZER, FEE ARRANGEMENTS AND NEGOTIATION

21 Law & Soc.Rev. 341, 341–47 (1987).

My central argument is that discussions of the settlement process, and particularly of manipulations of that process, must consider the interests of *all* involved in litigation. Regular participants in litigation are well aware of this point. In my series of interviews with corporate lawyers and their clients in Toronto regarding the impact of fees and fee shifting a number of respondents mentioned the importance of taking into account the interest of the opposing lawyer. For example, a litigation partner in a firm with one hundred lawyers said, "If you can satisfy the lawyer [with regard to his fee], you'll be a lot closer to settlement." A lawyer for a large retailer similarly stated that to achieve settlement, "you need to provide an incentive for the [opposing] lawyer." Yet despite the evidence that litigation lawyers do not selflessly ignore their own interests, little attention has been paid to how these interests affect settlement and negotiation.

I am not suggesting that lawyers engage in questionable actions for financial gain. The argument is more subtle: Lawyers, like all of us, when forced to make a choice for which there is no definitive answer, will tend to select the option that is in their own interest. In other words, the financial incentives of their work will often influence the decisions, and it is not coincidental that they will personally benefit from these choices. Thus, although the plaintiffs' bar may truly believe that the contingent fee is the poor man's key to the courthouse door, this belief is shaped by the fact that the key to the courthouse also brings clients—and therefore a livelihood—to the plaintiffs' lawyers. Elsewhere I have pointed out that the relationship between lawyers and clients is shaped by professional, personal, and business considerations, the last, at their most basic, meaning income (and income streams). But what is the significance of this type of analysis for settlement and negotiation?

In the last few years there has been increasing attention on the means of improving the negotiation process.

None of this literature takes into account one of the central ... facts of everyday litigation in the United States: that some lawyers work on an hourly fee basis while others work on a contingent or percentage fee basis. While contingent fees are most often thought of in regard to personal injury cases, they are in fact widely used in most cases in which the plaintiff is an individual, the major exception being domestic relations. Under a contingent fee, the lawyer is paid a portion of the recovery (plus expenses), and the recovery is often sent directly to the lawyer (who then extracts her fee and expenses, passing the balance on to the client) or jointly to the lawyer and the client. My argument is that the contingency arrangement has very important implications for the lawyer-negotiator.

In my introduction, I alluded to the theoretical argument that contingent fee lawyers in cases with modest amounts at stake have an incentive to arrive quickly at a settlement, even if that settlement is not the best for the client. Whether this means that the fee arrangement directly affects the amount of time the lawyer spends on settlement negotiations (although I could in fact find no systematic difference in time spent on such activities between hourly and contingent fee lawyers), the same theoretical considerations apply to the content of the actual negotiation. Specifically, since the contingent fee lawyer is to receive a share of the ultimate recovery, she has an incentive to see to it that the recovery can in fact be shared.

A contingent fee lawyer who sought nonmonetary resolutions of her clients' cases, even if those resolutions were better from the clients' perspective, would soon go out of business unless some alternate payment method were available for such settlements (e.g., fee shifting, whereby the defendant pays the plaintiff's attorney for his time, or a central fund, created by taxing'' contingent fees, from which the lawyer could receive compensation).

... Although lawyers are professionals who are concerned with the needs and interests of their clients, their behavior is nonetheless influenced (note the use of *influenced* rather than *determined*) by the forces of economic rationality or necessity or both, and this influence is felt as well in the lawyers' means of negotiating. If we want lawyers to consider actively what Menkel–Meadow calls the problem-solving approaches to negotiation, we must insure that their livelihood is not dependent upon adversary approaches to negotiation.

EVANS v. JEFF D.

Supreme Court of the United States.
475 U.S. 717, 726–38, 754–59, 106 S.Ct. 1531 (1986).

CASE INTRODUCTION

[In 1980, Charles Johnson, a lawyer for the Idaho Legal Aid Society, brought a class action alleging deficiencies in that State's treatment facilities for emotionally and mentally handicapped children. He sought a mandatory injunction ordering improvements in education and health care services, and costs and attorney fees as permitted by the federal Civil Rights Attorney's Fees Awards Act of 1976 (42 U.S.C. § 1988). The State agreed to make the requested changes regarding educational services, but negotiations broke down over the allegation of inadequate treatment facilities.

On the eve of trial, after extensive discovery and motion work, the State offered to settle the case. The settlement proposal "offered virtually all of the injunctive relief" the lawyer had requested, and more than the District Court had indicated it was prepared to grant. The State conditioned its settlement offer upon a waiver by plaintiffs of claims for statutory attorney's fees. Johnson felt compelled to accept the settlement on behalf of his clients.

The District Court approved the settlement, and denied Johnson's motion to submit a fee bill notwithstanding the waiver. Johnson argued that the waiver provision exploited the lawyer's ethical duty by "forcing" him to forego his fees in order to accept an offer favorable to his clients. On appeal, the Court of Appeals agreed with Johnson's argument. It affirmed the settlement, but invalidated the waiver. The case was remanded to the District Court for a determination of reasonable attorneys fees under the civil rights fees statute. The State of Idaho appealed to the United States Supreme Court. Justice Stevens wrote for the majority:]

II

The disagreement between the parties and amici as to what exactly is at issue in this case makes it appropriate to put certain aspects of the case to one side in order to state precisely the question that the case does present.

The options available to the District Court were essentially the same as those available to respondents: it could have accepted the proposed settlement; it could have rejected the proposal and postponed the trial to see if a different settlement could be achieved; or it could have decided to try the case. The District Court could not enforce the settlement on the merits and award attorney's fees anymore than it could, in a situation in which the attorney had negotiated a large fee at the expense of the plaintiff class, preserve the fee award and order greater relief on the merits. The question we must decide, therefore, is whether the District Court had a duty to reject the proposed settlement because it included a waiver of statutorily authorized attorney's fees.

That duty, whether it takes the form of a general prophylactic rule or arises out of the special circumstances of this case, derives ultimately from the Fees Act rather than from the strictures of professional ethics. Although respondents contend that Johnson, as counsel for the class, was faced with an "ethical dilemma" when petitioners offered him relief greater than that which he could reasonably have expected to obtain for his clients at trial (if only he would stipulate to a waiver of the statutory fee award), and although we recognize Johnson's conflicting interests between pursuing relief for the class and a fee for the Idaho Legal Aid Society, we do not believe that the "dilemma" was an "ethical" one in the sense that Johnson had to choose between conflicting duties under the prevailing norms of professional conduct. Plainly, Johnson had no ethical obligation to seek a statutory fee award. His ethical duty was to serve his clients loyally and competently. Since the proposal to settle the merits was more favorable than the probable outcome of the trial, Johnson's decision to recommend acceptance was consistent with the highest standards of our profession. The District Court, therefore, correctly concluded that approval of the settlement involved no breach of ethics in this case.

The defect, if any, in the negotiated fee waiver must be traced not to the rules of ethics but to the Fees Act. Following this tack, respondents argue that the statute must be construed to forbid a fee waiver that is the product of "coercion." They submit that a "coercive waiver" results when the defendant in a civil rights action (1) offers a settlement on the merits of equal or greater value than that which plaintiffs could reasonably expect to achieve at trial but (2) conditions the offer on a waiver of plaintiffs' statutory eligibility for attorney's fees. Such an offer, they claim, exploits the ethical obligation of plaintiffs' counsel to recommend settlement in order to avoid defendant's statutory liability for its opponents' fees and costs. . . . [W]e are not persuaded that Congress has commanded that all such settlements must be rejected by the District Court. Moreover, on the facts of record in this case, we are satisfied that the District Court did not abuse its discretion by approving the fee waiver.

. . .

Most defendants are unlikely to settle unless the cost of the predicted judgment, discounted by its probability, plus the transaction costs of further litigation, are greater than the cost of the settlement package. If fee waivers cannot be negotiated, the settlement package must either contain an attorney's fee component of potentially large and typically uncertain magnitude, or else the parties must agree to have the fee fixed by the court. Although either of these alternatives may well be acceptable in many cases, there surely is a significant number in which neither alternative will be as satisfactory as a decision to try the entire case.[23]

The adverse impact of removing attorney's fees and costs from bargaining might be tolerable if the uncertainty introduced into settlement negotiations were small. But it is not. The defendants' potential liability for fees in this

---

23. It is unrealistic to assume that the defendant's offer on the merits would be unchanged by redaction of the provision waiving fees. If it were, the defendant's incentive to settle would be diminished because of the risk that attorney's fees, when added to the original merits offer, will exceed the discounted value of the expected judgment plus litigation costs. If, as is more likely, the defendant lowered the value of its offer on the merits to provide a cushion against the possibility of a large fee award, the defendant's offer on the merits will in many cases be less than the amount to which the plaintiff feels himself entitled, thereby inclining him to reject the settlement. Of course, to the extent that the merits offer is somewhere between these two extremes the incentive of both sides to settle is dampened, albeit to a lesser degree with respect to each party.

kind of litigation can be as significant as, and sometimes even more signifi-cant than, their potential liability on the merits. This proposition is most dramatically illustrated by the fee awards of district courts in actions seeking only monetary relief. Although it is more difficult to compare fee awards with the cost of injunctive relief, in part because the cost of such relief is seldom reported in written opinions, here too attorney's fees awarded by district courts have "frequently outrun the economic benefits ultimately obtained by successful litigants." Indeed, in this very case "[c]ounsel for defendants view[ed] the risk of an attorney's fees award as the most signifi-cant liability in the case." Undoubtedly there are many other civil rights actions in which potential liability for attorney's fees may overshadow the potential cost of relief on the merits and darken prospects for settlement if fees cannot be negotiated.

The unpredictability of attorney's fees may be just as important as their magnitude when a defendant is striving to fix its liability. Unlike a determi-nation of costs, which ordinarily involve smaller outlays and are more suscep-tible of calculation, "[t]here is no precise rule or formula" for determining attorney's fees. ... It is therefore not implausible to anticipate that parties to a significant number of civil rights cases will refuse to settle if liability for attorney's fees remains open, thereby forcing more cases to trial, unnecessari-ly burdening the judicial system, and disserving civil rights litigants. Respon-dents' own waiver of attorney's fees and costs to obtain settlement of their educational claims is eloquent testimony to the utility of fee waivers in vindicating civil rights claims. We conclude, therefore, that it is not neces-sary to construe the Fees Act as embodying a general rule prohibiting settlements conditioned on the waiver of fees in order to be faithful to the purposes of that Act.

The question remains whether the District Court abused its discretion in this case by approving a settlement which included a complete fee waiver. [The Court concluded that it did not.]

Justice Brennan, with whom Justice Marshall and Justice Blackmun join, dissenting.

The Court begins its analysis by emphasizing that neither the language nor the legislative history of the Fees Act supports "the proposition that Congress intended to ban all fee waivers offered in connection with substan-tial relief on the merits." I agree. There is no evidence that Congress gave the question of fee waivers any thought at all. However, the Court mistaken-ly assumes that this omission somehow supports the conclusion that fee waivers are permissible. On the contrary, that Congress did not specifically consider the issue of fee waivers tells us absolutely nothing about whether such waivers ought to be permitted. It is blackletter law that "[i]n the absence of specific evidence of Congressional intent, it becomes necessary to resort to a broader consideration of the legislative policy behind th[e] provi-sion...."

It seems obvious that allowing defendants in civil rights cases to condi-tion settlement of the merits on a waiver of statutory attorney's fees will diminish lawyers' expectations of receiving fees and decrease the willingness of lawyers to accept civil rights cases. Even the Court acknowledges "the possibility that decisions by individual clients to bargain away fee awards may, in the aggregate and in the long run, diminish lawyers' expectations of statutory fees in civil rights cases." The Court tells us, however, that "[c]omment on this issue" is "premature at this juncture" because there is not yet supporting "documentation." The Court then goes on anyway to observe that "as a practical matter the likelihood of this circumstance arising is remote." I must say that I find the Court's assertions somewhat difficult to understand. To be sure, the impact of conditional fee waivers on the availability of attorneys will be less severe than was the restriction on fee awards created in *Alyeska* [an earlier Supreme Court decision on attorneys' fee awards in civil rights suits]. However, that experience surely provides an indication of the immediate hardship suffered by civil rights claimants whenever there is a reduction in the availability of attorney's fee awards. Moreover, numerous courts and commentators have recognized that permitting fee waivers creates disincentives for lawyers to take civil rights cases and thus makes it more difficult for civil rights plaintiffs to obtain legal assistance.

But it does not require a sociological study to see that permitting fee waivers will make it more difficult for civil rights plaintiffs to obtain legal assistance. It requires only common sense. Assume that a civil rights defendant makes a settlement offer that includes a demand for waiver of statutory attorney's fees. The decision whether to accept or reject the offer is the plaintiff's alone, and the lawyer must abide by the plaintiff's decision. As a formal matter, of course, the statutory fee belongs to the plaintiff, and thus technically the decision to waive entails a sacrifice only by the plaintiff. As a practical matter, however, waiver affects only the lawyer. Because "a vast majority of the victims of civil rights violations" have no resources to pay attorney's fees, lawyers cannot hope to recover fees from the plaintiff and must depend entirely on the Fees Act for compensation.[10] The plaintiff thus has no real stake in the statutory fee and is unaffected by its waiver. Consequently, plaintiffs will readily agree to waive fees if this will help them to obtain other relief they desire. As summed up by the Legal Ethics Committee of the District of Columbia Bar:

> "Defense counsel ... are in a uniquely favorable position when they condition settlement on the waiver of the statutory fee: They make a demand for a benefit that the plaintiff's lawyer cannot resist as a matter of ethics and one in which the plaintiff has no interest and therefore will not resist." Op. No. 147, reprinted in 113 Daily Washington Reporter, at 394.

Of course, from the lawyer's standpoint, things could scarcely have turned out worse. He or she invested considerable time and effort in the case, won, and has exactly nothing to show for it. Is the Court really serious

10. Nor can attorneys protect themselves by requiring plaintiffs to sign contingency agreements or retainers at the outset of the representation. Amici legal aid societies inform us that they are prohibited by statute, court rule, or Internal Revenue Service regulation from entering into fee agreements with their clients. Moreover, even if such agreements could be negotiated, the possibility of obtaining protection through contingency fee arrangements is unavailable in the very large proportion of civil rights cases which, like this case, seek only injunctive relief. In addition, the Court's misconceived doctrine of state sovereign immunity precludes damages suits against governmental bodies, the most frequent civil rights defendants. Finally, even when a suit is for damages, many civil rights actions concern amounts that are too small to provide real compensation through a contingency fee arrangement. Of course, none of the parties has seriously suggested that civil rights attorneys can protect themselves through private arrangements.

in suggesting that it takes a study to prove that this lawyer will be reluctant when, the following week, another civil rights plaintiff enters his office and asks for representation? Does it truly require that somebody conduct a test to see that legal aid services, having invested scarce resources on a case, will feel the pinch when they do not recover a statutory fee?

And, of course, once fee waivers are permitted, defendants will seek them as a matter of course, since this is a logical way to minimize liability. Indeed, defense counsel would be remiss not to demand that the plaintiff waive statutory attorney's fees. A lawyer who proposes to have his client pay more than is necessary to end litigation has failed to fulfill his fundamental duty zealously to represent the best interests of his client. Because waiver of fees does not affect the plaintiff, a settlement offer is not made less attractive to the plaintiff if it includes a demand that statutory fees be waived. Thus, in the future, we must expect settlement offers routinely to contain demands for waivers of statutory fees.[12]

The cumulative effect this practice will have on the civil rights bar is evident. It does not denigrate the high ideals that motivate many civil rights practitioners to recognize that lawyers are in the business of practicing law, and that, like other business people, they are and must be concerned with earning a living. The conclusion that permitting fee waivers will seriously impair the ability of civil rights plaintiffs to obtain legal assistance is embarrassingly obvious.

Because making it more difficult for civil rights plaintiffs to obtain legal assistance is precisely the opposite of what Congress sought to achieve by enacting the Fees Act, fee waivers should be prohibited.

---

12. The Solicitor General's suggestion that we can prohibit waivers sought as part of a "vindictive effort" to teach lawyers not to bring civil rights cases, a point that the Court finds unnecessary to consider is thus irrelevant. Defendants will seek such waivers in every case simply as a matter of sound bargaining. Indeed, the Solicitor General's brief suggests that this will be the bargaining posture of the United States in the future.

Chapter 11

CRITIQUES OF SETTLEMENT ADVOCACY

Perhaps it is too melodramatic for someone to admit remembering where they were when first reading a provocative law review article by Owen Fiss. After all, how could anyone be "Against Settlement"? Nonetheless, it is true. The date was 1984, a period early in the Messianic Period of Alternative Dispute Resolution archeology. Fiss' article, the ideas it spawned, and the discussion it provoked, deepened our understanding of dispute settlement as a social process in a democratic state.

We should note that the materials in this chapter raise questions different from—though related to—those we encountered when assessing the utility of distributive and integrative bargaining strategies. The readings in this chapter examine the role of law and legal norms and the attorney's professional responsibility for dispute processing. They amplify our consideration of the role of the lawyer as negotiator.

David Luban comes to the arguments raised by Fiss against settlement after a fifteen-year period of intense discussion of the implications of that work. Much has been written about Fiss' thesis; most has been critical. Luban recognizes that not all litigation provides an opportunity for courts to engage in what Fiss calls "social transformation." Much litigation is routine, even mundane. Nonetheless, Luban broadens Fiss' thesis by arguing that settlement privatizes and makes secret what should be public discourse in a healthy democracy. His question is not "against settlement" but "how much settlement?"

Our next reading is by Kevin McMunigal. Where David Luban looked at the systemic consequences of settlement advocacy from a macroscopic frame, McMunigal looks at its effects on members of the practicing Bar. He challenges us to rethink the assumption that lawyers take cases to trial. In fact, litigators settle cases rather than try them. McMunigal believes this unexamined but fundamental alteration of the attorney's task has caused atrophied trial skills and has diminished the lawyer's overall expertise in advocacy skills and predictive evaluation.

Carrie Menkel–Meadow responds directly to Luban's analysis. She is a longtime and eloquent proponent of "problem solving" approaches to negotiation and the attorney-client relationship. We considered her approach in

Chapter Four. In this reading, she again reframes the question under consideration from "for or against" settlement to settlement *"when, how, and under what circumstances"* settlement? Menkel–Meadow's comments are fueled by an appreciation of contemporary American civil litigation practice and her own experience as a participant in the Dalkon Shield mass tort litigation. She asks whether those who argue against settlement suffer from "litigation romanticism" by stressing the institutional and social values represented by disputant's claims rather than the needs of individual parties in conflict.

Readings

1. Owen M. Fiss, *Against Settlement*, 93 Yale L.J. 1073 (1984).
2. David Luban, *Settlements and the Erosion of the Public Realm*, 83 Geo.L.J. 2619, 2621–42 (1995).
3. Kevin C. McMunigal, *The Costs of Settlement: The Impact of Scarcity of Adjudication on Litigating Lawyers*, 37 UCLA L.Rev. 833, 834–61 (1990).
4. Carrie Menkel–Meadow, *Whose Dispute Is It Anyway?: A Philosophical and Democratic Defense of Settlement (In Some Cases)*, 83 Geo.L.J. 2663, 2663–85 (1995).
5. For Further Reading
    a. Richard Abel, ed., The Politics of Informal Justice (2 vols. 1982).
    b. Albert W. Alschuler, *The Changing Plea Bargaining Debate*, 69 Cal.L.Rev. 652 (1981).
    c. Wayne D. Brazil, *Protecting the Confidentiality of Settlement Negotiations*, 39 Hastings L.J. 955 (1988).
    d. Jules Coleman & Charles Silver, *Justice in Settlements*, 4 Soc.Phil. & Pol'y. 102 (1986).
    e. Robert J. Condlin, *Bargaining in the Dark: The Normative Incoherence of Lawyer Dispute Bargaining Role*, 51 Md.L.Rev. 1 (1992).
    f. John E. Coons, *Approaches to Court Imposed Compromise: The Uses of Doubt and Reason*, 58 Nw.U.L.Rev. 750 (1964).
    g. Richard Delgado, *Fairness and Formality: Minimizing the Risk of Prejudice in Alternative Dispute Resolution*, 1985 Wis.L.Rev. 1359.
    h. Hon. Harry T. Edwards, *Alternative Dispute Resolution: Panacea or Anathema*, 99 Harv.L.Rev. 668 (1986).
    i. Owen M. Fiss, *The Social and Political Foundations of Adjudication*, 6 Law & Hum.Behav. 121 (1982).
    j. Owen M. Fiss, *Out of Eden*, 94 Yale L.J. 1669 (1985).
    k. Marc Galanter, *The Quality of Settlements*, 1988 J.Disp.Resol. 55.
    l. Marc Galanter & Mia Cahill, *"Most Cases Settle": Judicial Promotion and Regulation of Settlements*, 46 Stan.L.Rev. 1339 (1994).
    m. Trina Grillo, *The Mediation Alternative: Process Dangers for Women*, 100 Yale L.J. 1545 (1991).
    n. Samuel R. Gross & Kent D. Syverud, *Getting to No: A Study of Settlement Negotiations and the Selection of Cases for Trial*, 90 Mich.L.Rev. 319 (1991).
    o. Herbert M. Kritzer, *Fee Arrangements and Negotiation*, 12 Law & Soc'y Rev. 341 (1987).

p.   William M. Landes & Richard A. Posner, *Adjudication as a Public Good,* 8 J.Legal Stud. 235 (1978).

q.   Lisa G. Lerman, *Mediation of Wife Abuse Cases: The Adverse Impact of Informal Dispute Resolution on Women,* 7 Harv.Women's L.J. 57 (1984).

r.   David Luban, *Bargaining and Compromise: Recent Work on Negotiation and Informal Justice,* 14 Phil. & Pub.Aff. 397 (1985).

s.   David Luban, *The Quality of Justice,* 66 Denv.U.L.Rev. 381 (1989).

t.   Carrie Menkel–Meadow, *For and Against Settlement: Uses and Abuses of the Mandatory Settlement Conference,* 33 UCLA L.Rev. 485 (1985).

u.   Carrie Menkel–Meadow, *Pursuing Settlement in an Adversary Culture: A Tale of Innovation Co-opted or "The Law of ADR",* 19 Fla.St.L.Rev. 1 (1991).

v.   Carrie Menkel–Meadow, *Ethics and the Settlement of Mass Torts: When the Rules Meet the Road,* 80 Cornell L.Rev. 1159 (1995).

w.   Andrew W. McThenia & Thomas L. Shaffer, *For Reconciliation,* 94 Yale L.J. 1660 (1985).

x.   Laura Nader, *Controlling Processes in the Practice of Law: Hierarchy and Pacification in the Movement to Re–Form Dispute Resolution,* 9 Ohio St.J.Disp.Res. 1 (1993).

y.   Mitchell Polinsky & Daniel Rubinfeld, *The Deterrent Effects of Settlements and Trials,* 8 Int'l Rev.L. & Econ. 109 (1988).

z.   Judith Resnick, *Managerial Judges,* 96 Harv.L.Rev. 374 (1982).

aa.   Judith Resnick, *Failing Faith: Adjudicatory Procedure in Decline,* 53 U.Chi.L.Rev. 494 (1986).

bb.   Judith Resnick, *Many Doors? Closing Doors? Alternative Dispute Resolution and Adjudication,* 10 Ohio St.J.Disp.Res. 211 (1995).

cc.   Judith Resnick, *Procedural Innovations, Sloshing Over: A Comment on Deborah Hensler,* 73 Texas L.Rev. 1627 (1995).

dd.   Lauren K. Robel, *Private Justice and the Federal Bench,* 68 Ind.L.J. 891 (1993).

ee.   H. Lee Sarokin, *Justice Rushed is Justice Ruined,* 38 Rutgers L.Rev. 431 (1986).

ff.   Steven Shavell, *Alternative Dispute Resolution: An Economic Analysis,* 24 J.Leg.Stud. 1 (1995).

gg.   Susan Sibley & Austin Sarat, *Dispute Processing in Law and Legal Scholarship: From Institutional Critique to the Reconstruction of the Juridical Subject,* 66 Den.U.L.Rev. 437 (1989).

OWEN M. FISS, AGAINST SETTLEMENT

93 Yale L.J. 1073 (1984).

I do not believe that settlement as a generic practice is preferable to judgment or should be institutionalized on a wholesale and indiscriminate basis. It should be treated instead as a highly problematic technique for streamlining dockets. Settlement is for me the civil analogue of plea bargaining: Consent is often coerced; the bargain may be struck by someone without authority; the absence of a trial and judgment renders subsequent judicial involvement troublesome; and although dockets are trimmed, justice may not be done. Like plea bargaining, settlement is a capitulation to the conditions of mass society and should be neither encouraged nor praised.

. . .

The disparities in resources between the parties can influence the settlement in three ways. First, the poorer party may be less able to amass and analyze the information needed to predict the outcome of the litigation, and thus be disadvantaged in the bargaining process. Second, he may need the damages he seeks immediately and thus be induced to settle as a way of accelerating payment, even though he realizes he would get less now than he might if he awaited judgment. All plaintiffs want their damages immediately, but an indigent plaintiff may be exploited by a rich defendant because his need is so great that the defendant can force him to accept a sum that is less than the ordinary present value of the judgment. Third, the poorer party might be forced to settle because he does not have the resources to finance the litigation, to cover either his own projected expenses, such as his lawyer's time, or the expenses his opponent can impose through the manipulation of procedural mechanisms such as discovery.

. . .

THE ABSENCE OF AUTHORITATIVE CONSENT

The argument for settlement presupposes that the contestants are individuals. These individuals speak for themselves and should be bound by the rules they generate. In many situations, however, individuals are ensnared in contractual relationships that impair their autonomy: Lawyers or insurance companies might, for example, agree to settlements that are in their interests but are not in the best interests of their clients, and to which their clients would not agree if the choice were still theirs. But a deeper and more intractable problem arises from the fact that many parties are not individuals but rather organizations or groups. We do not know who is entitled to speak for these entities and to give the consent upon which so much of the appeal of settlement depends.

Some organizations, such as corporations or unions, have formal procedures for identifying the persons who are authorized to speak for them. But these procedures are imperfect: They are designed to facilitate transactions between the organization and outsiders, rather than to insure that the members of the organization in fact agree with a particular decision. Nor do they eliminate conflicts of interests. The chief executive officer of a corporation may settle a suit to prevent embarrassing disclosures about his managerial policies, but such disclosures might well be in the interest of the shareholders. The president of a union may agree to a settlement as a way of preserving his power within the organization; for that very reason, he may not risk the dangers entailed in consulting the rank and file or in subjecting the settlement to ratification by the membership. Moreover, the representational procedures found in corporations, unions, or other private formal organizations are not universal. Much contemporary litigation, especially in the federal courts, involves governmental agencies, and the procedures in those organizations for generating authoritative consent are far cruder than those in the corporate context. We are left to wonder, for example, whether the attorney general should be able to bind all state officials, some of whom are elected and thus have an independent mandate from the people, or even whether the incumbent attorney general should be able to bind his successors.

These problems become even more pronounced when we turn from organizations and consider the fact that much contemporary litigation involves even more nebulous social entities, namely, groups. Some of these groups, such as ethnic or racial minorities, inmates of prisons, or residents of institutions for mentally retarded people, may have an identity or existence that transcends the lawsuit, but they do not have any formal organizational structure and therefore lack any procedures for generating authoritative consent. The absence of such a procedure is even more pronounced in cases involving a group, such as the purchasers of Cuisinarts between 1972 and 1982, which is constructed solely in order to create funds large enough to make it financially attractive for lawyers to handle the case.

THE LACK OF A FOUNDATION FOR CONTINUING JUDICIAL INVOLVEMENT

The dispute-resolution story trivializes the remedial dimensions of lawsuits and mistakenly assumes judgment to be the end of the process. It supposes that the judge's duty is to declare which neighbor is right and which wrong, and that this declaration will end the judge's involvement (save in that most exceptional situation where it is also necessary for him to issue a writ directing the sheriff to execute the declaration). Under these assumptions, settlement appears as an almost perfect substitute for judgment, for it too can declare the parties' rights. Often, however, judgment is not the end of a lawsuit but only the beginning. The involvement of the court may continue almost indefinitely. In these cases, settlement cannot provide an adequate basis for that necessary continuing involvement, and thus is no substitute for judgment.

The parties may sometimes be locked in combat with one another and view the lawsuit as only one phase in a long continuing struggle. The entry of judgment will then not end the struggle, but rather change its terms and the balance of power. One of the parties will invariably return to the court and again ask for its assistance, not so much because conditions have changed, but because the conditions that preceded the lawsuit have unfortunately not changed. This often occurs in domestic-relations cases, where the divorce decree represents only the opening salvo in an endless series of skirmishes over custody and support.

The structural reform cases that play such a prominent role on the federal docket provide another occasion for continuing judicial involvement. In these cases, courts seek to safeguard public values by restructuring large-scale bureaucratic organizations. The task is enormous, and our knowledge of how to restructure on-going bureaucratic organizations is limited. As a consequence, courts must oversee and manage the remedial process for a long time—maybe forever. This, I fear, is true of most school desegregation cases, some of which have been pending for twenty or thirty years. It is also true of antitrust cases that seek divestiture or reorganization of an industry.

In our political system, courts are reactive institutions. They do not search out interpretive occasions, but instead wait for others to bring matters to their attention. They also rely for the most part on others to investigate and present the law and facts. A settlement will thereby deprive a court of the occasion, and perhaps even the ability, to render an interpretation. A court cannot proceed (or not proceed very far) in the face of a settlement. To be against settlement is not to urge that parties be "forced" to litigate, since that would interfere with their autonomy and distort the adjudicative process; the parties will be inclined to make the court believe that their bargain is justice. To be against settlement is only to suggest that when the parties settle, society gets less than what appears, and for a price it does not know it is paying. Parties might settle while leaving justice undone. The settlement of a school suit might secure the peace, but not racial equality. Although the parties are prepared to live under the terms they bargained for, and although such peaceful coexistence may be a necessary precondition of justice, and itself a state of affairs to be valued, it is not justice itself. To settle for something means to accept less than some ideal.

I recognize that judges often announce settlements not with a sense of frustration or disappointment, as my account of adjudication might suggest, but with a sigh of relief. But this sigh should be seen for precisely what it is: It is not a recognition that a job is done, nor an acknowledgment that a job need not be done because justice has been secured. It is instead based on another sentiment altogether, namely, that another case has been "moved along," which is true whether or not justice has been done or even needs to be done. Or the sigh might be based on the fact that the agony of judgment has been avoided.

The Real Divide

To all this, one can readily imagine a simple response by way of confession and avoidance: We are not talking about *those* lawsuits. Advocates of ADR might insist that my account of adjudication, in contrast to the one implied by the dispute-resolution story, focuses on a rather narrow category of lawsuits. They could argue that while settlement may have only the most limited appeal with respect to those cases, I have not spoken to the "typical" case. My response is twofold.

First, even as a purely quantitative matter, I doubt that the number of cases I am referring to is trivial. My universe includes those cases in which there are significant distributional inequalities; those in which it is difficult to generate authoritative consent because organizations or social groups are parties or because the power to settle is vested in autonomous agents; those in which the court must continue to supervise the parties after judgment; and those in which justice needs to be done, or to put it more modestly, where there is a genuine social need for an authoritative interpretation of law. I imagine that the number of cases that satisfy one of these four criteria is considerable; in contrast to the kind of case portrayed in the dispute-resolution story, they probably dominate the docket of a modern court system.

Second, it demands a certain kind of myopia to be concerned only with the number of cases, as though all cases are equal simply because the clerk of the court assigns each a single docket number. All cases are not equal. The Los Angeles desegregation case, to take one example, is not equal to the allegedly more typical suit involving a property dispute or an automobile accident. The desegregation suit consumes more resources, affects more people, and provokes far greater challenges to the judicial power. The settlement movement must introduce a qualitative perspective; it must speak to these more "significant" cases, and demonstrate the propriety of settling them. Otherwise it will soon be seen as an irrelevance, dealing with trivia rather than responding to the very conditions that give the movement its greatest sway and saliency.

DAVID LUBAN, SETTLEMENTS AND THE EROSION OF THE PUBLIC REALM

83 Geo.L.J. 2619, 2621–42 (1995).

Fiss's opposition to settlements arises because of his unexpected dissent from the conventional wisdom that trials signal pathologies—his belief that adjudication may be a sign of health rather than a drastic cure for disease. This view is counterintuitive and wildly unpopular in a culture in which lawyer-bashing has become a national hobby, lawsuits a lightning rod for talk show resentniks, and the civil justice system a cherished target of rage and demagoguery. Yet the arguments for adjudication are neither eccentric nor frivolous. The first group of arguments, which is less controversial and more familiar, is instrumental in nature. These arguments do not commend adjudication as a good in itself, but rather as a necessary condition for fulfilling other values that our culture accepts. The second argument, at once less familiar and more controversial, considers adjudication an intrinsic good, a process that is as much a sign of a healthy society as free elections.

THE INSTRUMENTAL ARGUMENTS

[S]ettlements, like private adjudications, produce no rules or precedents binding on nonparties. Rules and precedents, in turn, have obvious importance for guiding future behavior and imposing order and certainty on a transactional world that would otherwise be in flux and chaos. Even those who favor settlement over adjudication generally rank order and certainty very high on the scale of legal values. Indeed, one of Fiss's criticisms of the alternative dispute resolution (ADR) movement is that its proponents value peace over justice. Settlements bring peace whereas adjudication, though perhaps more just, creates disruption. Regardless of whether Fiss is right that to be prosettlement is to value peace over justice, the present argument yields a surprising result: adjudication may often prove superior to settlement for securing peace because the former, unlike the latter, creates rules and precedents.

. . .

Civil adjudication can create other public goods besides rules and precedents. For example, it may develop the advocacy skills of litigating attorneys. Kevin McMunigal has noted that, as the number of civil trials declines, litigators' advocacy skills tend to atrophy. Ironically, this degeneration may distort not only trials but the settlement process as well: litigators without adequate trial experience are less able to evaluate cases accurately and are more likely to settle out of fear of their own inadequacy. If McMunigal is correct, the attorney skills developed through trials are a public good that will lead to settlements that better reflect the value of a case.

. . .

Even the authority of courts may be conceptualized as a public good furthered by adjudication. Whenever disputants rely on the final and public judgment of a court to resolve their controversy, they enhance the courts' claim as an authoritative resolver of controversies. However, when disputants turn elsewhere for resolution—private arbitration, nonjudicial government agencies, or private bargaining—the salience of adjudication fades and the authority of courts weakens. Each litigant who proceeds to judgment and acquiesces in it thereby subsidizes a judicial authority that is available for future litigants.

. . .

THE INTRINSIC ARGUMENTS: ADJUDICATION AS AN ELABORATION OF PUBLIC VALUES

The first of the preceding arguments emphasized that adjudication, which produces rules and precedents, is instrumentally useful because these provide a normative framework for future transactions. However, legal rules and precedents are valuable not only as a source of certainty, but also as a reasoned elaboration and visible expression of public values. Law on this view amounts to what Hegel called "objective spirit"—the spirit of a political community manifested in a public and objective form.

. . .

Against Settlement belongs to a series of articles in which Fiss distinguishes between two very different models of adjudication: adjudication as dispute resolution and adjudication as structural transformation. Dispute resolution, he explains, presupposes two neighbors of roughly equal capacity (perhaps the mythical Coasean farmer and rancher, or the cowboys and the farmers in *Oklahoma!*) quarreling in a state of nature and turning to a third party as an alternative to shooting irons. It is our addiction to the dispute resolution picture, Fiss believes, that underlies the drive to settlement.

However, we do not live in the world portrayed by the dispute resolution model. Rather, our lives and fortunes are everywhere mediated by large, bureaucratic institutions—not only government bureaucracies, but corporations, HMOs, schools, and unions. When these institutions become oppressive, we need structural transformations and not stopgap dispute resolution, which falsely presupposes disputants of roughly equal bargaining power. In Fiss's view, adjudication as structural transformation—exemplified by the class action suit to desegregate a school district—is a more important paradigm of what adjudication means in the modern world. Fiss, one should remember, is an expert on the injunctive process, particularly the civil rights injunction. Haunting his opposition to settlements is an unspoken question: *Where would we be if* Brown v. Board of Education *had settled quietly out of court?*

The problem with posing the argument this way is that it narrows and excessively marginalizes the constitutive role of adjudication. Class action lawsuits are rare, and are becoming rarer. Class actions for structural transformation injunctions are rarer still, not only because the federal judiciary has become hostile to such forms of judicial activism, but also because of the difficulties of financing such litigation. More generally, in cases in which statutory attorneys' fees are unavailable, parties and attorneys will be overwhelmingly likely to monetize disputes rather than to seek other forms of relief. Plaintiffs need a *res* to compensate their attorneys, attorneys need a *res* to get paid by their clients, and defendants faced with the alternative of paying money or transforming their own structure will be very likely to opt for the less intrusive option of paying monetary damages. Nowadays, the most important class actions, whose settlements most need examination, are mass torts, which remain a prominent part of the docket, rather than structural transformation suits.

In response to the objection that structural transformation suits compose only a tiny part of the universe of litigation, Fiss argues that the importance of structural transformation suits more than compensates for their infrequency. He argues as well that even nonstructural transformation suits can have public significance. Yet I do not believe that he has fully explained the philosophical basis of that significance, and the declining salience of structural transformation suits makes his argument against settlements seem somewhat anachronistic. As a result, he has been understood as focusing exclusively on public law litigation, rather than as aiming to call into question the meaningfulness of the public/private distinction. For this reason, the argument that follows is only partly Fissian in spirit, and hardly at all in detail. It aims to make explicit the implicit philosophical premises of Fiss's argument.

Let us first consider two "pure" accounts of the legitimacy of government and of the judicial role.

· · ·

The public-life and the problem-solving conceptions each offer justification for the legal system and the judicial function. The problem-solving conception of adjudication is broadly Hobbesian in character. Peacekeeping and coordination require governmental monopoly or near-monopoly on the use of violence and coercion. Justifying this monopoly, in turn, requires government to engage in the business of adjudicating disputes, because dispute resolution is effective only when the state's coercive power backs it up. In principle, of course, private arbitrators could carry out adjudication, with the state merely stepping in to enforce the result. However, because the losing party to the private arbitration could contest its legitimacy, the state would eventually have to readjudicate to decide whether to enforce the decision of the private arbitrator. The state inevitably would engage in the adjudication business somewhere down the line. The centralization of legal authority arises from the government's possession of the guns. Best of all, of course, is if it never has to use them, and the wisdom of the judge consists not in issuing the wisest orders, but in facilitating the quickest and most painless resolution of disputes. Rather than debating principles, the judge tries to wrestle the interests of the parties into alignment.

On the public-life conception, by contrast, the values realized in laws are a kind of public morality—objective spirit—and even ostensibly private disputes between apolitical citizens may have a public dimension engaging these values. Because the law is the visible residue of public action (shortly we shall see what this means), the law elevates private disputes into the public realm. Fiss defines adjudication as "the process by which the values embodied in an authoritative legal text, such as the Constitution, are given concrete meaning and expression," and he adds that these "public values" are "the values that define a society and give it its identity and inner coherence." As

Fiss explains: "[C]ourts exist to give meaning to our public values, not to resolve disputes." Adjudication, then, is necessary to define and redefine the conditions of the public space. Furthermore, in line with the public-life conception's view of public life as reasoned deliberation, Fiss insists that the unique genius of the courts is their twin requirements of independence and dialogue. Independence guarantees an impartial use of reason, and dialogue guarantees that courts must listen to all comers and reply with reasoned opinions.

If I am right, Fiss's view emerges out of the public-life conception. The difference between the public-life and problem-solving pictures is that for the public-life conception all adjudications are public in significance—they are political, inevitably embroiling the meaning and legitimacy of government. In Fiss's words: "Civil litigation is an institutional arrangement for using state power to bring a recalcitrant reality closer to our chosen ideals." For the problem-solving conception, by contrast, government gets involved only by unhappy necessity in the private ordering of human affairs. On this view, judicial involvement in a dispute is a necessary evil, whereas for the public-life conception it is an essential good.

. . .

At this point, we can see why Fiss finds nothing to celebrate in settlements. When a case settles, it does so on terms agreeable to its parties, but those terms are not necessarily illuminating to the law or to the public. Indeed, those terms may be harmful to the public. Instead of reasoned reconsideration of the law, we often find little more than a bare announcement of how much money changed hands (often accompanied by a disclaimer of actual liability)—unless the settlement is sealed, in which case we don't even find that out. It is true that settlement information has some precedential value: both plaintiffs' lawyers and defense lawyers share information about settlements to evaluate cases for future settlements. However, settlement information offers no reasons or reasoning, nothing to feed or provoke further argument. The relationship between settlements and judgments is like the relationship between a signal (such as a cry of unhappiness) and an explanation (such as a description of why I am unhappy). Both reveal information, but only the latter provides a basis for further conversation. A world without adjudication would be a world without public conversation about the strains of commitment that the law imposes.

. . .

A PROVISIONAL CONCLUSION

The thought-experiments of the two preceding sections were meant to show that, for either the public-life conception or the problem-solving conception of state legitimacy, both adjudication and settlement serve indispensable purposes. This conclusion, however, does not resolve the argument. Proponents of the problem-solving conception desire the minimum amount of adjudication necessary to create bargaining-shadows and adjudicatory authority. Proponents of the public-life conception, on the other hand, desire the maximum amount of adjudication consistent with respect for the parties, who may be reluctant to go to trial. Thus, the locus of disagreement changes from the question *for or against settlement?* to the question *how much settlement?*

Rephrased in these terms, Fiss's title should not have been *Against Settlement* but rather *Against So Much Settlement.*

KEVIN C. McMUNIGAL, THE COSTS OF SETTLEMENT: THE IMPACT OF SCARCITY OF ADJUDICATION ON LITIGATING LAWYERS

37 UCLA L.Rev. 833, 833–61 (1990).

Vivid images exert a powerful influence on our thinking. The gripping televised images of John Hinckley's shooting of Ronald Reagan and his highly publicized acquittal on insanity grounds provide an anecdotal instance of this phenomenon. The case spurred Congress and the legislatures of half the states to reshape the insanity defense. Vivid images often overshadow more accurate and representative data, such as statistics, which are in a pallid form.

. . .

Our thinking about lawyers is also shaped by vivid images. Lawyers try cases. They prove their clients' claims and challenge witnesses through cross-examination. They argue questions of law to judges and persuade juries in closing argument. Or so prevailing popular, theoretical, and professional conceptions of lawyers would have us believe. These conceptions reflect the influence of the concrete and emotionally compelling images generated by the process of adjudication, conveying that the lawyer's essential function is adjudicating legal rights and claims in an adversarial context. And trial is our most vivid form of adversarial adjudication.

. . .

The image of the courtroom lawyer, however, has little in common with the personal experience of most of today's lawyers. This is true not only for the substantial number of non-litigating lawyers, but also for many lawyers who specialize in litigation. Traditional adjudication in the form of trial and appeal appears to be an increasingly rare experience: the vast majority of cases are currently resolved by negotiated civil settlements and guilty pleas rather than by trials. For litigating lawyers, therefore, the role of negotiator is much more common than the role of advocate at trial. Negotiation is pervasive not only in litigation, but in virtually all areas of practice. Yet, the image of the lawyer as negotiator has not displaced the image of the trial lawyer as our primary conception of a lawyer's role.

. . .

A. Advocacy Skills

Perhaps the most obvious impact one would expect from scarcity of trial experience is a diminution in lawyer competence in the forensic skills used to try a case, such as cross-examination and closing argument. The task of accurately assessing the quality of advocacy is mired in the difficulties of defining standards for quality and gathering hard data to measure performance against such standards. Nonetheless, the quality of advocacy of American trial lawyers has attracted a great deal of attention. The ABA termed lawyer competence "the single dominant issue" for the legal profession in the 1980s. This concern was sparked by the criticisms of a number of prominent judges who decried a lack of competence among trial lawyers. Their complaints gave rise to numerous investigative committees, empirical studies, and a growing literature on the subject.

. . .

1. *Reduced Opportunities*

First, such a scarcity reduces the opportunities for lawyers to obtain and retain basic advocacy skills by actually trying cases. A premise of our present approach to teaching advocacy skills in simulation and clinical courses is that one learns best by actually engaging in the activity one seeks to learn or in a close approximation of that activity.

. . .

2. *Reduced Incentives*

Scarcity of trials may threaten advocacy skills in a second and different way. Actual trials are not the only way to obtain trial skills. Lack of opportunity to learn through real trials can in part be remedied by providing substitute learning experiences, such as trial simulation courses.

. . .

An increasing time and cost conscious legal environment, however, threatens to undermine the incentives for lawyers to use such alternatives. As trials become scarcer, incentives for a lawyer to invest resources in forensic training mechanisms may actually decrease rather than increase. Advocacy courses are often time consuming and expensive, and as the opportunities for using trial skills become more infrequent and remote, devoting money and precious billable hours to the development of those skills may increasingly appear an unsound investment. If the lawyer practices in a group setting such as a firm, these disincentives may be reflected in group or organizational norms devaluing seldom used skills. One wonders, for example, whether a law firm in which "litigators" rather than "trial lawyers" are the dominant breed would place a high value on trial skills.

. . .

B. SETTLEMENT DISTORTION

Proponents of adjudication have criticized settlement on a number of grounds. One point of attack has been the validity of the assumption of settlement proponents that the terms of a settlement accurately reflect the relative merits of each party's position. The tendency of a settlement to reflect the likely outcome on the merits at trial may be distorted, sometimes quite dramatically, by inequalities between the parties in areas other than the strength of their claims or defenses. Imbalance in financial resources, for example, may impair one party's ability to conduct adequate investigation. Consequently, one party's lack of knowledge may render it unable to predict accurately the likely outcome at trial and to bargain on that basis. Even if the party knows the likely outcome, the settlement may be distorted by a different sort of resource imbalance: the ability to tolerate the delay and expense of litigation.

. . .

1. Prediction

The process of settling cases involves both evaluation and bargaining. The element of evaluation requires predictions about liability and damages involving factual issues and tactical considerations such as a jury's likely reaction to particular witnesses, evidence, or arguments. One would expect a lawyer lacking in trial experience to operate at a disadvantage in assessing the prospects at trial in terms of both liability and damages. The broader the range of variation among individual juries, the broader the range of trial experience a lawyer would need to provide truly representative information about likely jury reactions. As in the area of advocacy skills, an ethical issue of competence arises, but this time in the form of competence to render advice on the advisability of settlement. Incompetence resulting in inaccurate predictions may impose the same sort of settlement distortion as lack of financial resources to conduct adequate investigation. Both hinder accurate prediction of the outcome of a trial and thus hamper the ability of the settlement to reflect the relative merits of the parties' positions.

2. Conflict of Interest

Impairment of the ability to predict outcome at trial might cause a lawyer lacking in trial experience to err either by being more optimistic or more pessimistic in predicting the outcome at trial than the merits of the case actually warrant. Which is the more likely direction of error?

Many factors unrelated to the merits of a case may influence an attorney's outlook toward settlement. Some have noted that attorneys in an adversary system may adopt a "litigation mentality" in which they magnify the legal and factual aspects of the case favorable to their own position, making them more disinclined toward settlement than the merits of the case warrant.

Lack of trial experience creates a similar potential for conflict of interest between attorney and client. Take, for example, a young partner in the litigation section of a firm whose experience places her in the category of litigator rather than trial lawyer. Her firm handles exclusively commercial matters usually resolved by settlement. She has "second chaired" a few trials in her ten years of practice but has tried none by herself. She has significant litigation experience, but it has primarily involved discovery, motion practice, and negotiating the settlement of cases. One would expect that such a lawyer would be reluctant to put the client's money as well as her own reputation, ego, and ability to attract future clients at risk on uncertain and untested trial skills and would thus urge settlement. Trial entails a public display of those skills, or the lack thereof, in front of the client, the judge, the firm's associates, and possibly other partners.

It seems more likely that our hypothetical lawyer, confronted with the pressures inherent in this scenario, will evaluate a particular settlement offer by inflating both the advantages of settlement and the risks of trial than if the case were being handled by an experienced trial lawyer. She is more likely to recommend settlement for several reasons. First, she may simply think about the outcome at trial and quite consciously and rationally conclude that her lack of trial experience decreases the chances for success. Or she may unconsciously magnify the risks and uncertainties at trial because of fear of the unknown. In either case, the lawyer's lack of trial competence introduces an additional element of risk unrelated to the merits and decreases the settlement value of the case.

Second, the lawyer may think about her own performance at trial. Fearing her own embarrassment in the process of trying the case—quite apart from an assessment of the likely outcome—she may either consciously or unconsciously inflate the attractiveness of a particular settlement.

. . .

For a younger lawyer, the lack of trial experience may create a similar conflict between attorney self-interest and client interest, but one which pushes the lawyer to be less rather than more trial-averse than the client. Take, for example, a young lawyer at a large firm who knows that the opportunities for trial experience in her regular workload are limited. The firm, however, takes on small *pro bono* cases, partly to satisfy the firm's ethical obligations but also to provide their younger lawyers with trial experience. In advising such a *pro bono* client about the relative advantages of accepting a settlement offer versus taking the case to trial, the young lawyer's desire to gain trial experience may put her own self-interest in gaining trial experience at odds with the client's interest in settlement, particularly since the case is one in which the monetary exposure and visibility of the case are much lower than in her regular paying work.

. . .

3. *Bargaining Credibility*

In settlement negotiations, fear of trial weakens one's bargaining position, since the strength of one's bargaining position is in part a function of one's willingness to try the case. Willingness to proceed with trial turns in part on a comparison of the potential risk and return of trial with the terms of settlement. Reluctance to try a case may stem from the weakness of one's position on the merits, the amount of damages at stake, or, as pointed out above, the cost and delay entailed in pursuing the case through trial and appeal. It may also stem, however, from a lawyer's lack of confidence in her own ability to try a case.

CARRIE MENKEL–MEADOW, WHOSE DISPUTE IS IT ANYWAY?: A PHILOSOPHICAL AND DEMOCRATIC DEFENSE OF SETTLEMENT (IN SOME CASES)

83 Geo.L.J. 2663, 2663–85 (1995).

INTRODUCTION

I have often thought myself ill-suited to my chosen profession. I love to argue, but I am often too quick to say both, "yes, I see your point" and concede something to the "other side," and to say of my own arguments, "yes, but, it's not that simple." In short, I have trouble with polarized argument, debate, and the adversarialism that characterizes much of our work. Where others see black and white, I often see not just the "grey" but the purple and red—in short, the complexity of human issues that appear before the law for resolution.

In the last decade or so, a polarized debate about how disputes should be resolved has demonstrated to me once again the difficulties of simplistic and adversarial arguments. Owen Fiss has argued "Against Settlement"; Trina Grillo and others have argued against mediation (in divorce cases and other family matters involving women); Richard Delgado and others have questioned whether informal processes are unfair to disempowered and subordinated groups; Judith Resnik has criticized the (federal) courts' unwillingness to do their basic job of adjudication; Stephen Yeazell has suggested that too much settlement localizes, decentralizes, and delegalizes dispute resolution and the making of public law; Kevin C. McMunigal has argued that too much settlement will make bad advocates; and David Luban and Jules Coleman, among other philosophers, have criticized the moral value of the compromises that are thought to constitute legal settlements. On the other side, vigorous proponents of alternative dispute resolution, including negotiation, mediation, arbitration, and various hybrids of these forms of preadjudication settlement, criticize the economic and emotional waste of adversarial processes and the cost, inefficiency, and political difficulties of adjudication, as well as its draconian unfairness in some cases.

In my view, this debate, while useful for explicitly framing the underlying values that support our legal system, has not effectively dealt with the realities of modern legal, political, and personal disputes. For me, the question is not "for or against" settlement (since settlement has become the "norm" for our system), but *when, how, and under what circumstances* should cases be settled? When do our legal system, our citizenry, and the parties in particular disputes need formal legal adjudication, and when are their respective interests served by settlement, *whether public or private?*

. . .

Those who criticize settlement suffer from what I have called, in other contexts, "litigation romanticism," with empirically unverified assumptions about what courts can or will do. More important, those who privilege adjudication focus almost exclusively on structural and institutional values and often give short shrift to those who are actually involved in the litigation. I fear, but am not sure, that this debate can be reduced to those who care more about the people actually engaged in disputes versus those who care more about institutional and structural arrangements. I prefer to think that we need both adjudication and settlement. These processes can affect each other in positive, as well as negative ways, but in my view, settlement should not be seen as "second best" or "worst case" when adjudication fails. Settlement can be justified on its own moral grounds—there are important values, consistent with the fundamental values of our legal and political systems, that support the legitimacy of settlements of some, if not most, legal disputes. These values include consent, participation, empowerment, dignity, respect, empathy and emotional catharsis, privacy, efficiency, quality solutions, equity, access, and yes, even justice.

. . .

To summarize, it seems to me that the key questions implicated in the ongoing debate about settlement vs. adjudication are:

1. In a party-initiated legal system, when is it legitimate for the parties to settle their dispute themselves, or with what assistance from a court in which they have sought some legal-system support or service?

2. When is "consent" to a settlement legitimate and "real," and by what standards should we (courts and academic critics) judge and permit such consent?

3. When, in a party-initiated legal system, should party consent be "trumped" by other values—in other words, when should public, institutional, and structural needs and values override parties' desire to settle or courts' incentives to promote settlement? In short, when is the need for "public adjudication" or as Luban suggests, "public settlement" more important (to whom?) than what the parties may themselves desire?

· · ·

A. *Settlement is Not Necessarily Unprincipled Compromise*

· · ·

The concern that settlements deprive both litigants and the larger public realm of normatively based solutions lies at the core of Luban's and Fiss's criticisms. Yet I would argue that a settlement process may actually be more "just" in the need for both less compromise and less narrowing of legally cognizable issues. That the parties will "compromise" without principle assumes two things: First, that items in dispute are valued equally by the parties, and second, that agreement requires giving them up. The legal system that Luban, Fiss, and others extol, however, is largely responsible for reducing most legal disputes, not to disputes of public values and resource allocation, but to monetized disputes about dollars. When they are submitted to judges and juries with such legal principles as comparative negligence, these monetized disputes are just as likely to result in "split-the-difference" results in court as settlement. Noncompromise settlements offer the promise that more than money can be at stake and that the parties can negotiate such other items as future relationships and conduct, apologies, in-kind trade, new contracts, etc. In my view, it is litigation, not settlement, that has led to monetization of disputes, for money has become the proxy for all legal harms and hurts. Judges and juries award dollars when they cannot order behavior that parties will agree to undertake on their own.

More often and more troubling to those who are concerned about justice, a litigated outcome will produce binary win-lose results that often do not capture the "just reality." As John E. Coons argued so elegantly many years ago, compromise (or at least nonbinary solutions) may represent more "precise justice" when we cannot be absolutely certain about the facts, or when competing principles of law dictate different and sometimes opposed underlying values. Coons argued that courts (as well as settling parties) should be allowed to render fifty-fifty or other allocative verdicts when either unresolved factual doubt or legal ambiguities or contradictions make winner-take-all results unjust. Thus, for me, until litigation is permitted to recognize the ambiguities and contradictions in modern life by developing a broader "remedial imagination," settlement offers the opportunity to craft solutions that do not compromise, but offer greater expression of the variety of remedial possibilities in a postmodern world.

· · ·

B. *Settlement Does Not Preclude the Use or Creation of Precedent*

Those who critique the lack of rules and principles and the "mushiness" of nondefinitive rulings also lament what they perceive to be the absence of precedent in settlement processes. Implicit in Owen Fiss's classic article (and one of the most trenchant of his criticisms) is the concern that too many settlements will reduce the making of law or provide an insufficient "sample" of cases from which the courts will draw to fashion rules to govern human behavior. Settlement, it is argued, is used to avoid both of the key elements of a legal system based on stare decisis—governance by existing rules and the enunciation of new rules from the public application of rules to new facts. Indeed, one could extend this argument and be concerned, as is David Luban, Laura Nader, and others, that it is precisely the important "public" sort of cases that are increasingly being shielded from formal court treatment, by the recent increased use of settlements in mass torts and consumer class actions.

· · ·

Once again, these concerns are based on different understandings of the role of courts and dispute resolution. For those, like Luban, who see adjudication as our public discourse, a case, once filed, becomes the property of the polity and is the *matériel* out of which we fashion our social, legal, political, and maybe even moral contracts. For those who regard our legal system as a public service for private dispute resolution, or as a "democratic and participatory" party initiated system, the dispute and its resolution remain the property of the parties and can be removed from the system in any way, as long as the parties consent. In a sense we could ask: "Whose Dispute Is It, Anyway?" To whom does a dispute belong when it enters the legal system? Whose "property" is a particular dispute, and who should decide how it should be treated?

However these important jurisprudential issues are resolved, it is important to observe here that settlements *are* affected by precedent—both in the *ratio decidendi* of arriving at particular solutions and in the creation of new precedents. Precedent makes its voice heard and power felt in every settlement, if only because one reason the parties may choose to settle is to avoid the effects of previous lawmaking. Yet just as often, settlement may be based on the uncertainty of knowing the legal result, especially if precedent is unclear or contradictory. To charge that settlement is ungoverned by precedent is to be grossly insensitive to the contexts in which settlements occur. For example, repeat play arbitrations and mediations are sensitive not only to the "norms" created by numerous repeat cases, but increasingly to published reports of settlements. In the last ten years, a variety of legal publishing services have begun to report the results, not only of verdicts, but of settlements as well. While these reports tend to be simply of monetary amounts and vary enormously by region and other contextual factors, they are used by practicing lawyers to guide their demands, settlements, and litigation decisions just as reported decisions are. These reports may not include the kind of elaborated legal reasoning contemplated by David Luban's public discourse about the law, but they provide at least as much guidance as jury verdicts and unreported judicial decisions.

· · ·

C.   The Perils and Necessity of Secrecy in Settlements

.   .   .

[W]hile critics like Luban and others call for the full public airing of the fact-finding and discovery process, as well as outcomes in settlements, they focus exclusively on the needs and interests of those other than the immediate parties to the particular dispute.   Professor Luban argues that settlements, like "[a]ll actions relating to the rights of other human beings are wrong if their maxim is incompatible with publicity."   Luban states that this "publicity principle lies at the core of democratic political morality."   Though I will not argue that every litigant has a right to keep his or her settlement totally private, I think it is antidemocratic and ultimately harmful to our legal and political system to insist that all disputes be publicly aired.   Some would draw the distinction that once a case is filed in a public forum, such as a court, the parties have waived their rights to privatize their disputes.   To the extent that many parties now use private dispute resolution providers, such as JAMS–ENDISPUTE, to avoid public decisionmaking, one draws a dangerous line because parties seeking to privatize their disputes will simply avoid the public courts completely, and we will defeat the very purposes Luban wishes to serve by public settlements.   If, as Luban suggests, secret settlements cause parties to "fob off" the costs of their settlements on to others (externalizing settlements by passing on costs to consumers, or forcing all litigants to bear the costs of discovery for similar transactions), then a legal system that requires full disclosure of all discovered facts and all the terms of settlements in every case likely will lead to a "private market" in dispute resolution (if it hasn't already, assisted by other factors such as the cost and delay in the public dispute resolution system).

.   .   .

Not all settlements can be public, or they simply will not occur.   Thus, the harder issue is to decide how we can regulate settlements so that both public and private values of our legal and political system can be accommodated.   From my perspective, Luban glosses too quickly over the question of what should be made the subject of public discourse in legal dispute resolution.   To the extent that good settlement (and here I am referring to my own "problem-solving conception," criticized by Luban as a merely "instrumentalist" conception of dispute resolution) requires the revelation of what I call "nonlegally relevant facts," such as the parties' real and underlying needs and interests (including such factors as emotional needs and motives, future business needs, financial data, trade secrets, psychological and social issues like risk aversion, and precedential effects for other employees or family members), open settlement processes will severely limit the willingness of parties to settle cases for "other factors" than those that are simply legal.

.   .   .

MAKING THE CASE FOR BETTER SETTLEMENTS IN
BOTH THE PRIVATE AND PUBLIC REALM

To recapitulate, I have tried to argue that settlements are not inherently inferior to adjudicated outcomes, as critics like Professor Luban seem to suggest.   (Even with his more narrowed focus on privacy in settlements, Luban continues to see settlements as a necessary evil.)   Just as adjudication is often romanticized when set off against settlement, and its better features are elaborated, I have here tried to make the following arguments on behalf of the "best" aspects of settlement:

1.   Settlements that are in fact consensual represent the goals of democratic and party-initiated legal regimes by allowing the parties themselves to choose processes and outcomes for dispute resolution.

2.   Settlements permit a broader range of possible solutions that may be more responsive to both party and system needs.

3.   What some consider to be the worst of settlement, that is, compromise, may actually represent a moral commitment to equality, precision in justice, accommodation, and peaceful coexistence of conflicting interests.

4.   Settlements may be based on important nonlegal principles or interests, which may, in any given case, be as important or more important to the parties than "legal" considerations.   Laws made in the aggregate may not always be appropriate in particular cases, and thus settlements can be seen as yet another "principled" supplement to our common law system.

5.   Settlement processes may be more humanely "real," democratic, participatory, and cathartic than more formalized processes, permitting in their best moments, transformative and educational opportunities for parties in dispute as well as for others.

6.   Some settlement processes may be better adapted for the multiplex, multiparty issues that require solutions in our modern society than the binary form of plaintiff-defendant adjudication.

7.   Despite the continuing and important debates about discovery and information exchange in the litigation process, some settlement processes (mediation and some forms of neutral case evaluation and scheduling) may actually provide both more and better (not just legally relevant) information for problem-solving, as well as "education" of the litigants.

8.   When used appropriately, settlement may actually increase access to justice, not only by allowing more disputants to claim in different ways, but also by allowing greater varieties of case resolutions.

Chapter 12

ETHICAL CONSIDERATIONS IN LAWYER'S NEGOTIATIONS— THE PARADOX OF CANDOR

Truth poses particular problems for negotiators. While the conventional wisdom lauds truthfulness in negotiation, many bargaining strategies are premised upon selective disclosure, omission to state, puffing, and even outright misrepresentation of fact. All of this bargaining takes place in a process that is largely immune from external scrutiny. Given this context, there is a broad terrain in which negotiators may lie, omit to state, or mislead by conduct.

The lawyer as negotiator faces unique issues regarding truth telling. Official rules governing the bargaining process and norms of professionalism are awash with ambiguity about the requirement of scrupulous adherence to veracity. For the past fifteen years the profession has engaged in a debate over whether ethical rules governing negotiation behavior are desirable or even warranted. To some, promulgating formal rules might well disadvantage rule-abiding attorneys. They could be falsely lulled into acting on the assumption that their more competitive counterparts were behaving similarly, at a cost to their clients.

Further confounding the boundary of professional responsibility and negotiation ethics, there is a clear potential for conflict between the attorney's own values and the perceived duty of single-minded zealous advocacy on behalf of the client's interests. Some clients may want counsel to use bargaining tactics that support shading the truth. Even by insisting that their attorney not volunteer to provide any information not compelled by court order or by comprehensive discovery, clients may compel their lawyers to swim in ethically murky waters. For all these reasons it is difficult to make prescriptive statements about truth telling and lawyers.

Take, for example, the section headings of a provocative article by Gerald Wetlaufer as an initial taxonomy of the truth telling quandary:

I Didn't Lie;

I Lied, if You Insist on Calling it That, but it Was an Omission of a Kind that is Presumed to be Ethically Permissible;

I Lied But It Was Legal;

I Lied But it Was on an Ethically Permissible Subject;

I Lied but It Had Little or No Effect;

I Lied but It Was Justified by the Very Nature of the Negotiations;

I Lied but It Was Justified by the Nature of My Relationship to the Victim—The Adversary's and Competitor's Excuses;

I Lied but It Was Justified Under the Special Ethics of Lawyering;

I Lied but It Was Permissible Because of the Bad Conduct or the Incompetence of My Adversary; and

I Lied but It Was Justified by the Good Consequences It Produced.

This bewildering array of possible responses to whether lying is appropriate demonstrates the complexity of the issue for lawyers in negotiation. The readings in this chapter provoke us to consider whether the profession should attempt to police lying in legal negotiation.

The first two readings in this chapter, by Eleanor Holmes Norton and James White, set the stage for our analysis of the acceptability of deception in lawyer's negotiation. From these excerpts we can see the difficulties inherent in attempting to impose formal regulatory constraints on attorneys on what may be undetectable and sometimes arguably justifiable conduct.

The next series of readings outlines the history of these regulatory attempts. The Bar has a lengthy history of debating the wisdom of efforts to require truth in negotiation, whether precatory or binding. The Kutak Commission's proposal in the early 1980's, and several responses to it, provide provocative food for thought.

Because the Kutak Commission's proposal was not adopted, a newer generation of writers have asked: If not rules, what about norms? Are there situations in which people expect candor, even without a formal requirement of candor, when they bargain? First, Eleanor Holmes Norton presents four justifications for truth telling in negotiation. She gives several examples to demonstrate the complexities of knowing when deception might be situationally acceptable. Next, David Lax and James Sebenius acknowledge that negotiators frequently use tactics designed in part to mislead their bargaining opposite as to their ultimate settlement point. The authors offer criteria that help determine when using these tactics is acceptable.

In the last reading in this group of three, Steven Hartwell alerts us to the importance of the context in which a deception may be practiced. Each negotiation occurs in a context of assumptions about how the parties will be bargaining. For example, if I am negotiating with an insurance claims representative over the amount of a payment for damage to my automobile, I will expect us to be doing distributive bargaining rather than problem solving or interest-based negotiation. Hartwell suggests that deception practiced *within* a bargaining context is less potentially harmful than deception *about* a context.

Finally, the chapter closes with three provocative case studies of the consequences of truth telling issues in negotiation.

Readings

The Problem Highlighted

1. Eleanor Holmes Norton, *Bargaining and the Ethic of Process,* 64 N.Y.U.L. Rev. 493, 506–08 (1989).
2. James J. White, *Machiavelli and the Bar: Ethical Limitations on Lying in Negotiation,* 1980 Am.Bar Found.Res.J. 926, 926–38.

The Bar's Attempts at Official Positions

3. Model Rules of Professional Conduct, Rule 4.1 and Comment (1983).
4. ABA Comm'n on Evaluation of Professional Standards (Kutak Commission), Model Rules of Professional Conduct (Proposed Final Draft, Jan. 30, 1980), Proposed Rule 4.2(a) & (b) and Comment.
5. Eleanor Holmes Norton, *Bargaining and the Ethic of Process,* 64 N.Y.U.L.Rev. 493, 538 (1989).
6. Geoffrey C. Hazard, Jr., *The Lawyer's Obligation to be Trustworthy When Dealing with Opposing Parties,* 33 So.Car.L.Rev. 181, 192–96 (1981).
7. Gary Lowenthal, *Truthful Bargaining by Lawyers,* 2 Geo.J. of Legal Ethics 411, 423–27 (1988).
8. Comment, Robert Gordon, *Private Settlement as Alternative Adjudication: A Rationale for Negotiation Ethics,* 18 U.Mich.J. of Law Reform 503, 530–36 (1985).

If Not Rules, What About Norms?

9. Eleanor Holmes Norton, *Bargaining and the Ethic of Process,* 64 N.Y.U.L.Rev. 493, 524–25, 535–36 (1989).
10. David A. Lax & James K. Sebenius, *Three Ethical Issues in Negotiation,* 2 Negot.J. 363–70 (1986).
11. Steven Hartwell, *Understanding and Dealing With Deception in Legal Negotiation,* 6 Ohio St.J. on Disp.Res. 171, 182–87 (1991).

Case Studies

12. Geoffrey Peters, *The Use of Lies in Negotiation,* 48 Ohio State L.J. 1, 8–13 (1987).
13. James J. White, *Machiavelli and the Bar: Ethical Limitations on Lying in Negotiation,* 1980 Am.B.Found.Res.J. 926, 931–35.
14. Rex Perschbacher, *Regulating Lawyers' Negotiations,* 27 Ariz.L.Rev. 75, 77–9, 137–38 (1985).
15. For Further Reading
    a. Richard Abel, *Why Does the ABA Promulgate Ethics Rules,* 59 Texas L.Rev. 639 (1981).
    b. Sisela Bok, Lying: Moral Choice in Public and Private Life (1978).
    c. Richard K. Burke, *"Truth in Lawyering:" An Essay on Lying and Deceit in the Practice of Law,* 38 Ark.L.Rev. 1 (1984).
    d. Lloyd Burton, Larry Farmer, Elizabeth Gee, Laurie Johnson & Gerald Williams, *Feminist Theory, Professional Ethics and Gender–Related Distinctions in Attorney Negotiating Styles,* 1991 J.Disp.Resol. 199.
    e. Jerard J. Clark, *Fear and Loathing in New Orleans,* 17 Suffolk U.L.Rev. 79 (1983).

f. Charles P. Curtis, *The Ethics of Advocacy*, 4 Stan.L.Rev. 3 (1951).

g. Scott S. Dahl, *Ethics on the Table: Stretching the Truth in Negotiations*, 8 Rev.Litig. 173 (1988).

h. Roger Fisher, *A Code of Negotiation Practices for Lawyers*, 1 Negot.J. 105 (1985).

i. Donald Gifford, *A Context–Based Theory of Strategy Selection in Legal Negotiation*, 46 Ohio St.L.J. 41 (1985).

j. Thomas F. Gurnsey, *Truthfulness in Negotiation*, 17 U.Rich. L.Rev. 99 (1982).

k. Steven Hartwell, *Moral Development, Ethical Conduct and Clinical Education*, 35 N.Y.L.Sch.L.Rev. 131 (1990).

l. Steven Hartwell, *Promoting Moral Development Through Experiential Teaching*, 1 Clinical L.Rev. 505 (1995).

m. Peter R. Jarvis & Bradley F. Tellam, *A Negotiation Ethics Primer for Lawyers*, 31 Gonzaga L.Rev. 549 (1996).

n. Reed Elizabeth Loder, *Moral Truthseeking and the Virtuous Negotiator*, 8 Geo.J. of Legal Ethics 45 (1994).

o. Gary Lowenthal, *The Bar's Failure to Require Truthful Bargaining by Lawyers*, 2 Geo.J. of Legal Ethics 411 (1988).

p. David Luban, Lawyers and Justice: An Ethical Study (1988).

q. Carrie Menkel–Meadow, *Lying to Clients for Economic Gain or Paternalistic Judgment: A Proposal for a Golden Rule of Candor*, 138 U.Pa.L.Rev. 761 (1990).

r. Alvin B. Rubin, *A Causerie on Lawyer's Ethics in Negotiation*, 35 La.L.Rev. 577 (1975).

s. Michael H. Rubin, *The Ethics of Negotiations: Are There Any?*, 56 La.L.Rev. 447 (1995).

t. Murray L. Schwartz, *The Professionalism and Accountability of Lawyers*, 66 Calif.L.Rev. 669 (1978).

u. Christopher S. Shine, *Deception and Lawyers: Away From a Dogmatic Principle and Toward a Moral Understanding of Deception*, 64 Notre Dame L.Rev. 722 (1989).

v. Walter W. Steele, Jr., *Deceptive Negotiating and High–Toned Morality*, 39 Vand.L.Rev. 1387 (1986).

w. John Tomlinson, *Opening Statement: Conducting Negotiations*, 13 Litigation 1 (1987).

x. Gerald B. Wetlaufer, *The Ethics of Lying in Negotiations*, 76 Iowa L.Rev. 1219 (1990).

THE PROBLEM HIGHLIGHTED

ELEANOR HOLMES NORTON, BARGAINING AND THE ETHIC OF PROCESS

64 N.Y.U.L.Rev. 493, 506–08 (1989).

Negotiation is neither a profession (though professionals often engage in negotiation), nor a discrete activity with a defined mission. Rather, negotiation is a process that takes place in a multitude of contexts, extraordinary in their variety and range. However, negotiation is not simply another means of human discourse. Bargaining is a unique process in which the parties engage in stylized strategic behavior and use practices such as bluffing, puffing, and withholding information as a matter of course. Such behavior needs to be probed and understood in the context of the process within which it occurs.

The first step toward sorting out unacceptable or unlawful behavior and aligning negotiation practices with ethical aspiration is more explicit recognition of the connections among strategy, law, and ethics. This requires an understanding of the context in which ethical decisions are made, because no convincing bargaining ethic can be abstracted from the everyday realities of this ubiquitous process. Even behavior by negotiators that appears inappropriate, excessive, or contrary to stated rules or law is unlikely to be questioned or changed if this would entail the alteration of indispensable characteristics of the negotiation process itself.

There has been little evidence of or interest in coherent standards or express norms for appropriate behavior in negotiations. It is difficult to articulate limits for a process whose chief benefits include its flexibility and its freedom from rules. Negotiation raises questions of ethics, strategy, and law that are sometimes peculiarly embroidered together and difficult to unravel. What appears strategically sound during the course of bargaining may not be ethically or even legally appropriate. For example, a person with only a slight injury to the neck may choose to wear an unnecessary neck brace to the negotiation session where her injury will be considered. The action is strategic, because even without saying anything about her injury, the claimant creates the impression of a condition serious enough to warrant compensation. The action is unethical, and probably illegal, because it transmits the false impression that she has been seriously injured.

Such ethical problems arise as a natural consequence of the inherent incentives to capitalize on negotiation skill and the near absence of express limits on the uses of that skill. Yet, traditional controls, such as codes and regulations, clearly do not fit a free-form, privately policed, and pervasive market process.

. . .

Truthfulness connotes the authenticity of the information conveyed. Without truthfulness, human relations would be impossibly cumbersome, because nobody could be believed and the trust essential to the accomplishment of all tasks would be impossible. In much the same way, truthfulness is vital to negotiations, but there are additional reasons for its necessity in this context. First, the assumption of truthfulness underlies the choice of negotiation by the parties; the parties would be unlikely to choose negotiation without the belief that the process would result in an agreement that would be carried out according to its terms. Second, each party to a negotiation needs information that may be possessed by only one of them. Third, the validity of the agreement itself is premised on truthfulness; an agreement based on false information may be declared fraudulent and therefore unenforceable.

Yet, the concept of truthfulness in negotiation raises unique ethical questions because in most circumstances candor is not necessarily required. Ethical clarity is taxed in a process in which both truthfulness and deception have standing. The legal doctrine of misrepresentation requires that the facts under negotiation be true. However, puffing as to these facts is legal, and aspects of puffing have recently been recognized as a specific exception to an attorney's ethical responsibility to be truthful. Deception may include a wide range of practices, from withholding information that need not be shared to misrepresentation that can invalidate an agreement. Between these poles are many deceptive practices: for example, an offer of inaccurate information concerning settlement price or concerning whether one is prepared to sue rather than settle at the terms offered; and silence concerning an important piece of information. The legitimacy, even necessity, of at least some deception in many traditional modes of bargaining makes it difficult to apply ordinary ethical notions of truthfulness in a systematic fashion. The available evidence confirms the notion that truthfulness is a particular sort of ethical tension in negotiation.

JAMES J. WHITE, MACHIAVELLI AND THE BAR: ETHICAL LIMITATIONS ON LYING IN NEGOTIATION

1980 Am.Bar Found.Res.J. 926, 926–38.

The difficulty of proposing acceptable rules concerning truthfulness in negotiation is presented by several circumstances. First, negotiation is non-public behavior. If one negotiator lies to another, only by happenstance will the other discover the lie. If the settlement is concluded by negotiation, there will be no trial, no public testimony by conflicting witnesses, and thus no opportunity to examine the truthfulness of assertions made during the negotiation. Consequently, in negotiation, more than in other contexts, ethical norms can probably be violated with greater confidence that there will be no discovery and punishment. Whether one is likely to be caught for violating an ethical standard says nothing about the merit of the standard. However, if the low probability of punishment means that many lawyers will violate the standard, the standard becomes even more difficult for the honest lawyer to follow, for by doing so he may be forfeiting a significant advantage for his client to others who do not follow the rules.

The drafters appreciated, but perhaps not fully, a second difficulty in drafting ethical norms for negotiators. That is the almost galactic scope of disputes that are subject to resolution by negotiation. One who conceives of negotiation as an alternative to a lawsuit has only scratched the surface. Negotiation is also the process by which one deals with the opposing side in war, with terrorists, with labor or management in a labor agreement, with buyers and sellers of goods, services, and real estate, with lessors, with governmental agencies, and with one's clients, acquaintances, and family. By limiting his consideration to negotiations in which a lawyer is involved in his professional role, one eliminates some of the most difficult cases but is left with a rather large and irregular universe of disputes. Surely society would tolerate and indeed expect different forms of behavior on the one hand from one assigned to negotiate with terrorists and on the other from one who is negotiating with the citizens on behalf of a governmental agency. The difference between those two cases illustrates the less drastic distinctions that may be called for by differences between other negotiating situations. Performance that is standard in one negotiating arena may be gauche, conceivably unethical, in another. More than almost any other form of lawyer behavior, the process of negotiation is varied; it differs from place to place and from subject matter to subject matter. It calls, therefore, either for quite different rules in different contexts or for rules stated only at a very high level of generality.

A final complication in drafting rules about truthfulness arises out of the paradoxical nature of the negotiator's responsibility. On the one hand the negotiator must be fair and truthful; on the other he must mislead his opponent. Like the poker player, a negotiator hopes that his opponent will overestimate the value of his hand. Like the poker player, in a variety of ways he must facilitate his opponent's inaccurate assessment. The critical difference between those who are successful negotiators and those who are not lies in this capacity both to mislead and not to be misled.

Some experienced negotiators will deny the accuracy of this assertion, but they will be wrong. I submit that a careful examination of the behavior of even the most forthright, honest, and trustworthy negotiators will show them actively engaged in misleading their opponents about their true positions. That is true of both the plaintiff and the defendant in a lawsuit. It is true of both labor and management in a collective bargaining agreement. It is true as well of both the buyer and the seller in a wide variety of sales transactions. To conceal one's true position, to mislead an opponent about one's true settling point, is the essence of negotiation.

Of course there are limits on acceptable deceptive behavior in negotiation, but there is the paradox. How can one be "fair" but also mislead? Can we ask the negotiator to mislead, but fairly, like the soldier who must kill, but humanely?

. . .

Pious and generalized assertions that the negotiator must be "honest" or that the lawyer must use "candor" are not helpful. They are at too high a level of generality, and they fail to appreciate the fact that truth and truthful behavior at one time in one set of circumstances with one set of negotiators may be untruthful in another circumstance with other negotiators. There is no general principle waiting somewhere to be discovered as Judge Alvin B. Rubin seems to suggest in his article on lawyer's ethics. Rather, mostly we are doing what he says we are not doing, namely, hunting for the rules of the game as the game is played in that particular circumstance.

The definition of truth is in part a function of the substance of the negotiation. Because of the policies that lie behind the securities and exchange laws and the demands that Congress has made that information be provided to those who buy and sell, one suspects that lawyers engaged in SEC work have a higher standard of truthfulness than do those whose agreements and negotiations will not affect public buying and selling of assets. Conversely, where the thing to be bought and sold is in fact a lawsuit in which two professional traders conclude the deal, truth means something else. Here truth and candor call for a smaller amount of disclosure, permit greater distortion, and allow the other professional to suffer from his own ignorance and sloth in a way that would not be acceptable in the SEC case. In his article Rubin recognizes that there are such different perceptions among members of the bar engaged in different kinds of practice, and he suggests that there should not be such differences. Why not? Why is it so clear that one's responsibility for truth ought not be a function of the policy, the consequences, and the skill and expectations of the opponent?

Apart from the kinds of differences in truthfulness and candor which arise from the subject matter of the negotiation, one suspects that there are other differences attributable to regional and ethnic differences among negotiators. Although I have only anecdotal data to support this idea, it seems plausible that one's expectation concerning truth and candor might be different in a small, homogeneous community from what it would be in a large, heterogeneous community of lawyers. For one thing, all of the lawyers in the small and homogeneous community will share a common ethnic and environmental background. Each will have been subjected to the same kind of training about what kinds of lies are appropriate and what are not appropriate.

Moreover, the costs of conformity to ethical norms are less in a small community. Because the community is small, it will be easy to know those who do not conform to the standards and to protect oneself against that small number. Conversely, in the large and heterogeneous community, one will not have confidence either about the norms that have been learned by the opposing negotiator or about his conformance to those norms.

The differences that may result in perceptions about "truth and candor" often come to the surface in my negotiations seminar at the Michigan Law School, where there will be students from all parts of the country, from large and small cities, and from a variety of ethnic backgrounds. One such seminar involved a discussion between two students who had engaged in a mock negotiation that had been heated and had resulted in an unsatisfactory outcome for both. Each student had grown up in Manhattan; one was black, the other was Jewish. Their discussion in the seminar about their personal reactions to negotiation, about their experience as children and young adults in the art of negotiation, and about their personal reactions to it was illuminating. The Jewish student, one of the best in the class, was more at ease with the negotiation process, more comfortable with the ambiguity it produced, and more experienced as a negotiator. The black student, also a good student, reported that an extended negotiation without some event to relieve the tension caused him tremendous anxiety. He reported that his youthful negotiations were short and often concluded in explosive behavior. For example, if there were an argument about where two groups would play baseball (on my lot or yours), the typical negotiation would last a few minutes and, if it were not quickly resolved, would be concluded by a fight. At the conclusion of that fight the game would be played on the winner's lot. Although the anecdote does not show systematic ethical differences between the two students, it does reveal systematically different attitudes about the negotiation process as a whole, and there is no reason to believe that there are not similar and systematic differences about the appropriate level of candor and honesty among the various ethnic and regional subgroups in our society. That is not to say that one norm is correct, only that the rules of the game played by one group are not the same as the rules played by another.

THE BAR'S ATTEMPTS AT OFFICIAL POSITIONS

MODEL RULES OF PROFESSIONAL CONDUCT

American Bar Association.

RULE 4.1   TRUTHFULNESS IN STATEMENTS TO OTHERS

In the course of representing a client a lawyer shall not knowingly: (a) make a false statement of material fact or law to a third person; or (b) fail to disclose a material fact to a third person when disclosure is necessary to avoid assisting a criminal or fraudulent act by a client, unless disclosure is prohibited by Rule 1.6.

Comment

. . .

Misrepresentation

A lawyer is required to be truthful when dealing with others on a client's behalf, but generally has no affirmative duty to inform an opposing party of relevant facts. A misrepresentation can occur if the lawyer incorporates or affirms a statement of another person that the lawyer knows is false. Misrepresentations can also occur by failure to act.

Statements of Fact

This Rule refers to statements of fact. Whether a particular statement should be regarded as one of fact can depend on the circumstances. Under generally accepted conventions in negotiation, certain types of statements ordinarily are not taken as statements of material fact. Estimates of price or value placed on the subject of a transaction and a party's intentions as to an acceptable settlement of a claim are in this category, and so is the existence of an undisclosed principal except where nondisclosure of the principal would constitute fraud.

Fraud by Client

Paragraph (b) recognizes that substantive law may require a lawyer to disclose certain information to avoid being deemed to have assisted the client's crime or fraud. The requirement of disclosure created by this paragraph is, however, subject to the obligations created by Rule 1.6.

MODEL CODE COMPARISON:

Paragraph (a) is substantially similar to DR 7–102(A)(5), which stated that "[i]n his representation of a client, a lawyer shall not ___ [k]nowingly make a false statement of law or fact."

With regard to paragraph (b), DR 7–102(A)(3) provided that a lawyer shall not "[c]onceal or knowingly fail to disclose that which he is required by law to reveal."

AMERICAN BAR ASSOCIATION COMM'N ON EVALUATION OF PROFESSIONAL STANDARDS (KUTAK COMMISSION), MODEL RULES OF PROFESSIONAL CONDUCT

(Proposed Final Draft, Jan. 30, 1980), Proposed Rule 4.2 and Comment.

4.2   FAIRNESS TO OTHER PARTICIPANTS

(a) IN CONDUCTING NEGOTIATIONS A LAWYER SHALL BE FAIR IN DEALING WITH OTHER PARTICIPANTS.

(b) A LAWYER SHALL NOT MAKE A KNOWING MISREPRESENTATION OF FACT OR LAW, OR FAIL TO DISCLOSE A MATERIAL FACT KNOWN TO THE LAWYER, EVEN IF ADVERSE, WHEN DISCLOSURE IS:

(1) REQUIRED BY LAW OR THE RULES OF PROFESSIONAL CONDUCT; OR

(2) NECESSARY TO CORRECT A MANIFEST MISAPPREHENSION OF FACT OR LAW RESULTING FROM A PREVIOUS REPRESENTATION MADE BY THE LAWYER OR KNOWN BY THE LAWYER TO HAVE BEEN MADE BY THE CLIENT, EXCEPT THAT COUNSEL FOR AN ACCUSED IN A CRIMINAL CASE IS NOT REQUIRED TO MAKE SUCH A CORRECTION WHEN IT WOULD REQUIRE DISCLOSING A MISREPRESENTATION MADE BY THE ACCUSED.

(c) A LAWYER SHALL NOT:

(1) ENGAGE IN THE PRETENSE OF NEGOTIATING WITH NO SUBSTANTIAL PURPOSE OTHER THAN TO DELAY OR BURDEN ANOTHER PARTY;

(2) ILLEGALLY OBSTRUCT ANOTHER PARTY'S RIGHTFUL ACCESS TO INFORMATION RELEVANT TO THE MATTER IN NEGOTIATION;

(3) COMMUNICATE DIRECTLY WITH ANOTHER PARTY WHO THE LAWYER KNOWS IS REPRESENTED BY OTHER COUNSEL, EXCEPT WITH THE CONSENT OF THE PARTY'S COUNSEL OR AS AUTHORIZED BY LAW.

COMMENT:

Fairness

Fairness in negotiation implies that representations by or in behalf of one party to the other party be truthful. This requirement is reflected in contract law, particularly the rules relating to fraud and mistake. A lawyer involved in negotiations has an obligation to assure as far as practicable that the negotiations conform to the law's requirements in this regard.

Disclosure

Under the usually accepted conventions of negotiation, the parties have only limited duties of disclosure to each other. Generally, a party is not required to apprise another party of background facts or collateral opportunities for gain that may accrue as a result of a transaction between them. Facts that must be disclosed do not include estimates of price or value that a party places on the subject of a transaction, or a party's intentions as to an acceptable settlement of a claim, or the existence of an undisclosed principal except where nondisclosure would constitute fraud. A party is permitted to suggest advantages to an opposing party that may be insubstantial from an objective point of view. The precise contours of the legal duties concerning disclosure, representation, puffery, overreaching, and other aspects of honesty in negotiations cannot be concisely stated. They have changed over time and vary according to circumstances. They also can vary according to the parties' familiarity with transactions of the kind involved. Thus, the modern law of commercial transactions places duties of disclosure on sellers that go well beyond the classic rule of caveat emptor, and modern securities transactions often must conform to elaborate disclosure rules. It is a lawyer's responsibility to see that negotiations conducted by the lawyer conform to applicable legal standards, whatever they may be.

In negotiation as in litigation, a lawyer generally has no duty to inform an opposite party of relevant facts and circumstances. However, it is the lawyer's duty to be forthcoming when the lawyer or the client has misled another party with respect to a matter of fact or law, for in such circumstances the failure to act is the equivalent of actively misleading the other party. A lawyer should not induce a belief that the lawyer is disinterested in a matter when in fact he or she represents a client.

Whether there should be a further burden of disclosure on a lawyer has long been a matter of some controversy. Canon 41 of the Canons of Ethics required, in general terms, that "when a lawyer discovers that some fraud or deception has been practiced he should endeavor to rectify it," if necessary by undertaking to "inform the injured person or his counsel." A more limited requirement was imposed by DR 7–102(B) of the ABA Model Code of Professional Responsibility. The competing considerations are clear but difficult to resolve. A lawyer could properly be regarded as having a professional responsibility to see that negotiations under his or her auspices are informed on all sides. However, to make a lawyer responsible for an opposing party's information about the matter in negotiation exposes the lawyer to charges of misfeasance that can be easily contrived, and exposes the transaction to additional risk of being legally avoided on the ground of mistake. The likelihood of these consequences is especially severe when the facts concerning the matter in negotiation are inherently uncertain or complex, or where there is substantial discrepancy between parties' access to information about the matter. Counsel for the accused in a criminal case is subject to constraint against disclosing during negotiations facts that might incriminate the client. See also Rule 1.7.

Tactics

Negotiation is ordinarily a voluntary process. The parties usually determine the agenda and procedure of negotiation, without the constraint of externally imposed rules or an external authority, such as a judge, to enforce them. The principal sanction supporting standards of decorum and fairness is that of breaking off negotiations, although in some situations, such as collective bargaining, there may also be legal sanctions to compel bargaining.

There are, however, limitations that should be observed by a lawyer in conducting negotiations. As an aspect of the duty to deal fairly with other parties, a lawyer should not engage in the pretense of negotiation when the client has no real intention of seeking agreement. In particular, it is dishonest to pretend to negotiate when the real purpose is to prevent the other party from pursuing an alternative course of action. More generally, a lawyer acting as negotiator should recognize that maintaining a fair and courteous tenor in negotiation can contribute to a satisfactory resolution. This is particularly true when the parties to the negotiation have a continuing relationship with each other, as in collective bargaining or in negotiations between divorcing parents concerning child custody. An agreement that is the product of open, forbearing, and fair-minded negotiation can be a demonstration by the lawyers of the conduct that the parties themselves should display toward each other.

ELEANOR HOLMES NORTON, BARGAINING AND THE ETHIC OF PROCESS

64 N.Y.U.L.Rev. 493, 538 (1989).

The addition of the comment to the Model Rules is an important breakthrough because it is the first suggestion in the history of legal ethics that bargaining may require some adjustment in the application of the otherwise uniform requirement of truthfulness. However, the comment opens rather than settles the issue. This addition depends on a set of examples and does not purport to be a coherent principle. The stated rationale for the change—that deceptive information about price, value, settlement terms, and the existence of a principal are part of a widely accepted category—creates the impression of a self-evident and coherent group of exceptions to the requirement of truthfulness in bargaining. However, it is not clear what the category is. Price deception usually takes place in a bidding process; deception concerning a settlement point often is offered as a bluff; and the existence of a principal is deliberately withheld, although the comment does not indicate whether, upon inquiry, the principal's existence could be denied. These are significantly dissimilar forms of deception, and placing them in a category called "accepted conventions" does not make their kinship any clearer or make it possible to analogize to other examples. The withholding of the existence of a principal, in particular, is a misrepresentation of a material fact and should therefore be the model for few if any similar exceptions. Thus reliance on "accepted conventions" in a field where the conventions have not been systematically examined injects pragmatism into the Rules without justifying this standard or examining its consequences.

GEOFFREY C. HAZARD, JR., THE LAWYER'S OBLIGATION TO BE TRUSTWORTHY WHEN DEALING WITH OPPOSING PARTIES

33 So.Car.L.Rev. 181, 192–96 (1981).

The idea underlying the Kutak Commission's original proposal was not very complicated: the lawyer, as the instrument of a transaction, should be the guardian of its integrity. The proposal did not purport to hold lawyers strictly liable for the integrity of transactions or even burden them with a duty of reasonable care. Their only duty was to disclose facts of which an opposing party was obviously ignorant and which might affect the integrity of the transaction.

Much more fundamental objections were leveled at the proposal, particularly at the requirement that lawyers be "fair." Many members of the Commission and certainly the Reporter were surprised at the vehemence of the objections. "Vehemence" is the correct word, since much more heat than light was forthcoming in the reaction to the proposal. The Commission's surprise was compounded because the proposal seemed appropriate to the lawyer's role and appeared to reflect one interpretation of the lawyer's duty as established in the decisional law.

Although the explanation of the bar's aversion to the January 1980 proposal is complex, some concerns can be identified. First, many members of the bar do not realize or are unwilling to accept the fact that the law at large applies to lawyers. Perhaps these members of the bar believe an immunity attaches to lawyers against the civil liabilities imposed by the law on other intermediaries such as real estate brokers or securities underwriters. More subtly, perhaps lawyers recognize that the law at large applies to them but do not wish to be accountable for that obligation in the context of professional discipline.

Still subtler concerns were involved. The fundamental difficulty appears to stem from the lack of a firm professional consensus regarding the standard of openness that should govern lawyers' dealings with others and the lack of settled and homogeneous standards of technique in the practice of law. This lack of consensus indicates that lawyers, at least nationally, do not share a common conception of fairness in the process of negotiation. The lack of this consensus means that lawyers lack the language to express norms of fairness in negotiation and the institutional means to give effect to these norms.

The underlying disagreement about standards of fairness is not difficult to understand. Lawyers' standards of fairness are necessarily derived from those of society as a whole, and subcultural variations are enormous. At one extreme lies the "rural God-fearing standard," so exacting and tedious that it often excludes the use of lawyers. At the other extreme stands "New York hardball," now played in most larger cities using the wall-to-wall indenture for a playing surface. Between these extremes are regional and local standards and further variations that depend on the business involved, the identity of the participants, and other circumstances. Against this kaleidoscopic background, it is difficult to specify a single standard that governs the parties and thus a correlative standard that should govern their legal representatives.

The second area of disagreement concerns professional technique. Lawyers differ widely in the technical sophistication they expect of themselves and of others with whom they deal. As a result, their expectations regarding their own or their opponents' knowledge in the context of a given transaction may vary widely. Among practitioners having a very high level of technique, it is expected that a lawyer has carefully investigated and compiled relevant information, is familiar with recent developments in applicable law, recognizes all tax implications of a transaction, and anticipates secondary transactions likely to be involved in the transaction at hand. At another level of technique, lawyers may use a standard form for a transaction and hope for a satisfactory result.

Professional transactions within any given level of technique proceed according to implicitly understood conventions that allay all but ordinary anxiety on the part of the lawyers. Professional transactions that combine diverse levels of technique pose much greater difficulties. Lawyers accustomed to less sophisticated techniques are understandably fearful that they will be outmatched or even hoodwinked, with the possibility of loss to their clients and humiliation or even worse for themselves.

Lawyers accustomed to more sophisticated techniques have a correlative but perhaps less apparent dilemma. First, signs of bumbling on the other side cannot necessarily be taken at face value; there is such a thing as country-slickering and it occurs even in the city. Second, sophisticated lawyers are at risk precisely because of their technical sophistication. High-level technicians recognize aspects of transactions that lawyers of lesser sophistication may overlook. But what is to be done with that knowledge? If it is withheld, the transaction becomes vulnerable to rescission because of the lawyer's nondisclosure. The lawyer's professional competence, if not fully deployed for the benefit of the opposing party, thus becomes a potential infirmity for the transaction. Conversely, if the lawyer's competence is deployed for the benefit of the opposing party, where does the deployment properly stop, short of a takeover of the transaction and assumption of responsibility for the interests of both parties?

In the ebb and flow of practice, lawyers can and do adjust to these exigencies. The high level technicians deal with each other with circumspection but confidence. Lawyers in other strata of the professional community have their own conventions. When levels are crossed, the less sophisticated lawyer must decide whether to trust the opponent or to associate someone else, research into the night, or perhaps even abort the transaction. The more sophisticated lawyer must decide whether to risk later recriminations about the transaction if the bargain is too hard, whether to make particular disclosures to protect the deal but at the risk also of killing the deal, or whether to handle the transaction for both sides.

This range of possibilities is difficult to govern by regulation. A rule based on the premise that the legal profession is substantially homogeneous in technical sophistication would put the technically sophisticated lawyer in a hopeless dilemma when dealing with an unsophisticated opposing counsel. Such a lawyer could straightforwardly be a partisan of his own client unless it became evident that the other side was inadequately represented. But in that case, the superior technician would have to assist the other side to guard against the risk of a subsequent charge of nondisclosure or fraud. Yet until a transaction is well underway, a lawyer cannot know which course of action is required. At the same time, the lawyer who is unsophisticated or is simply acting according to his idea of the applicable conventions of openness would be in jeopardy of giving away his client's position. Thus, in a situation where the opposing lawyers differ substantially in technical sophistication, a rule requiring reciprocal disclosure could not yield genuine reciprocity.

On the other hand, it would be practically impossible to formulate a general rule that accounts for variations in technical sophistication. Consider the difficulties with the concept of specialization and with the definition of specialization once the concept was accepted, or with the problem of "incompetence" among the trial bar. Could we imagine rules of disclosure that were based on a distinction between Type A Lawyers and Type B Lawyers? Anyone who is sanguine about overcoming these difficulties should try drafting the criteria by which to differentiate the technically sophisticated practitioner from the bar at large.

In light of these constraints, legal regulation of trustworthiness cannot go much further than to proscribe fraud. That is disquieting but not necessarily occasion for despair. It simply indicates limitations on improving the bar by legal regulation.

GARY LOWENTHAL, TRUTHFUL BARGAINING BY LAWYERS

2 Geo.J. of Legal Ethics 411, 423–27 (1988).

MISREPRESENTING SETTLEMENT AUTHORITY AND MAKING FALSE DEMANDS

One form of misrepresentation deserves separate discussion because it raises unique and difficult problems in defining the appropriate contours of ethical behavior. Some negotiators, believing that they are conforming to accepted bargaining conventions, make untruthful statements concerning their settlement authority or the legitimacy of their bargaining demands. For example, assume that the plaintiff in a damage action has indicated to his attorney that he will accept a settlement of $50,000, but feels he is entitled to $75,000 and requests his lawyer to negotiate for a sum that is as close to that figure as possible. The defense lawyer informs plaintiff's counsel that the defendant is prepared to offer $53,000 if the plaintiff will settle the claim for that amount, and then asks: "Will your client accept a $53,000 offer?" Knowing that an affirmative response will end the plaintiff's chances for a settlement closer to $75,000, the lawyer's reply is: "No."

A similar problem occurs when a negotiator makes a bargaining demand solely for purposes of leverage. Assume that a dispute between two neighbors, Smith and Jones, concerns debris from Jones' tree falling in Smith's backyard swimming pool. Smith alleges that broken limbs and leaves from the tree have ruined his pool skimmer and threaten to damage the pool's plaster surface and surrounding deck. The neighbors have been feuding about the tree for years and substantial animosity exists between them. Smith informs his lawyer that he has no desire for remuneration; he would gladly forego any damages for the skimmer if Jones would remove the tree. Smith's lawyer suspects (correctly) that Jones might be amenable to removing the tree because it drops debris into Jones' yard also. Like most people, however, Jones does not want to give up "something for nothing." Therefore, Smith's lawyer presses for damages in addition to the tree's removal, as a bargaining chip to be given up later to allow Jones to save face. To make the bargaining chip seem realistic, the lawyer asserts that Smith intends to sue Jones for the damages Smith has suffered, even though the lawyer knows that Smith has no such intent.

Both illustrations depict a lawyer-negotiator deliberately misrepresenting a fact to induce another party to enter into an agreement that meets the needs of the negotiator's client. In each case the misrepresented fact relates to the negotiation process itself, rather than to a circumstance or event surrounding the underlying dispute or transaction. In the first illustration, the lawyer lies about his settlement authority; in the second, the lawyer makes a claim that he has no intention of pursuing. Are practitioners who make such false statements about the bargaining process acting unethically?

Lawyers' views of the propriety of these untruths vary remarkably. Some would condone the statements in the two illustrations, either because they are "tactics" rather than lies, or because a lawyer is sometimes "duty bound" to lie on behalf of a client. Others—most notably Roger Fisher and Judge Alvin Rubin—reason that a lie is a lie and an ethics code that permits such deception in negotiation is "risky for clients, bad for lawyers, and bad for society." James White would treat the two hypotheticals differently. Agreeing with Fisher and Rubin in the first case, White sees the misrepresentation of settlement authority as a "lie," and believes it is unethical. However, he concludes that the false negotiation demand is acceptable behavior because its use is "standard" for experienced bargainers in some contexts.

Considering the bar's propensity to adopt negotiation ethics rules that permit deception by lawyers, it is not surprising that the *Model Rules* take the position of their Reporter, Geoffrey Hazard. Hazard believes that although it is "desirable" for lawyers to be truthful in negotiation, "conventions governing social intercourse" give lawyers license to make false statements concerning bargaining demands and settlement authority. The Comment to Rule 4.1 similarly concludes that statements regarding "a party's intentions as to an acceptable settlement of a claim" ordinarily are not statements of material fact, and thus may be misrepresented, according to "generally accepted" conventions of negotiation. Presumably the thoughts of leading commentators like Fisher, Rubin and—in part—White are outside Professor Hazard's notion of "generally accepted" wisdom. The *Model Rules* adopt the hard-line position that when negotiators make assertions about their settlement authority or the legitimacy of demands they are making, they do not vouch for the truthfulness of their assertions, regardless of how sincere they may seem. If a gullible person on the other side of the table believes a negotiator's false statement about a bargaining position, the fault lies with the person who is ignorant of the rules, and not with the one who intentionally misleads.

How or why the bar concludes that a negotiation morality that rewards dishonesty is "generally accepted" is never stated. The conclusion is certainly not based on existing empirical evidence. Indeed, James White, normally an advocate of hard-nosed, competitive bargaining, opines that: "Some might say that the rules of the game provide for [misrepresenting the limit of one's authority to settle], but I suspect that many lawyers would say that such lies are out of bounds and not part of the rules of the game." My own experience as a long-time observer of the negotiation process is that, at least in the first of my illustrations, most lawyer-negotiators will avoid answering the question without resorting to a lie. Moreover, regardless of empirical verification, an ethics code should not condone conduct merely because it is "generally accepted." Ethics rules should be principles of desirable conduct that are morally binding on the conscience of a professional.

There appear to be at least two alternatives that make more sense than the bar's approach to lying about the bargaining process. First would be to make clear in the comment to Rule 4.1 that there is no exception to the prohibition against knowingly misrepresenting facts when the facts in question refer to such matters as a negotiator's settlement authority or the legitimacy of a bargaining demand. Requiring honesty in negotiators' factual assertions does not mean that negotiators must make full disclosure of their room to make concessions. Instead, it means that when a lawyer-negotiator does assert that a client will not accept a particular settlement offer or that a client is committed to a certain course of action, the lawyer's words should be truthful.

This approach to ethics does not put the honest lawyer at a disadvantage in a zero sum negotiation; one can be a principled negotiator and still be firm. For example, when the lawyer negotiating on behalf of the damage claimant is asked if he has authority to accept a $53,000 settlement, he might respond resolutely that the question itself is inappropriate. The lawyer could also explain why $53,000 is an undesirable or inadequate figure or argue why the plaintiff believes that the claim is worth $75,000, rather than $53,000. Another response that sidesteps the inquiry is an assertion that the parties need to discuss the merits of the case more thoroughly before discussing specific amounts. Without lying, a lawyer can still press for a settlement that is favorable to the client.

A second alternative to the bar's approach would be to adopt a rule to the effect that whether it is unethical to make an untruthful statement about one's settlement authority or the legitimacy of a claim depends on the circumstances in which the statement is made. Factors that would have a bearing on the propriety of such statements might include the type of negotiation involved, prevailing practices in the locale and—most important—the opposing party's understanding of those practices. Untruthful posturing would be permissible only where both parties are aware that a negotiator's statements regarding the acceptability or legitimacy of settlement terms may be false. Under such an approach, the burden of knowing the other party's assumptions concerning the rules on truthfulness in negotiation should rest on the shoulders of a party who chooses to make untruthful statements. Although an ethics rule of this nature would condone untruthful statements in certain contexts, it would protect the innocent victims of a lawyer's lying, unlike the standard adopted by the bar.

COMMENT, ROBERT GORDON, PRIVATE SETTLEMENT AS ALTERNATIVE ADJUDICATION: A RATIONALE FOR NEGOTIATION ETHICS

18 J. of Law Reform 503, 530–36 (1985).

FAIRNESS TO OTHER PARTICIPANTS

In conducting settlement negotiations,

(A) A lawyer shall at all times act in good faith and with the primary objective of resolving the dispute without court proceedings;

(B) A lawyer shall not

(1) Knowingly make any statement that contains a misrepresentation of material fact or law or that omits a fact necessary to make the statement considered as a whole not materially misleading;

(2) Knowingly fail to

    (a) Disclose to opposing counsel such material facts or law as may be necessary to correct manifest misapprehensions thereof; or, alternatively,

    (b) Give reasonable indication to opposing counsel of the possible inaccuracy of a given material fact or law upon which opposing counsel appears to rely. Such indication may take the form of statements of unwillingness to discuss a particular matter raised by opposing counsel.

Comment

This Rule is designed to promote basic truthfulness in private settlement negotiations. Its precise objective is to make a lawyer's duty of truthfulness in the negotiation setting coextensive with his duty of candor toward a tribunal. Accordingly, the following interpretive guidelines are suggested.

1. Good Faith—The good faith commanded by subsection (A) requires that a lawyer in negotiation conduct himself in such a way as will maximize the potential for reaching a fair and expeditious settlement. This includes, but is not limited to, a duty to reciprocate the candor of opposing counsel with like candor, but in no instance with less truthfulness than that prescribed in subsection (B), and a duty to use information obtained in the course of the negotiation in a way constructive to fair settlement.

. . .

3. Statements of fact—The Rule is intended to apply to statements of law or fact, and does not reach statements of conjecture, theory, or opinion. No duty of truthfulness extends to expressions of this kind.

Example 4—Lawyer (L) and Opposing Counsel (OC) are negotiating a claim of medical malpractice. L states to OC, "I'm convinced your clients were negligent in the performance of their surgery on my client." In fact, L has conferred with an expert witness, both concluding that the operation was probably conducted with due care. Because the statement refers to the personal belief of L, rather than to any material fact, the misrepresentation does not violate the Rule.

4. Duty to disclose or give reasonable indication of inaccuracy—Subsection (B)(2) gives the lawyer an option when faced during negotiation with an adversary laboring under a manifest misapprehension of material fact or law. He may either: (a) disclose such information as is necessary to disabuse the adversary of his misconception, or (b) give some reasonable indication of the possible inaccuracy of material information upon which opposing counsel appears to rely.

Example 5—Lawyer (L) represents a prominent golf pro (G) who suffered a disabling back injury when he slipped on a ball negligently left in a dark clubhouse corridor. Although the newspapers reported G's injury as permanent, G has spent the past month abroad receiving medical treatment with positive results. He now works out, practices daily, and doctors have given assurances that he will be back on the playing circuit within a year. G informs L of these developments prior to the commencement of settlement talks. During negotiation, however, it is clear that Opposing Counsel (OC) still believes that the damage to G's back is irreversible. He states, "What has happened to your client is a terrible thing, and we want to do right by him. Suffering as he is now, his career gone forever, we want to do all we can to ease the pain."

In this situation, subsection (B)(2) of the Rule gives L an option. Since G's physical condition is a matter of material fact, and OC's misapprehension as to the true status of this condition is manifest, L must either: (a) tell OC about the treatment G has been receiving and the likelihood of his being able to return to the pro circuit; or (b) give OC such reasonable indication as to put him on notice of the possible inaccuracy of his perception of G's health. Although L need not inform OC of the exact prognosis for G's recovery, he may not permit OC's misperception of this critical fact to go completely unchecked. His second option, therefore, would be to make some statement to indicate nonassent to the misapprehended fact. He may say, for example: "I'm not willing to discuss either the extent of my client's suffering or his future career prospects." Or, he might say, "If you want to depose my client or his doctors to find out the extent of the injuries, you may. We're only here to discuss settlement."

Statements such as these satisfy the dictates of subsection (B)(2)(b), as they put OC on notice that information upon which he appears to rely may be inaccurate. Although such statements amount to at least partial disclosure, it is important that a lawyer be able to keep some cards close to the chest without violating his duty of truthful negotiation behavior. No rule of negotiation ethics should oblige a lawyer to submit to cross-examination by his adversary. Yet neither should rules of professional conduct permit one attorney to profit unfairly from the manifest misapprehensions of opposing counsel. Subsection (B)(2)(b) strikes a compromise. The notice it ensures prevents a settlement from being negotiated on the basis of misinformation. Yet the form this notice takes allows a lawyer to remain in the negotiation without giving up facts he would rather force his adversary to discover independently. Given that candor toward opposing counsel will be reciprocated with like candor, the wisdom of making statements like the foregoing is questionable. But the Rule takes account of the varying tactical predilections of legal negotiators, and allows lawyers to conduct truthful settlement without having to research for their adversaries. Such a compromise affords lawyers a certain amount of strategic freedom when negotiating, yet at the same time safeguards the integrity of information that will ultimately produce settlement.

IF NOT RULES, WHAT ABOUT NORMS?

ELEANOR HOLMES NORTON, BARGAINING AND THE ETHIC OF PROCESS

64 N.Y.U.L.Rev. 493, 524–25; 535–36 (1989).

[After a detailed exploration of four prominent justifications for professional rules on truthtelling, Professor Norton summarizes:]

These four approaches, in part because of an insufficient focus on the operational features of the bargaining process, do not adequately satisfy the demands of a workable aspirational ethic for bargaining. Each, however, offers relevant insights. Universalism insists that negotiators not allow the special responsibilities of partisan advocacy to distort their ethical obligations. Without diminishing the importance of universalist aspirations, however, long and instructive experience with legal ethics cautions that there are limits to the usefulness of universal ethical rules in a specialized process. The need to accommodate individualist notions of partisan protection inherent in our legal system has produced a special lawyer's ethic. Similar partisan considerations are at work in bargaining.

Traditionalism most closely approximates the instinctive partisanship of classical competitive negotiations. In legal matters, traditionalism stresses both the right of the individual to partisan loyalty from an attorney and the importance of the adversarial system in obtaining justice. No such overriding values characterize generic negotiations. What remains, therefore, is partisanship, a virtually instinctive characteristic that needs no reinforcement in negotiation ethics. The legal system, in which the partisan posture has been submitted to detailed analysis, teaches that partisanship brings ethical pressure. Unexposed to public monitoring, traditionalism would intensify the private struggle that the unpoliced bargaining process already encourages.

Relativism is useful in the search for an appropriate negotiation ethic because it directs attention to the actual purposes such an ethic would serve. Probing the function of a given aspect of legal practice is useful to the search for a feasible bargaining ethic. However, relativism that goes no further than the classic division between advocates and nonadvocates obscures the possibility that in negotiations, the two may harbor as many similarities as differences.

Pragmatism offers experience rather than theory as the basis for a bargaining ethic. However, the absence of systematic data revealing existing bargaining ethics seriously impedes this approach. If experience with bargaining ethics could be satisfactorily documented, pragmatism might point toward an ethic that is sensible, coherent, and practical. Even then, however, pragmatism would not ameliorate unethical practice if it rested on the lowest common denominator of ethical experience. In any case, pragmatism raises unprecedented methodological difficulties in determining how, and even whether, to credit existing experience as a legitimate basis for a bargaining ethic.

. . .

The assumptions of the functionalist model [which Norton develops] may be summarized as follows:

1. Bargaining is indispensable to the functioning of society.

2. The fundamental purpose of bargaining is to achieve a valid agreement.

3. Practices that threaten the validity of an agreement violate the fundamental purpose of the process.

4. Bargaining is an adversarial market process in which willing opponents use partisan strategic dealings (bargaining techniques) to arrive at accurate information and to obtain fair treatment.

These assumptions underlie the use of the internal resources of the process to achieve truthfulness and fairness in bargaining. The result is a minimal but functional ethic. This ethic is best understood through an explanation of its operation to induce truthfulness and fairness and through an analysis of appropriate illustrations.

Truthfulness is important in negotiations because it encourages trust between opponents and thus facilitates agreement. However, adherence to the ethical standard of truthfulness in bargaining does not require a negotiator to abandon the assumptions of the process. Parties to a negotiation may use bargaining techniques, including strategic dealings, in order to arrive at accurate information concerning factual matters and the true intentions of an opponent, as well as to limit information offered to an opponent.

False information is not usually recognizable as a bargaining technique and therefore closes off the opportunity for an opponent to arrive at accurate information through the use of his own bargaining techniques. Thus, giving false information in a negotiation violates the assumption that bargaining techniques will elicit accurate information. False information also undermines the basic purpose of the bargaining process, to achieve a valid agreement. However, false information necessary for a mode of bargaining to occur is an exception because of the assumption that bargaining is necessary to the functioning of society. Generally, though, information that is necessary for bargaining to occur is also recognizable as a bargaining technique. Such false information does not threaten the validity of an agreement because it may be uncovered during the course of bargaining through the use of bargaining techniques so as to facilitate the eventual discovery of more accurate information. Thus, deceptive offers and counteroffers, as well as settlement point deception may be considered either bargaining techniques that invite counter-techniques or false information that is necessary for a form of bargaining to occur. The withholding of the name of a principal, however, cannot be uncovered readily through the use of bargaining techniques and therefore can be justified only as necessary for bargaining to occur. Often deceptive exchanges are not misrepresentations as the term is commonly understood because the true asking price or the settlement point may become clear to the parties only as a result of the process of bargaining itself.

Several examples may be helpful to show how the assumptions apply to truthfulness. Avoiding a direct answer is a bargaining technique when it limits information to an opponent without undermining the validity of an agreement. Failing to volunteer information is a bargaining technique when it limits information to an opponent unless, for example, silence about the particular facts undermines the validity of the agreement. Other examples of bargaining techniques are puffing concerning the quality of goods and bluffing concerning calling off negotiations. The process assumes that negotiators will use partisan strategic dealings to arrive at truthful information, and that the statements made will not keep opponents from using bargaining techniques to arrive at truthful information. Such deceptive information is not inconsistent with the assumptions of the process. When it is offered in such a way as to allow strategic responses that can arrive at more accurate information, it is necessary for bargaining to occur.

DAVID A. LAX AND JAMES K. SEBENIUS, THREE ETHICAL ISSUES IN NEGOTIATION

2 Negot.J. 363–70 (1986).

The agent for a small grain seller reported the following telephone conversation, concerning a disagreement over grain contracted to be sold to General Mills:

> We're General Mills; and if you don't deliver this grain to us, why we'll have a battery of lawyers in there tomorrow morning to visit you, and then we are going to the North Dakota Public Service [Commission]; we're going to the Minneapolis Grain Exchange and we're going to the people in Montana and there will be no more Muschler Grain Company. We're going to take your license.

Tactics mainly intended to permit one party claim value at another's expense inescapably raise hard ethical issues. How should one evaluate moves that stake out positions, threaten another with walkout or worse, misrepresent values or beliefs, hold another person's wants hostage to claim value at that person's expense, or offer an "elegant" solution of undeniable joint benefit but constructed so that one side will get the lion's share?

. . .

The essence of much bargaining involves changing another's perceptions of where in fact one would settle. Several kinds of tactics can lead to impressions that are at variance with the truth about one's actual position: persuasive rationales, commitments, references to other no-agreement alternatives, calculated patterns of concessions, failures to correct misperceptions, and the like. These tactics are tempting for obvious reasons: one side may claim value by causing the other to misperceive the range of potentially acceptable agreements. And both sides are generally in this same boat.

Such misrepresentations about each side's real interests and the set of possible bargaining outcomes should be distinguished from misrepresentations about certain aspects of the substance of the negotiation (e.g., whether the car has known difficulties that will require repair, whether the firm being acquired has important undiscussed liabilities, and so on). This latter category of tactics, which we might dub "malign persuasion," more frequently fails tests of ethical appropriateness. Consider two such tests.

ARE THE "RULES" KNOWN AND ACCEPTED BY ALL SIDES?

Some people take the symmetry of the bargaining situation to ease the difficulty of ethical choice. The British statesman, Henry Taylor, is reported to have said that "falsehood ceases to be falsehood when it is understood on all sides that the truth is not expected to be spoken." In other words, if these tactics are mutually accepted as within the "rules of the game," there is no problem. A good analogy can be found in a game of poker: Bluffing is expected and thus permissible, while drawing a gun or kicking over the table are not. Yet often, the line is harder to draw.

For instance, a foreigner in Hong Kong may be aware that at least some tailors bargain routinely, but still be unsure whether a particular one—who insists he has fixed prices—is "just bargaining." Yet that tailor may reap considerable advantage if in fact he bargains but is persuasive that he does not. It is often self-servingly easy for the deceiver to assume that others know and accept the rules. And a worse problem is posed if many situations are often not even recognized as negotiation, when in fact they exhibit its essential characteristics (interdependence, some perceived conflict, opportunistic potential, the possibility of explicit or tacit agreement on joint action). When, as is often the case in organizational life, such less acknowledged negotiation occurs, then how can any "rules" of the game meet the mutual "awareness and acceptance of the rules" test?

CAN THE SITUATION BE FREELY ENTERED AND LEFT?

Ethicist Sissela Bok (1978) adds another criterion: For lying to be appropriate, not only must the rules be well-understood, but the participants must be able freely to enter *and* leave the situation. Thus to the extent that mutually expected, ritual flattery or a work of fiction involve "lying," there is little problem. To make an analogy between deception and violence: though a boxing match, which can involve rough moves, meets this criterion, a duel, from which exit may be impossible, does not.

Yet this standard may be too high. Bargaining situations—formal and informal, tacit and explicit—are far more widespread than many people realize. In fact, a good case can be made that bargaining pervades life inside and outside of organizations, making continual free entry and exit impractical. So if bargaining will go on and people will necessarily be involved in it, something else is required.

OTHER HELPFUL QUESTIONS

When it is unclear whether a particular tactic is ethically appropriate, we find that a number of other questions—beyond whether others know and accept it or may leave—can illuminate the choice. Consider several such questions:

Self-image. Peter Drucker (1981) asks a basic question: When you look at yourself in the mirror the next morning, will you like the person you see? And there are many such useful queries about self image, which are intended to clarify the appropriateness of the choice itself and not to ask about the possible consequences (firing, ostracism, etc.) to you of different parties being aware of your actions: Would you be comfortable if your co-workers, colleagues, and friends were aware that you had used a particular tactic? Your spouse, children, or parents? If it came out on the front page of the *New York Times* or the *Wall Street Journal?* If it became known in ten years? Twenty? In the history books?

Reciprocity. Does it accord with the Golden Rule? How would you feel if someone did it to you? To a younger colleague? A respected mentor? A member of your family? (Of course, saying that you would mind very much if it were done to another need not imply that the tactic is unethical; that person may not be in your situation or have your experience—but figuring out the reason you would be bothered can give a clue to the ethics of the choice.)

Advising Others. Would you be comfortable advising another to use this tactic? Instructing your agent to use it? How about if such advice became known?

Designing the System. Imagine that you were completely outside the setting in which the tactic might be used, but that you were responsible for designing the situation itself: the number of people present, their stakes, the conventions governing their encounters, the range of permissible actions, and so on. The wrinkle is that you would be assigned a role in that setting, *but* you would not know in advance the identity of the person whose role you would assume. Would you build in the possibility for the kind of tactics you are now trying to evaluate? A simpler version of this test is to ask how you would rule on this tactic if you were an arbitrator, or perhaps an elder, in a small society.

Social Result. What if everybody bargained this way? Would the resulting society be desirable? These questions may not have obvious answers. For example, hard, individual competition may seem dehumanizing. Yet many argue that, precisely because competition is encouraged, standards of living rise in free-market societies and some forms of excellence flourish.

Alternative Tactics. Are there alternative tactics available that have fewer ethical ambiguities or costs? Can the whole issue be avoided by following a different tack, even at a small cost elsewhere?

Taking a Broader View. In agonizing over a tactic—for instance, whether to shade values—it is often worth stepping back to take a broader perspective.

First, there is a powerful tendency for people to focus on conflict, see a "zero sum" world, and primarily aim to enlarge their individual shares. Such an emphasis on "claiming" is common yet it can stunt creativity and often cause significant joint gains to go unrealized. In such cases, does the real problem lie in the ethical judgment call about a tactic intended to claim value, or is it a disproportionate focus on claiming itself? If it is the latter, the more fruitful question may be how to make the other face of negotiation—moves jointly to "create value"—more salient.

Second, does the type of situation itself generate powerful tendencies toward the questionable tactics involved? Is it an industry in which "favors" to public officials are an "expected" means for winning good contracts? If so, evaluating the acceptability of a given move may be less important than deciding (1) whether to leave the situation that inherently poses such choices, or (2) which actions could alter, even slightly, the prevalence of the questionable practices.

. . .

CONCLUSION

The overall choice of how to negotiate, whether to emphasize moves that create value or claim it, has implications beyond single encounters. The dynamic that leads individual bargainers to poor agreements, impasses, and conflict spirals also has a larger social counterpart. Without choices that keep creative actions from being driven out, this larger social game tends toward an equilibrium in which everyone claims, engages constantly in behavior that distorts information, and worse.

Most people are willing to sacrifice something to avoid such outcomes, and to improve the way people relate to each other in negotiation and beyond. The wider echos of ethical choices made in negotiation can be forces for positive change. Each person must decide if individual risks are worth general improvement, even if such improvement seems small, uncertain, and not likely to be visible. Yet a widespread choice to disregard ethics in negotiation would mark a long step down the road to a more cynical, Hobbesian world.

STEVEN HARTWELL, UNDERSTANDING AND DEALING WITH DECEPTION IN LEGAL NEGOTIATION

6 Ohio St.J. on Disp.Res. 171, 182–87 (1991).

A. Environmental Cues to Context

Ordinarily, the environment itself cues people to the appropriate context for decoding information. When I hear a trilled "r" accompanied by bodily gestures characteristic of latin culture, I know to "decode" the sounds I hear as Spanish. When I enter a theater, environmental cues such as the stage and the seating tell me that the action to follow is "theater." The words "once upon a time" cue a child that what follows is merely a story. We can, of course, make mistakes about context. The language I hear may be Portuguese, not Spanish. Modern theater sometimes plays with context, having actors step out of the theater audience so that the theater context does not tell us for sure whether they are actors or not. Although becoming socialized within a culture entails the ability to quickly and accurately identify social contexts, we all occasionally misidentify contexts even within cultures we know very well. Most all of us have experienced the jitters while attending an unfamiliar social occasion because we fear we will misunderstand or be misunderstood.

Context can clarify an otherwise ambiguous conversation. Consider, for example, over-hearing this simple statement: "John shot two bucks." The first necessary contextual decision is that the language is English and that the sentence should be understood according to the rules of the English language. Without any other contextual markers, the sentence might mean that John shot a gun and struck two deer or that John gambled away two dollars. Context would ordinarily be provided by our knowledge of John (he is a renowned hunter), the speaker (she is only interested in gambling), the general subject matter of the conversation (they have been talking all morning about hunting) or perhaps the location (they are at a casino). In the same manner, negotiation styles or contexts serve as contextual markers that help us identify the probability that certain statements are intended as deceptive.

B. Negotiation Contexts

"Negotiation" is the name of a context and, as well, the name of a set of contexts. When two opposing attorneys meet on the courthouse steps just before trial, the environment cues them that what they say in the next few minutes should be interpreted as within the 'context "negotiation." Only a naive attorney would interpret the greetings, inquiries about parking problems, and other such topics as merely conversation within the context of polite social intercourse. Negotiation, however, is a complex context containing within it several different contexts. The meaning of certain words or gestures in one of these contexts may differ from their meaning in another context. The context of a "courthouse steps" negotiation differs from the collegial "office" context of negotiating among one's peers within a law firm or law school faculty. The contextual interpretation of "deception" in one such context may differ from the contextual interpretation in another. Environmental cues and the language employed guide us in the appropriate interpretation of deceptive language and conduct. In order to understand better how these deceptions are interpreted, we need to review briefly the three major contexts that constitute most negotiations.

Professor Thomas Gifford has recently offered a comprehensive typology of negotiation contexts. His typology identifies three explicit contexts: competition, cooperation and integration (often called "collaboration"). The first context, competition, is marked by high demands, limited disclosure of information, threats, apparent commitments to positions, and deception. Asserted opening demands, bottom lines, constraints on authority to bargain, the identity of one's principal, and the seriousness of threats should all be taken as potentially deceptive. For example, a statement by one negotiator that "One million dollars is the least we will accept to settle this case" should, given a competitive context, be interpreted as a high demand and a probable deception. The opponent would undoubtedly err if he were to interpret this statement as a candid offer.

The characteristic pattern that identifies the second context, cooperation, is the pattern of alternating and sequential concessions directed toward a compromise. Each party typically opens with offers that are less than what they expect at a final settlement. Given the above statement in a cooperative context, the opponent should interpret it as a signal inviting a counter-offer with the expectation that the opponent will then make a lesser demand. The speaker does not intend to deceive as he might in a competitive context, but intends that the statement encourage a sequence of concessions in which he himself intends continued participation. Plea bargaining between experienced prosecutors and defense counsel typically follows a cooperative context.

With the third context, integration, the negotiators engage in problem solving to satisfy their common interests. Given the "one million dollar" statement, the opponent should interpret it as candid, and designed to help both negotiators resolve their common problem. The two negotiators may have, for example, two million dollars to resolve a certain problem. The speaker does not intend to deceive or to induce a counter-offer. Integration differs from cooperation in several respects. Cooperation typically presumes a zero-sum situation in which your gain is my loss. The pattern of sequential concessions is intended to reach a fair division of a fixed pie. Integration typically presumes a non-zero sum situation, that is, a situation in which the pie can be made larger or in which the parties can abandon the original pie and, by working together, construct a new and tastier pie.

C. Deception of Context

A major thesis of this paper is that the kind of deception that threatens a negotiation is a deception *about* a context and not a deception *within* a context. As long as each negotiator accurately identifies the negotiation strategy (that is, the negotiation context) of the other, and appropriately anticipates the kind of candidness and deception which that negotiation context entails, deception will not derail the negotiation. If, for example, both negotiators knowingly employ a competitive context, then each will interpret the other's statements as presumptively deceptive. A negotiator who understands the negotiation context as competitive cannot rationally walk out of a competitive negotiation in a rage over a deception. Similarly, if both negotiators knowingly engage in a integratively-contexted negotiation, neither should ever intentionally deceive the other because it is not in their own self-interests to do so. However, negotiations are complex events and negotiators sometimes misread the context of a negotiation and consequently misinterpret the language of their opponents. At other times, negotiators act irrationally by refusing to recognize a patently obvious context, a type of negotiation pathology. . . .

1. Why We React More Strongly to Deception of Context

Good reasons compel negotiators to react more strongly to deception about a context than to deception within a context. Deception about context is potentially much more harmful than deception within a context. To be deceived about a context is to misinterpret every piece of information within that context. Consider the feeling of discovering that a person whom we thought to be a friend (that is, a person within a "friend context") has, from the very beginning, been a false friend. This sudden realization means that we have misunderstood everything this person has said to us. We have been deceived not once but numerous times. We may feel painfully humiliated. The difference between deception within a context and deception about a context is the difference between merely falling short and betrayal, between Peter and Judas.

2. Embarrassment and Shame

We intuitively express the difference between deception within a context and deception about a context with the social concepts of embarrassment and shame. Embarrassment is always context dependent. What is embarrassing in one context (belching in the faculty dining room, a deception in an integrative negotiation context) may not be embarrassing somewhere else (belching at home in front of one's long suffering family, a deception in a competitive negotiation context). Embarrassment is a negotiator's typical reaction to being caught in an inadvertent deception within a context that does not permit deception, such as a deception within an integrative context. Someone is embarrassed because he has not acted consistently with the context he wishes to project. The deceiver's embarrassment (flushed face, stammering) signals his opponent that he did not mean to deceive (that is, that he momentarily and inadvertently slipped from his role as an integrative negotiator). Sometimes negotiators are embarrassed when they discover they have been deceived because the deception indicates that they have not been the astute, sophisticated negotiators they thought themselves to be.

3. Shame

In contrast to embarrassment, shame typically entails intentional deception *about* a context. Shame is not being the person one claims to be in some fundamental way. Shame entails the violation of some general principle of civil conduct. To be a false friend and betray another is shameful.

CASE STUDIES

GEOFFREY M. PETERS, THE USE OF LIES IN NEGOTIATION

48 Ohio St.L.J. 1, 8–13 (1987).

DISTINGUISHING LYING FROM OTHER DECEPTIONS

A Bargain for Frances, is a children's book about negotiation. The story concerns two children, Frances and Thelma. Frances is characterized as being trusting, naive, and virtuous. Thelma is a con artist. Frances goes to Thelma's house, where the two play with Thelma's plastic tea set with red flowers on it. Frances tells Thelma that she has saved $2.17 towards the purchase of a china tea set with blue flowers. Thelma convinces Frances to buy her plastic tea set with red flowers for a price of $2.17. She uses the following tactics:

1. Thelma argues that plastic tea sets are better than china tea sets even though Thelma secretly prefers china tea sets.

2. Thelma tells Frances that she does not believe china tea sets are available anymore, while Thelma knows that there is one for sale in the nearby candy store for $2.07.

3. When Frances expresses interest in buying Thelma's tea set, Thelma says she does not want to sell it. The reader is left with the impression that Thelma secretly did want to sell it, even as she was telling Frances the contrary.

Upon returning home with the plastic tea set, Frances soon learns how Thelma has tricked her. Frances sets out to return the favor, but she does not sink to Thelma's level to do so. Thelma has used lies to trick Frances. Frances decides to trick Thelma back by using other forms of deception.

At this point Frances becomes very clever. She puts a penny in the plastic sugar bowl. She calls Thelma and points out to her that the "no backsies" clause in their sales agreement covers any contents as well as the set itself. She suggests to Thelma that there is something in the sugar bowl. Thelma concludes that what is presently in the sugar bowl was left there by her (Thelma). Frances has been able to create this impression without ever actually saying anything that is untrue in the absolute, objective, scientific sense. Thelma continues lying. She claims that she left a ring in the bowl. Frances says it is not a ring. Then Thelma lies that she left some birthday money in the bowl. Frances admits that there is money in the bowl, but she does not have to tell Thelma how much. She does not respond to Thelma's guesses of $2.00 and then $5.00. Under the rules of no backsies, the only way Thelma can get back whatever was in the sugar bowl when she sold it to Frances is to buy the set back. She no longer has Frances' $2.17, having spent $2.07 of it on the china set with blue pictures. Frances agrees to take the china set plus ten cents for returning the plastic set to Thelma.

The reader is left with the sense that Frances has taught Thelma a lesson while maintaining her own virtue. She has not lied to Thelma. She has simply allowed Thelma to be misled by her own greed and deviousness. It is revenge at its sweetest. The bully has punched herself in the nose. Frances does not consider either kind of trickery to be "nice," but there is an unmistakable sense that Frances' trickery was within ethical bounds whereas Thelma's was not.

Legal literature dealing with negotiation makes the same distinction. Because lawyers function in a world structured by judges and legislatures, we should not be surprised to find rules designed to govern lawyers in their negotiations, and accompanying text regarding the special difficulty of using rules to regulate negotiation. But they are general and ill-defined enough to permit a very wide range of interpretations regarding appropriate negotiating behavior. Statutes require that certain negotiations be conducted in an open and candid manner. The American Law Institute's *Restatement of the Law* contains sanctions against dishonest negotiating, but it does not specify what is to be considered "dishonest." The *Model Rules of Professional Conduct* prohibit lawyers from lying in negotiations. Rule 4.1(a) provides that a lawyer, in the course of representing a client, cannot "[m]ake a false statement of material fact or law to a third person."

Scholarly and instructional writing in the area rarely addresses the distinction directly, although it is often implicit in their writings. Although I find the idea of definitions dangerous, I will offer working definitions of "lying" and "deception" here to facilitate the recognition of the distinction in writings about negotiation. A "lie" is a false statement made by one who knows its falsity and with the intent to deceive another as to the truth. A "deception" is any other method of concealing the truth, including silence.

Kronman analyzes the famous case of *Laidlaw v. Organ* in his analysis of the law of fraud. According to Kronman, the case involved Organ's sale of tobacco to Laidlaw. The War of 1812 had driven the price of tobacco down. At the time of the formation of the contract to sell, Organ knew that the war had just ended and that Laidlaw did not know. As soon as the news of the war's ending got out, the price of tobacco rose dramatically. Before entering into the contract to sell, Laidlaw had "asked if there was any news which was calculated to enhance the price or value of the article about to be purchased." Kronman then distinguishes between two possible responses, each of which would have succeeded in protecting his ability to exploit his knowledge that the war had ended. Organ could have answered that he had no such knowledge—a lie, or he could have somehow cleverly avoided answering in such a way that the suspicions of Laidlaw would not have been aroused—a deception. Kronman notes that the path of clever avoidance would be sanctioned by the law, while the path of direct denial would have been disapproved of as a fraud.

Wenke says,

> It is common for a party to alter a position that earlier has been represented as nonnegotiable. This practice is considered to be *bluffing* rather than *lying*.

It is important to note, as Wenke does, that what distinguishes puffing from lying is that the statement is not expected to be believed in what might be considered a "literal" sense. For example, the rug salesman at Bok's Eastern bazaar does not lie when he says the rug is a priceless heirloom that you would be lucky to buy at the asking price. The reason is that the salesman does not expect you to believe the literal meaning of the statement. He expects that his statement will make you believe that the salesman probably is unwilling to reduce his price much. The statement would not be a lie, even if the salesman is, in fact, willing to come down dramatically. Yet the statement is meant, like all puffing, to deceive.

I think Raiffa and Sperber can be interpreted similarly. Raiffa says:

> A common ploy is to exaggerate the importance of what one is giving up and to minimize the importance of what one gets in return. Such posturing is part of the game. In most cultures these self-serving negotiating stances are expected, as long as they are kept in decent bounds. Most people would not call this "lying," just as they would choose not to label as "lying" the exaggerations that are made in the adversarial confrontations of a courtroom. I call such exaggerations "strategic misrepresentations."

Sperber says:

> Most negotiators use tactics which to outsiders could be considered lying and therefore dishonest. The criteria for judging an action is not what some third party believes but what is actually meant or perceived by the parties conducting the negotiations. If the other side understands the representation is merely an exaggeration and not a representation, then it is a perfectly acceptable tactic [whose effectiveness nonetheless depends on its ability to deceive] to be utilized. If in fact the other side accepts the proposal because of its belief in what is being said, then it is a misrepresentation of a material fact, it is unethical, and the result is an unenforceable agreement.

Fisher and Ury evidence their disapproval of lying by including such statements in their list of "dirty tricks." Fisher and Ury use "deliberate deception" where I would use "lie." This can be seen from the language following immediately after the heading "Deliberate deception," which reads,

> Perhaps the most common form of dirty trick is misrepresentation about facts, authority, or intentions. . . . The oldest form of negotiating trickery is to knowingly make some false statement: "The car was driven only 5,000 miles by a little old lady from Pasadena who never went over 35 miles per hour."

Fisher and Ury list two other examples of deceptions, each of which involve lies. They refer to the "dirty trick" of "announc[ing] that they [the dirty tricksters] must take it [a purported agreement] to someone else for approval," and to the "dirty trick" of falsely asserting one's intention to comply with an agreement. Having disapproved of these lies, Fisher and Ury approve of other methods of deception in their approval of intentional concealment of the truth. "Good faith negotiation does not require total disclosure."

Dudley addresses the problem faced by a negotiator with a weak position. The simplest and most effective way to conceal that weakness would be to lie about it, claiming a strong position. Instead he suggests concealing the weakness "under extra details and the affect of style. . . . This style deflects the specific inquiry as well as it aids the inflation of your meager strengths."

All of this is meant to show that although the rules of negotiations among lawyers are not elaborately set out in a single governing statute, it is possible to discern conventions of a less formal nature that govern nonetheless.

Among these conventions, which have something in common with rules of etiquette and good manners, is one that forbids the telling of lies while it approves the use of other deceptive tactics aimed at concealing the truth.

JAMES J. WHITE, MACHIAVELLI AND THE BAR: ETHICAL LIMITATIONS ON LYING IN NEGOTIATION

1980 Am.Bar Found.Res.J. 926, 931–35.

FIVE CASES

Easiest is the question that arises when one misrepresents his true opinion about the meaning of a case or a statute. Presumably such a misrepresentation is accepted lawyer behavior both in and out of court and is not intended to be precluded by the requirement that the lawyer be "truthful." In writing his briefs, arguing his case, and attempting to persuade the opposing party in negotiation, it is the lawyer's right and probably his responsibility to argue for plausible interpretations of cases and statutes which favor his client's interest, even in circumstances where privately he has advised his client that those are not his true interpretations of the cases and statutes.

A second form of distortion that the Comments [to proposed Model Rule 4.2] plainly envision as permissible is distortion concerning the value of one's case or of the other subject matter involved in the negotiation. Thus the Comments make explicit reference to "puffery." Presumably they are attempting to draw the same line that one draws in commercial law between express warranties and "mere puffing" under section 2–313 of the Uniform Commercial Code. While this line is not easy to draw, it generally means that the seller of a product has the right to make general statements concerning the value of his product without having the law treat those statements as warranties and without having liability if they turn out to be inaccurate estimates of the value. As the statements descend toward greater and greater particularity, as the ignorance of the person receiving the statements increases, the courts are likely to find them to be not puffing but express warranties. By the same token a lawyer could make assertions about his case or about the subject matter of his negotiation in general terms, and if those proved to be inaccurate, they would not be a violation of the ethical standards. Presumably such statements are not violations of the ethical standards even when they conflict with the lawyer's dispassionate analysis of the value of his case.

A third case is related to puffing but different from it. This is the use of the so-called false demand. It is a standard negotiating technique in collective bargaining negotiation and in some other multiple-issue negotiations for one side to include a series of demands about which it cares little or not at all. The purpose of including these demands is to increase one's supply of negotiating currency. One hopes to convince the other party that one or more of these false demands is important and thus successfully to trade it for some significant concession. The assertion of and argument for a false demand involves the same kind of distortion that is involved in puffing or in arguing the merits of cases or statutes that are not really controlling. The proponent of a false demand implicitly or explicitly states his interest in the demand and his estimation of it. Such behavior is untruthful in the broadest sense; yet at least in collective bargaining negotiation its use is a standard part of the process and is not thought to be inappropriate by any experienced bargainer.

Two final examples may be more troublesome. The first involves the response of a lawyer to a question from the other side. Assume that the defendant has instructed his lawyer to accept any settlement offer under $100,000. Having received that instruction, how does the defendant's lawyer respond to the plaintiff's question, "I think $90,000 will settle this case. Will your client give $90,000?" Do you see the dilemma that question poses for the defense lawyer? It calls for information that would not have to be disclosed. A truthful answer to it concludes the negotiation and dashes any possibility of negotiating a lower settlement even in circumstances in which the plaintiff might be willing to accept half of $90,000. Even a moment's hesitation in response to the question may be a nonverbal communication to a clever plaintiff's lawyer that the defendant has given such authority. Yet a negative response is a lie.

It is no answer that a clever lawyer will answer all such questions about authority by refusing to answer them, nor is it an answer that some lawyers will be clever enough to tell their clients not to grant them authority to accept a given sum until the final stages in negotiation. Most of us are not that careful or that clever. Few will routinely refuse to answer such questions in cases in which the client has granted a much lower limit than that discussed by the other party, for in that case an honest answer about the absence of authority is a quick and effective method of changing the opponent's settling point, and it is one that few of us will forego when our authority is far below that requested by the other party. Thus despite the fact that a clever negotiator can avoid having to lie or to reveal his settling point, many lawyers, perhaps most, will sometime be forced by such a question either to lie or to reveal that they have been granted such authority by saying so or by their silence in response to a direct question. Is it fair to lie in such a case?

Before one examines the possible justifications for a lie in that circumstance, consider a final example recently suggested to me by a lawyer in practice. There the lawyer represented three persons who had been charged with shoplifting. Having satisfied himself that there was no significant conflict of interest, the defense lawyer told the prosecutor that two of the three would plead guilty only if the case was dismissed against the third. Previously those two had told the defense counsel that they would plead guilty irrespective of what the third did, and the third had said that he wished to go to trial unless the charges were dropped. Thus the defense lawyer lied to the prosecutor by stating that the two would plead only if the third were allowed to go free. Can the lie be justified in this case?

How does one distinguish the cases where truthfulness is not required and those where it is required? Why do the first three cases seem easy? I suggest they are easy cases because the rules of the game are explicit and well developed in those areas. Everyone expects a lawyer to distort the value of his own case, of his own facts and arguments, and to depreciate those of his opponent. No one is surprised by that, and the system accepts and expects that behavior. To a lesser extent the same is true of the false demand procedure in labor-management negotiations where the ploy is sufficiently widely used to be explicitly identified in the literature. A layman might say that this behavior falls within the ambit of "exaggeration," a form of behavior that while not necessarily respected is not regarded as morally reprehensible in our society.

The last two cases are more difficult. In one the lawyer lies about his authority; in the other he lies about the intention of his clients. It would be more difficult to justify the lies in those cases by arguing that the rules of the game explicitly permit that sort of behavior. Some might say that the rules of the game provide for such distortion, but I suspect that many lawyers would say that such lies are out of bounds and are not part of the rules of the game. Can the lie about authority be justified on the ground that the question itself was improper? Put another way, if I have a right to keep certain information to myself, and if any behavior but a lie will reveal that information to the other side, am I justified in lying? I think not. Particularly in the case in which there are other avenues open to the respondent, should we not ask him to take those avenues? That is, the careful negotiator here can turn aside all such questions and by doing so avoid any inference from his failure to answer such questions.

What makes the last case a close one? Conceivably it is the idea that one accused by the state is entitled to greater leeway in making his case. Possibly one can argue that there is no injury to the state when such a person, particularly an innocent person, goes free. Is it conceivable that the act can be justified on the ground that it is part of the game in this context, that prosecutors as well as defense lawyers routinely misstate what they, their witnesses, and their clients can and will do? None of these arguments seems persuasive. Justice is not served by freeing a guilty person. The system does not necessarily achieve better results by trading two guilty pleas for a dismissal. Perhaps its justification has its roots in the same idea that formerly held that a misrepresentation of one's state of mind was not actionable for it was not a misrepresentation of fact.

In a sense rules governing these cases may simply arise from a recognition by the law of its limited power to shape human behavior. By tolerating exaggeration and puffing in the sales transaction, by refusing to make misstatement of one's intention actionable, the law may simply have recognized the bounds of its control over human behavior. Having said that, one is still left with the question, Are the lies permissible in the last two cases? My general conclusion is that they are not, but I am not nearly as comfortable with that conclusion as I am with the conclusion about the first three cases.

Taken together, the five foregoing cases show me that we do not and cannot intend that a negotiator be "truthful" in the broadest sense of that term. At the minimum we allow him some deviation from truthfulness in asserting his true opinion about cases, statutes, or the value of the subject of the negotiation in other respects. In addition some of us are likely to allow him to lie in response to certain questions that are regarded as out of bounds, and possibly to lie in circumstances where his interest is great and the injury seems small. It would be unfortunate, therefore, for the rule that requires "fairness" to be interpreted to require that a negotiator be truthful in every respect and in all of his dealings. It should be read to allow at least those kinds of untruthfulness that are implicitly and explicitly recognized as acceptable in his forum, a forum defined both by the subject matter and by the participants.

REX R. PERSCHBACHER, REGULATING LAWYERS' NEGOTIATIONS

27 Ariz.L.Rev. 75, 77–9, 137–38 (1985).

Although there is no lawyers' code of negotiation ethics, there are rules regulating how negotiations may be conducted and how negotiators must conduct themselves with their clients and their adversaries. Two examples illustrate the problem of the possible gulf between technically effective and ethically proper negotiation conduct. The lawyer representing a defendant in a civil case has been instructed by her client to accept any settlement offer under $100,000. The plaintiff's lawyer tells her, "I think $90,000 will settle this case. Will your client give $90,000?" The defendant's lawyer is in a bind. If she answers truthfully she forecloses further negotiation and the possibility of a much lower settlement. If she lies about what her client will do, she may well benefit her client. But is it proper for the lawyer to lie?

Consider further the case of a lawyer representing the proposed buyer of a financially distressed business. After initially showing an interest in accepting the seller's asking price of $90 million, the lawyer and his client, knowing there are no other likely buyers, agree on a strategy of delay in reaching final agreement in order to take advantage of the seller's deteriorating business prospects. As a result, the seller eventually accepts the buyer's offer of $45 million. As a bargaining technique the strategy is successful; the buyer has obtained the business at half the original asking price. But in doing so the lawyer may have breached a duty of fairness owed to others in negotiations to bargain in good faith.

These cases are difficult because the lawyers' roles as client advocate and ethical practitioner appear inconsistent and lead to different results. But they are difficult only on the assumption that the law does not resolve the conflict of roles. A factor is missing from these cases, one usually as important to the lawyer as knowing what technique will be most effective and what the rules of professional ethics will allow. That factor is the law—the legal effects of each of the choices involved. The choices may not be any easier, but would not the litigation lawyer want to know whether misrepresenting her client's instructions to the plaintiff may, if discovered, make the resulting agreement voidable or expose her or her client to an action for fraud? Would she not want to know whether, by making the misrepresentation, she risked a suit by her own client for failing to follow instructions, or whether she may be liable for malpractice if no settlement results and the case must be tried?

Similar issues arise for the buyer's lawyer. Will the agreement finally reached be enforceable, or can it be avoided by the seller on the ground of duress? Does the lawyer, alone and with the buyer, risk liability to the seller for the economic harm that is suffered? Is the lawyer liable for malpractice if the agreement is avoided or if the buyer is found liable to the seller?

The examples pose basic questions regarding a lawyer's responsibility for the conduct of negotiations—the kinds of questions a "law of lawyers' negotiations" should answer. The examples also disclose the basic relationships such a law must address: (1) negotiators' relations with their clients, and (2) negotiators' relations with adversaries and other third parties.

. . .

When lawyers act as negotiators for their clients they are themselves subject to the commands of the law. To determine what the law requires, a lawyer-negotiator needs to consider two sets of obligations—those owed to the client, and those owed to other parties to the negotiation. In dealing with clients, the rules of contract, torts, and agency law regulate and restrict lawyers' freedom to act independently and require close consultation with clients. Lawyers must act within their authority and obey reasonable instructions from their clients, who possess final decisionmaking responsibility over the objectives of the representation. Lawyers must provide clients with all material information to make those decisions, keep them informed of the progress of the negotiations, and act competently and diligently in pursuing clients' interests.

Thus the lawyers in the two cases mentioned at the beginning of this Article must act according to their clients' instructions and overall objectives. If settlement for $100,000 (or less) is possible in the civil case, the lawyer must settle; if the client buyer in the business sale hypothetical wants negotiations prolonged, the lawyer must follow that instruction unless he determines it is unreasonable or unethical. The lawyer's professional obligation gives him a privilege to refuse to obey improper directions and instead withdraw as counsel. Apart from any specific instructions, lawyers are free to conduct the negotiations using reasonable judgment so long as they act for the benefit of their clients. The civil defendant's lawyer in the opening hypothetical should convey the significant information just learned from the plaintiff's lawyer—that the plaintiff is willing to settle for $90,000 (or less)—to her client if it is reasonable to do so. The facts suggest the plaintiff's lawyer wants an immediate answer. Hence, bargaining for a better settlement is a reasonable method of proceeding so long as the defendant's lawyer does not jeopardize the acceptable settlement already offered. Acting within these limits satisfies these lawyers' obligations to their clients under the circumstances.

. . .

Under these standards, the litigation lawyer and business lawyer discussed above are each at risk in dealing with their adversaries. Respectively, the hypotheticals raise serious legal issues of negotiator misrepresentation and coercive bargaining practices in negotiations. This Article points out that the hypotheticals raise the equally troublesome issue of lawyers' misrepresentations in negotiations. With the limited facts available, there is no sure answer to the question whether this conduct may expose the lawyers to liability for damages to the other parties. However, in the hypothetical civil case it is clear that if the defendant's lawyer misrepresents her client's intention—"No, my client won't give $90,000"—the lawyer has made a fraudulent misrepresentation by which she hopes to obtain a settlement more favorable to her client. If she does do better than $90,000, in part because of the misrepresentation, whether it makes the settlement voidable or not in turn depends upon whether plaintiff's reliance was justified.

. . .

In the hypothetical sale of business case, there is a strong possibility that the application of economic pressure and delay for the purpose of enhancing that pressure will make the agreement voidable for duress. On the other hand, there is no real likelihood that the lawyer faces monetary exposure to the third party for his conduct.

It is more difficult to gauge lawyers' potential liability to their clients for their actions. In the hypothetical civil litigation case, if the defendant's lawyer is candid with her opponent, the client could possibly show the lawyer was acting unreasonably in not seeking a more favorable settlement and that a more favorable settlement was possible using adversarial bargaining. In the sale of business example, if the buyer's lawyer chooses the pressure strategy and it taints the agreement, he faces a potential malpractice claim. The argument would be that a reasonably skillful lawyer should know the limits of coercive bargaining (the law of duress) and apply enough pressure to be effective, but not enough to endanger the agreement. In both cases the lawyers' difficulties are easily avoided by consulting the clients in advance and discussing possible strategies in the negotiations. As is often the case, lawyers' real problem with their clients is lack of communication, not incompetence.

Becoming familiar with the legal regulation of negotiation will not solve many of the dilemmas lawyers encounter there. What it does do, however, is to give lawyers their most valuable tool—the law—to take into account while calculating the consequences of their conduct for their clients, other parties, and, most importantly, for themselves. Lawyer-negotiators need to be as rigorous, as thorough, and as dispassionate in examining the legal consequences of their alternative courses of action as they are in assessing the legal consequences of the client's choices.

Section IV

BIBLIOGRAPHY

General Books on the Subject of Negotiation

a. Karl Albrecht & Steve Albrecht, Added Value Negotiating (1993).
b. Kenneth Arrow, et al., eds., Barriers to the Negotiated Resolution of Conflict (1994).
c. Samuel Bachrach & Edward Lawler, Bargaining: Power, Tactics and Outcomes (1981).
d. Max H. Bazerman & Roy Lewicki, eds. Negotiating In Organizations (1983).
e. Brams, Negotiation Games (1990).
f. J. William Breslin & Jeffrey Z. Rubin, eds., Negotiation Theory and Practice (1991).
g. Herb Cohen, You Can Negotiate Anything (1980).
h. Daniel Druckman, ed., Negotiations: Social–Psychological Perspectives (1977).
i. Joel Edelman & Mary Beth Crain, The Tao of Negotiation (1993).
j. Guy O. Faure & Jeffrey Z. Rubin, eds., Culture and Negotiation (1993).
k. Roger Fisher, William Ury & Bruce Patton, Getting to Yes: Negotiating Agreement Without Giving In (2nd ed. 1991).
l. Roger Fisher & Scott Brown, Getting Together: Building a Relationship that Gets to Yes (1988).
m. Barbara Gray, Collaborating: Finding Common Ground for Multiparty Problems (1989).
n. Paul Gulliver, Disputes and Negotiations: A Cross Cultural Perspective (1979).
o. Fred Jandt, Win–Win Negotiating: Turning Conflict Into Agreement (1985).
p. Chester Karras, The Negotiating Game (1970).
q. Chester Karras, Give and Take: The Complete Guide to Negotiating Strategies and Techniques (1974).
r. Gavin Kennedy, Field Guide to Negotiation (1994).
s. Leonard Koren & Peter Goodman, The Haggler's Handbook: One Hour to Negotiating Power (1991).
t. Roderick M. Kramer & David M. Messick, eds., Negotiations as a Social Process (1995).
u. David Lax & James Sebenius, The Manager as Negotiator: Bargaining for Cooperation and Competitive Gain (1986).
v. Richard Ned Lebow, The Art of Bargaining (1996).
w. Roy Lewicki & Joseph A. Litterer, Negotiation: Readings, Exercises and Cases (2nd ed. 1993).
x. Laura Nader & Harry F. Todd, eds., The Disputing Process: Law in Ten Societies (1978).
y. Gerald Nierenberg, Fundamentals of Negotiating (1974).

z.   Dean Pruitt, Negotiation Behavior (1981).
aa. Linda Putnam & Michael E. Roloff, Communication and Negotiation (1992).
bb. Howard Raiffa, The Art and Science of Negotiation (1982).
cc. H. Lawrence Ross, Settled Out of Court: The Social Process of Insurance Claims Adjustment (2nd ed. 1980).
dd. Mark H. Ross, The Management of Conflict (1993).
ee. Jeffrey Z. Rubin & Bert Brown, The Social Psychology of Bargaining and Negotiation (1975).
ff. Thomas Schelling, The Strategy of Conflict (1960).
gg. Anselm Strauss, Negotiations: Varieties, Contexts, Processes and Social Order (1978).
hh. William Ury, Jeanne Brett & Steven Goldberg, Getting Disputes Resolved: Designing Systems to Cut the Costs of Conflict (1988).
ii. William Ury, Getting Past No: Dealing With Difficult People (1991).
jj. Richard E. Walton, Managing Conflict: Interpersonal Dialogue and Third–Party Roles (1987).
kk. Richard E. Walton & Robert B. McKersie, A Behavioral Theory of Labor Negotiations: An Analysis of a Social Interaction System (1965).
ll. Richard E. Walton, Joel E. Cutcher–Gerschenfeld & Robert B. McKersie, Strategic Negotiations (1994).
mm. H. Peyton Young, ed., Negotiation Analysis (1991).
nn. I. William Zartman & Maureen Berman, The Practical Negotiator (1982).

Legally Oriented Books on Negotiation

a.   Robert Bastress & Joseph Harbaugh, Legal Interviewing, Counseling and Negotiation: Skills for Effective Representation (1990).
b.   Gary Bellow & Bea Moulton, The Lawyering Process: Negotiation (1981).
c.   Charles B. Craver, Effective Legal Negotiation and Settlement (1993).
d.   Ted Donner & Brian Crowe, Attorney's Guide to Negotiations (2nd ed. 1995).
e.   Hon. Harry Edwards & James J. White, Problems, Readings and Materials on the Lawyer as a Negotiator (1978).
f.   Donald Gifford, Legal Negotiation—Theory and Applications (1989).
g.   Roger Haydock, Negotiation Practice (1995).
h.   Herbert Kritzer, The Justice Broker: Lawyers and Ordinary Litigation (1990).
i.   Herbert Kritzer, Let's Make a Deal: Understanding the Negotiation Process in Ordinary Litigation (1991).
j.   Douglas Rosenthal, Lawyer and Client: Who's In Charge (1978).
k.   Phillip Schrag & Michael Meltsner, Public Interest Advocacy: Materials for Clinical Legal Education (1974).
l.   E. Wendy Trachte–Huber & Stephen K. Huber, Alternative Dispute Resolution: Strategies for Law and Business (1996).
m.   Gerald Williams, Legal Negotiation and Settlement (1983).

†